ROUTLEDGE LIBRAR
HISTORIOGR/

Volume 14

THE DIVERSITY OF HISTORY

THE DIVERSITY OF HISTORY

Essays in honour of Sir Herbert Butterfield

Edited by

J. H. ELLIOTT AND H. G. KOENIGSBERGER

LONDON AND NEW YORK

First published in 1970 by Routledge and Kegan Paul Ltd

This edition first published in 2016
by Routledge
2 Park Square, Milton Park, Abingdon, Oxon OX14 4RN

and by Routledge
711 Third Avenue, New York, NY 10017

Routledge is an imprint of the Taylor & Francis Group, an informa business

British Library Cataloguing in Publication Data
A catalogue record for this book is available from the British Library

ISBN: 978-1-138-99958-9 (Set)
ISBN: 978-1-315-63745-7 (Set) (ebk)
ISBN: 978-1-138-19490-8 (Volume 14) (hbk)
ISBN: 978-1-138-19492-2 (Volume 14) (pbk)
ISBN: 978-1-315-63863-8 (Volume 14) (ebk)

Publisher's Note
The publisher has gone to great lengths to ensure the quality of this reprint but points out that some imperfections in the original copies may be apparent.

Disclaimer
The publisher has made every effort to trace copyright holders and would welcome correspondence from those they have been unable to trace.

THE DIVERSITY OF HISTORY

Essays
in honour of
Sir Herbert Butterfield

edited by
J. H. Elliott
and
H. G. Koenigsberger

Routledge & Kegan Paul London

Published in Great Britain 1970
by Routledge and Kegan Paul Ltd
Broadway House, 68–74 Carter Lane
London, E.C.4
Printed in Great Britain by
Western Printing Services Ltd
Bristol

ISBN 0 7100 6942 1

Contents

page

Frontispiece: portrait-photo of Sir Herbert Butterfield

Foreword vii

1 Sir Herbert Butterfield as a Historian: an Appreciation 1
Sir Denis Brogan

2 St Augustine 17
Dom David Knowles

3 Music and Religion in Modern European History 35
H. G. Koenigsberger

4 Venetian Diplomacy before Pavia: from Reality to Myth 79
Felix Gilbert

5 The Statecraft of Olivares 117
J. H. Elliott

6 Time, History and Eschatology in the Thought of Thomas Hobbes 149

J. G. A. Pocock

7 On the Historical Singularity of the Scientific Revolution of the Seventeenth Century 199

A. Rupert Hall

8 History and Reform in the Middle of the Eighteenth Century 223

Franco Venturi

9 The Duke of Newcastle and the Origins of the Diplomatic Revolution 245

The late D. B. Horn

10 Cavour and the Tuscan Revolution of 1859 269

Denis Mack Smith

11 Bibliography of Sir Herbert Butterfield's Writings (to 1968) 315

R. W. K. Hinton

Index 327

Foreword

This volume is intended as an expression of affection and appreciation for Sir Herbert Butterfield on the occasion of his seventieth birthday. Professor Butterfield's range of interests has been so wide, and the company of his friends and admirers so great, that the editors found themselves in some difficulty as to the best means of commemorating the event. They finally decided in favour of a volume containing a relatively small number of essays, each of which would touch upon some kind of history or historical theme which Professor Butterfield has illuminated, and which has been dear to his heart. This decision necessarily meant that many of Sir Herbert's friends and former students could not be represented in the volume, although they would certainly wish to be associated with the intention behind it. They and others will recognize in the diversity of the contributions here printed a reflection of the remarkable diversity of interests of Sir Herbert himself. This diversity precludes any unity of theme, other than that which derives from the desire to do honour to the recipient—to express admiration for the historian, and affection for the man.

The editors wish to thank the contributors for their understanding co-operation, which has notably lightened their task. It is a matter of special regret to them that Professor Horn should not have lived to see his essay in print. They also wish to express their thanks to Mr J. R. Harrison of the Cambridge University Library for his assistance to Dr Hinton in the preparation of the bibliography.

Photographer Edward Leigh

Sir Herbert Butterfield

One

Sir Herbert Butterfield as a Historian: an Appreciation

by

Sir Denis Brogan

The contributions of Herbert Butterfield to 'history' are not only remarkable for their quality, but for their variety, and it is for that reason that I have put 'history' in inverted commas. There is the obvious paradox that one of the most remarkable of Sir Herbert Butterfield's books, *The Origins of Modern Science, 1300–1800*, is at first sight an odd choice of subject for one who began his research under the direction of that very eminent but orthodox diplomatic historian, the late Harold Temperley. But the book itself is an ingenious, indeed a subtle, criticism of certain types of historical priorities as exemplified in the writing of what one may call standard narrative history. Indeed, although some of Sir Herbert's works are pioneering and masterly expositions of the traditional aims and achievements of formal historiography, especially of diplomatic historiography, there is none of his books, not even the earliest, which does not display an originality of approach and judgment which, without in any way weakening their scholarly force in the traditional sense of the term, yet give his books a novel and a very exciting flavour of their own.

Re-reading, sometimes after a very long interval, the *œuvre* of Sir Herbert Butterfield, I have been struck by two permanent, highly personal, and extremely important attitudes in his writings on all topics. The first of these is his gentle but firm stress on the importance of the historical phenomenon called 'sin'. Nothing is more penetrating in his numerous notes on Lord Acton than his friendly irony at the identification which Acton made between Providence and Progress. For long before this naïve view that Providence and Progress were working hand in hand or that in any real sense Progress was progressing, long before Belsen and Hiroshima, Herbert Butterfield's own Christian position, one might say his Christian pessimism, had saved him from the innocence which many of Acton's judgments reveal. Indeed, having had to re-read recently for totally different purposes some of the essays of Macaulay, I was struck by the fact that although the rhetorical style of Macaulay is very unlike that of Acton, a great deal of Macaulay could be translated straight into Actonese, and vice versa. Macaulay, we may assume, believed in 'the religion of all sensible men'. We have the recent testimony of Mr Douglas Woodruff that Acton's Catholic belief and piety were deep. But the gap between ourselves and the optimistic agnostics and the optimistic Christians of the nineteenth century is so great, that even the most friendly account of Macaulay or of Acton underlines what must seem to us a curious credulity. And the credulity is seen peculiarly clearly when it is contemplated by a believing Christian like Sir Herbert Butterfield, who believes (I have no personal authority for this) in the permanence of the meaning of original sin and does not believe it can be exorcized or ended by any form of political change or, indeed, by any form of new psychological technique. I suspect, again without any personal authority, that Sir Herbert Butterfield may, among other reasons for doubting the judgment of Sir Lewis Namier, have been affected by the discovery that Namier had a somewhat credulous belief in the utility of modern psychological theory applied to historical personalities and so to historical problems. Again and again, and not only in a book like *Christianity and History*, Sir Herbert Butterfield reveals the degree to which his Christian pessimism and his consciousness of evil and not merely of misjudgment is a part of history that can only be wished away or dodged with great historical lies. This is not to say that Sir Herbert Butterfield is as confident as Acton was and as Macaulay was that the duty of the historian is to give historical judgments on past figures in history. Even Macaulay, who was far more willing to allow for the different standards of morality of different ages, did not doubt that although allowances had to be made, allowances of a kind that Acton would not have made, the historian was a judge of the morality of past historical figures.

Of course, Sir Herbert Butterfield is not indifferent to the moral character of past historical figures. Their real or alleged morality is, after all, a part of their public 'image', to use a word which he himself never uses, and so is part of the historical record. But the kind of ethical judgment he makes is very far indeed, on the one hand, from the brusque hanging judgments of a Macaulay or an Acton and on the other from the almost perfect ethical neutrality of Creighton. Sir Herbert's ethical judgment is, to me, entirely free from the naïve censoriousness of so many 'Anglo-Saxon' historians, a censoriousness now more common in the United States than in Great Britain. Indeed, I have only once seen a trace of this moral *naïveté*, and that is in his parallel between Hitler and Napoleon. For by a carelessly designed sentence, Sir Herbert may lead some naïve or careless readers to think that Hitler was a more moral, ethically admirable character than was Napoleon, because he believed deeply in the murderous Germanic nonsense which he put into effect.

This seems to me to be on the edge of the English heresy that it is most important that a statesman should be 'sincere' without sufficiently reflecting what he should be sincere about. Here I am on the side of Napoleon against Hitler as Hallam was on the side of Napoleon against Cromwell. But this is the only instance of the English mind in its less lucid moments. And if in *George III, Lord North, and the People, 1779–80*, there are signs of Yorkshire patriotism, this, I think, actually improves the book because, as Henry Adams had had to point out, Yorkshire was, or perhaps still is, a society, a sub-nationality, within the English nationality. And to take Yorkshire seriously is not to be a jingo, but a rational judge!

But at least equally important, perhaps more important and more revealing, is a metaphor that Sir Herbert Butterfield uses again and again—perhaps more often than he fully realizes. Again and again, in discussing a historical problem or a scientific problem, he points out that a solution was delayed, sometimes delayed for a very long time, because the searcher for the solution—Descartes or Acton—did not take hold of 'the other end of the stick'. It should be noted that Sir Herbert Butterfield does not say the *right* end of the stick. All sticks have two ends, and it is necessary to contemplate both of the ends. But sometimes the stick is picked up in what 'operationally' is a wasteful way, to avoid the misleading word 'wrong'. Indeed, profound and accurate but irrelevant learning may be an obstacle to a solution. The Renaissance belief in the solution of a great many problems by the Greeks perhaps delayed the development of a spontaneous Western study of problems, and less learned experimenters might have gone further. More than that, less learned experimenters had the great advantage of not having to get out of their system a great deal of ingenious intellectually impressive but irrelevant theorizing—for example, in problems of astronomy. If Descartes had been less of a genius, he might not have gone off the rails so completely as he sometimes did. And in one of the most acute examinations of a historical problem Sir Herbert Butterfield has made, his discussion of the origins of the Seven Years War, he points out that the great increase in historical knowledge which led to the belief that Frederick the Great was in no danger from a coalition against him was highly misleading, but highly misleading because the original conspiratorial theme had broken down when the methods of modern scholarship were applied. But the real clue was that it was not the Empress Maria Theresa who was anxious for an immediate war against Frederick, but the Empress Elizabeth of Russia, and this is a most elegant example (to use a mathematical metaphor) of the stick being picked up by the less useful end. If the same scholarship had been devoted to studying St Petersburg as was devoted to studying Vienna, the problem would in fact have almost disappeared.

In the same way, the bitterly fought-over question of whether Catherine de' Medici had planned the Massacre of St Bartholomew long before the event, a controversy in which Acton went badly wrong, was bedevilled by the failure to accept the fact that Catherine de' Medici was such a liar that she even lied to her own disadvantage and charged herself with what would seem today, as it seemed to Acton, an elaborate, criminal conspiracy when in fact the Massacre of St Bartholomew was the last desperate expedient of a woman at her wits' end. And, although the problem is not so elaborately developed, Bismarck in his old age gave testimony to his own detriment, trying to show that he had planned his policy, which is not now universally admired, from the very beginning: whereas, as Sir Herbert Butterfield points out, Bismarck's real reflections on the problems of any long-term diplomatic plan were far wiser, far more interesting, and far more relevant.

Indeed, for the professional historian one of the most fascinating parts of Sir Herbert Butterfield's work is his breakdown of sources and his refusal of a dogmatic preference for one source over another. Nothing, for example, could be more convincing and nothing more educational than Sir Herbert Butterfield's discussion of the historical value of the testimony of Horace Walpole, though he firmly refuses to deny the value of Horace Walpole's *Memoirs* of George III. He points out the competing value, and occasionally the superior value, of the contemporary letters that Walpole was writing. Here it is a question of picking up the stick by both ends, if such an Irish bull can be permitted.

Once or twice Sir Herbert asserts his belief in the nearly supreme value for the young research student of dealing with a narrow and precise problem in diplomatic history. Here I am in a difficulty, for diplomatic history is a part of the art which appeals to me very little, which I have practised only with great reluctance, and whose status and successes I have to take largely on trust. And, indeed, contemplating Sir Herbert's first important book, *The Peace Tactics of Napoleon, 1806–1808*, one is tempted to believe that Sir Herbert has to some extent been deceived by the brilliance and originality of that book into thinking that diplomatic studies done by much less able young men, having a far less general and generous view of historical problems, can have anything like the same value. They may educate the young man, but they often seem to me to do no more than that, and do not educate the reader, professional or common. Indeed, *The Peace Tactics of Napoleon* is a book of great revelatory power. It is obviously written in a style which owed a great deal to Harold Temperley. It is dramatic, it is florid, it is probably excessively metaphorical. But whereas Sir Herbert Butterfield got over that style and has, in fact, been reproached with the austerity of his later writing, Harold Temperley, as his last book shows, never did. Actually, I am prepared to defend the style of *The Peace Tactics of Napoleon* because it brings out the complexity of the problem with which the young Herbert Butterfield was faced. It would have been easy for him, even then, with his mastery of the techniques of diplomatic history, to have examined and settled a great many of the problems created by the events leading up to the Treaty of Tilsit. Indeed, he did settle one important problem by applying the stick method. For he noticed that it was assumed by nearly everyone that at Tilsit Napoleon seduced Alexander, who was deceived by the astonishing subtlety and charm of the Emperor of the French. We have plenty of evidence that Napoleon delighted to charm when he wanted to. But it was noted that historians, perhaps led astray by anti-Napoleonic bias, assumed that Alexander was not capable of seduction and of deceit. He was, after all, the grandson of Catherine the Great, and that was more important than his putative descent from the Czar Paul I. He was a pupil of La Harpe; but the Winter Palace was not a place in which the only source of education was an enlightened Swiss tutor. And if the young Bonaparte had his period of being an *idéologue*, there are people who hold (I am one of them) that he never quite got over some of his Jacobin biases. Here, quite rightly contemplating and accepting the possibility or probability that the stick had two ends and ought to be handled at both, the young Herbert Butterfield reduced the problem of Tilsit to something like rationality.

But much more important, and with one exception (which I shall come to) the almost unique example in his work, Sir Herbert Butterfield did much more in *The Peace Tactics* than study the narrow diplomatic problem and the narrow diplomatic solution. Although few people are less attracted by the magic of military glamour than he, he insisted that Tilsit was not a diplomatic conference in the manner, let us say, of Vienna or of Berlin. It came at the end of a particularly savage and, in some ways, demoralizing military campaign. The French Army, fighting and winning a very doubtful victory at Eylau in the horrors of an East Prussian winter, was not the French Army that had won Austerlitz in the comparative mildness of the Moravian winter. The morale of the French army was not, in fact, irreparably damaged, but it was damaged as it had not been damaged before under the Emperor's command. There is a famous story of a soldier dying in the snow in the retreat from Moscow in 1812 and murmuring, 'It's a long way to Carcassonne.' A great many French soldiers at Eylau must have said the equivalent, even if they survived and finally got back to Carcassonne. And (again I have not consulted Sir Herbert Butterfield on the point) we have the evidence of *War and Peace* that the Russian army, much more used to the climate and much more used, in fact, to a totally ruthless use of the Czar's military resources, itself suffered a great deal in the campaign through the hardships caused, not only by the battle itself, but by the breakdown of supplies and the general frustration of the winter campaign. After all, Tolstoi had seen something like the equivalent of this ordeal and its results when he was with the Russian army outside Sebastopol. It seems to me that one of the most effective parts of Sir Herbert's historical achievement is conveying to us with a mastery worthy of a good novelist, if not quite worthy of Tolstoi, the degree to which the victorious Napoleon's power of free action was limited by the state of the French army. Friedland could retrieve but could not abolish the winter campaign, and at Tilsit both Emperors had Eylau in mind as well as Friedland.

The other lengthy historical narrative which Sir Herbert Butterfield has provided is *George III, Lord North, and the People*, and, of course, the problems of the revolutionary crisis of 1780 are very different from those of the brief settlement of the world by the two Emperors in 1807. Nevertheless, the problem which Sir Herbert Butterfield set himself in the later book has some things in common with the problems he set himself as a very young man in *The Peace Tactics of Napoleon*. For just as in his first book he broke the narrow bounds of straight diplomatic history as exemplified, for example, in Robert Lord's book on the origins of the War of 1870, in this second book he saw that the historical challenge produced by the publication, in 1929, of Namier's *The Structure of Politics at the Accession of George III* would have to be met. If Namier's book was a revolution, there is a sense in which *George III, Lord North, and the People* is a counter-revolution. And, of course, the narrative of *George III* cannot be separated from the other writings on the historiographical problems presented by the varying traditions of the role of George III in the first half of his reign. The history and the historiography of the reputation of George III is a necessary part of the total problem and of Sir Herbert Butterfield's solution of the problem presented by this special case of the Whig tradition in history.

George III and the Historians (1957) is a lesson to undergraduates, to graduates, and, one feels, to the late Sir Lewis Namier on the importance of seeing how and when and in what forms historiographical tradition dominates historical narrative. Although Sir Herbert does not stress this, he notes, as other people have done, that the late Sir Lewis Namier ignored or avoided or dodged the problem of writing narrative history. It was, of course, dodged with the highest motives and with immense technical skill. But it is Sir Herbert's view (it is also my view, which is quite unimportant) that by dodging the problems of narration, Sir Lewis Namier not only saved himself some trouble, but confused the issues and, in the not very long run, diminished the value of his pioneering work. Here I am perhaps stressing the point more than Sir Herbert Butterfield would do; but few celebrated historical works have a more deceptive title than *England in the Age of the American Revolution.* 'England' is a vague and general term, and it is reduced to a narrow and technical and, in some ways, sterile term in this still useful and once celebrated book. It would be idle to deny that if Sir Herbert Butterfield is right, a great deal of the reputation of Sir Lewis Namier deserves reconsideration, and here it is impossible to avoid the impression (again I am speaking solely for myself) that Sir Herbert Butterfield was convinced of the limitations of Sir Lewis Namier which were caused in great part by his origins. I think this is perhaps revealed in Sir Herbert's discussion of Albert von Ruville. He shows the advantage that von Ruville had in coming to the study of English history without accepting the complacent traditions of English historiography. As he points out, but does not, I think, stress enough, this was not because von Ruville was a noisy, patriotic German redressing an Anglo-Saxon distortion of European history. After all, it was von Ruville who provided the most effective defence of George III and Bute against the common Prussian charge that they had betrayed Frederick the Great by making peace with France. But at the same time, von Ruville, looking at English institutions and still more at English views of those institutions, was concerned to cut English vanity—and the belief of the English in the uniqueness of their inheritance—down to size. (In the same way, Sir Herbert points out how much rational study of English medieval constitutional history owed to an outsider like, for example, Petit-Dutaillis.) True, the revolutionary interpretation of Magna Carta was mainly due to that eminent Glasgow *savant* McKechnie: but then Sir Herbert realizes that the Scots are not English. There is no doubt, and Sir Herbert makes it plain, that Sir Lewis Namier contributed a great deal to an understanding of eighteenth-century political practice. But I think there is no doubt as well that Sir Herbert feels that the drawbacks imposed on Sir Lewis Namier by his origins were almost as great as the advantage he got by standing outside the English tradition of his period to see the undiscussed premises which lay behind so much English historiography and also to notice that these premises were often very shaky foundations, if this mixed metaphor can be permitted. Here it should be noted that Sir Herbert, usually so bland, does not conceal the fact that he thinks the *epigoni* of the Namier school are not as impressive as was the founder of the school. It may even be that he feels that what he regards as the inadequacy of Sir Lewis's pupils and imitators tells us a good deal about Sir Lewis himself.

What does it tell us? Here there is a sharp division of political bias between the late Sir Lewis Namier and Sir Herbert Butterfield. No one is less a victim of the idols of the left-wing forum than Sir Herbert Butterfield; but he believes (again, I am glossing his writings without consulting him) that the famous kindly maxim, *tout comprendre, c'est tout pardonner*, is false. *Tout comprendre* is simply *tout comprendre.* If a general pardon follows the comprehension, that is an uncovenanted good. Consequently, he resists the Namierian temptation to feel that a profound, acute, and technically accurate account of English political institutions in the first years of the reign of George III justifies these institutions or, to put it in another way, condemns the critics of these institutions. Of course, no one is less likely to fall for the naïve version of Whig tradition than Sir Herbert Butterfield. No one is less likely to fall for the naïve version of its descendants of the so-called liberal or left tradition of today. But he is not willing to accept the view that the critics of the 'system' of George III were foolish, ignorant or merely destructive. Of course, he does not for a moment accept the naïve hagiography of a book like George Otto Trevelyan's *Early History of Charles James Fox.* He has his admiration for the Rockingham Whigs well under control. He is not a blind admirer of Edmund Burke. But there is, I think he feels, in the Namier achievement a devotion to a *status quo* which had a great many faults and which was under very serious threats in the last years of the American War of Independence.

Sir Herbert Butterfield is too polite to comment on Sir Lewis Namier's disadvantage as a foreign student of English history, as he commented favourably on the advantage of Albert du Ruville; but I find it difficult to believe that he has not reflected on the thwarted ambition of Sir Lewis Namier—first of all, the thwarted ambitions of his father to make him a member of the Polish gentry, and his own ambition to be accepted as a prose poet of the English aristocratic establishment. Therefore the great literary enterprise (apart from the history of Parliament) ran quickly into the sands. History without ideas and a political system based entirely on more or less edifying mechanical operations does not appeal to Sir Herbert Butterfield.

Here I think I shall be pardoned for intruding a personal remark. It seems to me that Sir Lewis Namier's description of English politics in the eighteenth century is curiously unrealistic under the guise of a rigorously scientific realism. I myself have had occasion to tell various graduate students that they must remember that even a Sachem of Tammany Hall has an ideology which does not always work to his immediate advantage and to which he feels a confused but inexorable and genuine loyalty. It is not merely a matter of *omertà*. It is probably not a matter of mere *omertà* even in some members of the Honoured Society!

Sir Lewis Namier was so busy divesting himself of ideologies that he may, in the absence of ideologies, have accepted an absolute which is as blinding as the credulity of the traditionalists.

It has been rumoured for a very long time that one ambition of Sir Herbert Butterfield was to write a life of Charles James Fox, and there are moments when I have felt that this was a very mistaken ambition, since there are many aspects of Mr Fox's career which not only must have shocked Sir Herbert Butterfield more than they did me, but would have brought him in contact with types, political and activist, whom he would find it hard to enjoy. I have even dared to suspect he does not know the role in the history of Fox played by a Soho public house called 'The Intrepid Fox'. On the other hand, when he insists that there was a real meaning in the devotion to the Whig tradition in the light mind of Horace Walpole, he is, I think, insisting on something that was real and meant a great deal to Horace Walpole. That he was proud of two prints, one of the text of Magna Carta and the other of the death sentence of Charles I, which he called *major carta*, is something which Sir Lewis Namier could hardly have understood. Nevertheless, they were important for Horace Walpole, and for a good many other people—for example, Boswell's father, Lord Auchinleck.[1] There has never been so much consensus in English political life as Sir Lewis Namier, contemplating with very natural disgust the anarchy of the Polish Republic, was anxious to find.

It is impossible, and would, indeed, be absurd, to ignore a side of Sir Herbert's historical activities on which my own opinion is of even less value than it is on diplomatic history or the history of England in the eighteenth century. Yet I suppose I could say that *The Origins of Modern Science* is the book of Sir Herbert's which I read and re-read most often, have enjoyed most, and have felt I have gained most from. He has done for me what he has done for many others. He has destroyed naïve ideas of the 'Renaissance'. The real turning-point in modern history does

[1] The few surviving readers of *Tom Brown at Oxford* will remember that young Mr Brown, when he went up from Rugby to Oxford, adorned his rooms with a facsimile of the death sentence of Charles I to show, not that he was a Whig, but that he was a Radical.

not come with the flight of the Greek scholars from Constantinople. It may even be that the sudden shot in the arm that classical tradition got from these refugees prevented the development of a more promising attitude to natural science visible in Paris in the fifteenth century. It is not accidental that in several books we are reminded of the importance of the University of Padua in the development of natural science, with the implication that we have devoted too much time or too much thought to (I am choosing the names not all at random) Politian, Petrarch, and the rest.

That the great turning-point in the intellectual history of Western Europe which transformed the whole role of Western Europe in the world comes later than the revival of Greek is, of course, not an invention or a discovery of Sir Herbert Butterfield's, but it has never been put with more elegance or quality or more convincingly than it is in his very remarkable lectures. And I cannot help thinking that there is a deliberate Puckish humour (which is extremely well known to his friends) in some of the dates on which he lays stress. Again and again, he notes by implication the comparative unimportance or irrelevance of the kind of turning-points in history, etc., which are inflicted on schoolboys. Sometimes he makes us note the parallel for ourselves; sometimes he underlines it; and one of the parallels—perhaps the most impressive of the parallels—which he does not need to underline is the conjunction in the year 1687 of that moderately important event, the Declaration of Indulgence of King James II, and the publication of Newton's *Principia.* Of course, this has been done by other people in less dramatic contrasts: for example, the Declaration of Independence, *The Decline and Fall of the Roman Empire*, and *The Wealth of Nations* were all published to a candid world in the same year. But no one who has read, digested, and re-digested *The Origins of Modern Science* will ever think as naïvely again of what is important in history as he did in the simple old days of *1066 and All That.* (I hasten to add that there is a great deal of intelligent criticism of history-teaching embodied in *1066 and All That.*)

I permit myself the liberty of not sharing the great warmth of Sir Herbert Butterfield's admiration for Lord Acton: but then

I know comparatively little about the works of Lord Acton, and only moderately admire what I do know of him. I am sometimes fascinated by information that Sir Herbert provides to which he quite rightly does not give much importance, like some of the slogans of the Protestant Irish in the great crisis which led to the creation of 'Grattan's Parliament'. I sometimes wonder if he knows of the poetical importance of Dungannon, which was not only the birthplace of the Irish Volunteers, but the locus of a celebrated Protestant Ulster song still in circulation. Perhaps, although Sir Herbert is extremely tolerant of the mistakes made both by scientists and by historians, led astray by a dominant theory of which they have not managed to clear their minds completely, he is more tolerant of corrigible errors than I am. Himself setting an example of great intellectual candour and moral impressiveness in his own historical work, and so destroying a great many idols, he is perhaps too kind to idol-worshippers still with us—and not all of them Whigs. But we cannot all be hanging judges as well as great judges of the court of historical appeal. And I think few people reading Sir Herbert Butterfield can doubt that, if we are to have a court of historical appeal, it is very much better presided over by him than by Macaulay, Acton, Michelet, or even by the excessively neutral Ranke, who carried his scientific attitude almost to the point of being itself a new form of bias. All history has to be re-written in each generation; all history is contemporary history, even if one does not follow out Croce completely in this argument; and all contemporary history, now and for a long time past, would have been better written—and not only in the English tongue—if more people had gone to school to the former Master of Peterhouse.

Two

St Augustine

by

David Knowles

These pages on St Augustine may not be out of place in a book dedicated to Herbert Butterfield, for he is in more than one way himself an Augustinian. The judgments throughout his lectures on Christianity and History have as their foundation his consciousness of the sinfulness of all men, even if he might not accept Augustine's celebrated and terrible phrase, *massa damnata*, for the human race of old. Augustine, also, is a supreme example of the rare saint included by Butterfield in his world-view who escapes from the circumstances of his world by a conversion that sets him above circumstance. Moreover, the great historian and the great religious thinker who have often caused him to stray from Parliament and chanceries, Lord Acton and Cardinal Newman, are themselves Augustinian characters, Acton by his thirst for justice amid the sins of popes and potentates and Newman by his awareness of the say the heart has in the counsels of the mind. Indeed, reject him or ignore him how we will, Augustine remains, alike in his condemnation and in his revelation of human nature, one of the greatest moulders of thought and one of the most richly endowed personalities in the history of the Christian Church.

Of all the great men whose writings have influenced the religious life and thought of the Western world, St Augustine of Hippo (A.D. 354–430) is probably the least familiar to the world of today. It may be doubted whether one out of ten educated men and women in Britain or America has read a page of his works, or could give even the briefest account of his genius. Yet it would be no exaggeration to say that, apart from the writers of the Scriptures, no one has influenced Christian life and thought throughout the centuries more deeply than Augustine. If he is virtually unknown today outside universities and seminaries, this is partly because neither theology nor traditional philosophy is among the major intellectual interests of the contemporary world, but partly also because much of Augustine's thought, like that of St Paul, has sunk so deeply into the Christian consciousness that its origin has been wholly forgotten.

Yet from his lifetime until the middle of the eighteenth century his writings were ceaselessly working like yeast in Europe. First as the Doctor of Grace, then as the patron and guide of numerous religious orders, such as the Augustinian canons, the Austin friars, the Dominicans and others, then as the reputed founder of an influential school of thought, Augustinism, then as the authority invoked in different senses by Luther, by Calvin, and by the Catholic theologians of the Counter-Reformation, and lastly as the immense figure looming dimly behind Jansenism in Antoine Arnauld's manifesto, *Augustinus*—in all these avatars Augustine was at the heart of one great controversy after another. Doctor of the Church, did we say? Or half-heretic? For, unlike any other of the Fathers, St Augustine has been called in aid by both parties in a succession of theological quarrels throughout the ages, and even in the modern world of the late seventeenth century the production of a critical edition of his works caused an earthquake both in the Roman *curia* and at the Court of Versailles when, as in the days of Arius in the early Church, a single letter in a single word in a treatise of Augustine on grace could ruin or reveal a Jansenist.[1] Even today we are being told by 'progressive' theologians that the Church has been in bondage to Augustine even until now, and that his attitude to sin, to women and to marriage has been weighing us down these fifteen hundred years.

Add to this his influence on political thought and the theory of government, in which his greatest work, *The City of God*, was a textbook for kings and theorists in circumstances very different

[1] Cf. the celebrated sentence in the *Enchiridion*, ch. 95: 'Nec utique Deus injuste noluit salvos fieri, cum possent salvi esse, si vellent.' The variant reading 'vellet' shifts the sense from human choice to divine predestination.

from those familiar to its author, from the days of Charlemagne to the early Renaissance. Add, finally, his influence on language and style, which probably has no parallel in Western literature. For almost a millennium his voluminous works were also the most ubiquitous, after the Bible, throughout Europe, and there is scarcely a writer of fame (unless Bede be one) who does not take something of the Augustinian manner and style. Even such literary giants as Anselm and Bernard owe half their style, as well as more than half their ideas, to him, and there is a series of writers of unknown or consciously concealed identity, from the fifth to the twelfth century, whose works were attributed to him in manuscripts and printed among his writings until one by one they have been separated in the acid-bath of modern criticism.

Augustine stands with a foot in each of two worlds, the ancient and what we call, for want of a better word, the medieval. In his childhood and early manhood the Roman Empire, though battered, was still a unity reaching from northern England to Persia and the Sahara; education was still the watery, late-Roman version of a system derived from ancient Athens and Alexandria; Christianity was ubiquitous, but the culture of the governing classes was still largely classical and pagan. Augustine's father was not a Christian, and he sent his son to the public school of the town; Augustine himself was for long a member of the heretical sect of the Manichees, and then a free-thinking professor of rhetoric and student of philosophy. Yet Augustine lived to see Rome sacked and his native Africa invaded by northern hordes; his mother was a Christian and he himself became a Christian bishop. If his early life was spent among the remains of the literary and intellectual heritage of Greece and Rome, his later years were devoted to explaining the gospel teaching to an African city congregation and in leading theological crusades against schismatics and masked heretics.

The division of interests between the early and later parts of his life corresponded to a difference of careers and aims. Till his thirty-third year Augustine was a man of the ancient world, and his goal was the career of a successful teacher of literature and rhetoric, which often ended, as does at times an academic career today, in a call to high office in the state. After his conversion, his mind and heart were given entirely to the service of God, first in retirement, then as a priest, and finally as Bishop of Hippo at a time of turbulence, schism and threatening heresy, and finally of invasion and destruction. It is something of a paradox that this convert man of letters, self-taught in divinity, should have become the profoundest and most universal doctor of the Church, in whose writings can be found not only the most fruitful speculation on the mysteries of the Trinity, of grace, of predestination, of free will and of the presence of Christ in the Eucharist, but also a host of details in the daily life of Christian piety that are revealed by no other writer of the age.

Of the many aspects of the life's work of this richly versatile man there is space here to consider only four: those of the doctor of grace, of the preacher, of the Christian philosopher and of the political thinker.

The great theological controversy which occupied the last phase of Augustine's life came upon him unexpectedly. The New Testament, especially the letters of St Paul and early Christian documents, are full of allusions to the mysterious, God-given capacity of believing and acting as a Christian, and thereby deserving eternal life. This capacity was known by the name of 'grace', a term meaning no more than a free gift, or a gift of God. St Paul had posed some of the problems of man's capability, liberty and destiny, but the Church as a whole had preferred to consider the riches and rewards of the adopted sons of God rather than the fate and problems of individuals until Pelagius, a British monk then in Italy, taking up a famous saying of Augustine himself—'O God, give me what thou biddest, and bid then what thou wilt' ('*Da quod jubes, et jube quod vis*')[2]—posed as a champion of free will and high endeavour and, in effect, put virtue and its eternal reward within the power of man unaided by any additional gift of God. Augustine took up the challenge and the engagement continued for years. Augustine, unable to forget the uncovenanted mercy of his own release from sin and unbelief,

[2] *Confessions*, bk. X, par. xxix (40). Pelagius held that man should by dint of his own effort keep the unchanging law of God. Augustine (so he thought) asked God both for a special commandment and the power to keep it.

emphasized, perhaps with exaggeration, the utter sinfulness and weakness of mankind, and the irresistible efficacy of God's foreknowledge and grace, and between them the disputants explored all the tremendous problems of predestination and free will that were to drive so many souls in a later century to the brink of despair. Augustine's teaching was adopted in large part by the Western Church, but some of his hardest sayings were never canonized, and theologians throughout the ages have been divided for and against him. Dominicans and Jesuits, Calvinists and Anglicans, Jansenists and Catholics have all been at odds, and all have claimed Augustine as their master.

Augustine was for forty years Bishop of a sea-coast town in Africa. Till very recently the 'composition of place' was wholly lacking for our meditations on his life at Hippo Regius, but part of the ancient town has been excavated recently, and we can see the floor of Augustine's church and the foundations of what was probably his house next-door. Still more recently, Mr Peter Brown, in an admirable biography,[3] has given particular attention to Augustine's environs and pastoral methods, which we can glimpse in the numerous details scattered about his letters and sermons.

It has been said that if the Bible had been lost in the Middle Ages we could reconstruct it in great part from Augustine's quotations. The Scriptures, as we know, were for him the crown of all other studies. He preached on them regularly, even daily, though to modern readers he seems to lack entirely the interest of his contemporary, Jerome, whose critical, down-to-earth comments and wide linguistic and historical knowledge, together with his keen observation, are so arresting. We may sometimes even have thought that his genius was wasted on a small provincial audience, who seem, to judge by his letters, to have been quarrelsome and petty, but it can surely have been no ordinary congregation that sat or stood day by day during their bishop's slow progress through the Fourth Gospel. Augustine usually treats his text as a basis for a theological or moral explanation, with occasional excursions into symbolism and allegory, and lapses into his foible, the mystique of numbers. Certainly he uses all the resources of rhetoric, and his short sentences, his frequent

[3] *Augustine of Hippo: a Biography* (Oxford, 1967).

questions, and his jingle of assonances must have ensured attention. Some of his sermons on the Psalms, on the Gospels, and above all on St John, are among the most precious jewels of Christian exegesis. He excels in his devotional power, and he can occasionally touch the chords that vibrate with such rich overtones in the *Confessions*:

> *Come to me all ye that labour.* Why is it that we all labour if not because we are mortal men, frail, sick and bearing vessels of clay which straiten each other's movements? But if the earthly vessels are straitened, there is greater room for charity. Why then does he say, *Come to me all ye that labour,* if not to ease our labour? And his promise is nigh at hand, because he has called those who labour. . . . Do they ask what reward they will have when they are called? *And I,* he says, *will give you rest. Take my yoke upon you and learn of me*—not to make the world, not to create all things visible and invisible, not to work wonders in the world and to raise the dead, but—*for I am meek and humble of heart.* Do you wish to be great? Begin then with little things. Are you planning something vast and tall? Then think first of the foundations at its base. . . . What is the top of the fabric we are toiling at? How high is its summit? I can say it in a word—as high as is the vision of God. To see God—how marvellous! how sublime! He who desires this knows what I say and what the words mean. Christ promises us the sight of God, the true God, the supreme God. It is a wonderful thing to see Him Who Sees. For they that worship false gods can see them when they wish, but what they see have eyes and see not; but to us is promised the vision of the living God, the God who sees all.[4]

Augustine, the eminent orator, the stylist who had been captivated by Cicero and Virgil, had long ago been repelled by the rough phrases and plain language of the Bible, but now he takes up its cadences and weaves them into his own work:

> *No one can come to me unless the Father draw him.* Do not think that you will be drawn unwillingly; love also can

[4] Sermo 10, *De Verbis Domini.*

draw you. Do not be dismayed by those who see nothing but words and cannot comprehend spiritual things. They will pick up the words of the gospel and say to us: 'How can I be free in believing if I am drawn?' I answer, you will be drawn not only freely [*voluntate*] but joyfully [*voluptate*]. What do I mean by joyfully? I mean, *delight in the Lord, and he will grant what your heart desires.* For there is a heart's delight for one who savours that heavenly food. Yes, if the poet can say, *Each one is drawn by what delights him*[5]—not by force, but by joy, not by obligation, but by delight—ought we not to say that a man who loves truth, who loves happiness, who loves justice, who loves eternal life, that such a one is drawn far more powerfully to Christ, for he is all these things? Shall we say that the bodily senses know what joy is, and that the mind does not? If the mind has not its joy, how can the words be true, that *the children of men shall put their trust under the shadow of thy wings. Thou shalt make them to drink of the river of thy pleasures. For with thee is the fountain of life; in thy light we shall see light.* Show me one who loves; he knows what I say. . . . If then earthly delights and pleasures, when they are seen, draw men who love them, since it is true that *each one is drawn by what delights him*, will not Christ, shown to us by the Father, draw? What can the soul desire more fiercely than truth?[6]

Augustine had been led to Christ by Greek philosophy. He was, and he remained, an intellectual, and when he became a Christian he sought to explain God and the universe by christianizing Plato. He was not the first to see Plato as a prophet of Christ among the Gentiles. Origen, Basil the Great and others had used Greek philosophy in expounding and defending Christianity. Nevertheless, Augustine was the first of the great Western Fathers to assume throughout his writings that there was a basis of human reasoning, certain and unchanging, from which the Christian theologian started and upon which he could lay the fabric of revealed truth. It was he who began a tradition, that was

[5] Virgil, *Eclogues*, ii, 65.

[6] *Tractatus in Johannem*, XXVI, 4.

to continue unbroken for 900 years, that there is a body of natural truth, moral as well as metaphysical, ascertainable by all men of intelligence and reliable within its limits, that was crowned and not contradicted by the revealed truths of the Old and New Testaments. The Orthodox Church has never looked upon the relationship of philosophy to theology precisely in this light, but in the West, though the harmony of the schools was broken in the fourteenth century, the Roman Catholic Church has never in principle abandoned the conception of a single body of truth, in part ascertainable by reason, in part revealed, and it is from Augustine that this outlook is in the last resort derived.

Unfortunately, perhaps, Augustine had little or no direct knowledge of Plato's works and none at all of those of Aristotle. What he took for Platonism was in fact what was later called Neoplatonism, and the Platonic writings to which he refers were those of Plotinus and Proclus. Consequently, Augustine was himself in general a Neoplatonist, and this was to have a lasting, and in some ways an unfortunate, influence upon Christian thought. For Plotinus had transformed Plato's system into a theology, almost into a religion; this it was that had appealed to Augustine, and this the outlook that he adopted. The result was not altogether a happy one. Plotinus was not a pantheist, but in his view all that was not God proceeded from him by emanation, not by creation. There was no room in his system for a distinction between natural and supernatural, revelation and rational knowledge. Augustine stood firmly for creation and revelation, but his Neoplatonist sympathies, and his habit of considering all human problems in terms of the individual Christian soul—one had almost said, of his own soul—and not in terms of abstract humanity, led throughout his writings to a blending of natural and supernatural. This acceptance of the existential reality of the individual soul enhances his appeal to the reader and adds to its practical value for the Christian life, but it often makes interpretation of his words difficult. Ultimately, indeed, it drove his system off the market in the later Middle Ages and the modern world, whereas the Aristotelian outlook of Aquinas can be comprehended and discussed, even if not adopted, by philosophers of any school.

Besides his genius as a philosopher, Augustine is also the creator of medieval political thought and of the philosophy of history. In 410 Alaric the Visigoth captured and sacked Rome. This unprecedented disaster profoundly shocked the whole civilized world, and though Alaric died almost immediately and Rome was rehabilitated, contemporaries and historians have agreed to regard the event as a point of no return in the history of the later Empire. Augustine had lived and worked in Rome before his conversion, and to him the fall of the city came as a judgment not only upon an Empire, but upon a whole civilization and way of life. The catastrophe inspired his greatest work, *The City of God*, which for all its daunting bulk and its disorderly ramifications is one of the small group of books, such as Adam Smith's *Wealth of Nations* and Rousseau's *Confessions*, that have profoundly influenced both thought and political action in Europe. At first sight his division of human society into the City of God and the City of the Devil seems an arbitrary and unbending confrontation of Church and State, even of clerical and lay dominion, and it is easy to see the Church of the medieval Papacy as the logical child of Augustine's thought, while some of his celebrated aphorisms, such as 'What are kingdoms but magnified gangster rule?' seem to leave little room for any idealization of kingship or patriotism or even for the naturalism of a democratic or social state. Yet such a simplification is wholly inadequate. Augustine's teaching is far more true and practical, if it is also more subtle and difficult to grasp. In his treatment of grace he seems at first to separate men into a mass of vice and damnation on the one hand, and a divinized minority on the other, yet in fact he is regarding the individual with his warring faculties, his aspirations and the action upon him of God's providence. So here in the *City of God* the Christian Church is only the visible framework of an ever-moving, ever-shifting procession of souls, while the unregenerate kingdoms are only the visible homes of evil men; in each visible body there may be those who in spirit and desire belong elsewhere. Here as always is that baffling confusion, as it seems to some of his readers, between classes and individuals, and the presence of what is ultimately Augustine's only interest, the journey of the individual soul from the City of the Devil (the love of self and contempt of God) to the City of God (the love of God and contempt of self); from darkness to the daylight of the vision of God. But in his treatment of that theme what riches are not thrown up from the depths of that great mind!

Augustine is the first writer to see historical events as a progress in time from the creation to the ultimate reign of Christ, as opposed to the conception of a series of cyclic processes or of the dramatic fortunes of a kingdom, a city, or a man. Time always fascinated him, and here again he characteristically defined it with reference to the individual mind, remembering or foreseeing events before or after the instant of present vision. As memory plays an essential part in recognizing time, this too is a subject to which he returns again and again. He is the first, and still remains the greatest philosopher of memory, and the familiar threefold division of the faculties of the soul into memory, understanding and will is his; it was later to be ousted by the Aristotelian twofold division of understanding and will.

Thus far we have considered Augustine as a theologian, a philosopher and an historian. His strongest claim upon our attention has yet to be recalled. In the spiritual literature of the Church two books of widely different scope and character stand apart from all others. One, the *Imitation of Christ*, is probably the most widely read religious book in the world, the Bible alone excepted; the other, the *Confessions* of St Augustine, may have fewer readers at the present day, but it is, what the *Imitation* is not, one of the acknowledged literary masterpieces of the world, and it has been, at least since the later Middle Ages, one of the great formative books of Europe, moulding the spirits of men within and without the Christian Church and exercising a most powerful influence in more than one realm of thought.

It would, indeed, be hard to exaggerate the significance of the book in the history of Christian sentiment. Alone from out the vast bulk of the writings of the Greek and Latin Fathers, it has passed into the literature of the world as a classic; it is the only work of a Father of the Church which a man of wide culture may be expected to have read. But it has a significance greater than this. It is the first, and it remains the greatest, complete autobiography in Western literature; it is the first great masterpiece of psychological analysis; it is in many ways the most modern, actual, work of the ancient world, anticipating, by almost a thousand years, phases of sentiment, traits of character, and turns of language that we associate with the new Europe that has grown out of the Middle Ages.

As an autobiography, it surpasses all others by reason alike of the personality of its author and the breadth of its appeal. Its writer was the philosopher and theologian who stands in the history of Western thought before the modern age in the small group which counts among its members Plato, Aristotle, Plotinus and Thomas Aquinas. Its pages describe the stages leading to a conversion from error and sin to Christendom more pregnant with consequences than that of any other man before or since, with the single exception of St Paul.

Yet though the writer was a philosopher and a theologian who had said farewell to all secular interests, the *Confessions* surpasses all other autobiographies in the breadth of its appeal. In every spiritual progress there must be some mixture of the moral and intellectual elements, but almost all the great autobiographies stress one of these at the expense of the other. In St Teresa of Avila, and in Ste Thérèse of Lisieux, it is the moral and spiritual elements that predominate; in Newman, the intellectual holds the field. In the *Confessions* mind and will, head and heart, constantly interact, now thwarting, now impelling the spirit of Augustine in its passage from evil and error to goodness and truth and the love of God, and though it is a saint, and not the least, who writes, the extraordinary and the marvellous have no place here; God's influence, though intimate and compulsive, is unseen and secret.

Finally, we owe it to the *Confessions* that the rich, many-sided, intensely human personality of Augustine, smothered from sight elsewhere to all but the keenest scrutiny by the vast and often forbidding mass of his own writings, stands out clearly defined for all time, and that with it we see, as under a lightning-flash, the whole world in which he lived, his mother Monica, his friends, the university and urban life of Africa, so soon to disappear for ever, the groups, Christian and secular, in the Milan of Ambrose and Theodosius. And yet, though the writer is Augustine, the Bishop and doctor, the passages that remain clearest in the memory, apart from the pages describing the crisis of conversion and the last days and death of Monica, are those in which he looks back at the trivial incidents and characteristics of childhood and boyhood, or those which he consecrates to the memory of a friend taken from him too soon.

The *Confessions* were written in or about the year 400, some fifteen years after the last event they describe, and when their author was forty-six years old. Augustine, the first great analyst of the memory, himself had one that was most tenacious and exact. A memory of persons and emotions of the past is a *sine qua non* of vivid autobiography; this Augustine had in full measure, but he had also an exact memory, keener even than Newman's, for the changing phases of his own past intellectual positions and problems. To the majority of his readers, no doubt, the absorbing interest of the *Confessions* is the moral struggle—the struggle of higher and lower within Augustine himself, and the struggle of a mother's love for her son which overcame both his wayward resistances and her own deeply seated prejudices and habits. Those, however, to whom the philosophy and culture of the ancient civilization is a living interest, must find a fascination without parallel in literature in watching the formation and purification of that wonderfully subtle and receptive mind. How receptive, how capacious that mind was can, indeed, only be fully appreciated by those who, while reading of its entanglement in the meshes of materialism and its flights hither and thither in the ether of Neoplatonism, bear in mind also the learned and to us unreal Biblical exegesis of the last pages of this selfsame book, as well as the adamantine masses of Augustine's treatises on grace, and the calm and panoramic reflection of Catholic tradition in his later writings. Without the *Confessions*, indeed, Augustine would be for the world of all time what he was to many in the early Middle Ages and to not a few theologians, Catholic and Protestant, Calvinist and Jansenist, since that time —the austere Bishop of his biographer Possidius and the relentless enemy of Pelagius and human nature, who could see no hope of salvation for the generations of the past, and who could consign infants to torment without pity. 'Ah, but that's the world's side.' The keenest sight might have been able to divine, from a page here and there in the letters, in the commentary on the Psalms and St John, and in an occasional sermon *de Tempore*, the presence of

> the other side, the novel
> Silent silver lights and darks undreamed of.

This, the intimate, the real Augustine, was revealed in its fullness

> Once, and only once, and for One only,

in the *Confessions*.

Hence it is that, for all the strange seas of thought and emotion in which the writer of these pages voyages, every reader finds in Augustine, even more than in Hamlet or Werther, his own likeness. 'I seem to be reading the history of my own wanderings',[7] wrote the sophisticated, fastidious Petrarch. 'When I began to read the *Confessions* I thought I saw myself there',[8] said a woman of a very different character and range of experience, Teresa of Avila. In the twelfth century the book, first read at the Court of King David of Scotland, was the only one remaining beside the Gospel of St John in the cell of the dying Cistercian abbot, Ailred of Rievaulx, to whom the great doctor of grace was always 'my Augustine'. In our own age Cambridge and Tübingen, the Italian free thinker and the Carmelite nun, have found wisdom and life in its pages. For Augustine, conscious of sin, yet still more conscious of God's providence, speaks throughout to God alone, not to man, in an intimacy that silences all criticism and sets the reader, unawares, himself in the presence of his Creator, begging with hope, in Augustine's own most celebrated words, for a new heart and a right spirit: 'Give what thou biddest, then bid what thou wilt.'[9]

The style and language, as all else in the *Confessions*, at once announce the dissolution of the classical culture and anticipate the sentiment of the distant future. Words never failed Augustine; they streamed from his lips and from his pen, as from Cicero's,

[7] Petrarch, *De contemptu mundi*, Dialogus I.

[8] *The Life of St Teresa of Jesus by Herself*, ch. ix (tr. E. A. Peers, in *Works*, I, p. 56).

[9] *Confessions*, bk. X, par. xxix (40), twice.

throughout his long life, as the volumes of Migne bear witness. Already in him we can see and regret that diffuseness, that love of digression, that lack of the old nervous energy of Plautus and Caesar, that were to be such marks of all Latin prose literature between Leo the Great and Petrarch. Yet for all the verbal artificiality that came from the schools of rhetoric, there are deep murmurs and pure melodies in the *Confessions*, where the new cadences of phrase match the new wine of Christian sentiment. They are heard best, perhaps, in the unforgettable moment when Augustine is lying beneath the fig tree in the Milanese garden, but they are present throughout beneath the surface of the words, from the first page, with its familiar and celebrated postulate, to one of the latest, with its poignant cry of regret:

> Great art thou, O Lord, and exceedingly to be praised: great is thy power and of thy wisdom there is no reckoning. And man, indeed, one part of thy creation, has the will to praise thee: yea, man, though he bears his mortality about with him . . . even man, a small portion of thy creation, has the will to praise thee. Thou dost stir him up, that it may delight him to praise thee, for thou hast made us for thyself, and our hearts are restless till they find repose in thee.[10]
>
> Too late have I loved thee, O beauty ever ancient and ever new, too late have I loved thee! And behold! Thou wert within and I without, and it was without that I sought thee. Thou wert with me, and I was not with thee. Those creatures held me far from thee which, were they not in thee, were not at all. Thou didst call, thou didst cry, thou didst break in upon my deafness; thou didst gleam forth, thou didst shine out, thou didst banish my blindness; thou didst send forth thy fragrance, and I drew breath and yearned for thee; I tasted and still hunger and thirst; thou didst touch me, and I was on flame to find thy peace.[11]

Would that Augustine had always written at that level of emotion and expression. There are long periods in his works

[10] *Confessions*, bk. I, par. i (1).

[11] *Confessions*, bk X, par. xxvii (38).

where he is dull, and others where he yields to a love of assonance and repetition that betray the teacher of rhetoric in a decaying empire, or to ingenious attempts to find an allegorical sense in the number of years of the man at the Pool of Bethesda or of the miraculous draught of fishes in the last chapter of St John. Yet again and again, and often when least expected, a thought or a word strikes a spark in his mind, and a burning chain of words shoots upwards like a rocket. Augustine can often be flat or dry, but he is one of the rare masters who can also touch sublimity. The bishop who wrangled with Pelagius could also utter the two phrases that echo throughout his works: 'Unchanging God, to know myself is to know Thee',[12] and 'Only love, and then do what thou wilt'.[13]

[12] *Soliloquies*, II, i: 'Noverim me, noverim Te'.

[13] *Tractatus in Johannem*, VII, 8: 'Dilige et quod vis fac'.

Three

Music and Religion in Modern European History

by

H. G. Koenigsberger

. . . and playing with all the dexterousness of the art of Musick, he shewed upon the Pipe, what notes were fit for the herds of Cowes and Oxen, what agreed with the flocks of Goats, what were pleasing to the sheep. The tones for the sheep were soft and sweet, those of the herds were vehement; and for the Goats were sharp and shrill.

Longus, *Daphnis and Chloe*[1]

Sic praedicavit Deus evangelium etiam per musicam. . . .

Luther, *Table Talk*, 1528[2]

[1] Longus, *Daphnis and Chloe*, tr. G. Thornley (1657) (London, 1925), bk. II, p. 102.

[2] Quoted in F. Blume, *Geschichte der evangelischen Kirchenmusik* (2nd ed., Kassel, 1965), p. 7.

In the introduction to *The Protestant Ethic and the Spirit of Capitalism*, Max Weber listed music as one of the fields which distinguished European civilization from all others. It was not that the ears of other peoples were musically less sensitive, Weber wrote; perhaps rather the contrary. It was rather that only the Europeans developed a rational harmony and counterpoint, the standardized musical instruments of the modern orchestra and, above all, musical notation, without which both the composition and playing of modern music would have been impossible.[3] Weber did not go beyond this brief paragraph, with its implication that it was the rational element of European music which primarily distinguished its development from that of music in other civilizations. Nor did Weber say very much about this particular problem of the uniqueness—I am deliberately avoiding the word 'superiority'—of European music in his later essay, *The Rational and Sociological Foundations of Music*;[4] yet it is as striking a phenomenon as the uniqueness of modern European capitalism or science. The present essay is not intended to give a complete explanation of this phenomenon. It seeks only to analyse one condition (though, I believe, a very important one) of this peculiar development of music in modern European history. Music, as Weber knew well,[5] was in practically all cultures

[3] M. Weber, 'Die protestantische Ethik und der Geist des Kapitalismus', *Gesammelte Aufsätze zur Religionssoziologie* (Tübingen, 1934), i, 2.

[4] M. Weber, *Die rationalen und soziologischen Grundlagen der Musik* (Munich, 1921).

[5] *Ibid.*, p. 30.

intimately linked with religious worship and ceremonial. It was so in classical and early Christian Europe, no less than in Asian and African civilizations. But in Europe the power of religion and religious sensibility declined, slowly and almost imperceptibly, from the later Middle Ages and the Renaissance, more and more rapidly, and very perceptibly, from the end of the seventeenth century.

This growing secularization of European civilization is well known, and I shall here take it for granted. I shall argue that the extraordinary development of music in Europe is closely linked with this phenomenon of secularization. More specifically, I will try to show that, as religious sensibilities declined, there appeared a new psychological need in men, a kind of emotional void, and that this need or void was filled primarily by music. Music found itself rarely in direct opposition to religion, and when this did happen the initiative came from the side of certain religious leaders. More normally, it was the very alliance of religion and music which allowed music to play an increasingly important and, eventually, even preponderant role in the European psyche.

The Renaissance was passionately concerned with the relative merits of different art forms. Sometimes as a kind of intellectual parlour game in princely courts, more commonly in treatises and other writings with a high philosophical intent and a sharp social purpose, men (and women) debated the ideal ranking order of poetry, painting, sculpture and music, and of the social status of those who practised these arts. The arguments varied, but among the most common was the power which works of art exerted on men's minds. For Leonardo, for instance, painting was, understandably, the supreme art:

> Painting will move the senses more readily than poetry . . . [he wrote in his notebooks]. An artist painted a picture that whoever saw it at once yawned, and went on doing so as long as he kept his eyes on the picture, which represented a person who also was yawning. Other artists have represented acts of wantonness and lust which kindled these passions in the beholders. Poetry could not do as much.

> And if you write a description of Gods, such writing will never be worshipped in the same way as a painting of the deity. For to the picture many offerings and prayers will incessantly flow, many generations will flock to it from distant lands and from the eastern seas and they will ask help from such a painting, but not writing.[6]

Leonardo placed music, too, above poetry because it can produce 'simultaneous harmony', but below painting, because sound does not last and because the eye is better than the ear.[7]

The type of argument which Leonardo used is typical for the period, although the conclusions of different writers tended to vary with their professions or predilections, and not all such discussions were necessarily in the form of a competition between the arts. The discussion of music was closely bound up with a persistent literary-philosophical tradition that went back to the Greeks. This tradition had three aspects. The first was the powers ascribed to music and celebrated by historians and poets. Thus music had power to quieten infants, as everyone knew. It had also tamed wild beasts, as Orpheus and Arion had demonstrated. Amphion's lyre had made the very rocks move to form the walls of Thebes, and Asclepiades and many others, like David with his harp, had used music to heal or calm madmen and drunkards.

The second aspect in the discussion of music was the theory of the different types of music and of their respective effects on the listener. Plato had taught that the Dorian and Lydian modes gave men courage and strength, but that most of the other modes had enervating and demoralizing effects. What was worse, such debilitating music was most pleasant to the ear and could insinuate itself into the mind of a virtuous and strong man,

> pouring into his soul through the funnel of his ears those sweet and soft and melancholy airs . . . and his whole life is passed in warbling and the delights of song . . . if he

[6] L. da Vinci, *The Literary Works*, ed. J. P. and Irma A. Richter (Oxford, 1939), 2nd ed., i, 64.

[7] *Ibid.*, pp. 77ff.

> carries on the softening and soothing process, in the next stage he begins to melt and waste, until he has wasted away his spirit; and he becomes a feeble warrior.[8]

Any musical innovation, Plato therefore argued, was harmful to the State and should be prohibited; for when the modes of music change, the fundamental laws of the State will change with them.[9]

It seems that not all of Plato's contemporaries agreed with him. He blamed the poets themselves:

> They were men of genius, but they had no perception of what is just and lawful in music; raging like Bacchanals and possessed with inordinate delights . . . ignorantly affirming that music has no truth and, whether good or bad, can only be judged rightly by the pleasure of the hearer. And by composing such licentious works, they have inspired the multitude with lawlessness and boldness, and made them fancy that they can judge of themselves about melody and song.[10]

Plato's theory of the difference between good and bad or, rather, moral and immoral music has had, in one form or another, an extraordinarily long and successful career and is, perhaps even now, not completely dead; but it celebrated its greatest triumphs in the sixteenth century. How did music have such powers for good or evil?

The answer to this question provides the third aspect of the tradition which the Renaissance inherited, and again it went back to the Greeks; this time, however, to the Pythagorean theory that musical harmony was of the same nature or, at least, that it reflected the mathematical harmony and structure of the universe. In its more than two-thousand-year history, from Pythagoras and Plato to Kepler and Leibniz, this theory took many forms, not least in importance being that of the music or harmony of the

[8] Plato, *The Republic*, III, 411. *The Dialogues*, tr. B. Jowett (Oxford and London, 1892), 3rd ed., iii, 99.

[9] *Ibid.*, IV, 424, 112.

[10] Plato, *Laws*, III, 700. *Dialogues*, vol. v, pp. 82–3.

spheres.[11] More generally, the exact relationship between musical and cosmic harmony was posited, but left vague, as it was, for instance, in Boethius's enormously influential treatise on music.[12]

During the Middle Ages the theory of the existence of this relationship was never lost: music, together with arithmetic, geometry and astronomy, formed the *quadrivium* in the study of the liberal arts. During the Renaissance the theory received a great impetus through the revival of Neoplatonism. It was naturally, though somewhat uneasily, linked to the tradition of the *laudes musicae*, the praises of the powers of music, and to the Platonic distinctions between moral and immoral music. The so-called musical humanists of the latter half of the sixteenth century faced some difficult practical problems in their attempts to re-create ancient music with all its virtues. In the first place, no one really knew how far the Platonic modes coincided with the modes as they were known in the sixteenth century, and therefore which of them were permissible and which were not. This was not, perhaps, as important as it might seem; for every musical humanist was certain that he himself had the correct interpretation, even if it differed from that of his colleagues. In the second place, modern music did not really display the wonderful effects which the ancients had described or, at least, not in quite the same, very specific, way. The musical humanists thought they saw the logical reason for this shortcoming of modern music in the tendency of contemporary counterpoint to obscure the words of vocal music. They were not concerned with purely instrumental music, partly because there was, as yet, relatively little of it; but, more important, because they (wrongly) thought that the ancients had no purely instrumental music. It seemed to them that it was the words, with their impact heightened by music, which were

[11] Shakespeare, *The Merchant of Venice*, V, 1:

There's not the smallest orb which thou behold'st
But in his motion like an angel sings,
Still quiring to the young-eyed cherubins.

[12] Boethius, *De Institutione Musica*, ed. A. Damerini (Florence, 1949), ch. 3, p. 30: 'Sed quorsum istaec [i.e. the powers of music]? Quia non potest dubitari, quin nostrae animae et corporis status eisdem quodammodo proportionibus videatur esse compositus, quibus arminicas modulationes posterior disputatio coniungi copularique monstrabit.'

responsible for the famous effects.[13] They therefore felt it necessary to break with the late-medieval polyphonic tradition and to place music strictly into the service of words.

The lengths to which some musical humanists were willing to go in this direction were shown by the French poet Jean-Antoine de Baïf and his friend, the musician Thibault de Courville. These two attempted nothing less than to mould the rather refractory French language into the metrical pattern of Greek and Latin verse and then to set them to music as a '*musique mesurée*' which followed the metre of the verse as closely as possible. It seems that, with the support of the King, Charles IX, they thought they could 'reform' the musical life of France according to Platonic ideals. They hoped to do this through the educative efforts of an academy of poetry and music.[14] Charles IX's letters patent for this academy, in 1570, show clearly the Platonic assumptions about the powerful but ambiguous effects of music:

> . . . il importe grandement pour les mœurs des Citoyens d'une Ville [runs the preamble] que la Musique courante et usitée au Pays soit retenue sous certaines loix, dautant que la pluspart des esprits des hommes se conforment et comportent, selon qu'elle est; de façon que où la Musique est désordonnée, la volontiers les mœurs sont dépravez, et où elle est bien ordonnée, là sont les hommes bien moriginez.[15]

[13] D. P. Walker, 'Musical Humanism in the 16th and Early 17th Centuries', *The Music Review* (1941), vol. 2, pp. 7–13, 111–27, 289–308; vol. 3, pp. 64ff. It is possible, as Dorothy Koenigsberger has suggested to me, that the musical humanists emphasized the importance of the words in singing because their effects were predictable and controllable, whereas those of pure music were not. There were certainly many in the sixteenth century who were afraid of the effects of music and hence sought to subordinate it to the word. But this attitude is clearer with the theologians than the humanists.

[14] D. P. Walker, 'The Aims of Baïf's *Académie de Poésie et de Musique*', *Journal of Renaissance and Baroque Music*, i (1946–7), pp. 91–100.

[15] Quoted in F. Yates, *The French Academies of the Sixteenth Century* (London, 1947), p. 319.

The Italian musical humanists did not go quite so far. But they were as firmly convinced as the French that it was the words which determined the meaning and effects of music. Girolamo Mei, generally regarded by his contemporaries as the greatest authority on Greek music, was emphatic on this point. It was quite wrong to think that the music of the ancients was meant to delight the ear with its harmony, he wrote to Vincenzo Galilei in 1572; it was rather meant to 'express entirely and powerfully all that speaking intends to express by means of a high- or low-pitched voice'.[16]

Theologians and religious moralists had long since come to similar conclusions and they had done this for fundamentally similar, though not always equally antiquarian, reasons. Music which delighted the ear was suspect, at least in church; for it would distract the worshipper from the word of God or, worse still, lead his thoughts into worldly, even lustful directions. 'We have introduced an artificial and theatrical music into the church . . . ', complained Erasmus. 'Horns, trumpets, pipes vie and sound along constantly with the voices. Amorous and lascivious melodies are heard such as elsewhere accompany only the dances of courtesans and clowns. The people run into the churches as if they were theatres, for the sake of the sensuous charm of the ear.'[17] The English scene was, it seems, particularly bad: 'What else is heard in monasteries, colleges and almost all churches, besides the clamour of voices?'[18] There is, clearly, some awareness here of the powers of music independent of the words set. But Erasmus's main point was a moral one, and he thought of certain melodies as 'amorous and lascivious' because, like so much church music of the time, they were parodies, i.e. they had started life as tunes for popular songs and, even after the words were changed, tended to remind the listener of the original words. As one would expect from Erasmus, he also quoted the ancients and the laws they were

[16] G. Mei, *Letters on Ancient and Modern Music to Vincenzo Galilei*, ed. C. V. Palisca (American Institute of Musicology, 1960), p. 116.

[17] Comment on 1 Corinthians i, 14. Quoted in G. Reese, *Music in the Renaissance* (New York, 1954), p. 448.

[18] Quoted in C. A. Miller, 'Erasmus on Music', *Musical Quarterly*, lii, no. 3 (1966), pp. 338–9.

supposed to have enacted to prevent music from corrupting the minds of the citizens.[19]

Calvin was even more uneasy about music than Erasmus. Some of his friends may well have condemned music altogether, for Calvin thought it necessary to defend the art. It serves our enjoyment rather than our need, he wrote, but 'it ought not on that account to be judged of no value; still less should it be condemned'.[20] Did not God 'render many things attractive to us, apart from their necessary use'?[21] As long as he could stay on such rational grounds, Calvin seems to have felt safe. Thus he argued that it was God who lightened Saul's melancholy, and not the therapeutic effects of David's harp.[22] Nevertheless, the powers of music were too well attested, and that by the highest authorities: Calvin could not simply write music off as a matter for mere 'enjoyment'. In his Preface to the *Geneva Psalter*, Calvin wrote: 'Car à grand peine y a il en ce monde qui puisse plus tourner ou fléchir çà et là les mœurs des hommes, comme Plato l'a prudemment consyderé. Et de fait, nous experimentons qu'elle a une vertu secrette et quasi incredible à esmouvoir les cueurs en une sorte, ou en l'autre. . . .' For while it is true that wicked words pervert good customs, yet 'quand la mélodie est avec, cela transperce beaucoup plus fort le cueur, et entre dedans tellement que comme par un entonnoir le vin est iesté dedans le vaisseau, aussi le venin et la corruption est distillé iusques au profond du cueur, par la melody'.[23] This is pure Plato, even to the metaphor of the funnel. But Calvin's emphasis was on the negative aspect of the power of music. The flute and the tambourin are to be condemned only in their abuse, he said in a sermon on the Book of Job; but this is just what usually happens, 'car il est certain que iamais le tambourin ne sonne pour faire resiouir les hommes, qu'il n'y ait de la vanité, ie ne di point

[19] *Ibid.*, p. 348.

[20] J. Calvin, Commentary of Genesis iv, 20, quoted in *The Institutes of the Christian Religion*, tr. F. L. Battles, vol. 2 (Philadelphia, 1960), p. 721, n. 4.

[21] Calvin, *Institutes*, III, x, 721.

[22] H. P. Clive, 'The Calvinist Attitude to Music', *Bibliotèque d'Humanisme et Renaissance*, xix (1957), p. 87.

[23] Quoted in *ibid.*, p. 86.

superflue, mais comme brutale, car voilà les hommes qui sont transportez tellement qu'ils ne s'esgayent point d'une ioye moderée . . .'.[24]

It is difficult to escape the impression that Calvin was profoundly uneasy about music, that he was frightened by its dionysiacal powers of giving men joy beyond moderation.[25] It is therefore not surprising that the only music he would allow in divine service was the unaccompanied singing of psalms. The Jews of the Old Testament had admittedly praised the Lord with drums and cymbals and trumpets, but these instruments had performed an educative function, because of the spiritual weakness of the Jews. Since the coming of Christ they were no longer needed. And thus Calvin banished musical instruments from his church.[26]

The immediate course of events seemed to justify his decision. Psalm-singing came to be a most powerful, because highly popular, weapon in the spread of Calvinist ideas in western Europe. Its long-term effects on musical life as a whole were a different matter.

The Calvinists spoke slightingly of 'popish music'; but the musical puritanism of the age made itself felt in all denominations. In England, for instance, Bishop Coverdale lamented the profanity of popular music-making:

> Would God that our minstrels had none other thing to play upon, neither our ploughmen other things to whistle upon save psalms, hymns and such like godly songs . . . and if women at the rocks and spinning at the wheels had none other songs to pass their time withal than such as Moses' sister sang before them, they should be better occupied than with 'Hey Nonny Nonny', 'Hey Trolley lolly', and such like fantasies.[27]

[24] *Ibid.*, p. 93, n. 4.

[25] See also Calvin's Commentary on Genesis iv, 20: 'Damnanda quidem est voluptas, nisi cum Dei timore, et communi humanae societas utilitate sit coniuncta.' Quoted in Clive, 'The Calvinist Attitude to Music', p. 93, n. 4.

[26] *Ibid.*, pp. 90ff.

[27] Preface to the *Goostly Psalms* (1539), quoted in C. Garside, 'Calvin's Preface to the Psalter: A Re-appraisal', *Musical Quarterly*, xxxvii (1951), 572n.

Catholics were less concerned with the iniquities of popular music; but a long line of theologians and church councils condemned over-elaborate and 'lascivious' church music, such as was practised by the Netherlands school of polyphonic composers. It made the words of the liturgy unintelligible, they claimed, and seduced men's minds from attention to the word of God.[28] In the Netherlands the tradition of elaborate polyphony in church music was strong enough to resist the attacks of those who wanted to subordinate music completely to words. But even the tolerant Netherlands Church authorities would not allow their composers to assimilate the chromaticism of contemporary Italian secular music for the sake of heightening the emotional impact of their own religious music. Unwilling to give up their aims completely, some of the Netherlands composers adopted a method of musical notation which involved a double meaning: one, openly apparent, which accorded with the traditional rules of the church modes, and the other, secret or concealed, which was understood only by the initiated.[29]

The deviousness of this method of composition is surprising, even in an age as passionately devoted to allegories, anagrams and hidden meanings as was the Renaissance. Its practitioners appear to have come mainly from those Erasmian circles whose religious orthodoxy was often suspect, but who never chose openly to break with the Catholic Church. It seems unlikely, however, that Erasmus himself would have been pleased with this victory of the power of music over the power of the word.

The orthodox Catholic position was summarized by the decrees of the Council of Trent, in September 1562 and November 1563, prohibiting the use of 'lascivious, impure and profane' music in church,[30] and insisting that the function of church music was not to delight the ears but to strengthen the impact of the words of the liturgy and to incline the hearts of the listeners towards a longing for heavenly harmony and the contemplation of

[28] Clive, 'The Calvinist Attitude to Music', pp. 98ff.

[29] E. Lowinsky, *Secret Chromatic Art in the Netherlands Motet*, Columbia University Studies in Musicology, vi (New York, 1946).

[30] *Canones et Decreta Sacrosancti oecumenici et generalis Concilii Tridentini* (Venice, 1564), p. 112.

the joys of the blessed.[31] The decrees, however, were silent on detail and left room for different interpretations. Palestrina's splendid unaccompanied masses fulfilled to perfection the demands of the Council of Trent, even in a fairly rigorous interpretation of its decrees. Some churchmen went further. It is told of St Carlo Borromeo that he attracted excellent musicians to Milan by paying them good salaries, but that he insisted on a reformed music in which the words would be clearly understood. All instruments except the organs were banished from the churches in his diocese.[32] But such austerity was far from universal, and the phase of acute musical puritanism in the Catholic Church did not outlast the end of the sixteenth century.

In all this discussion of music during the sixteenth century something seems to be missing. Either, some of the would-be authorities on music are not really very musical, are uneasy about it or even afraid of it, and seem to acknowledge its value only because the ancients did. Perhaps Erasmus, certainly Calvin and many of his followers fit into this category. Or, where they were genuinely sensitive to music, as were presumably the musical humanists and churchmen, such as Borromeo, their thinking was predetermined by Platonic categories of good and bad music, by humanist and theological insistence on the need to subordinate music to words and, by a tradition going back to the early Church Fathers, of hostility towards 'heathenish' instruments in church. Thus they all sought to limit and confine music, to force it into patterns whose origins were philosophical or theological rather than musical, and above all to control the fearful powers of music over men's souls by making it the servant of the much more easily controllable word.

These efforts were never wholly successful. In spite of the continual and often strident demands for its subordination, music constantly tended to escape from all such attempts to harness it to a purely moral purpose. Practising composers and musicians,

[31] K. G. Fellerer, 'Church Music and the Council of Trent', *Musical Quarterly*, xxxix (1953), 576.

[32] G. P. Giussano, *Vita di S. Carlo Borromeo* (Rome, 1610), p. 89. I would like to thank Professor Gordon Griffiths of the University of Washington for drawing my attention to this source.

even at times the ultra-orthodox Palestrina himself, often remained stubbornly impervious to the demands of the moralists, and so did much of the general public. It is inconceivable that the famous school of Flemish contrapuntalists would have retained its fame throughout Europe for generation after generation if their sonorous and complex, but in the eyes of the moralists frivolous, music had not appealed to a wide and influential audience. The moralists themselves sadly recognized that people flocked into the churches to hear music rather than the word of God. Practical musicians, moreover, even when they were also theorists, found it hard to accept the more extreme of the Neoplatonist views. Zarlino, Choirmaster of St Mark's, Venice, as well as author of one of the most famous treatises on music,[33] agreed with the moralists that music should have a moral purpose and that words gave music ultimate force;[34] but he was sceptical about knowing the genuine Greek modes and caustic about 'those who are ignorant of a subject and therefore misrepresent it; as we see with someone who, being unmusical but delighting in the study of humane letters, much prefers to hear the words in the cantilena . . . than its harmony; perhaps because he has no ear for it'.[35] This reproof was directed especially against Vincenzo Galilei and Girolamo Mei.

It is clear that there had always been men, and even 'men of genius', who, as Plato had lamented, 'had no perception of what is just and lawful in music';[36] in other words, men for whom music as such was more important than any moral implications it might have. And there were also those whom music affected in this way but who had a bad conscience about it. One of these was St Augustine. 'Yet when it happens to me to be more moved by the singing than by what is sung', he wrote in his *Confessions*, 'I confess myself to have sinned criminally, and then I would rather not have heard the singing.'[37] Augustine's regrets have

[33] *Istitutioni Armoniche* (Venice, 1558).

[34] D. P. Walker, 'Musical Humanism', *The Music Review*, ii, 227; iii, 63.

[35] *Ibid.*, p. 66.

[36] See above, p. 40.

[37] St Augustine, *The Confessions*, tr. J. G. Pilkington (New York, 1943), x, 33, 257.

nothing to do with Platonic notions of moral and immoral music, nor with patristic and later theological and humanist objections to the subordination of words to music. It was the power of music itself, its ability to distract him from the word of God, however clearly heard, which frightened St Augustine. It was the sort of power which Leonardo da Vinci saw in painting and which many, in the Renaissance, saw in poetry.

Even those who valued the power of words above music might still understand the independent power of music as Augustine understood it. To Ficino, music was a kind of living, moving air which directly affected man's spirit, that corporeal vapour which, it was believed, flowed from the brain through the nervous system.[38]

> . . . Musical sound by the movement of the air moves the body [he wrote in his commentaries on Plato's *Timaeus*]; by purified air it excites the aerial spirit which is the bond of body and soul: by emotion it affects the senses and at the same time the soul: by meaning it works on the mind: finally, by the very movement of the subtle air it penetrates strongly: . . . by the conformity of its quality it floods us with wonderful pleasure: by its nature, both spiritual and material, it at once seizes, and claims as its own, man in his entirety.[39]

Since Ficino, as a good Platonist, also believed that musical harmony reflected the mathematical harmony of the universe, he was doubly convinced of its power. Unlike most of the musical humanists of the sixteenth century, Ficino was willing to use music not only, in conjunction with words, for moral purposes, but also as a powerful means for working natural magic. The planets have certain qualities, beneficial or dangerous to man. These can be attracted in various ways, but especially by music:

> Thus from the tones chosen by the rule of the stars, and then combined in accordance with the stars' mutual

[38] D. P. Walker, *Spiritual and Demonic Magic. From Ficino to Campanella*, Studies of the Warburg Institute (London, 1958), xxii, 4.

[39] Quoted *ibid.*, p. 9.

> correspondences, a sort of common form can be made, and in this a certain celestial virtue will arise. It is indeed very difficult to judge what kind of tones will best fit what kind of stars, and what combinations of tones agree best with what stars and their aspects. But, partly by our own diligence, partly by divine destiny . . . we have been able to accomplish this.[40]

The magical effects which Ficino sought to accomplish were designed only to affect his own mind and, in particular, to effect a proper proportion and balance of the bodily humours and relieve it from excessive melancholy. For Ficino, as for the sixteenth-century humanists, the words of his song held, eventually, a predominant position; for they could influence the mind, whereas music alone, without words, could influence only man's spirit. But it was not the text which gave music its great, and sometimes magical, power; it was rather the combination of music and words in song; for song affected the whole person, mind and spirit equally.[41] I can see no good reason to doubt that Ficino's musical magic often had the effects which he claimed for it, at least on himself. Whether the causes he posited for these effects were correct is a different matter.

Dr D. P. Walker, on whose work I have relied heavily for the passage on Ficino, suggests that Ficino's astrological singing 'came near to being a religious rite'.[42] The effects which Ficino desired, Dr Walker argues, a Christian would look for in the action of God on man's soul. But if these effects could really be achieved by natural magic, as Ficino claimed, i.e. without the intervention of God and only from the natural powers existing in the universe, then such magic would constitute a real threat to Christianity; for its logical consequence would be atheism or deism.[43]

Natural magic, for all its importance in the intellectual history of the Renaissance and even of the seventeenth century,[44] remained

[40] Quoted *ibid.*, p. 16.

[41] *Ibid.*, p. 21.

[42] *Ibid.*, p. 20.

[43] *Ibid.*, pp. 83–4.

[44] Cf. A. R. Hall, 'On the Historical Singularity of the Scientific Revolution in the Seventeenth Century', see below, pp. 219ff.

an esoteric cult. But its chief emotional ingredient, music, was accessible to all. Music, moreover, did not need the paraphernalia of magical practices to exert its own, quasi-magical powers. The question was: How far could it be allowed to do so?

The one great theologian of the Renaissance period who gave an unqualified affirmative answer was Luther. 'What a conscience St Augustine had!' Luther commented on the saint's reference to music in his *Confessions*. 'When he had pleasure in music and was made cheerful by it, he thought he had done wrong and had sinned.' And he added, with characteristic egocentricity: 'He [Augustine] was a fine, pious man; if he lived in the present time he would be one of us.'[45] It was not the relation of music to the harmony of the universe which was important to Luther; although, as a former student of the traditional *quadrivium*, he certainly knew of this connection. What mattered to Luther was rather the sound of music and its effect on man's mind. Time and again, in his table talk, in his writings and, not least, in his own practice of music in church and home, he comes back to this point: 'One of the most beautiful and magnificent gifts of God is music.' Princes should foster it and spend money on it.[46] Or again: 'The devil is a sad spirit and makes people sad and therefore he does not like gaiety. That is why he flies from music as far as he can, and does not stay when people sing, especially religious songs.'[47]

If religious songs were best, that did not mean that for Luther there was a Platonic distinction between moral and immoral music. On the contrary, since music as such was a gift of God to man, there was no harm in musical parody, the adaptation of secular songs to religious purposes; for why, Luther asked, should the devil have all the best tunes? The famous chorale, '*Vom Himmel hoch da komm ich her*', derived from the song '*Aus fremden Landen komm ich her*' and, even more alarmingly, from '*Mit Lust tret ich an diesen Tanz*'. The Lutheran hymnal was full of such transformations. Music and the joy it gave men, Luther claimed, were the foretaste of the much greater joys of Heaven; for

[45] Quoted in Clive, *The Calvinist Attitude to Music*, p. 101, n. 1.

[46] M. Luther, *Tischreden* (Weimar, 1912), 1, 968.

[47] *Ibid.*, no. 194.

music was near theology: it made the words come alive.[48] Luther's friend and collaborator, the musician Johannes Walter, set the tone for the long line of *cantors* of the Evangelical Church in a *laus musicae*, published in 1538:

> Sie ist mit der Theologie
> Zugleich von Gott gegeben hie/
> Gott hat die Music fein bedeckt
> in der Theologie versteckt/
> Er hat sie beid im fried geschmückt
> Das kein der andern ehr verrückt/
> Sie sin inn freundschafft nahe verwandt
> Das sie für schwestern wern erkandt/[49]

Theology and music, then, were heavenly sisters and neither would touch the other's honour; there could be no antagonism nor rivalry. In this firm belief generations of Lutheran pastors and *cantors* practised the art and allowed it freely to develop in their churches. It did not occur to them, as it did not occur to Walter and Luther, that one of the heavenly sisters would suffer an all but fatal decline in her appeal and that, without overt antagonism or rivalry, this decline would leave the other sister in a commanding position over men's hearts.

It did not occur to Luther; Zwingli, however, knew it well and feared it, even in his own time. A fine musician himself and able to perform on quite a variety of musical instruments, Zwingli would allow no singing in church at all. Had not the prophet Amos said: 'Take thou away from me the noise of thy songs; for I will not hear the melody of thy viols' [v. 23]? And what would

[48] *Ibid.*, no. 968: 'Weil unser Herr Gott in dies Leben, das doch ein lauter Schmeishaus ist, solche edle Gaben geschütt und uns gegeben hat, was wird in jenem ewigen Leben geschehen, da Alles wird aufs Allervollkommenste und Lustigste werden; hie aber ist nur *materia prima*, der Anfang . . . Die Musica ist eine schöne herrliche Gabe Gottes, und nahe der Theologie . . . Die Noten machen den Text lebendig.' A recent historian even suggests that music as a means of communication is possessed, for Luther, both of a theological dimension and of theological power: C. Garside, 'Some Attitudes of the Major Reformers Toward the Role of Music in the Liturgy', *McCormick Quarterly*, xxi (1967), 153.

[49] J. Walter, *Lob und Preis der löblichen Kunst Musica 1538* (Kassel, 1938).

he not have said today to all the singing and dancing, and to the choristers who come to the altar in their silken shirts?[50] In practice, music in church led to vanity and hypocrisy, for not one in a hundred could understand the mumbling of the singing nuns.[51]

Such criticism of music in church was traditional enough. But Zwingli went much further. Prayer was valuable only when said with complete concentration on its meaning. This was difficult enough, even under the most favourable circumstances, for 'when one prays, mouth and mind are not long on the same track'. Zwingli then drew the apparently inescapable conclusion: 'much less so mind and song'.[52] The power of music over men's minds was too great to allow it to compete with the word of God in church.[53] Unlike Calvin, Zwingli believed that it really was David's music, and not God's intervention, which had freed Saul, at least temporarily, from the visitations of the Devil.[54] But since God had nowhere actually commanded the use of music in his service, Zwingli could come to only one conclusion: music must be banished completely from church and become a purely secular art.

It is possible that Zwingli's thinking on church music continued to develop and that he might have reintroduced a reformed song into his Church if he had not been killed at Cappel.[55] In actual fact, however, singing ceased in those Swiss churches which were most directly influenced by Zwingli's teaching, and in Zürich and Berne the organs of the churches were destroyed or sold[56]—it is claimed, with the approval of the congregations.[57] Not until 1598 was singing of a very simple kind allowed again in the services of the Reformed Church in Zürich. There has

[50] H. Reimann, *Huldrych Zwingli—der Musiker* (Neujahrsblatt der Allgemeinen Musikgesellschaft Zürich, 1960), cxliv, 16.

[51] *Ibid.*

[52] C. Garside, *Zwingli and the Arts* (New Haven and London, 1966), p. 49.

[53] *Ibid.*, p. 49.

[54] *Ibid.*, p. 67.

[55] Reimann, *Zwingli—der Musiker*, pp. 17ff.

[56] W. Blankenburg, 'Die Kirchenmusik in den reformierten Gebieten', Blume, *Geschichte der evangelischen Kirchenmusik*, p. 344.

[57] Garside, *Zwingli and the Arts*, pp. 61ff.

never been a clearer, nor a more devastating, acknowledgment of the power of music in its ambivalent relations with religion.

It is not surprising that Switzerland played little part in the great triumphs of music in the eighteenth and nineteenth centuries. Probably until the end of the seventeenth century and, quite likely, well beyond it, church music formed the bulk of all music that was composed and played. Cut off church music, and the chances were that secular music would be stunted, too. That, at least, seems to have been the feeling of many in the sixteenth and seventeenth centuries as they contemplated the austere services of the Calvinists and the even bleaker ones of the Zwinglians and of those Anabaptists who rejected or restricted church music. In England there appeared a voluminous and spirited defence of music, at the turn of the sixteenth century, ranging from Shakespeare's famous thrust against

> The man that hath no music in himself,
> Nor is not moved with concord of sweet sounds,
> Is fit for treasons, stratagems and spoils,[58]

to the crude but forceful verse of Samuel Rowley:

> The dulcet tongue of musicke made the stones
> To move, irrational beasts and birds to dance.
> And last the trumpet's musicke shall awake the dead,
> And clothes their naked bones in coates of flesh
> T'appeare in that high house of parliament,
> When those that gnash their teeth at musicke's sound
> Shall make that place where musicke ne'er was found.[59]

A generation later, with the tide of puritanism running more strongly than ever, the battle was still continuing. Sir Thomas Browne was still convinced of the existence of the harmony of the spheres which,

> though they give no sound unto the ear, yet to the understanding they strike a note most full of harmony. Whosoever is harmonically composed delights in harmony;

[58] Shakespeare, *The Merchant of Venice*, v, i.

[59] Quoted in J. Hutton, 'Some English Poems in Praise of Music', *English Miscellany* (Rome, 1951), ed. M. Praz, ii, 41.

> which makes me distrust the symmetry of those heads which declaim against all Church-Musick. For myself . . . I embrace it: for even that vulgar and Tavern-Musick, which makes one man merry, another mad, strikes in me a deep fit of devotion, and a profound contemplation of the first Composer.[60]

Leonardo da Vinci had seen that painting has an enormous psychological power, a numinous power—or a demonic one, as the Calvinist iconoclasts thought. Music has this power to an even greater degree, and there had always been musicians, writers and listeners who had recognized this. Yet during the Renaissance for many the clear recognition of this phenomenon was obscured by a too one-sided evaluation of the relationship between words and music, and its discussion was side-tracked into the arid, and eventually meaningless, attempt to resurrect the Platonic distinctions between moral and immoral music. But by 1600, outside those areas strongly influenced by Zwingli and Calvin, music was emerging triumphantly from the attacks of the musical moralists, both secular and clerical. In Venice, where the *capella* of St Mark's depended on the secular authorities, puritanism in music was never looked upon with any greater favour than any other type of puritanism. The Netherlander Willaert had introduced the use of multiple choirs in St Mark's, and his successors accompanied these with organ, trombones and strings. Towards the end of the sixteenth century, Andrea and Giovanni Gabrieli composed church and secular music, indifferently, and with a richness of texture that matched contemporary Venetian painting. This, it seems, was the way in which the painters saw it. In his *Marriage of Cana*, now in the Louvre, Veronese painted a group of musicians in the very centre of his composition and immediately below the figure of Christ: they were Titian playing a string bass, Tintoretto and Veronese himself playing viols, and Bassano playing the flute. Here were music and painting at the feet of Christ, without the intervention of the word except in so far as the painting told the well-known Biblical story. This was indeed

[60] Sir Thomas Browne, *Religio Medici*, II, ix; also quoted in W. Mellers, *Music and Society*, 2nd ed. (London, 1950), pp. 104f.

a different conception of the role of music (and painting) from that of Baïf or Borromeo.

In the seventeenth century some theorists, such as Mersenne, continued to argue as the sixteenth-century humanists had done. But, effectively, musical puritanism was being transformed by being channelled into opera, the invention of Vincenzo Galilei and his circle. For in opera the primacy of words over music, which they had so earnestly striven for, could be happily combined with the rich sonorities of Venetian instrumental music and the intricate part writing and emotional subtleties of the madrigalists. In Catholic church music the precepts of the Council of Trent were gradually forgotten. By 1628 Orazio Benevoli was commissioned to write, for the consecration of the new Cathedral of Salzburg, a mass for twelve separate choirs and fifty-three voices. As in every other form of Baroque art, the total effect of a complete and complex work on the senses and sensibilities of the beholder or listener came to be regarded as more important than the effects or values of any of its parts.

Such an attitude may also help to explain the rapidly growing popularity of different forms of religious or spiritual music—*geistliche Musik*—as distinct from traditional church and liturgical music. Their origins were varied. *Laude spirituali* (spiritual songs), for instance, were popular already in the sixteenth century, and their Catholic publishers were as liberal as Luther in parodying secular songs.[61] St Filippo Neri, in the second half of the sixteenth century, introduced music as a devotional exercise into his oratory in Rome and, at first, with all the musical puritanism of the Counter-Reformation. But, precisely because such music was not part of a regular church service, it rapidly developed considerable freedom. Thus was launched oratorio on its immensely successful career, culminating in the sustained popular apotheosis of Handel's *Messiah* in England, and leading to the philologically absurd but culturally quite logical genre of secular oratorio in the twentieth century. Thus also developed spiritual concerts, organ introductions to church services, motets and cantatas. The dividing-line between these free forms of religious music and liturgical or church music properly speaking was by no means

[61] G. Reese, *Music in the Renaissance*, p. 453.

always clear nor rigidly observed. In the Lutheran Church it was hardly made at all; in the Catholic Church it varied with place and time. But everywhere this religious music developed according to purely musical rules and tastes, with barely a curtsy towards the rigid rules which sixteenth-century theologians and humanists had wanted to impose upon it. The brilliant orchestration of secular and courtly dance suites with their concertante solo instruments, the emotional and dramatic effects of Italian opera with its *da capo* arias and its coloratura singing—in short, all the splendours of secular Baroque music—were easily adapted to religious purposes, either by being given a slightly solemn or sentimental tinge or, more commonly, by simply being supplied with appropriate religious texts. Large sections of the European public, especially the educated classes, seem to have wanted to take their religion with a large admixture of music and, what is more, with the most dramatic, exciting and affecting music that was being composed. So strong was this longing that even the Calvinist and Zwinglian parts of Europe could not resist it. *Geistliche Abendmusiken*, religious musical evenings, spread from the Netherlands throughout northern Germany and became immensely popular. Zürich itself, the city which had abolished church music altogether, found that it could not do without 'music in church'.[62]

From about the middle of the seventeenth century some theoreticians of music began to emancipate the art from moral and theological values. For the Italian, Marco Sacchi, music was to be performed no longer *ad maiorem Dei gloriam*, but *ad maiorem musicae artis gloriam*. It was not an altogether original notion: Plato had been enraged by those who thought that music could 'only be judged rightly by the pleasure of the hearer'.[63] Naturally, it had not been a fashionable idea among Renaissance Neoplatonists. But by the early eighteenth century there was a whole school of music theoreticians in Germany who saw the end and justification of music in the pleasure it gave the listener.[64] More important,

[62] Reimann, *Zwingli—der Musiker*, p. 19.

[63] Cf. above, p. 40.

[64] P. Bernary, *Die deutsche Kompositionslehre des 18. Jahrhunderts* (Leipzig, 1955), p. 37.

however, from our point of view, than the emancipation of music as an art was the fact that for most musicians and theoreticians it continued to be linked in some way with religion and with the essential nature of the universe. For instance, Andreas Werckmeister, writing about 1700, saw music as 'a tool of the Holy Ghost by which He awakens all sorts of pious and elevating emotions in the human heart'.[65] It was as if man had his divine image of himself presented to him by music, Werckmeister argued, for music represented the order which God had created.[66]

This type of simplified Neoplatonism dominated also the prevalent French school of musical aesthetics which saw music as an essentially imitative art, able to reproduce in the listener specific emotional and even visual effects existing in the outside world. This theory of imitation worked well enough for painting and poetry. It could still be reasonably applied to songs and opera. But what effects did a symphony or sonata reproduce? The solution to this difficulty seemed to lie again in the old Pythagorean and Neoplatonic theory of a world harmony based on numbers which, in some way, was mirrored by music.[67] Leibniz put it succinctly: 'Musica est exercitium arithmeticae occultum nescientes se numerare animi' (music is a concealed practice of mathematics of a soul not consciously calculating).[68]

It is against the background of these shifting attitudes towards music that we have to see the towering and enigmatic figure of Johann Sebastian Bach. Not entirely surprisingly, the interpretation of Bach's own attitude towards music has become highly controversial in the last twenty years.[69] There is, of course, no

65 Quoted in H. Goldschmidt, *Die Musikästhetik des 18. Jahrhunderts und ihre Beziehungen zu seinem Kunstschaffen* (Zürich and Leipzig, 1915), p. 53.

66 *Ibid.*

67 J. Écorcheville, *De Lulli à Rameau 1690–1730. L'Esthétique Musicale* (Paris, 1906), p. 31.

68 Quoted in H. H. Dräger, 'Musik-Ästhetik', *Musik in Geschichte und Gegenwart*, ed. F. Blume (Kassel, 1961), ix, col. 1,012.

69 See, for instance, out of an enormous literature, G. Herz, 'Bach's Religion', *Journal of Renaissance and Baroque Music*, i (1946–7); W. Blankenburg, 'Bach, geistlich und weltlich', *Musik und Kirche*, xx (1950), and 'Das Parodieverfahren Bachs', *ibid.*, xxxii (1962); F. Smend, *Luther und Bach* (Berlin, 1947); F. Blume, 'Bach, Johann Sebastian', *Musik in*

question of Bach's deep religious convictions. But it does seem that it was music itself which was the centre of his religious convictions and which largely determined their form. He was hostile to the Pietists because of their puritanical attitude towards music, and not for theological reasons. Or, rather, music itself was part of his theology. Here Bach was undoubtedly within the Lutheran tradition, but it is clear that music's twin sister, theology, had already suffered a marked eclipse. As in the case of Sir Thomas Browne, it was music itself, and not necessarily or specifically church music, which was man's *laudatio Dei* and *recreatio cordis.*

Thus Bach could accept, as some modern scholars believe, the Leibnizian Neoplatonic view of the relation of music to a fundamental world order and even incorporate a highly complex and esoteric number symbolism in some of his compositions.[70] More important still, it enabled him to compose, without apparent qualms of conscience, music for Catholic church services and, most significant of all, to transform much of his own immense output of secular music into church cantatas, oratoria and even parts of the *St Matthew Passion*, and all this on a scale greater than anyone realized until quite recently. It is not necessary to suppose that Bach's thinking about music was completely consistent throughout his life. If nothing else, the last variation of the *Goldberg Variations*, with themes from the popular song

Kraut und Rüben
Die haben mich vertrieben

(Cabbage and turnips
Have driven me from home)

[70] Smend, *Luther und Bach*, pp. 16–20; Blankenburg, 'Bach, geistlich und weltlich', pp. 41ff.

Geschichte und Gegenwart (Kassel, 1949–51), i, and 'Umrisse eines neuen Bach-Bildes', *Musica*, xvi (1962), controverted by A. Dürr, 'Zum Wandel des Bach-Bildes', *Musik und Kirche*, xxxii (1962), and answered by Blume, *ibid.* For an attempt at a completely Pythagorean interpretation of Bach see P. T. Barford, 'The Concept of Bach', *Music Review*, xxiii (1962). The most recent attempt at an orthodox interpretation that I have seen is J. Widmann, 'Johann Sebastian Bach. Musik zwischen Gott und Gemeinde', *Musik und Kirche*, xxxviii (1968). See also Blume, *Kirchenmusik*, pp. 168–213.

should warn us against an altogether too solemn interpretation of Bach's attitude towards his greatest works. It seems perhaps most sensible to assume (for we cannot prove it conclusively) that Bach saw no essential difference between secular and church music. For Bach, I believe, all music was sacred, the *Brandenburg Concertos* as much as the organ preludes, the Catholic Magnificat as much as the Protestant cantatas, the coloratura aria 'Prepare thyself, Zion' as much as the chorale 'Oh Haupt voll Blut und Wunden'. If Descartes's God was the great artificer, worshipped most appropriately through mathematics, Bach's God was the great creator of harmony, worshipped most fittingly through music. The metaphors and analogies involved in both beliefs were not as far apart as has often been thought.

In the course of the eighteenth century the last remnants of philosophical and religious puritanism disappeared from musical thought. 'To enjoy music fully, we must completely lose ourselves in it', wrote Rameau.[71] It was just this power of music to make the listener lose himself in it which had terrified Plato and his Renaissance disciples. Worse still, from the traditional point of view: Rameau thought that words might actually get in the way of a proper understanding and appreciation of music.

> We must not think but let ourselves be carried away by the feeling which the music inspires [he urges, and then adds (in what I take to be a somewhat ironic bow towards the fashionable philosophy of the age):] As for reason, everybody possesses it nowadays; we have just discovered it in the bosom of nature itself. We have even proved that instinct constantly recalls it to us. . . . When reason and instinct are reconciled, there will be no higher appeal.[72]

If music could be reconciled with reason it could also, *a fortiori*, still be reconciled with religion. Music, as we have seen,

[71] 'Observations sur notre instinct pour la musique et sur son principe' (1734), quoted and translated by S. Morgenstern, *Composers on Music* (New York, 1956), p. 43.

[72] *Ibid.*, pp. 44–5.

has a numinous power, like painting, and it has this perhaps to an even greater degree. It is this fact which caused the analogy between the two arts to break down in the eighteenth century. As the strength and fervour of traditional religious beliefs declined, the quality of religious painting began to decline too; for it was, in the end, bound to the artist's (and perhaps also his patron's) convictions in this matter. With some few exceptions, notably in the work of Tiepolo and Blake and, arguably, Goya, the eighteenth and nineteenth centuries produced very little great religious painting—that is, painting comparable as religious painting with the work of Renaissance and seventeenth-century artists, and comparable simply as painting with the work of the great painters of secular subjects, from Watteau to Renoir.

But music was different. Nearly all the great composers, from Handel through Haydn, Mozart and Beethoven to Verdi, Brahms and Fauré, poured some of their finest musical thought into masses, requiems and spiritual songs. It was not only the advantage which music had over painting, in that its exercise preserved something of the spirit of communal worship of an earlier, more orthodox age; it was its ability to create this spirit even when it was no longer clear what, if anything, was being worshipped.[73] It did not even matter very much whether this religious music used liturgical texts or not. Its impact was primarily on the emotions and it could accommodate any intellectual content. It could encompass Handel's astonishing fusion of Anglo-German Biblicism with an Italian and Baroque sense of drama just as easily as Mozart's masonic deism or the great

[73] The late Professor E. J. Dent realized this very clearly: 'It has often been maintained that the Church "inspired" the art of European music; it would be more true to say that music inspired the Church. The Church was the first great utilizer of music, and it sought to utilize it because, as we learn from St Augustine, it was afraid of music. The history of church music shows us plainly from the earliest days down to the *Motu proprio* of Pope Pius X that the so-called "hand-maid of the Church" very soon asserted herself, and continued to do so unabashed, as a *serva padrona*': Introduction to A. Yorke-Long, *Music at Court* (London, 1954), pp. xiii–xiv. I came across this passage after I had written the first draft of this essay. As far as I know, Dent never elaborated this point, which comes very near to the central thesis of this essay.

paean to God the Creator of the world and of its order and harmony which is Haydn's *Creation*.

Later, in the nineteenth and early twentieth centuries, the Churches found it difficult to accept such works as church music. The author of the article on church music in the *Catholic Encyclopaedia* (1911) criticized particularly the church music of Haydn, Mozart and Beethoven and of the Protestant composers Bach and Handel. He distinguished, quite reasonably, between religious and church music and then stated categorically that these composers 'do not fulfil the requirements of the Church'.[74]

No one, however, demonstrated the capacity of music to create its own religious feelings more clearly than Beethoven. There is little doubt that when Beethoven wrote his *Mass in C*, Op. 86 (1806) and his *Missa Solemnis* (1819–23) he set out to write proper church music. He studied Gregorian chant, medieval hymns and Palestrina's masses with care, and incorporated elements of these styles in his work. But the work was clearly so far removed from the traditional mass and so individual in its conception that, during Beethoven's lifetime, only the *Kyrie*, *Credo* and *Agnus Dei* were performed, and this, moreover, in German translation, as *Drei grosse Hymnen* (Three Great Hymns), in order to avoid clerical censure.[75] But of its impact on the listener there has never been any question: 'Von Herzen—möge es zu Herzen gehen' (From the heart, may it go to the heart), as Beethoven wrote over the *Kyrie*.

But it was not just Beethoven's church music which has had this effect. It was the whole of his work. It seems that he himself believed that music, especially his own music, had transcendental qualities.

[74] G. Gietmann, 'Church Music', *The Catholic Encyclopaedia*, x, 650. Presumably, so as not to appear as a philistine, Gietmann added: 'The musical fame of these masters is thereby in nowise diminished.' In fairness, it should be pointed out that F. J. Molek, writing the equivalent article in the *New Catholic Encyclopaedia*, x (1967), is very much more perceptive about, and not in the least critical of, Haydn's and Mozart's church music.

[75] G. Schuhmacher, 'Beethoven's geistliche Werke', Schallplatte und Kirche, Beiheft 1 zu *Musik und Kirche*, xxxvii (1967), 6.

> When I lift my eyes [he said] I must sigh; for what I see is contrary to my religion, and I must despise a world which does not perceive that music is a higher revelation than all wisdom and philosophy; it is the wine which rouses to new creations, and I am the Bacchus who presses this glorious wine for men and makes them spiritually drunk; when they are sober again they will have fished up much which they can keep on dry land.

Thus Bettina Brentano reported her conversation with Beethoven to Goethe in 1810.[76] A few days later Beethoven elaborated his views to Bettina, especially for Goethe's benefit:

> Talk to Goethe about me; tell him he should listen to my symphonies and he will agree with me that music is the only incorporeal entrance [*unverkörperte Eingang*] into a higher world of knowledge which encompasses man but which he cannot encompass.... Thus art always represents the deity, and man's relation to art is religion....

As the seed needs the wet, soft electrical soil to grow, he continued, so music is the electrical soil in which the spirit lives, thinks and creates. Music gives the spirit its relationship to harmony and unity. All that is electrical stimulates the spirit to musical, pulsing, outflowing creation. 'I have an electrical nature', he exclaimed at the end—and then rushed Bettina off to a rehearsal. She wrote it all down, that night, and when she showed it to him the next morning he said: 'Did I say that? Well then I must have been in a trance [*Nun dann hab ich einen Raptus gehabt*].'[77]

The authenticity of Bettina's account has often been doubted, ever since she published it, in 1835, in her undoubtedly romanticized account of her friendship and correspondence with Goethe. But most modern scholars tend to accept that Beethoven did say something like what she wrote. The very confusion of ideas, the faint echoes of Platonic harmony, the misunderstanding of contemporary scientific notions about electricity, all this seems highly

[76] Bettina von Arnim (Brentano), *Goethes Briefwechsel mit einem Kinde*, ed. G. Konrad (Frechen-Köln, 1960), p. 246.

[77] *Ibid.*, pp. 247–9.

likely for a man unused to finding words for his deepest thoughts about music. Goethe was evidently taken aback, but kept his Olympian calm.

> It has been a great pleasure to me [he wrote in answer to Bettina's account] to receive this picture of a true genius without wanting to classify him. . . . From what can be understood from these [i.e. Beethoven's] manifold utterances, I must confess that ordinary common sense might perhaps find contradictions in them: but what is uttered by one possessed by such a daemon must cause reverence in the layman . . . for here the gods are at work, sowing seeds for future understanding. . . .[78]

Goethe's view of music was not a romantic one. Music could move him deeply. After a recital of Bach's *Well-tempered Clavier* he wrote: 'I said to myself: it is as if the eternal harmony was conversing with itself, as it might have happened in God's heart just before the creation.'[79] But principally he sought to understand music intellectually and to construct a theory of tones, in analogy to his theory of colours, involving both the mathematical elements and the psychological effects of music.[80] Characteristically, Bettina thought this a waste of time.[81] For her the matter was quite simple. 'Look out, Frau Rat,' she claimed to have said to Goethe's mother, 'that the angels will not beat you about the head with their fiddlesticks until you have realized that heaven is music.'[82]

Bettina Brentano is important because her simple, romantic equation of music and the divine, and more especially of Beethoven's music and the Deity, was characteristic for much of the musical sensibility of the nineteenth and even twentieth centuries. It really mattered little what Beethoven himself had said or thought. His listeners felt themselves well able to interpret the master's meaning. It started in his lifetime, and before anyone but

[78] *Ibid.*, p. 250.

[79] Quoted in F. Blume, *Goethe und die Musik* (Kassel, 1948), p. 65.

[80] *Ibid.*, pp. 70ff. and *passim*.

[81] Bettina von Arnim, *Goethes Briefwechsel*, p. 142.

[82] *Ibid.*, p. 128.

Goethe had read his conversation with Bettina. 'Even if you do not believe it, you are being glorified', a certain Hofrat Peters wrote into Beethoven's conversation book in 1823. 'You will rise with me from the dead and you will conduct the choirs while I pray.'[83] Beethoven's answer is not recorded.

After Beethoven's death, the minor Romantic poets celebrated his divinity in reams of almost unbelievably bad verse. Nikolaus Lenau was, relatively, better than most:

> In der Symphonien rauschen,
> Heiligen Gewittergüssen,
> Seh ich Zeus auf Wolken nahn und
> Christi blut'ge Stirne küssen;
>
> Hört das Herz die grosse Liebe
> Alles in die Arme schliessen,
> Mit der alten Welt die neue
> In die ewige zerfliessen.[84]

Wagner, although he was sceptical of Bettina's account of her conversation with Beethoven, was completely uninhibited in his own interpretation of Beethoven's music. 'A deaf musician!' he exclaimed. 'Could one imagine a blind painter? But a blind seer we do know. Teiresias, who was shut off from the world of appearances but who is able to perceive the reason of all appearances with his inner eye—like him, the deaf musician listens to the harmonies of his inner being. . . .' His inner light reflects on the world of appearances and gives it back its childlike innocence: ' "Today thou wilt be with me in Paradise"—who does not hear this word of the Redeemer when he listens to the *Pastoral Symphony*?' Never has any art created anything so joyful, Wagner continues, as Beethoven's symphonies in A and F (i.e. No. 7 and No. 6, the *Pastoral*). Their effect on the hearer is that of freeing him from all guilt and their after-effect, when he returns to the

[83] Quoted in A. Schmitz, 'Die Beethoven-Apotheose als Beispiel eines Säkularisierungsvorganges', *Festschrift Peter Wagner* (Leipzig, 1926), pp. 186–7.

[84] Quoted in L. Hirschberg, 'Beethoven und die Dichtung', *Die Musik*, x, 37 (1910–11), 350.

world of appearances, is that of paradise lost. 'Thus these wonderful works preach repentance and penance in the deepest sense of a divine revelation.'[85]

The high point of the deification of Beethoven's music, and even of the composer himself, was reached in the Beethoven biographies of the early twentieth century. Paul Bekker wrote in 1912: 'Thus he regards himself as a vessel of supernatural revelation—as the hero, the conqueror who had suffered, had let himself be crucified, had descended to the dead and had risen and felt God awaken in himself.'[86] Romain Rolland, in 1903, had put it more elegantly, but only a little less fancifully: 'Et à mesure qu'il était plus seul, veuf d'amitiés et d'amours, et qu'il s'acheminait vers le complet détachement de cette vie . . . Dieu remplissait en lui tout l'espace: il épousait sa triple forme: la Force, l'Amour et la Lumière. Il s'identifiait avec la Toute-Puissance créatrice, en même temps qu'avec la tremblante humilité de la créature.'[87]

A German musicologist, A. Schmitz, has called this Beethoven-apotheosis an example of a process of secularization.[88] This seems to me true in so far as this phenomenon could occur only in an age of a rapid weakening of traditional religious feeling. But, essentially, the attitude of the Beethoven worshippers was not a secular one at all. It was, on the contrary, quite consciously religious and was expressed deliberately in religious language. It seems to me, therefore, that a kind of transference had occurred. Music and its emotional appeal, even the persons of the composers of music, had become identified with religion and were held to speak the language of religion, thus providing an emotional satisfaction which the traditional church service could no longer provide.

This becomes very clear from the persistent tendency, even in most recent times, for Beethoven's music to be interpreted in

[85] R. Wagner, 'Beethoven', *Gesammelte Schriften und Dichtungen*, ed. W. Golther (Berlin, n.d.) viii, 92–3.

[86] P. Bekker, *Beethoven*, 2nd ed. (Berlin, 1921), p. 89. Also quoted in Schmitz, 'Die Beethoven-Apotheose', p. 184.

[87] R. Rolland, *Beethoven, Les Grandes Epoques Creatrices. Le Chant de la Resurrection* (Paris, 1937), p. 364.

[88] Schmitz, 'Die Beethoven-Apotheose', *passim*.

philosophical and religious terms. Aldous Huxley's comments, at the end of *Point Counterpoint*, on the slow movement of the Quartet, Op. 132, the *Holy Song of Praise of a Convalescent to the Deity*, are a typical literary example:

> It was as though heaven had suddenly and impossibly become more heavenly, had passed from admired perfection into perfection yet deeper and more absolute. The ineffable peace persisted; but it was no longer the peace of convalescence and passivity. It quivered, it was alive, it seemed to grow and intensify itself, it became an active calm, an almost passionate serenity. The miraculous paradox of eternal repose was musically realized.[89]

Even Stravinsky, the composer who claimed that composing was the ordering of a certain number of tones in certain interval relationships,[90] wrote recently: 'These [Beethoven's last] quartets are my highest article of musical belief (which is a longer word for love, whatever else), as indispensable to the ways and meanings of art, as a musician of my era thinks of art and has tried to learn it, as temperature is to life. They are a triumph over temporality. . . .'[91]

While no other composer has had quite such an effect on his hearers as Beethoven, the elevation of all music into a kind of religion was very much a part of the Romantic movement. It was given philosophical respectability by Schopenhauer. Ideas, Schopenhauer argued—that is, Platonic ideas—were the objectivization of the will, the basic principle of the world. It is the purpose of works of art to stimulate the recognition of these ideas by the representation of individual objects. Works of art therefore

[89] A. Huxley, *Point Counter Point* (Harmondsworth, 1955; 1st ed., 1928), p. 433. It is irrelevant for my argument whether this passage represented Huxley's own feelings or whether he intended it only to represent those of a character in his novel.

[90] H. F. Redlich, 'Strawinsky', *Musik in Geschichte und Gegenwart*, xii (1965), col. 1,512.

[91] Review of J. Kerman, *The Beethoven Quartets*, *New York Review of Books*, xi, 5 (26 September, 1968), 4.

objectivize or mirror the will only indirectly, i.e. through the ideas. Music, however, differs from all the other arts in that it is not the image of ideas, but the image of the will itself; which explains the extraordinary effect of music, an effect much greater than that of any other art. Music is, moreover, independent of the world and could exist without it.[92]

Melody especially, Schopenhauer argues, expresses the manifold striving of the human will, from wish to satisfaction and then to a new wish; for just so melody meanders away from the keynote and through a series of dissonances, before returning to it. As the quick succession of desires and satisfactions constitutes happiness and well-being, so a quick melody is, in general, cheerful. Slow melodies, with painful dissonances analogous to delayed satisfaction, are sad. Thus 'the composer reveals the inmost being of the world and speaks its deepest wisdom in a language which his reason does not understand'.[93] Music, Schopenhauer maintained, expresses in a very general language the essence of the world—it expresses joy or sorrow, jubilation or sadness, without anything contingent or particular attached to these 'abstract' emotions. Philosophy, however, is nothing else but a complete and correct repetition and expression of the nature (*Wesen*) of the world in general concepts. It therefore follows, always according to Schopenhauer, that a true explanation of music, i.e. a detailed repetition of what music expresses in concepts, would immediately be a sufficient repetition and explanation of the world, a real philosophy. Leibniz's epigram, 'Musica est exercitium arithmeticae occultum nescientes se numerare animi', should now really read 'Musica est exercitium metaphysices occultum nescientes se philosophari animi' (Music is a concealed practice of metaphysics by a soul that is not conscious of philosophizing).[94]

This was Platonism without tears; or, at least, without mathematics. For the theory of a mathematical equivalence or, at least, analogy between the structure of the universe and the nature of

[92] A. Schopenhauer, 'Die Welt als Wille und Vorstellung', *Sämtliche Werke*, i (Munich, 1911), 304.

[93] *Ibid.*, pp. 307f.

[94] *Ibid.*, pp. 308–13.

music (a theory which, rightly or wrongly and in however varying and attenuated forms, had constituted the hard core of the philosophy of music for some two thousand years), for this basically rational theory Schopenhauer substituted a deliberately non-rational and essentially romantic metaphysics of music. In detail, the results of Schopenhauer's views were inevitably arbitrary. Thus he quite seriously proposed an analogy between 'the four voices of all harmony, i.e. bass, tenor, alto and soprano, or keynote, third, fifth and octave' and the 'four gradations in the series of beings [*Wesen*], i.e. the mineral realm, flora, fauna and man'.[95]

Schopenhauer's metaphysics of music may have been philosophically shallow and musically naïve, but they managed very successfully to strike a certain mood of the nineteenth century. Never before had music been elevated so high above the other arts nor been identified so unequivocally with the self-expression of the Deity (Schopenhauer's 'will', at least as popularly understood). Wagner accepted Schopenhauer's philosophy with enthusiasm.[96] As a musician, and a very articulate one, he was, moreover, a great deal more specific than the philosopher: 'Just as Christianity arose in the international civilization of the Roman Empire, so music emerges out of the chaos of modern civilization. Both proclaim: "Our kingdom is not of this world." And this means: we come from within, you from without; we derive from the essence, you from the appearance of things.'[97]

While Wagner had put music and Christianity on the same level, their relationship to each other remained somewhat confused in his thought. The music of the Greeks had 'intimately penetrated the world of appearances and had fused with its scientific and social laws'. But this paradise had been lost—presumably in the despised 'international civilization' of the Roman Empire. Then, however, 'it was the spirit of Christianity which revived music'.[98]

[95] *Ibid.*, ii, 509.

[96] E.g. in his essay on Beethoven, pp. 66ff.

[97] Article 'Musik', *Wagner Lexikon*, ed. C. Fr. Glasenapp and H. v. Stein (Stuttgart, 1883), p. 497.

[98] *Ibid.*, p. 498.

This seems both orthodox and categorical. But immediately Wagner continues:

> Church music was sung to the words of the concepts of dogma: in its effects it dissolved these words and the concepts of dogma contained in them to the point where their very perception disappears, so that it [music] now conveys their pure emotive content to the entranced emotions of the hearer. In this sense we have to recognize that music reveals the essence of the Christian religion with unrivalled definiteness. . . .

In the painting of a Raphael Madonna, Wagner continues, we still have to say: *this means*. 'But music says to us: *this is*—because it abolishes the dichotomy between concept and feeling, and this through tonal form, a form which is wholly other than the world of appearances, yet one which fills our soul as by grace and which is not comparable to anything real.'[99]

Here were St Augustine's and the theologians' fears of the powers of music not only fulfilled but actually made to triumph over the words of the dogma as mere 'concepts'. For Wagner the function of song was not to give greater effect to words. The human voice itself was simply one more musical instrument designed to serve the functions of music. He praised Bach for using his choirs with the flexibility of an orchestra and approvingly characterized the *Missa Solemnis* as 'a purely symphonic work of the truest Beethovenesque spirit'. The only reason why the words of great church music do not disturb us is because 'they do not stimulate rational concepts, but rather (and as, indeed, their ecclesiastical character requires) they touch us only with the impression of well-known symbolic formulas of faith'.[100] Even Zwingli, in his most pessimistic moments about church music, could hardly have foreseen such a reversal of values.

Seeing in Beethoven's symphonies a language of such power and subtlety as had never previously been spoken, Wagner asked himself why music should have reached such heights in his own century. The answer, he thought, must be found in the growing

[99] *Ibid.*, pp. 498–9.

[100] Wagner, 'Beethoven', p. 103.

conventionality of the modern European languages which made the development of a completely new form of expression a 'metaphysical necessity'. The extraordinary popularity of even the most profound musical genres, the growing zeal in the introduction of music into the general system of education, all this showed the inner need of mankind for this new language.[101]

> Let everyone experience for himself how the whole modern world of appearances [*die ganze moderne Erscheinungswelt*], which inexorably encompasses him on all sides to the point of desperation, suddenly vanishes into nothingness as soon as the first bars of these divine symphonies [i.e. Beethoven's] resound. How would it be possible to listen to such music with even a little devotion [*Andacht*] in our modern concert halls (where indeed Turks and Zouaves would feel comfortable!) if the optical perception of our surroundings did not vanish? But this is, in its most serious sense, the effect of music with regard to our whole civilization; music supersedes it as daylight supersedes artificial light.[102]

Wagner had observed a real phenomenon, even if he had assigned to it a wrong and unhistorical reason; for the splendours of nineteenth-century European literature make his theory of the growing conventionality of the modern European languages quite unacceptable. The real reason for the extraordinary development of music must be sought rather in the decline of conventional religious beliefs and in the psychological inadequacy of the Churches in fulfilling the religious longings of large sections of the educated European public; for music was able to provide precisely these emotional satisfactions and, by a process of rationalization and justification, also, apparently, those eternal truths which the Churches used to provide. This explains Wagner's own consistent use of religious phraseology and metaphors when talking about music and musicians. After his famous interview with Rossini, in 1860, for instance, Wagner remarked: 'What might he not have produced if he had received a forceful and

[101] *Wagner Lexikon*, p. 497.

[102] *Ibid.*

complete musical education? Especially if, less Italian and less sceptical, he had felt within him the *religion of his art*?'[103] It also explains the conception and history of the Wagner Theatre in Bayreuth and the passionate feelings, for and against, which it aroused and sometimes still arouses. For this was not the 'modern concert hall where Turks and Zouaves would feel comfortable', but, deliberately, the worthy place of pilgrimage for those who wished to listen to the master's music 'with devotion'. Here the performance of Wagner's operas attained to an almost liturgical status, and it was not until after the Second World War that Wagner's grandsons finally dared to break with the tradition of stage production established by the master himself.

If Wagner's was an extreme case, it was the extreme of a very widespread feeling in the nineteenth and early twentieth centuries. Richard Strauss, while a much more sober personality than Wagner, continued until the end of his life to speak of music in that mixture of Platonic and Schopenhauerian terms which had been so fashionable in his youth. 'Poetic inspiration', Strauss wrote in 1940, 'can still have a connection with the intelligence, because it must externalize itself through words—melodic inspiration is the absolute revelation of final mysteries. . . .'[104] And again, in 1944, but this time with an admixture of Jungian concepts:

> In Susanna's garden aria, in Belmonte's and Ferrando's A major and Octavio's G major aria, Eros himself sings in Mozart's melodies, Love in its most beautiful, purest forms speaks to our feelings. . . . In the slow section of Donna Anna's so-called 'Letter' aria, in both arias of the Countess in *Figaro*, we have before us the creations of the Ideal which I can only compare with Plato's 'Ideas', the prototype of visions projected into real life . . . not to be recognized by the eye, not to be grasped by the understanding, but to be divined by consciousness as most godly which the ear is permitted to 'breathe in'. Mozartean

[103] Quoted in H. Weinstock, *Rossini, a Biography* (New York, 1968), p. 297. My italics.

[104] *Composers on Music*, ed. S. Morgenstern, p. 338.

> melody is detached from every earthy form—the 'thing in itself', like Plato's Eros, poised between heaven and earth, between the mortal and the immortal—liberated from the 'will', it embodies the deepest penetration of artistic imagination, of the unconscious, into the final mysteries, into the realm of the 'archetypes'.[105]

Characteristically for Strauss, and perhaps generally for the mid-twentieth century, the high point of musical expression is seen no longer in Beethoven, but in Mozart.

In such an atmosphere of musical emotion it is not surprising that someone should have taken the final logical step and formally proclaimed music as a religion. In 1905 Riccardo Canudo first published a book in Paris which, in 1913, appeared in England with the title *Music as a Religion of the Future.*[106] Canudo's arguments were neither original nor philosophically distinguished, and I do not think the book had any considerable impact. They summed up, however, a great deal of previous thinking and emotion about music. Canudo saw the secret of both art and religion in self-oblivion and he argued that music, alone among the arts, was capable of creating 'this indispensable condition of Oblivion which all Religions have bestowed on their faithful'.[107]

The ultimate step in the apotheosis of music, the *non plus ultra* of the claims for its powers, and for those of its composer, was made, not by a clever rationalist like Canudo, but by the Russian composer Alexander Scriabin. At the turn of the nineteenth century mystical and revolutionary ideas were fashionable in Russia.[108] Scriabin seems to have been receptive to all of them, from Marxist socialism to theosophy. By 1904 he was telling a friend in Geneva:

> There will be a fusion of all the arts, but not a theatrical one like Wagner's. Art must unite with philosophy and

[105] *Ibid.*, p. 341.

[106] R. Canudo, *Music as a Religion of the Future*, tr. B. D. Conlan (London and Edinburgh, 1913).

[107] *Ibid.*, pp. 15–24. Canudo's (or his translator's?) capitalization.

[108] M. Cooper, 'Scriabin's Mystical Beliefs', *Music and Letters*, 16 (1935), 110–15.

> religion in an indivisible whole to form a new gospel which will replace the old gospel we have outlived. I cherish the dream of creating such a 'mystery'. For it, it would be necessary to build a special temple—perhaps here, perhaps far away in India. But mankind is not yet ready for it. It must be preached to; it must be led along new paths. And I do preach. Once I even preached from a boat, like Christ. I have a little circle of people who understand me perfectly and follow me. Particularly one—a fisherman. He is simple, but a splendid fellow.[109]

More and more he wrote his music, and especially his orchestral works, as preliminaries for the great 'mystery'. The programme notes for Scriabin's orchestral work, *The Divine Poem*, written by his mistress, Tatiana Schlözer, speak of the evolution of the human spirit, emancipated from past beliefs and passing through pantheism to a 'joyous and intoxicated affirmation of its liberty and its unity with the universe, the divine Ego'.[110] In a later work for orchestra, *Prometheus: a Poem of Fire*, Scriabin developed his ideas of the conjunction of the different arts by introducing a *clavier à lumière* which was to throw coloured lights on to a screen during the performance of the work.

The nature of the final 'mystery' remained somewhat vague, both in theory and in the proposed details of its execution, although not, apparently, in the results it was meant to produce. Scriabin, it seems, saw the universe as dominated by an 'alternation of creative rhythms' or 'the breaths of Brahma'.[111] Two creative but opposite forces, evolution and involution, were to combine in an erotic act of love. This would result in a return to the primordial state of chaos and this, in its turn, would be followed by a new 'breath of Brahma'. Scriabin saw himself as the impresario or, rather, the creator of this great act which was

[109] Quoted by G. Abraham, 'Alexander Scriabin', in M. D. Calvocoressi and G. Abraham, *Masters of Russian Music* (New York, 1936), pp. 472–3.

[110] *Ibid.*, p. 475.

[111] L. Sabaneyeff, *Modern Russian Composers*, tr. J. A. Joffe (New York, 1927), p. 48.

to lift the world to a higher level. It was to take place in India, in a semi-spherical temple at the edge of a lake. Together with its reflection, this temple would then form the most perfect of all shapes, the sphere. Two thousand persons, all of them performers and none spectators, were to enact the 'supreme and final ecstasy' by means of all the known arts, music, dance, poetry and, even, light and scent. The artistic standards were to be superlative; for Scriabin considered the participation of Chaliapin and Karsanova, but rejected it, though, presumably, not for purely artistic reasons. Even so, this act seems to have been only the prologue, for which Scriabin actually wrote some of the poetry. It was to be followed by the 'mystery' itself, which was never clearly spelled out but which, Scriabin was convinced, would effect the end of the world as it existed and then initiate its transformation.[112]

It was characteristic of Scriabin's self-centred messianism that he actually welcomed the outbreak of the War of 1914–18 as a prelude to the great transformation. He died quietly in Moscow in 1915, while the outside world appeared to be nearing its end rather through wholesale slaughter than through the regenerative powers of his music and an ecstatic act of love. It is the final irony of Fate that Scriabin has remained alive as the composer of elegant short piano pieces while his grandiose orchestral works and his advanced theories of musical harmony have been forgotten, together with his mystical dreams.

It was only about the turn of the nineteenth century that the Churches finally reacted against this large-scale invasion of music into their own traditional fields of religion and religious emotion. The reason for this long delay, through practically the whole of the nineteenth century, was probably the essential ambiguity of the relations between music and religion; for they were never overtly hostile to each other and, as we have seen, nearly all the great composers of the century wrote superb and heartfelt religious music, even if it was mostly not strictly liturgical. In 1903, however, the recently elected Pope Pius X issued his famous *Motu proprio* with its call for a return to the traditions of Gregorian chant, its condemnation of secular elements in church music and

[112] *Ibid.*, pp. 59–60. G. Abraham, 'Alexander Scriabin', pp. 494–5.

its categorical declaration that music must remain 'the humble servant of the liturgy'.[113] About the same time there occurred a deliberate and self-conscious revival of Protestant church music, especially in Germany, which however looked for its models to the great period of Lutheran church music in the sixteenth and seventeenth centuries, rather than to Gregorian chant. In both the Catholic and the Protestant Churches, this seems to have been an attempt to rescue church music from absorption into secular music and to redraw sharp lines between them.[114]

It is not the function of this essay to evaluate the musical and religious results of these attempts. It is worth noting, however, that in most recent years the lines between church and secular music are being deliberately blurred again, and this is happening, just as it did in the seventeenth century, as part of an attempt to widen the appeal of church music. In contrast to the seventeenth century, however, the part played by church music in contemporary life has become quite small and, relatively, unimportant. The development of the psychological impact of music which we have traced was, up to the end of the nineteenth century, largely confined to the educated classes and to sophisticated, 'classical' music. But from about 1900 the decline of the religious appeal of the organized Churches began to spread to the mass of the uneducated or semi-educated population of Europe and America. The drastic decline of the figures for church attendance leave very little doubt of the reality of this phenomenon. Concurrently, it seems to me, there has occurred an enormous rise in the popularity and the sheer volume of performance, and through radio and gramophone in listening time, of all types of popular music. Is not the almost devout attendance of fans at jazz sessions comparable with the devout absorption of the mainly middle-class audiences at a Beethoven symphony concert? Is not the behaviour

[113] *Acta Sancta Sedis* (Rome, 1904), 36, 329–39.

[114] A. Adrio, 'Erneuerung und Wiederbelebung', ch. IV in Blume, *Kirchenmusik*. The difference in Catholic and Protestant attitudes was, however, not as great as it might appear; for the *Motu proprio* specifically singled out Palestrina's music as having attained 'the greatest perfection' in classical polyphony, the form of music which most clearly had the qualities that the Church demanded. *Acta Sancta Sedis*, xxxvi, 333.

of a teenage rock 'n' roll audience remarkably similar to that of the congregation of a revivalist preacher?

I have deliberately left these observations as questions because it is notoriously difficult for a historian to see the events of his own age in a correct historical perspective. But some contemporary observers and enthusiasts have, in fact, made far-reaching claims, not only for the aesthetic, but also for the ethical and even religious significance of the best of modern popular music.[115] No doubt this is philosophy and religion for teenagers; but is it not part of the phenomenon which is the theme of this essay, the rise of music to a quasi-religious status and cult, as a psychological compensation for the decline of all forms of traditional religion? And do not young people feel the need for non-material values with special intensity?

What then of the second part of my original question, Max Weber's argument of the uniqueness of the development of European music, and my suggestion that this development was linked with the progressive secularization of European civilization? I do not think that such a link can be proved conclusively, even less so, perhaps, than Weber's own hypothesis of a link between the Protestant ethic and capitalism. Much, perhaps most, of the development of European music can and must be explained by its own laws of development, by a certain logic inherent in the art of composition and by the physical and physiological determinants of the art; above all, perhaps, by the genius of a long line of great composers and musicians. Moreover, if music was a psychological substitute for religion, it was not the only one: painting, poetry, the natural sciences, even politics and the quest for power have, at some time or other, been elevated to religious or quasi-religious status. But all these remained marginal, the beliefs of cranks or, at best, of relatively small groups of intellectuals. Music, however, was never marginal in European life and, as Wagner rightly saw, has shifted more and more into its centre. This centre had formerly been occupied by religion, as it was so occupied (and, in contrast to Europe, has continued to be

[115] Cf. B. DeMott, 'Rock as Salvation', *The New York Times Magazine*, 25 August 1968. Cf. also the 1968 Beatles film, *The Yellow Submarine*.

so occupied, at least until very recently) in all non-European societies. The conclusion seems inescapable that here, indeed, there is a connection.

Four

Venetian Diplomacy before Pavia: from Reality to Myth

by

Felix Gilbert

In discussing the policy which Charles V ought to follow in Italy after his victory at Pavia, the Emperor's great Chancellor, Gattinara, spoke with particular scorn of the rulers of Venice; he emphasized that they should make particular efforts to support Charles V in order to make amends for their 'faults'.[1] This condemnation stands in strange contrast to the tributes usually paid to the wisdom of Venetian diplomacy. Gattinara, however, had good reasons for his contempt of Venetian policy because in the period before the Battle of Pavia it had pursued a disastrous course. At the beginning of the campaign between Spain and France which decided the fate of Italy, the Venetians had been the allies of the Emperor Charles V. The Venetians then broke this treaty and made an alliance with King Francis I of France; three months later Francis I was defeated and a prisoner of Charles V. The Venetians had, at a critical moment, broken an imperial alliance and sided with the French, who were to lose the struggle.

[1] 'Et quant aux Veniciens lhon pourra tresbien leur remonstrer qu'ilz n'ont bein tenu ce qu'ilz ont promys et que sa Maté ne seroit tenu plus avant à l'observance du traicté, ains luy pourroit demander comme infractairs du traicté toutz les dommaiges, interes, qui s'en sent ensuyz, et avec ce retourner aux premiers actions de tout ce qu'ilz ont u surpé de l'empire,—toutefois que sadite Mté pour le bien de la chrestienté entendoit pour le present supporter et excuser certe faulte. . . .' Report of Gattinara, published by Karl Brandi, 'Berichte und Studien zur Geschichte Karls V. XVII. Nach Pavia', *Nachrichten von der Gesellschaft der Wissenschaften zu Goettingen*, Philologisch-Historische Klasse, Fachgruppe II: Mittlere und Neuere Geschichte, Neue Folge, ii, 8.

Venetian foreign policy in the years 1524–5 certainly was 'faulty'. And the question might be raised whether the praises which have been sung to the wisdom of Venetian diplomacy in the seventeenth and eighteenth centuries should also be bestowed on the Venetian conduct of foreign affairs in the Renaissance.[2]

The sources on which judgments on the Renaissance period of Venetian diplomacy can be based are very scanty. But some papers preserved in the Biblioteca Correr contain the texts of speeches given in 1524 when the Pregadi debated whether Venice should change from the Spanish to the French side.[3] With the help of this material, it is possible to throw some light on this particular episode in the history of Venetian diplomacy. It was an episode which—probably because of the obvious mistake which the Venetians committed—has aroused the attention of many historians of the sixteenth century: Guicciardini, Morosini, Contarini, Paruta. All have treated in some detail the developments of Venetian foreign policy in the years 1523–5. Thus a new analysis of Venetian diplomacy before Pavia is of interest, not only because it might help to provide a factual basis for judgments on the quality of Venetian diplomacy in the Renaissance period; it will also be possible to gain some clearer view of the methods of Italian sixteenth-century historians and their concept of historical truth.

I

The decision of the Venetians to switch from the Spanish to the French side in 1524 was not the first breach of a treaty committed

[2] Donald E. Queller, *Early Venetian Legislation on Ambassadors* (Geneva, 1966), pp. 56–8, rightly raises this question. Willy Andreas, *Staatskunst und Diplomatie der Venezianer* (Leipzig, 1943), provides a useful survey in his first essay entitled 'Italien und die Anfänge der neuzeitlichen Diplomatie', but he is interested only in diplomatic representation abroad, not in the handling of foreign affairs by the government at home.

[3] These papers form part of the diary of Marcantonio Michiel, which is preserved in two volumes in Venice, *Biblioteca Correr*, Cod. Cicogna, 2848 and 2551. While the first volume is original, the second volume, to which these papers belong, is a later copy of sections of Michiel's diary; unfortunately, the codex is not paginated. A few excerpts concerned with Hungarian history were published in *Monumenta Spectantia Historiam Slavorum Meridionalium*, VI (1875), pp. 132–43; otherwise Michiel's diary has not been published nor, as far as I can see, been used.

by the Venetians in this period. In Blois on 23 March 1513 Venice concluded an alliance with the French King, Louis XII, in which the contracting parties promised each other assistance in the war which would bring Milan back under French rule and would restore to Venice its lost territories on the *terra firma*. This treaty settled the boundaries between Milan and Venice and established that 'sunt atque erunt perpetuis temporibus Amici et Confoederati'.[4] This treaty was reconfirmed and renewed on 8 October 1517. 'Ut omnes intelligant praefatos Serenissimum et Christianissimum regem et illustrissimum ducem et dominium Venetiarum arctissimo vinculo conjunctos esse.'[5] Changed circumstances, however, required some modifications. Francis I had succeeded Louis XII as King of France and he was in possession of Milan, so that the treaty now specified the number of troops which either of the contracting parties ought to provide for the defence of the existing situation.

This was the treaty which Venice broke when six years later, on 29 July 1523, it concluded an agreement with the Emperor Charles V, with the King of England, Henry VIII, with Archduke Ferdinand and with Francesco Sforza, who, in consequence of Spanish victories over the French, had been re-established as Duke of Milan.[6] Two clauses of this treaty were significant. Venice obtained from the Emperor and the Archduke recognition of all its territorial possessions, but agreed to pay to the Emperor 200,000 gold ducats in eight annual instalments of 25,000 ducats. Moreover, Venice and Charles V were to provide an equal number of troops to the defence of Milan; if Naples were attacked by a Christian ruler, Venice would send fifteen galleys to support the Neapolitans.

[4] Printed in DuMont, *Corps Universel Diplomatique* (Amsterdam, 1726), vol. iv, part i, 182–3.

[5] Printed in DuMont, *op. cit.*, pp. 263–4; see also the brief abstract in 'Libri Commemoriali' printed in Deputazione Veneta, *Monumenti Storici*, Serie Prima, Documenti (Venice, 1903), xi, 146.

[6] The full text of this treaty is printed in Marino Sanuto, *Diarii* (Venice, 1892), xxxiv, cols. 316–23, and for a summary in English see *Calendar of State Papers, Spanish*, ed. G. A. Bergenroth (London, 1866), ii, 570–1, or see the summary in 'Libri Commemoriali', *op. cit.*, pp. 171–3. For the negotiations on this treaty, see Francesco Guicciardini, *Storia d'Italia*, xv, ch. 2.

The conclusion of this treaty had been urged on Venice by Pope Hadrian VI. The Pope was no partner of this treaty, however, but concluded on 3 August 1523 a special agreement with Charles V for reciprocal defence.[7] A clause of this agreement stated that the treaty would remain in force one year beyond the death of either of the partners; payment for the troops which the signatories had agreed to provide would have to be renegotiated every three months. These arrangements are of importance for the events in the autumn of 1524. Hadrian VI died on 14 September 1523, one month after the conclusion of his agreement with Charles V. In the autumn of 1524, one year after Hadrian's death, the strange situation had come about that the Church-State, whose ruler had urged the Venetians to ally themselves with Charles V, was no longer tied by an alliance treaty to Spain because Hadrian's alliance with Charles V was no longer binding on Hadrian's successor, Clement VII.[8] The Venetians, however, remained allies of Charles V. Thus, when after the fall of Milan to the French in October 1524 Clement VII urged the Venetians to break with Spain and to join him in an alliance with the King of France, the Venetians were legally less free than the Pope. This represented an additional problem for the Venetian policy-makers when they began to deliberate about abandoning Charles V and allying themselves with Francis I in 1524.

II

The subject of the following is a description of the negotiations of 1524 which resulted in the conclusion of an alliance with France, but some discussion of the negotiations of the previous year which

[7] The best analysis of this treaty in Guicciardini, *op. cit.*, xv, ch. 3. The full text has never been published. See Stephan Ehses, 'Die Politik des Papstes Clemens VII bis zur Schlacht von Pavia', *Historisches Jahrbuch*, vi (1885), 561.

[8] It is a different question whether there was a moral obligation for Clement VII to remain on the side of Charles V; this problem has been well argued by Ehses, *loc. cit.*, p. 591; it may be added that, in the treaty of 1523, the Emperor was willing to guarantee to the Cardinal of Medici and the Medici family their territorial possessions; this meant that the Cardinal of Medici implicitly was a member of the alliance.

led to the Venetian change from the French to the Spanish side will help to clarify this situation.

Information about the negotiations in 1523 is much less extensive[9] than that about the events in the following year. The statements in Sanuto's diary show that the conclusion of the treaty with Charles V was bitterly fought in the Senate. The Senate encompassed a pro-Spanish and a pro-French party. Most vocal in recommending the alliance with Spain were Gabriele Moro and Domenico Trevisan, but also pro-Spanish were Alvise Mocenigo, Marcantonio Venier and Giorgio Corner, to whom the actual conduct of the negotiations was entrusted.[10] Continuation of the alliance with the French King was recommended by Marin Morosini—who, according to Sanuto, spoke like an advocate of the French King[11]—Gasparo Malipiero and Paolo Capello.[12] The most important figure among the advocates of the French alliance was Andrea Gritti. He was elected Doge in the midst of these negotiations, and Guicciardini maintained that the elevation of Gritti damaged the pro-French cause because, after his election, 'he never wished by words or acts to show his preference for any side'.[13] This statement cannot be regarded as entirely true, because Sanuto noted that, even as Doge, Gritti bestowed signs of approval on those who spoke for continuing the alliance with France.[14] Gritti's election, however, might have

[9] Sanuto, xxxiii, 536, 539–40, 554, 634; xxxiv, 49, 105, 115, 240, 264–5, 292, 295, 301, 306, 309, 311, 314. The negotiations started in the autumn of 1522; for the instructions given to the Venetian negotiators, see A.S.V., *Senato. Secreta*, Reg., xlix; these documents show that a minority steadily opposed these arrangements, see ff. 154v, 161v, 162r. Guicciardini's report about these negotiations will be discussed below (see pp. 107–9).

[10] Others of the same inclination were Leonardo Mocenigo, Girolamo da Pesaro, Francesco Bragadin, Luca Tron.

[11] Sanuto, xxxiv, col. 309, also xxxiii, col. 634: Morosini had to defend himself against the reproach that he was '*Francese*'; he stressed that he had not sent his son to study in Paris.

[12] Others on the French side were: Matteo Priuli, Andrea Trevisan, Sante Tron.

[13] Guicciardini, *op. cit.*, xv, ch. 2: '. . . egli, collocato in quel grado, lasciata meramente la deliberazione al senato, non volle mai più nè con parole nè con opere dimostrarsi inclinato in parte alcuna'.

[14] Sanuto, xxxiv, col. 309.

influenced the French cause unfavourably because Gritti was considered to be authoritarian, and his election might have strengthened the opposition to the French alliance because it implied a challenge to the influence of the Doge.

The struggle between the adherents of Spain and the adherents of France was not fought out in one great debate. The discussions extended throughout the nine months while the negotiations were being conducted. Even when the negotiators had finally agreed on a treaty and presented a text in the Pregadi, the adversaries of the alliance with Charles V still continued the struggle by insisting on a firm stand in details, demanding changes in formulations and in the amount of the payments to be made by Venice. The final vote at the end of a long day was 152 against 39 with 19 abstentions: 'Those who held to France were like dead.'[15]

The groupings and animosities which had developed in the course of these discussions about the usefulness of changing from the French to the Spanish side played their role when, fifteen months later, in October 1524, the issue reappeared in reverse, as a proposition to change from the Spanish to the French side.

The fundamental reason for a reconsideration of the Venetian course in foreign policy was the change in military fortunes which had occurred in the interval. In 1523 Spain had defeated the French and had the upper hand in northern Italy. But an advance into Provence in the spring of 1524 failed and Francis I was able to use the disorganization in the enemy's camp for a renewed invasion of Italy. On 24 October Milan was in French hands.

Most immediately and most critically affected by the re-appearance of the French in Italy was Pope Clement VII.[16] The independence of the Papacy seemed menaced if, as it seemed possible, the French King should become the master of the whole of Italy. The integrity of the Church-State was endangered because it could be expected that the French King would want to annex

[15] Sanuto, xxxiv, col. 315: '. . . quelli tien di Franza, come morti'.

[16] For a good exposition of the dangerous position of the Pope, see Ehses, *loc. cit.*, pp. 587–90, and on the precariousness of the Medicean position in Florence at this time see my article, 'The Venetian Constitution in Florentine Political Thought', *Florentine Studies*, ed. Nicolai Rubinstein (London, 1968), p. 495.

Parma and Piacenza to the Dukedom of Milan and would support the claims of the Duke of Ferrara on territories of the Church-State. Pope Clement VII was, however, particularly disturbed because an overthrow of the Medici rule in Florence was an obvious possibility. The Medici rule was precarious because of the lack of an adult Medici heir. Clement VII thought that immediate negotiations and an understanding with the King of France might reduce the dangers threatening the Church-State and the Medici rule in Florence. Even before the French had entered Milan the Venetian Ambassador in Rome, Marco Foscari, reported[17] a conversation in which the Pope indicated that he was inclined towards an agreement with the French King and hoped that the Venetians would act together with him; he wished to remain in close touch with Venice and asked the Venetians for advice on how to proceed.

This report arrived in Venice on 25 October; the Council of Ten and the Collegio drafted a reply to be sent to Foscari, and the Pregadi were assembled to give their approval to this instruction.[18] The main issue of this meeting, of course, was whether Venice should agree to negotiations with France—an issue which was regarded to be of such importance that the discussion in the Pregadi was treated as 'materia secretissima'.[19] The instruction which was submitted to the Pregadi for approval expressed pleasure about the willingness of the Pope to act in accord with Venice and stressed the Venetian confidence in the wisdom of the Pope. The Venetians emphasized that the situation had become more critical and urgent than it had been when the Pope had talked to Foscari, because since then Milan had fallen into French hands and this conquest had proved the great power of the

[17] See A.S.V., *Senato. Secreta*, Reg., 50, f. 107r, and v. Foscari's reports from Rome can be found in A.S.V., *Capi del Consiglio dei Dieci, Lettere di Ambasciatori* (Rome, 1515–38), busta no. 22, but this collection has no reports written between 23 July 1524 and 4 December 1524; moreover, the letters from December 1524 are chiefly concerned with the attitude of the Duke of Ferrara and contain no material about the negotiations of the Pope with France.

[18] A.S.V., *Senato. Secreta*, Reg., 50, ff. 107r–107v, also a summary in the second volume of Michiel's diary.

[19] Sanuto, xxxvii, col. 96.

French King. 'Et se a sua Beat^ne^ paresse, chel tempo necessiti de pratticar accordo con il Re Christianissimo, Nui siamo ben contenti: et ne par esser cusi stretti, et coniuncti insieme con sua San^ta^ che non si po far cosa, salvo a commun beneficio.' This was the key sentence of the instruction and it generated a vehement debate which set the tone for all the further discussions of this issue.[20] Girolamo Pesaro and Domenico Venier emphasized that the issue was of such importance that it needed lengthy and careful consideration. They moved that the debate be postponed till the next day. In 1523 Girolamo Pesaro had been an adherent of the alliance with Spain. It seems likely, therefore, that he wanted to prevent a panicky rush to a treaty with France. In this meeting, however—as also in all the following meetings—the main advocate of loyal adherence to the alliance with Charles V was Zaccaria Bembo, a *Savio* of the *terra firma.* Instead of the sentence which expressed approval if the Pope regarded an agreement with the French King necessary, Bembo suggested an innocuous phrase which purely emphasized that Venice and the Pope ought to act in accord and which assured the Pope that Venice would not conclude an agreement with Francis I without the Pope. The speech in which Bembo justified this altering of the wording of the instruction makes it clear that he intended to prevent Venice from changing sides. Bembo argued along a number of different lines. It was against Venetian tradition to break a commitment. The military situation of the army of Charles V and of his allies could not be considered as desperate; by abandoning Milan, the adversaries of France had been able to save their troops and to consolidate their position in Pavia, Lodi, Alessandria and Cremona. And if a battle should occur the outcome was uncertain. Without the help of Venice, the French King could not establish himself securely in Milan. There was no need for Venice therefore to humiliate itself, to abandon the Spanish alliance, and to implore the friendship of the French King.

Bembo's speech seems to have made a great impression; the alteration of the instruction which he suggested was not accep-

[20] My description of this discussion is based on the sources indicated in note 18.

ted,[21] but in the vote the opposition showed such strength that it was necessary to hold another meeting on the same issue the next day.

For this meeting a new instruction had been drafted and at the end the Pregadi accepted this revised version of the instruction.[22] The formulations of the new instruction were somewhat more favourable to the Spanish side than the draft voted on the previous day: now the Venetian Government expressed no opinion about the desirability of an alliance with France, but limited itself to saying that the Pope ought to decide soon what ought to be done, because delay might be dangerous. This draft carried the signatures of many of those who one year earlier had advocated the alliance with Charles V—namely, in addition to that of Zaccaria Bembo, those of Alvise Mocenigo and Girolamo Pesaro. The advocates of the French alliance moved unsuccessfully for an addition which contained an explicit statement that if the Pope decided on an alliance with Francis I Venice would join him. The proposed amendment was signed by old adherents of France like Paolo Capello, but had also the names of two influential patricians, Luca Tron and Leonardo Mocenigo, who in 1523 had favoured Charles V.[23] Their transition from the Spanish to the French side probably was a crucial factor in swinging the Ten and the Collegio over to the French side. However, the number of those who changed sides was limited. Although the instruction in its final form permitted negotiations with France, the opposition was strong enough to prevent any expression which would have been taken as a positive affirmation of the desirability of such an alliance.

Venetian reticence displeased the Pope. He expressed to Foscari his astonishment[24] that the Venetians had given no clear

[21] The majority for the draft was 74 against 70; the majority against Bembo's motion 101 against 84. Briefly, the draft did not get an absolute majority of those present (185). On voting procedures in the Pregadi, see Giuseppe Maranini, *La costituzione di Venezia* (Milan, 1931), pp. 255 *et seq.*

[22] For the meeting and the instruction, see A.S.V., *Senato. Secreta*, Reg., ff. 107v–108v.

[23] Both were candidates for the doganate when Gritti was elected; the amendment was also signed by Andrea Trevisan and Niccolò Bernardo.

[24] A.S.V., *Senato. Secreta*, Reg., 50, f. 109v.

answer to his request for an explanation of their views. His eagerness for an agreement with Francis I steadily increased. He explained to the Venetian Ambassador that Charles V could not reinforce his troops because of lack of money; the position of the French seemed to him overwhelmingly strong. For this reason, in the Pope's opinion, a quick decision was needed.

This report arrived in Venice on 28 October; it made evident that the Venetians could no longer delay a definite explanation of their attitude towards a treaty with France. And so, on 29 October, the Pregadi decided to instruct Foscari[25] that the Venetians were satisfied if the Pope negotiated with the French King in the manner which seemed appropriate. Foscari was given power to conclude, together with His Holiness, 'bona, et syncera Pace cum il Re Christianissimo'; the Venetian wish was for restoration of the *status quo* which had existed before the outbreak of the war between Venice and France. Furthermore, because the Pope had said that he wanted to negotiate and conclude 'intelligentia secreta fra lei, il Christian^mo^ Re, et la Signoria nostra', Venice was ready to make such a treaty after the conclusion of peace. In vain did Zaccaria Bembo attempt to achieve a postponement of this decision. Considering the cautiousness with which the Venetians moved and their great hesitations about changing sides, it is surprising to hear that Foscari—even before he had received this instruction—told the Pope that he could be sure of Venice's full agreement to an alliance with France, 'a rather unheard-of thing that an ambassador presumes so much without having received from the Senate instructions which might have been to the contrary'.[26]

The negotiations which now began were much more complicated than the Pope or even the Venetians expected when they entered upon them. Because Clement VII regarded the situation of the Spaniards to be desperate, he believed that Charles V

[25] A.S.V., *Senato. Secreta*, Reg., 50, ff. 109r–110v: the instruction included the formal document, empowering Foscari to conclude peace and make an alliance with the French King.

[26] 'Pare cosa nova, che un Imbas^re^ presumesse tanto senza ordine del Senato, essendosi di qui pronto deliberare il contrario', from Michiel's diary; but see also Sanuto, xxxvii, col. 110.

would welcome an end of the war; the Pope envisaged the negotiations with Francis I as a prologue for the establishment of peace between Charles V and Francis I, with the Pope himself as mediator.[27] The Venetians hoped the same.[28] But when the Pope's confidant, Matteo Giberti, visited the Spanish and the French camps in northern Italy, he discovered that neither the Spaniards nor the French were inclined towards an ending of hostilities.[29] The consequence was that if a treaty with the French King were concluded by Venice and the Pope it would imply a complete break and probably war with Charles V.

Under these circumstances many seem to have felt that the decision which had been taken at the end of October might have been over-hasty and that a reconsideration of Venice's position in the conflict between Charles V and Francis I was desirable. Simultaneously, however, the Venetians were made aware of the urgency to come to a decision. Characteristic was the scene which took place on 19 November. There appeared in the Collegio first the Ambassador of France emphasizing that the French King was anxious to be 'buon amico' with Venice; the Doge assured him of the great esteem in which the French King was held in Venice. Immediately afterwards the Ambassadors of Charles V and of Francesco Sforza appeared and demanded orders for the Venetian troops to join the imperial forces in accordance with the alliance existing between Charles V and Venice; the Doge assured them of Venice's friendly feelings.[30] The Pope was also put under pressure and even in a more direct way: the French threatened with an invasion of Naples. But while pressures mounted the decision which had to be taken became more

[27] See Ehses, *loc. cit.*, pp. 595–7.

[28] See the instruction to Foscari of 29 October, A.S.V., *Senato. Secreta*, Reg., 50, f. 110r: 'Nui sommaments laudamo, che sua Beat^ne^ trovi forma de reservar loco honorificentissimo alla prefata Cesarea Ma^tà^ et procurar, che la intri in ditta pace.'

[29] 'Donde superfluo e parlare di accordo dal quale l'una e l'altra parte tanto si discosti', Giberti to Cardinal Salviati, 12 November 1524, printed in *Negociations Diplomatiques de la France avec la Toscane*, ed. A. Desjardins (Paris, 1861), ii, 788. See also *Delle Lettere di Principi*, ed. G. Ruscelli, Venice, 1581, pp. 140r–145v.

[30] 'Di la bona mente di questo stado . . .', Sanuto, xxxvii, col. 171.

difficult; the panicky reaction produced by the French conquest of Milan was now followed by quieter considerations and the military situation appeared less certain and more balanced.

These problems came out into the open in crucial meetings of the Pregadi which took place in the middle of November. Their occasion was a report from Rome in which the Venetian Ambassador wrote about a conversation with the Pope and required an immediate answer. The Pope had told Foscari that he had come to the conclusion that if Pavia could withstand the French attack he would spin out negotiations with the French King and try to establish general peace. However, if the French succeeded in conquering Pavia then he would make an agreement with the King of France and ask Charles V to cede to France those parts of the Dukedom of Milan which the Spaniards were still holding. If Charles V refused it would be necessary to take up arms against him. The Pope was anxious to hear what the Venetian Government thought about these ideas.[31]

The debate in the Pregadi on the answer which ought to be given to the Pope lasted over two days and the speakers on both sides tried carefully to marshal all the arguments which could be made in favour of their cause. Because of the decisive importance of this debate, it deserves a somewhat extended description.[32]

On the first day, 15 November, the Collegio presented the draft of an instruction to Foscari. Controversy focused on one passage of this draft; it said that if the French should take Pavia the Venetian Government would approve of His Holiness making peace and coming to an agreement with the French King for himself and for Venice as it had been stated in the instruction of 29 October. The opposition suggested that this passage should be replaced by a formula which, if Pavia should fall, encouraged the Pope to continue negotiations with the French King, but no treaty should be concluded without special orders by the Venetian

[31] See Sanuto, xxxvii, col. 196, and the report on the meeting of 15 November in Michiel's diary.

[32] For these two meetings, see chiefly Michiel's diary, but also Sanuto, xxxvii, cols. 196, 202, and the drafts of the instructions, presented in Pregadi, A.S.V., *Senato. Secreta*, Reg., 50, ff. 113r–115r.

Government.[33] A proponent of this amendment and the chief opposition speaker was a *Savio* of the Consiglio, Alvise Mocenigo.[34] He reiterated[35] the reasons which had been brought up in previous deliberations on this issue—namely, that it was against Venetian tradition to break a treaty and that the military position of the Spaniards was strong; it would not even be desperate after a loss of Pavia. Mocenigo also added a new argument. The Pope's real intention was to get Ferrara. Alberto Pio da Carpi, the French Ambassador at the Papal Court, considered the Duke of Ferrara as his oldest and most deadly enemy. Carpi had set his heart on a joint enterprise of the French and the Pope against Ferrara and he had promised the Pope the possession of Ferrara if he would come over to the French side.[36]

Mocenigo's speech must have been very effective. The change in the draft which he had suggested was not adopted, but the instruction as it had been drafted also found no majority.

Thus, the deliberations had to be resumed the next morning. By then new reports had arrived. The Venetian Ambassador in Vienna wrote that Archduke Ferdinand intended to invade Italy with military forces. Foscari reported from Rome that the Pope did not intend to press the negotiations with France if Pavia should be held by the Spaniards. But if Pavia should fall he

[33] 'Vi dicemo cum Senatu, che ottenendo Francesi Pavia, laudamo che Sua Beat[ne] continui la prattica cum il Re Christianissimo: ma non devenire a conclusione senza ordine nostro', A.S.V., *Senato. Secreta*, Reg., 50, f. 113v.

[34] According to Sanuto, xxxvii, col. 196, the *Savi della terra firma* (Marcantonio Contarini, Zaccaria Bembo, Domenico Venier, Giovanni Francesco Badoer) also were unenthusiastic about the draft, and this may have influenced its rejection.

[35] For Mocenigo's speech, see Michiel's diary.

[36] The same story is reported by the Ambassador of Federigo Gonzaga from Rome on 28 November: 'A questi di intesi, ch'el re christianissimo proponeva Ferrara al papa vincta a sue spese se e'voleva farsi Francese, e questo lo diceva Alberto.' This report was published by Ludwig von Pastor, *Geschichte der Paepste* (Freiburg, 1907), iv, part 2, 738; on the influence of Alberto Pio da Carpi in Rome, see *ibid.*, pp. 186 *et seq.* The enmity between the Pios and the Estes, and particularly between Alberto Pio and the Duke of Ferrara, is a well-known historical fact. Because of his pro-French attitude, Alberto Pio lost Carpi, which was given by Charles V to the Duke of Ferrara in 1527.

would immediately conclude a treaty with Francis I. The majority of the *Savi* (Domenico Trevisan, Leonardo Mocenigo, Paolo Capello, Luca Tron, Andrea Trevisan, Niccola Bernardo of the *Savi di Consiglio*; Antonio Contarini, Domenico Venier, Giovanni Francesco Badoer of the *Savi della terra firma*) now submitted to the Pregadi the draft of an instruction which was rather similar to the one presented on the previous day; it was somewhat toned down, however, and emphasized the importance of the news about the possible coming of Archduke Ferdinand. Alvise Mocenigo and Zaccaria Bembo offered a different version, which stressed that even if Pavia should fall the Spaniards would remain strong and would receive reinforcements: briefly, one should then reconsider the entire situation.

Mocenigo again rose to speak in order to justify the version which he had drafted.[37] He enlarged on a statement which he had made the day before—namely, that the interests of the Pope were very different from those of Venice. The Pope might be strengthened by getting Ferrara, but in the case of a conflict with the Habsburgs Venice would be immediately exposed to great dangers: not only because of the possibility of an attack on the *terra firma* by the Austrian Archduke, but also because Venetian trade would suffer, since Venetian galleys would not be able to enter Spanish ports. Moreover, if foreigners had to exert control in Italy the rule of Charles V was much preferable to that of the French King. The French ruled as tyrants ('*tirannicamente*') because by nature they were arrogant and overweening.[38] Charles V, however, permitted Italians to rule themselves.[39]

Zaccaria Bembo, who supported Mocenigo, placed moral considerations in the foreground. It was against all traditions of Venetian policy to break faith: 'Our wise ancestors had at no time, in no calamity, at no opportunity, wanted to break faith with any prince, Christian or infidel, except when their state was

[37] See Michiel's diary for Mocenigo's speech, and for the other speeches described in the following.

[38] '. . . la natura de Francesi essere arrogantissima e molto superba . . .'.

[39] An allusion that the Spanish rule over Milan was somewhat disguised; it was exerted by means of the Sforza Duke, with Girolamo Morone as principal adviser.

placed in obvious danger.'[40] At first sight, it might appear most expedient to be the friend of the Emperor in his time of prosperity and to abandon him in the time of good fortune of the French King—briefly, to be always on the side of the victor. 'But such behaviour is so ruthless and unnatural that it can give no secure and solid basis.'[41] To this moral appeal Bembo added also political arguments. The King of France had no reason to love Venice, which in the year before had defected to Charles V. Thus, after a treaty with France Venice would be isolated, and if the Emperor wanted to revenge himself on Venice he could probably come to an understanding with the French at the expense of Venice; briefly, Bembo envisaged the possibility of another League of Cambrai. Because changing sides from the Spanish to the French was a most radical step[42] Bembo said he could regard it as neither unusual nor beyond reason to demand information from Rome about the contents of the treaty before giving Foscari permission to sign it.

With this last point, Bembo referred to remarks of Luca Tron, an advocate of the French alliance. Tron had said that if Venice withdrew from the position of 29 October—when it had given Foscari power to sign the treaty which the Pope might negotiate—confidence of the Pope in the Venetian Government would be destroyed. Venice would find all doors to negotiations with the French King closed; it would be left without allies. Other advocates of the French alliance, too, were perturbed by the possibility of friction with the Pope if the instruction of 29 October were withdrawn. Chiefly, however, emphasis was placed on the military strength of the French; it was also said that Mocenigo was wrong: French rule over Milan was less a threat to Venice than a rule of the Habsburgs.

A position somewhat in the middle was taken by Girolamo

[40] '. . . Savii Progenitori nostri, li quali in niun tempo, in ruina, calamità, per niuna occasione non vollero mai rompere la fede ad alcun Prencipe non pure Christiano ma infedele oltroche ponevano lo stato loro in manifesto pericolo.'

[41] '. . . questo però è un operar così violento e contra natura che non può havere in se stesso poco o nulla firmezza o fondamento . . .'.

[42] '. . . materia di tanta importanza di fare una pace nuova, e romper una Tregua vecchia ed una confederazione tanto solennemente giurata . . .'.

da Pesaro, one of the *Savi del Consiglio* who had signed neither of the two drafts. Pesaro stated that he was widely in accord with Mocenigo and Bembo, but he agreed with Tron that it was highly important not to shake the confidence of the Pope. In his opinion, the instruction given to Foscari on 29 October should not be withdrawn. However, the Pope ought to be told politely and moderately that French military superiority was not as great as it appeared; the Spanish troops were receiving reinforcements, so that even after a fall of Pavia the Spanish situation was not hopeless. So there was no desperate hurry about an agreement with France, and the Pope and Venice had not to bow to the wishes of the French King.

The mediating position of Girolamo da Pesaro carried the day, and he was asked to draft the instruction to Foscari. The instruction which resulted was in many respects very similar to that which Mocenigo and Bembo had drafted; it emphasized that even the conquest of Pavia would not make the French King all-powerful in Italy and that the possible appearance of Archduke Ferdinand in Italy deserved serious consideration. Nevertheless, the instruction left the final decision to the Pope[43] and did not withdraw the instruction of 29 October, which had given power to the Pope to conclude an agreement with Francis I in the name of Venice. The Venetian Government indicated, however, that they were anxious to get more information before a final decision was made. The Venetians warned against undue haste in coming to an agreement with Francis I. Clearly, this was a compromise intended to be acceptable to the diverging opinions of the members of the Collegio and the Pregadi.

The Pope disregarded the Venetian advice to go slow in the negotiations with France. His emissary, Giberti, had reported to him that he felt sure that the French King had decided on a campaign to conquer Naples.[44] The Pope believed he had to do

[43] '. . . il tutto remettemo al sapientissimo iudicio della Beat^{ne} Sua'. See A.S.V., *Senato. Secreta*, Reg., 50, f. 115.

[44] 'Ond'io non credo . . . che Sua Maesta sene voglia rimuovere, anzi pensa farlo con piu apparecchio . . .'. From a report, Giberti's from Parma on 25 November 1524, published in *Negociations*, ed. Desjardins, p. 739; Giberti's reports from the French camp show that he was highly impressed by the French King, for instance, *ibid.*, p. 787.

everything possible to avoid such an enterprise, fatal for the independence of the Papacy. Thus he decided on a last great attempt to establish peace between Charles V and Francis I. But since Clement VII was convinced of the superiority of the French, he felt that he had to make far-reaching concessions to the French King if he wanted to persuade him to keep away from Naples and to make peace. His proposal was to guarantee Charles V the possession of Naples, but Charles V would have to cede Milan to Francis I; if Charles V refused, the Pope was willing to go over to the French side.[45] In order to facilitate cession of Milan, the Pope was willing to make Francesco Sforza, the Duke of Milan, a cardinal.

When Foscari's report about these plans of Clement VII arrived in Venice the Venetians themselves had received a strong reminder of the urgency of the situation. On 23 November the Ambassadors of Charles V and of the Sforza Duke of Milan appeared before the Collegio and presented a note[46] in which they demanded that Venice fulfil its alliance obligations and command its troops to join those of Spain and Milan; the Ambassadors emphasized that such action was without great risks because Spanish and Milanese troops were superior in strength to those of Francis I.[47] Thus, when on Saturday, 26

[45] For these negotiations, see Ehses, *op. cit.*, pp. 598–601, and Pastor, *op. cit.*, pp. 185–8. There are some differences between the facts given in these books and those facts which arise from the Venetian material. For instance, the Venetian materials do not indicate that the Pope planned to give Milan to the second son of Francis I. On the other hand, only the Venetian materials seem to mention the idea of making Francesco Sforza a cardinal for abandoning his claims to Milan. In our context, however, these details are of no great significance, but I ought to mention that I see little justification for Ehses' view that Lannoy was willing to let the French have Milan; my interpretation of the relevant documents would be that he was playing for time because all his envisaged concessions were very much hedged in, and Lannoy's reports to Charles V from November and December 1524, published in Leon E. Halkin and Georges Dansaert, *Charles de Lannoy, Vice-Roi de Naples* (Paris, 1934), pp. 246–54, seem to me to confirm this interpretation.

[46] Printed in Sanuto, xxxvii, cols. 232–5.

[47] The note speaks of the 'vane voci et grandissime bravate' of the French and emphasized in contrast 'la consueta et da voi ben cognosciuta realità'

November, the Pregadi met to consider the answer which the Pope ought to receive they were aware that time was running out.[48] The instruction presented to the Pregadi bestowed high praise upon the Pope for his proposal to establish peace in Italy by guaranteeing Naples to Charles V and Milan to Francis I.[49] But this instruction was accompanied by a further instruction which said that even if Charles V would not agree the Venetian Government was willing to make a treaty with the French King, as the Pope desired. It was this second instruction which once again started a debate on the course which Venice ought to follow. Girolamo Pesaro and Zaccaria Bembo expressed misgivings about this second instruction. They tried to prevent the Venetian Government from taking any irrevocable step; both warned against unnecessary haste. Zaccaria Bembo urged them to honour the often-proved wisdom of using 'the benefit of time', and Pesaro reinforced him by referring to the proverb that 'Who rushes ahead in affairs of state will soon repent'.[50] Pesaro suggested that it might be possible to wait until one knew about Charles V's reaction to the Papal proposals. In any case both wanted a post-

[48] For the following, see A.S.V., *Senato. Secreta*, Reg., 50, ff. 116v–117r, and Michiel's diary.

[49] 'Ma quello, che nui da singular satisfactione è la resolutione divinitus fatta per Sua San^{tà} a questo effetto di pace, di far quella divisione delli dui stati de Napoli, et Milano: fra questi dui Re, excogitata da lei, stabiliendola, et firmandola con la confederatione . . .'; this is a 'salutifera opera'.

[50] '. . . aspettare il benefitio che sole portare il tempo . . .' and '. . . chi corre a furia nelle deliberationi delli stati, corre più presto al pentirsi . . .', from Michiel's diary.

of the Spaniards: '. . . gli francesi se vadino adiutando con voci et parole, poichè le cesarei procurano de adiutarsi con effetti'. According to the report in Michiel's diary, the Ambassadors gave exact account of the military strength of their troops. Until the alliance with France became public, the demands of the Spanish and Milanese Ambassadors continued to be pressed, and the Venetians took recourse to delaying tactics, even to what seems to have been a diplomatic illness of the Doge. Despite their continued demands, the Ambassadors seem to have had little illusions about a possible success and the audiences with them became very acrimonious and high words were exchanged. See Sanuto, xxxvii, cols. 252 ('*alta parola*'), 260, 273, 282, 299, 300, 302, 303; but see also Michiel's diary on a meeting with the Ambassadors on 2 December.

ponement of the decision until Monday, so that everyone would have time to consider the matter carefully and dispassionately.

Their views were opposed by Luca Tron, who put up a powerful defence of the instruction as it had been presented to the Pregadi. In Tron's opinion, nothing could happen that would change the situation; hesitation and delay could only arouse the resentment of the Pope. The suggestion of Clement VII to guarantee Charles V's rule in Naples and to give the French King a secure position in the north was excellent; if carried out, there would always be a counterweight against any attempt of the French King to make himself ruler of Italy and against any attempt of Charles V to become monarch of the world.[51] Luca Tron's views carried the day; the Pregadi accepted the draft in the form in which it had been proposed.

Clement VII now had the Venetians where he wanted them. He could act for them even if Pavia did not fall. He did not allow the Venetians to forget that they had bound themselves. When he heard about the requests of the Spanish Ambassador for support by Venetian troops and about the Venetian delaying answer, he showed a lively annoyance; in a letter of explanation and apology, the Venetian Government assured him that never under any circumstances would they separate themselves from His Holiness.[52] This instruction to Foscari also stated that in case the negotiations with the Spanish did not lead to an understanding which might establish general peace the Venetians were anxious that the Pope should go ahead with the secret agreement between the Pope, France and Venice.[53]

[51] '. . . potendo sempre con il contropeso dell'altro diffendersi, non volendo in alcuno tempo Li Cesarei che il Re di Francia sia il Signor della Italia, nè il Re Christianesimo che l'Imperatore sia Monarca del Mondo . . .', like all the quotations from speeches from Michiel's diary.

[52] Sanuto, xxxvii, col. 283, 5 December 1524, referring to an answer to a letter from Rome of 30 November, and see A.S.V., *Senato. Secreta*, Reg., 50, ff. 118r–119v for the instruction sent to Foscari. The meeting in the Pregadi of 5 December is also reported in Michiel.

[53] '. . . siamo contenti concorrere cum sua Beat^{ne} alla conclusione della ditta pace, et accordo secreto fra lei, il christianissimo Re, et la Signoria nostra, et usarete della faculta vi habbiamo data cum senatu a di XXIX ottobre . . .',

Actually the secret treaty by which Venice moved from the Spanish to the French side was signed on 12 December.[54] Before it was concluded, the matter came up once again in the Pregadi[55] in an almost indirect way: the issue was what ought to be said to the commander of the Spanish troops in reply to his renewed request for support by Venice.[56] The answer on which the Pregadi decided was negative, although the rejection was put in a diplomatic form. It emphasized the significance of the peace efforts of the Pope; of course, since these efforts involved the cession of Milan to France, the answer implied that Venice did not intend to fulfil its obligations to Charles V regarding the defence of Milan. The debate was short, but lively. The Spanish cause was defended by a new but powerful voice, that of Gabriele Moro.[57] He stated that Venice ought to say to the Viceroy that it was willing to come to his assistance and to defend Milan for Charles V. Moro's abortive intervention was memorable because it con-

[54] For the text, see Champollion-Figeac, *Captivité du Roi François I* (Paris, 1847), p. lxxviii, no. 5, or the abstract in Bergenroth, *op. cit.*, p. 684, and, in general, Ehses, *loc. cit.*, p. 602; the treaty renewed the alliance between Venice and France concluded in 1513. Venice was not obligated, however, to assist France in the present war for the conquest of Milan. This treaty was secret. It was followed by the public treaty between Clement VII and Francis I of 5 January 1525, published in Sanuto, xxxvii, cols. 418–20, which was joined by Venice, and which Charles V, Archduke Ferdinand and the English king were asked to join; this treaty implied the cession of Milan to France. See also the digest in the 'Libri Commemoriali', published R. Deputazione Veneta di Storia Patria, *Monumenti Storici*, Serie Prima, Documenti, vol. xi, under 1524, Dicembre 12.

[55] There was a further meeting on 9 December—see A.S.V., *Senato. Secreta*, Reg., 50, ff. 119v–120r—but it discussed only the best way to decline further military co-operation with the Spaniards.

[56] For this and the following, see Sanuto, xxxvii, col. 296, under 7 December, and A.S.V., *Senato. Secreta*, Reg., 50, ff. 119r–119v.

[57] Moro's speech is given at length in Michiel. It is directed primarily against the Pope, who had made no real attempt to conclude peace among the Christian princes, but, under the pretence of making peace, had pursued an anti-Spanish policy. Venice had committed a grave mistake in accepting the guidance of the Pope in its policy.

A.S.V., *Senato. Secreta*, Reg., 50, f. 118r; the vote was: *pro*, 125; *contra*, 21; undecided, 24.

tained a vehement outbreak of indignation against the leaders of Venetian policy. Four men, Moro maintained, dominated the Collegio and did not allow others to express themselves freely.[58] They were responsible for having brought Venice between 'hammer and anvil'. Even the Doge had tried to exert influence in favour of the French cause. But he, Gabriele Moro, was a man who was born in a free city, and so he said freely what he thought.[59]

Thus, the last debate about Venice's change of sides in the conflict between Spain and France brought out into the open that the issue had aroused deep passions[60] and that the opponents of the French alliance believed that Venice had been manœuvred into a fateful decision by a small, powerful group.

III

What do these negotiations reveal about the broader issue with which we are concerned, about the nature, the strength and the weaknesses of Venetian diplomacy in the Renaissance period?

In the conduct of foreign affairs before the Battle of Pavia the Venetians did not prove that they possessed any particular foresight or wisdom. In allying themselves with the French, who became the losers, they miscalculated the strength of the antagonists fighting for hegemony. This was a mistake, however, which almost all Italian rulers were prone to commit. Ever since 1494, when Charles VIII had made his triumphal march from the north of Italy to the south, the Italians overestimated French power.

The Venetians committed a tactical mistake as well. By giving

[58] Clearly these four were Luca Tron, Paolo Capello, Andrea Trevisan and Leonardo Mocenigo.

[59] '. . . per esser homo nassuto in città libera, dirà liberamente il sentimento suo, e per mal governo questo stado è tra l'ancadine e il martello', Sanuto, xxxvii, col. 296.

[60] In addition to his report on Gabriele Moro's speech in Sanuto, xxxvii, col. 296, see *ibid.*, col. 196, and see Michiel's diary, which describes Paolo Capello as speaking 'con grande collera'.

the Pope the power to negotiate on their behalf with the French King, the Venetians could not escape signing an agreement with the French when such an alliance suited the Pope because of the threatened French invasion of Naples, but when Venetian interests were no more endangered than before. If the Venetians had used the 'benefitio del tempo' as some of the *Savi* wanted, they would have been in an excellent bargaining position a few months later when the military strength of the Spaniards was increasing and the French King might have thought more highly of Venetian support.

The crucial but also the most questionable factor in the Venetians' attitude was their anxiety to maintain close co-operation with the Pope. Certainly, there were advantages in leaving the diplomatic initiative to Clement VII. With the Pope in Rome as chief negotiator, the Spanish could be kept longer in the dark about Venetian intentions. The mounting Turkish threat too made the Venetians eager to secure the goodwill of the Pope, the head of Christianity. But there seems to have been an almost irrational element in the Venetian eagerness for co-operation with the Pope. The Venetians seem to have been haunted by the memories of the League of Cambrai. Actually the Venetians had nothing to fear of the Pope, not only because Clement VII was no Julius II, but also because an alliance of Spain and France could not be arranged. In 1509 a coalition between the Spanish, German and French rulers at the expense of Venice had been possible; in 1524 it was not. Charles V, with his aspirations to world monarchy, could not permit a strengthening of his main enemy, the French King. Fundamentally the Venetians lacked awareness that, with the combination of German and Spanish powers in the hands of one family, the Habsburgs, a new situation had arisen in which the precedents of the previous decades had little relevance.

Obviously the difficulties of noticing the need for changes in basic assumptions are great. But because of the awe in which the wisdom of Venetian statesmen is held the point deserves to be made that the Venetians did not see further than other rulers in the Renaissance period. As the speeches made in the Pregadi show, their calculations were based on the same factors on which other

Italian governments relied in figuring out what they ought to do.[61] In measuring the strength of a power, its financial resources and its military assets were the prime consideration. But the size, the maintenance and the efficiency of an army was believed to depend entirely on the availability of funds for the pay of the troops. The Venetians had no doubt of the truth of the saying that 'Money is the nerve of war'. They also shared the *communis opinio* of the importance of psychological factors. The actions of a ruler were viewed as determined by such factors as his pride, his eagerness to revenge a defeat or his hostility towards an individual. Like other governments, the Venetians were much concerned with maintaining their 'reputation'. They were convinced that they had an outstanding record in carrying out commitments and in keeping treaties and they wanted to keep this record clean. Such protestations uttered by men who were contemporaries of Cesare Borgia and Niccolò Machiavelli may sound rather hollow and hypocritical. But every diplomatic negotiation of this period attests to the high value which was placed on acting within correct legal grounds in the conduct of foreign policy. The Florentine attitude is almost identical with that of the Venetians; the Florentines too were proud of the loyalty with which they observed the treaties which they had concluded. Legal considerations were a serious matter in diplomacy. For this reason the remark which one of the Venetian patricians made in these discussions—that treaties should be broken only when the State is placed in obvious danger—deserves attention. It probably expressed more correctly than Machiavelli the accepted opinion about the extent and the limits of the observation of legal obligations in foreign policy.

If the intellectual framework in which the Venetians thought about foreign policy was the customary one, their psychological attitude also does not seem to have been distinguished by cool and unbiased objectivity. Many of the speeches which were made in the course of the debates on the treaty with France were emotional and passionate. The entire discussion had somewhat the character

[61] For the similarity between the Venetian and the Florentine outlook on foreign affairs, see my article, 'Florentine Political Assumptions in the Period of Savonarola and Soderini', *Journal of the Warburg and Courtauld Institutes*, xx (1957), particularly 196–202.

of a replay of the fight which had taken place one year earlier when the alliance with Charles V was concluded. The advocates of Charles V in 1523—Gabriele Moro, Alvise Mocenigo, Girolamo Pesaro—now opposed the French alliance,[62] whereas the friends of France in 1523—Paolo Capello, Andrea Trevisan—spoke for the renewal of the ties with France. Those who in 1523 had advocated adherence to the French alliance were anxious to show that they had been right, and they were not willing to let anything stand in the way of a successful conclusion of the negotiations. The outburst of Gabriele Moro against the four men who had determined the course of events probably was a reflection of this feeling that the pro-French group believed that its hour had come and was ruthless in pointing out that it must be listened to because it had been right. A striking parallel is the pro-French and pro-Habsburg division in the Florentine ruling group when party rivalry and personal enmities also had been involved in the evaluation of the situation. Again, the necessary conclusion seems to be that the Venetian ruling group was neither more unified nor less emotional than that of other city-states of the Renaissance.[63]

Nevertheless, the detailed analysis of one particular diplomatic episode which we have attempted reveals some features peculiar to the Venetian system of government, and they might help to explain the reputation for secrecy, finesse and astuteness which Venetian diplomats were to gain over the course of centuries. In the princely states of the Renaissance decisions on foreign policy were made by the ruler, perhaps together with a few counsellors. In Medicean Florence foreign policy was the preserve of the head of the Medici family, who might act after deliberation with a few influential friends of the Medici régime.[64] Even in the Republican period of Florence, between 1494 and 1512, the Office of the Ten

[62] Zaccaria Bembo, who played such a role in 1524, was on the *terra firma* as *provveditore* in 1523.

[63] It would go far beyond the scope of this essay to investigate whether the attitude of the individuals was influenced by economic interest or other personal reasons, but I hope that this study suggests the possibility and the importance of such investigations.

[64] See Nicolai Rubinstein, *The Government of Florence under the Medici (1434–1494)* (Oxford, 1966), p. 227.

handled foreign affairs, perhaps after consultation, in a *pratica*, with a few members of the aristocratic ruling group; a large *pratica* in which a greater number of citizens participated was rare and hardly ever concerned with issues of foreign policy.[65]

In Venice reports from those sent on missions abroad were discussed by the Ten and the Collegio, and these officials then drafted a reply. In cases of decisions of importance the Pregadi were assembled, although those members of the Pregadi whom the issue might involve in a 'conflict of interest' were not permitted to participate in the deliberations. This meant that in the negotiations about the treaty with France—because the Pope was prominently involved—the Papalisti, i.e. those who were related to the Pope or to cardinals—were excluded. The relevant documents were presented to the Pregadi. Then the proponents of the draft defended it and its opponents explained their position and made their proposals for textual revision. In the debates on the French alliance almost only *Savi del Consiglio* and *Savi della terra firma* took the word.[66] At the end there was a vote which decided whether the draft should be approved, amended, or a new draft should be resubmitted the next day.

The most startling consequence of this procedure is that the number of those who knew about the secrets of state and foreign policy was quite large. There were leaks, of course, as is shown by the many laws threatening severe punishment of those who violated the rules of secrecy. Yet it is astounding that the system worked, and there is reason therefore for the frequent statements in which contemporaries expressed their admiration for the Venetian ability to keep secret Government affairs. But it is also remarkable to what extent the discussions were concerned, not only with broad questions about what course to take in foreign

[65] See my article mentioned in note 61.

[66] Of course, debates in the Pregadi had a strictly hierarchical aspect; those in the higher rank—the *Savi*—talked before the others, and if a *Savio* had opposed a proposal, the proposal had to be defended by a person of the same rank, i.e. also a *Savio*. It would seem that, because there was great difference in the Collegio about the course to follow, so many *Savi* became involved in the debate that it never went below this rank. For the organization of debates and voting in the Pregadi, see Maranini, *op. cit.*, pp. 246 *et seq.*, 255 *et seq.*

policy, but also with finding the most appropriate language in the formulation of an instruction or a treaty.

This aspect of the discussions on foreign policy in the Pregadi might help to explain the reputation which Venetian diplomats enjoyed. In the times of the Renaissance and in the following centuries as well the men who understood the technical details in the conduct of diplomacy were the secretaries, the members of the Chancellery, the slowly growing number of professional civil servants. Frequently they played an important role as advisers in diplomatic negotiations or as agents preparing the ground for a diplomatic action. But they had not enough status to head diplomatic missions of importance. Prestigious diplomatic tasks were entrusted to great nobles or, in the case of city-states, to members of the wealthy ruling group. They could learn their diplomatic tasks only slowly through practice; as the Florentine legislation on ambassadors shows, the preparation of the youth of the ruling group for diplomatic service was regarded as a constant problem never satisfactorily solved.[67] In Venice, however, presence at the discussions of the Pregadi must have served as ideal training for diplomatic duties. Even if the concepts of Venetian diplomacy were similar to those of other states and the Venetian statesmen no paragons of impartiality and far-sightedness, their experience in the Pregadi must have taught them to move in the diplomatic world with a finesse and subtlety which made them stand out.

IV

The political importance of the Venetian move from the Spanish side to the French side in 1524 is limited. It must have been the contrast between the much-vaunted reputation of Venetian diplomacy and its actual performance in this diplomatic episode which has attracted the attention of historians; for the conduct of Venetian diplomacy at the time of Pavia has been described by historians of the sixteenth century with great care. Their treatment has been so detailed that in the most recent study of Venetian

[67] See Giu seppe Vedovato, *Note sul Diritto Diplomatico della Repubblica Fiorentina* (Florence, 1946).

historiography this episode could be taken as a criterion for defining the differences among the Venetian historians of the sixteenth century.[68] However, on the basis of our reconstruction of the actual course of events some further contribution to a study of the manner in which these historians of the sixteenth century approached their task should be possible.

Actually the first sixteenth-century historian who dealt with these diplomatic events was not a Venetian, but a Florentine: Francesco Guicciardini in his *History of Italy*. Guicciardini was less interested in the decision of 1524 than in the events of the previous year when Venice had abandoned the French alliance and joined Charles V.[69] As we have seen, discussions in the Pregadi on this issue extended over a long period of time and were concerned with the formulation of instructions to be given to the negotiators. Like almost all the other sixteenth-century historians, Guicciardini attributed critical importance to one great debate between two speakers representing opposite points of view. The speaker in favour of the French alliance was Andrea Gritti; the speaker for Charles V was Giorgio Corner. Although a clash between Gritti and Corner in one great debate is most unlikely, because, if it had happened, Sanuto would have mentioned it, Guicciardini's choice of Gritti and Corner as advocates of the two opposing points of view is justifiable. Gritti was well known as 'Francese' and Giorgio Corner was one of the three Venetian statesmen selected to negotiate the treaty with the Ambassador of Charles V. Moreover, Gritti and Corner were the two most outstanding Venetian statesmen at this time; when the Doge Grimani died in the summer of 1523 and Gritti was elected his successor, Corner was his chief rival. The speeches of Gritti and Corner are beautiful examples of Guicciardini's technique in the composition and use of speeches. Guicciardini wanted to show clearly the dilemma by which Venice was faced. One argument was that Venice ought to try to establish a balance of forces by permitting France to rule in Milan and Charles V in

[68] Gaetano Cozzi, 'Cultura Politica e Religione nella "Pubblica Storiografia" Veneziana del '500', *Bollettino dell'Istituto di Storia della Societa e dello Stato Veneziano*, v/vi (1963–4), 267–90.

[69] Francesco Guicciardini, *Storia d'Italia*, xv, ch. 2.

Naples; consequently, Venice ought to support France. The counter-argument was that if France were settled in Milan, Venice would have a restless and ambitious prince as neighbour. From the Venetian point of view, it would be preferable to have Francesco Sforza, a weak and self-indulgent prince, as ruler in Milan. This could be done only with the help of Charles V, and thus spoke for an alliance with him. Historical events of the recent past were cited as proof for all these statements. The Italian campaigns of Louis XII, the origin of the League of Cambrai, the unreliability of the Swiss mercenaries—all were referred to in order to justify the speakers' theories about the future policy of the French and the Spanish.

The speakers also tried to gauge the changes of the military situation. By having the two speakers present a divergent estimate of the military strength of the Spaniards and the French, Guicciardini indicated the uncertainty which permeates all such calculations. In Gritti's opinion, the French King was strong enough to appear suddenly in Italy, and clearly this remark was meant to foreshadow what happened one year later. Many remarks in these speeches—the need for a balance of power between Francis I and Charles V, the emphasis on the crucial position of Milan, the fear of an 'impero di tutta Italia' under Charles V—evoke the entire complex of problems which would dominate Italian politics in the next five years. By reminding the reader of the experiences of the recent past, and by suggesting to him some of the events that were to happen, Guicciardini succeeds in placing the present as a transitional moment between past and future. But although these speeches have their function in the structure of Guicciardini's entire history, they do not go beyond what would be appropriate to the situation which Guicciardini described in this chapter. Certainly, Gritti and Corner in Guicciardini's presentation saw farther and said more than the speakers in the Pregadi did. But Guicciardini never allowed them to see or say anything that they could not have said or seen. He remained in the time and in the situation which he analysed. However, because Guicciardini's presentation implied that prudent men who had mastered trials in the past and were aware of the dangers of the future could not find a secure road, he prepared the reader for the fateful course which events would take in the coming years, and he expressed the grand theme of his work: the impotence of men before fate.

Guicciardini's attention is directed towards an explanation of the political changes which occurred in the first decades of the sixteenth century, and in his presentation of the dilemma of Venetian diplomacy he stressed those aspects which have bearing on the entire political scene. After Guicciardini, those historians who wrote on the diplomatic manœuvres before the Battle of Pavia were Venetians. They were officially appointed to write the history of their republic and were concerned with the political lessons which might be drawn from these events for the conduct of Venetian policy; if Guicciardini treated this episode as an example of the human predicament, the Venetian writers tried to use these events to decide whether moral principles or political pragmatism ought to guide statesmen. Certainly their interest in these aspects of the events was influenced by the time in which they wrote. Their works were composed later than Guicciardini's, in the second half of the sixteenth century, in the time of the Counter-Reformation.

Andrea Navagero, Venice's first official historian, had died in 1529 without having started on the work which he was commissioned to do.[70] And his successor, Pietro Bembo, had brought the official history only up to the year 1513 when he died in 1547. There was an intermission of thirteen years until the appointment of the next official historiographer, Daniele Barbaro, but he had composed only a discussion of the situation at the time of the League of Cambrai when he died. But all the next three holders of this position—Alvise Contarini (appointed 1577), Paolo Paruta (appointed 1580), and Andrea Morosini (appointed 1598)—discussed the events before the Battle of Pavia.

Alvise Contarini died a few years after his appointment and his history, which begins where Bembo stopped and ends in 1570, remained in rather rough form and has never been printed.[71] The

[70] For the history of Venetian public historiography, see the above-mentioned article by Gaetano Cozzi (note 68).

[71] Aloysii Contarini, 'Delineatio Historia, qua res gestas Venetorum complectitur, nulla diligentia contexta, iterum atque iterum expolienda et

manuscript gives attention, however, to the dilemma of Venetian diplomacy in the years of the struggle between France and Spain. Contarini clearly followed Guicciardini in the presentation of this episode. Like Guicciardini in the *History of Italy*, he focused on the decision of 1523, and his main antagonists are Gritti and Corner. But Contarini places the decision by which Venice was faced in a different framework than had Guicciardini. The disagreement of the speakers is about means; their aim is the same: to keep Venice neutral and thereby to secure peace for Italy. Interestingly enough, Contarini finds it necessary to stress that the Venetians were not egoists. In pursuing neutrality and peace they had in mind not only the interests of their commerce and material advantages; rather than the freedom of Italy. The observation of neutrality and peace is the morally superior course.[72]

Contarini's successor as official historiographer, Paola Paruta,[73] is not concerned with issues of morality or religion. His only interest is to draw from the past rules for the conduct of

[72] Cozzi, *loc. cit.*, pp. 250 *et seq.* discusses the relations between Agostino Valier and Alvise Contarini. Valier dedicated a book which outlined the 'perfect historian' (*Ricordi per Scriver le Historie della Repubblica di Venezia di Questi Tempi*) to Alvise Contarini, and he wrote a kind of outline of Venetian history, entitled *Dell'Utilita che si puo ritrarre dalle cose operate di Veneziani Libri XIV*, published, for the first time, Padua, 1787. This might be considered as a collection of examples, teaching the usefulness of following a moral and Christian course. On p. 275, Valier touches upon the negotiations before Pavia, he speaks of 'molte consulte, pretendendo alcuni che si dovesse anteporre l'amicitia del Re di Francia', but his description of events is brief, superficial and confusing. Cozzi, *loc. cit.*, p. 253, emphasizes the influence of Valier on Alvise Contarini, but he states that in Contarini's book the moral principles are somewhat more subdued. I must say that my view would be that Contarini had a much stronger political sense than Valier; the difference between the two seems to be greater than Cozzi assumes.

[73] For Paolo Paruta's *Historia Venetiana* and for Andrea Morosini's *Historia Veneta* I used the editions in *Istorici delle Cose Veneziane i quali hanno scritto per pubblico Decreto* (Venice, 1718–22); Paruta is printed in vols. iii and iv, Morosini in vols. v–vii.

---

debitis coloribus exornanda, in quatuordecim libros distincta', *Biblioteca Marciana*, cl. lat. x, cod. 285 (3,180); the most relevant passages are on ff. 24–5.

politics applicable to the present. The aim of using history for setting down his views about the right principles for Venetian politics is so dominating that Paruta shows a sovereign disregard for factual accuracy and a tendency to make the facts fit his intellectual aims. In Paruta's story[74] the two antagonists in a discussion on the treaty with France are Giorgio Corner and Domenico Trevisan. One might say that Paruta refrained from assigning Gritti a role in this debate because he knew that in 1524 Gritti was Doge and as such could not be the leading spokesman of a group in the Pregadi; Domenico Trevisan, who replaced Gritti in Paruta's story, was indeed an adherent of the French alliance. But it might be questioned whether Paruta would have selected him if in the meantime Domenico Trevisan had not risen in reputation as the father of a Doge.[75] Paruta's arbitrariness in the selection of speakers emerges from his making Giorgio Corner the other speaker. It is true that Corner was one of the most prominent Venetian statesmen of this period and had played an important role in 1523; but in 1524 he was sick and unable to appear in the Pregadi.[76] Moreover, as a relative of the two Cardinals from the Corner family he would have been excluded from most of the discussion as a 'Papalista'.

Paruta's tendentious arbitrariness is reflected in the manner in which he used this episode to strengthen and justify the anti-Papal course which Venice pursued in Paruta's time. Paruta throws the entire responsibility for the events of 1524 on Pope Clement VII. He makes the Pope the driving force in the negotiations with France. In order to show the Pope's zeal, Paruta places Giberti's mission to Francis I before the fall of Milan; he lets the Pope make the demand that the Venetians should give Foscari full power to sign the treaty which the Pope had negotiated, and according to Paruta the treaty was concluded by the Pope when the Pregadi assembled 'per venir all'ultima terminazione del negotio'.[77]

[74] Paruta's description of the diplomatic negotiations between 1523 and 1525 can be found in *Istorici*, iii, 360–89.

[75] Marc Antonio Trevisan, Doge, 1553–4.

[76] Sanuto, xxxvii, col. 85.

[77] *Istorici*, iii, 379. The speeches of Corner and Trevisan on pp. 379–89.

The purpose of the presentation of this episode in Paruta's book, and particularly of the speeches put into the mouths of Trevisan and Corner, is to give political instruction. They contain hardly any references to the factual situation which existed in 1524; emphasis on the uncertainty of the military situation is the most concrete issue which the speakers discuss. Paruta used his speeches to set forth his views about the appropriate approach to the management of foreign affairs. The first requirement was to consider such decisions in cool objectivity without passion or bias. The intellectual framework for such a rational consideration is formed by the concepts of 'interest', 'reason of state', 'balance of power'. Each state or prince will always follow his own interest. He will not subordinate political interests to a higher moral law. Politics has its own law: the reason of state. Venice's dominating interest is to prevent control over Italy falling into the hands of one great power. In particular, this means to maintain a balance of power between Spain and France. This can best be achieved by supporting always the one which at a given moment is weaker against the one which is stronger.[78] Venice should never follow a fixed course. Its foreign policy ought to be flexible, moving from one side to the other. The argument of the need to remain loyal to commitments has no value. In foreign policy reason of state is the highest principle.

Morosini, Paruta's successor as Venetian historiographer, took the almost opposite line. In his description of the debates which led to the decision in 1524 moral considerations are presented as decisive. The advocate of the French alliance said that the highest duty was to preserve the fatherland. Destruction threatened from iron and blood, force and rape. An adjustment to circumstances through an alliance with France was necessary.[79] His opponent emphasized that in the past the Venetians' loyalty to agreements was their highest pride.[80] Everything ought to be tried rather than

[78] *Ibid.*, p. 385.

[79] *Istorici*, v, 106: '. . . ii qui in rebus publicis, imperiisque regendis floruere consilia nonnumquam temporum rationibus accommodando patriam e summis pericolis eripuere . . .'. For Trevisan's speech, see pp. 104–7.

[80] *Ibid.*, p. 107: 'nemo sane ignorat qua fide integritate constantia sanctissimi illi viri, qui nobis florentissimam istam Rempublicam, atque imperium

to violate a treaty. The debate between the two speakers centred on the question whether the preservation of the life of the state and of its inhabitants or obedience to moral law is the highest duty, and the author's sympathy is clearly on the side of morality. But Morosini adds to his moral appeals also some practical considerations which correspond to the situation: he directs attention to the great man-power reserves of the Habsburg rulers. Moreover, Venice is not as free as the Pope, who has no alliance with France and whose position makes it easy for him to change from one side to the other. These were arguments which had actually been made in 1524. The speeches treat the issue as a problem of moral philosophy. But these theoretical discussions are embedded in a story of remarkable factual exactitude. If you are acquainted with the records of the Pregadi you can have no doubt that Morosini studied them before writing his story.[81] Like Paruta, he selected Domenico Trevisan as advocate of the French alliance. But Alvise Mocenigo, who in Morosini's story maintains the opposite point of view, was indeed, as we have seen, a vehement protagonist of loyalty to Spain. Morosini is also aware of the role and the attitude of Zaccaria Bembo, who, as Morosini says,[82] 'magna dicendi vi atque impetu animi contradicente' delayed the sending of an instruction which would have permitted Foscari to sign the treaty. But Morosini explained correctly that the next day such an instruction was sent and he acknowledged the crucial role of Girolamo Pesaro in effecting a compromise. It is striking, however, that in Morosini's presentation the story of 1524 has no ending. He never states that the outcome of the discussion was a change of sides and the conclusion of a treaty with France.

[81] I might mention that, as far as I can see, Morosini is the only writer who reports about the suggestion of the Pope to make Francesco Sforza a cardinal; see *ibid.*, p. 115. Cozzi's characterization of Morosini's historiography in Cozzi, *loc. cit.*, pp. 288–9, seems to me questionable because he is unaware of Morosini's careful use of sources. On Morosini's *Historia Veneta*, see also William J. Bouwsma, *Venice and the Defence of Republican Liberty* (Berkeley, 1968), pp. 557–61.

[82] *Ibid.*, p. 110.

veluti per manus tradidere, societates foederaque coluerunt'; p. 108: 'omnia prius experiri antequam . . . pacta infringeretis . . .'. For Mocenigo's speech, see pp. 107–9.

The analysis of the manner in which this episode was described in the writings of sixteenth-century historians should be of help for our understanding of the developments of historiography and of Venetian political thought. Guicciardini's superiority as a writer of history clearly stands out. The speeches which he composed form a necessary link in the explanation of events. They serve to provide a survey of all the ingredients which went into the making of a decision. In contrast, the contents of the speeches written by Venetian historians later in the sixteenth century are extraneous to the occasion at which they were supposed to be given. They are less rhetorical, less purely decorative than the abstract and moralizing reflections in speeches by humanist historians of the fifteenth century; the speeches of the Venetian historians of the sixteenth century at least remained in a political context; Paruta set forth principles of successful political conduct, Morosini discussed problems of the relation between morals and politics. But these speeches are not closely integrated with the historical narrative; they are inserts and appear somewhat like an alien element.[83] The historical narrative runs along independent from the speeches, and it depended on the author whether the narrative was shaped according to political purposes or was presented with concern for factual accuracy.

In explanation of the discrepancies between Guicciardini and the later Venetian historians, it might simply be said that Guicciardini was a greater historian; this is certainly a valid explanation, but not more than a partial explanation. The problems of morals and politics and the origin of the doctrine of

[83] Paolo Paruta, *Della Perfettione della Vita Politica* (edition, Venice, 1599), on pp. 212–19, deals with the significance of historical writing and discusses also in particular the question of the composition and the use of speeches by historians; Paruta regards speeches as inserts, he warns against speeches whose contents are entirely speculative and philosophical; speeches ought to remain somewhat connected with the events and ought to set forth in a general and abstract form what can be learned from the events described in the historical narrative. These theoretical views are rather close to Paruta's practice in his *Historia Venetiana*. For a description of Paruta's views on history in his *Della Perfettione* . . ., see also William J. Bouwsma, *op. cit.*, pp. 219–23, although Bouwsma's analysis seems to me to read into this work notions which it does not contain.

reason of state which emancipated politics from the subordination to the general laws of morality, were issues which the religious conflicts of the second part of the sixteenth century had raised. They were regarded as new problems causing deep concern, and historical writers were expected to take them up. Finally, it ought to be added that Paruta and Morosini were official historiographers and, as the decrees of their appointments say, their histories were expected to be of use in the conduct of government; they will have considered the abstracting of rules from the presentation of the past as inherent in the task of an official historiographer.

As official historiographers these Venetian writers were also custodians and transmitters of the Venetian myth[84]—that is, the further conclusion which can be drawn from the analysis of this episode. These writers did not admit that Venetian statesmen had ever acted without unusual wisdom, responsibility and foresight. That certainly is the reason why Morosini did not report about the outcome of the debate which he had described. Venetian statesmen did not commit acts of disloyalty or serious diplomatic mistakes. If in Venice the art of history had advanced in realism beyond the *Quattrocento*, in which humanist rhetorics had smothered the facts, historical truth was now limited by a myth which had become an integral part of Venetian political life.[85]

[84] Alvise Contarini, on f. 20 of his 'Delineatio', *Biblioteca Marciana*, cl. lat. x, cod. 285 (3,180), states that criticisms of Venice by historians have their origin in that they 'in invidiam adducunt et ut prudentiores aliis esse videantur calumniis opprimunt'. It is rather amusing, however, how belief in Venetian wisdom and righteousness has continued into modern treatments of this episode. Kretschmayr, *Geschichte von Venedig* (Gotha, 1934), iii, 12, combines Guicciardini, Sanuto and Paruta to a mixture which has no relation to facts, but also recent Italian historians, much more steeped in the sources, cannot get rid of the myth: Roberto Cessi, *Storia della Repubblica di Venezia* (Milan, 1946), ii, 83, and also Cozzi, *loc. cit.*, p. 289, propound the thesis that Venice really did not break the treaty with Charles V because it did not promise assistance to Francis I in the present war. But this thesis is untenable; as the speeches in the Pregadi or, later, Andrea Morosini show, the Venetians themselves did not claim that the treaty with Francis I was compatible with their alliance with Charles V.

[85] For the origin of the Venetian myth, see my article, 'The Venetian Constitution in Florentine Political Thought' in *Florentine Studies*, ed.

Whereas in the fifteenth and the early part of the sixteenth century the political role which Venice played was not very different from that of any other Italian government, now at the end of the sixteenth century Venice was in a unique position: it was the only Italian state which was not under the control of a great foreign power. But great powers were now dominating the political scene, and the Venetian role in foreign policy became reduced to that of an observer rather than that of a principal. Indeed, it was as outside observers that the Venetian diplomats really became what the Venetian historians claimed that they had always been: masters of penetrating and objective observations.

It was the Venetians' weakness which fostered and fortified the Venetian myth. In an age of competition among great powers, Venetian independence was due to toleration by others rather than to innate strength. It was natural for the Venetians, however —and perhaps necessary for their self-confidence—to refuse recognition of such a humiliating situation and to explain the preservation of Venice's independence as the work of age-old political wisdom by which Venice had always excelled all other states. Thus, the Venetian myth became an integral part of the Venetian reason of state.

Nicolai Rubinstein (London, 1968), pp. 466–72; the Venetian myth, of course, emerged long before the sixteenth century, in which it was 'codified'.

Five

The Statecraft of Olivares

by

J. H. Elliott

The political career of the Count Duke of Olivares exemplifies, perhaps more poignantly than that of any of his contemporaries, the dilemmas, the disappointments and the frustrated ambitions of the seventeenth-century statesman. Few, it seems, can have aimed so high, and yet have fallen so low and been so cruelly disillusioned. The man who had set out to restore the fortunes of the Spanish Monarchy found himself instead presiding impotently over its dissolution. This terrible intermingling of national and personal tragedy has always had about it something of the grandeur, and perhaps also the inevitability, of a classical drama—a drama of *hubris* and its punishment. The drama is full of ironies, and not the least of them is that its details will for ever escape us. Scraps and fragments, dispersed State papers and tantalizing snatches of correspondence are all that remain of Olivares's prodigious output. Perpetually haunted by the fear that he would die 'without having achieved anything of consequence',[1] he was to be defrauded even in his ambition of leaving something of himself to posterity. His hopes of succession were dashed by the death in 1626 of his daughter, his only child; his meticulous instructions for the preservation of his superb library were disregarded after his death;[2] and his archive of public and private papers was destroyed in an eighteenth-century fire. Nothing, it seemed, survived but a record of disasters and a series of anecdotes

[1] Quoted by A. Cánovas del Castillo, *Estudios del Reinado de Felipe IV* (Madrid, 1888), i, 168.

[2] G. Marañón, *El Conde Duque de Olivares* (3rd ed., Madrid, 1952), pp. 163–6.

sufficient to provide the material for an unflattering comparison with Cardinal Richelieu.[3]

Yet enough has survived for us to be able to reconstruct at least something of the man and his policies. Since Olivares first engaged the attention of Cánovas del Castillo[4] and Martin Hume,[5] old pieces of evidence have been reassessed and new pieces have come to light. His character, his private life and his personal relationships have been examined in Dr Marañón's ambitious psycho-analytical biography;[6] and a number of detailed studies have brought certain aspects of his domestic and foreign policies into sharper focus.[7] There is much that still remains to be investigated—the formative influences on his career, his methods of government, the identity and the character of his advisers and confidants. But his ideas, his hopes and his ambitions are a little better known than they were; and a few more clues have become available to his statecraft and his policies.

Olivares's approach to the problems of government was inescapably affected by the ambiguities of his position as favourite and principal minister of Philip IV of Spain.[8] The ambiguities,

[3] See the point-by-point comparison in Valdory's Preface to his compilation of anecdotes from the *Mercurio* of Siri, *Anecdotes du Ministère du Comte Duc d'Olivarés* (Paris, 1722).

[4] In his *Estudios del Reinado de Felipe IV* (1888), Cánovas shows himself markedly more sympathetic to Olivares than in his first study of the period, *Historia de la Decadencia Española* (Madrid, 1854).

[5] *The Court of Philip IV* (1st ed., London, 1907).

[6] First published Madrid, 1936.

[7] For his fiscal policies, see Antonio Domínguez Ortiz, *Política y Hacienda de Felipe IV* (Madrid, 1960); for his Catalan policy, J. Sanabre, *La Acción de Francia en Cataluña en la pugna por la hegemonía de Europa, 1640–1659* (Barcelona, 1956), J. H. Elliott, *The Revolt of the Catalans* (Cambridge, 1963), and E. Zudaire, *El Conde-Duque y Cataluña* (Madrid, 1964); for aspects of his foreign policy, A. Leman, *Richelieu et Olivarès* (Lille, 1938), J. M. Jover, *1635. Historia de una polémica y semblanza de una generación* (Madrid, 1949), M. Fernández Alvarez, *Don Gonzalo de Córdoba y la Guerra de Sucesión de Mantua y del Monferrato, 1627–1629* (Madrid, 1955), and R. Ródenas Vilar, *La Política Europea de España Durante La Guerra de Treinta Años, 1624–1630* (Madrid, 1967).

[8] Francisco Tomás Valiente, *Los Validos en la Monarquía Española del Siglo*

which were considerable, sprang from a deeply rooted historical distrust of favourites in Castile, and a lingering assumption, frequently disappointed but never totally abandoned, that it was the duty of kings to govern. By the seventeenth century the need for a principal minister was obvious. It was hardly consonant with royal dignity, as Philip IV himself pointed out in later life, for the King to go from one minister's house to another to find out whether his orders had been obeyed.[9] The clear necessity for such a minister, however, did little to reconcile Spaniards to the fact of his existence, although the profusion of treatises purporting to assist and advise the favourite suggests that he was reluctantly coming to be accepted as an indispensable part of monarchical government. In the circumstances, he could hardly avoid being a source of conflicting emotions to contemporaries. They at once admired the extent of his power, and felt deep resentment at its exercise. They were fascinated by the emphemeral character of a greatness so entirely dependent on royal caprice for its survival, while at the same time eagerly proffering advice to the favourite on how to remain in office.

Olivares himself shared the doubts and uneasiness of his contemporaries. He rejected the name of *privado* (favourite), preferring to style himself the 'minister' or 'faithful minister' of the King.[10] 'I never aspired to, nor worked for, the position which I hold', he wrote, with only a very moderate degree of truthfulness, to his future son-in-law. 'Establish your own reputation and do not count on my remaining in a position so subject to sudden change. . . . Now that I am in it, I am not so foolish as to let a single day pass without thinking that I may have lost it by the next morning. This is the truth, and anything said to the contrary is a baseless illusion.'[11] No doubt this *was* the truth. In spite of the

[9] Letter to Sor María de Agreda, 30 January 1647, quoted by Valiente, p. 181.

[10] Valiente, p. 75.

[11] University of California (Berkeley), Bancroft Library, MS. M–M 1755 (Varios Papeles), no. 15, 'Instrucción del Conde Duque de Olivares para su yerno', 9 October 1624, p. 186.

XVII (Madrid, 1963), is a valuable study of the favourite in the institutional life of seventeenth-century Spain. For contemporary ideas about the favourite, see J. A. Maravall, *Teoría Española del Estado en el Siglo XVII* (Madrid, 1944).

strong bond of confidence between Philip IV and his minister, Olivares harboured no illusions about the fate of favourites and the fickleness of kings.

In some ways, there was even a kind of perverse satisfaction to be derived from this nagging awareness of the supremely precarious character of a favourite's power. Anyone who exalted the majesty of kingship as Olivares exalted it could hardly take exception to the exercise of regal power implicit in the dismissal of a favourite and the personal assumption of his duties by the King. The paradox was inherent in the seventeenth-century conception of kingship, but Olivares savoured it to the full. He expected the King of Spain to take his duties seriously, and Philip IV's shortcomings in this respect during the early years of his reign were a source of genuine concern. In his famous admonition to Philip in September 1626, he reminded the King that he had repeatedly requested permission to retire, since his policies had no hope of success unless the King applied himself to business.[12] The ministers must be relieved of the burden of attending to individual petitioners—a task which properly belonged to the King. The resumption of this essential function of kingship, the exercise of patronage, would put an end to the use of the word *privado*, and to the most coveted features of the post. The King's ministers would then be left free to serve him in the proper manner—as his advisers on matters of government.

Seventeenth-century conditions made this attempt to distinguish between patronage and government totally unrealistic. Government was dependent upon patronage; and the fact that Olivares's contemporaries looked upon him, with good reason, as a *privado* is sufficient indication that he was well aware of this. But the desire to dispossess himself of the *privanza* was not necessarily hypocritical. For all the vituperation of his enemies, who saw in him an obsessive desire to accumulate wealth and favour, Olivares's own inclination was essentially towards the ministry rather than the *privanza*. At heart he was, and aspired to be, a professional in the art of government. At the same time he

[12] B(ritish) M(useum), Eg(erton) MS. 347, ff. 113–16 (*Papel del Conde Duque* . . . 4 September 1626). A version from Madrid printed as Appendix V of Valiente.

discovered, to his distress, that he was exposed to all the obloquy traditionally lavished on the *privado* of the King. This was a fate from which nothing could save him. All he could do was to urge the King to greater personal efforts, while himself resorting to the usual devices employed by favourites to keep themselves in power.

Olivares's enemies detected in him 'an insatiable desire to govern'.[13] This seems to have sprung less from personal ambitions than from that 'passion to command'—to dominate for its own sake—which has been seen as the key to his complex personality.[14] He devoted himself with absolute single-mindedness to the work of government, and he demanded the same sacrifices of others (including the King) that he demanded of himself. He was not, he warned his secretaries, a good man for whom to work. They should expect no special favours or preferments, and should remember the fate of one of their predecessors who died in office of overwork, and was given a pauper's burial. The ideal which he held constantly before his ministers, his secretaries and himself was service—'the King should be well served'.[15] The passionate intensity with which he pursued this ideal taxed to the limits his own extraordinary energies, and exhausted those of the lesser men around him. Between drafting memoranda, dictating letters, addressing council meetings, holding audiences, there was scarcely time for rest. 'During many nights without sleep and days of continuous cogitation, I have discovered with the help of some of my principal ministers certain means and devices. . . .'[16] And all too often, when there was a chance of a little sleep, it would not come. 'For many days now I have been unable to sleep by night or day. . . .'[17] Complaints of sleeplessness provided the continuous refrain to twenty-two years of personal government.

[13] B.M. Add(itional) MS. 25,689, ff. 166–70, 'Papel que se dió a SM. sobre la privanza del Conde Duque' (attributed to the Conde de Salinas, 1630), f. 167.

[14] See the Introduction to Marañón, *El Conde Duque de Olivares.*

[15] Berkeley, Bancroft MS. M–M 1755, pp. 173–5, 'Copia del orden del Conde Duque de Olivares que han de guardar . . . sus secretarios'.

[16] Domínguez Ortiz, *Política y Hacienda,* app. xxiii, 388.

[17] B.M. Add. MS. 14,007, f. 63v (to Cardinal Infante, 14 July 1636).

Olivares was not a man to let potential dramas go by default, and no doubt he derived a certain satisfaction from publicly parading the burdens of office. But the sense of duty was instinctive. As favourite, he was the essential intermediary between the King and the people, and this function carried with it unique responsibilities. He had to be able to listen to the people, in order to interpret their needs to the King; and he had to be able to advise the King in order to remedy the needs of the people. To achieve these ends to the best of his ability, he needed a store of political wisdom. He sought the advice of contemporaries, like the Prince of Carpiñano, of whom he enquired how he could best give audiences when he had only two or three hours at his disposal for such an important function.[18] But above all he sought the advice of the great authors of antiquity, and not least of Tacitus.

The excessive dependence of Olivares on maxims of state drawn from classical authors was, indeed, a principal charge levelled against him by that acute observer of the contemporary scene, Francisco Manuel de Melo:

> The political and historical books which he read had left him with a number of maxims which were unsuited to the humour of our times. From this sprang a number of harsh actions, whose only object was to imitate the ancients; as if Tacitus, Seneca, Paterculus, Pliny, Livy, Polybius and Procopius, of whom he took counsel, would not have altered their views if they had been alive now, considering the differences which every age introduces into the customs and the interests of men.[19]

Melo's insistence on the inapplicability of ancient wisdom to modern problems ran directly counter to the central argument advanced by the Spanish adherents of Tacitus, whose acknowledged leader for many decades was the former friend and

[18] B.M. Eg. MS. 2053, ff. 26–36 (*Preguntas del Conde Duque sobre las audiencias*). See also Enrique Tierno-Galván, 'Acerca de dos cartas muy poco conocidas del Conde-Duque de Olivares', *Anales de la Universidad de Murcia* (1951–2), pp. 71–6.

[19] Francisco Manuel de Melo, *Epanáforas* (ed. E. Prestage, Coimbra, 1931), p. 93. See also Marañón, *Olivares*, pp. 162–3.

disciple of Antonio Pérez, Baltasar Alamos de Barrientos.[20] In the dedication to his famous volume of translations and aphorisms from Tacitus, the *Tácito Español*, Alamos quoted with approval the words of the master: 'men may change, but not their habits'.[21] He quoted the same words again in a long paper offering advice to Olivares, with whom he appears at some periods of his life to have been closely associated. 'Read Tacitus,' he begged Olivares, 'and do not say that he offers nothing but impracticable metaphysics.' On the contrary, the essence of this science 'which they call the science of state' was eminently practical, for it taught men to understand the passions and motives of mankind.[22] In Tacitus, the 'singular master of this science', could be found those clues to human nature, the knowledge of which was the key to the successful practice of statecraft.

As taught by Alamos de Barrientos, the science of state was comparable to medical science. Because similar causes led to similar consequences, accurate diagnosis of the ills of the body politic could lead to the prevention and cure of disease.[23] No doubt there were insufficient rules to cover every conceivable contingency; but at least it was possible to provide a corpus of instructions, based on actual experience, which could furnish the statesman, like the physician, with general guidance in his art.

There are clear indications that Olivares accepted this approach to statecraft, and made it his own where it suited his purpose. For a man who possessed no previous political experience at the time of his elevation to a position of supreme power in the state, the political wisdom to be culled from extensive historical reading offered obvious attractions. At the same time, the political maxim represented an obvious device for accomplishing his most important duty as the royal favourite—to instruct his master, who

[20] For Alamos de Barrientos, see F. Sanmartí Boncompte, *Tácito en España* (Barcelona, 1951), pp. 72–4, and G. Marañón, *Antonio Pérez* (3rd ed., Madrid, 1951).

[21] (Madrid, 1614), *Dedicatoria*, f. 2.

[22] Hispanic Society of New York, MS. HC380/80, ff. 1–156v. 'Advertencias políticas sobre lo particular y público de esta monarchia', ff. 10–11v.

[23] *Tácito Español*. 'Discurso para la inteligencia de los Aforismos' (no page numbers).

was even less experienced than himself, in the art of government. The most famous of all his state papers—the great memorandum of December 1624 on the government of the Spanish Monarchy[24] —was designed, in his own words, to 'instruct the royal mind in certain general maxims concerning the government of Castile and of Spain . . . general maxims which conform to the rules of policy and state'.[25] But, like Alamos de Barrientos, he was willing enough to admit that general maxims could not hope to cover every contingency. 'Great and varied are the matters of government and state in these kingdoms of Castile . . . and to attempt to comprehend them all under fixed rules would be a vain ambition, and culpably presumptious.' It was therefore incumbent upon the king, duly enlightened by general maxims, to devise suitably appropriate measures to deal with each specific contingency.[26]

It must be admitted that Olivares's general maxims, like most general maxims, were far too general in character to be of any great service. The king must be loved by his vassals, but no king can be loved who is not just. To rule justly, he must have upright ministers, and must favour the virtuous man in all his appointments. He must distribute favours with great care and moderation. . . . All this, and much else, represented the usual small change of edifying advice to kings, and Olivares dispensed it as liberally as any other seventeenth-century favourite. But it is typical of Olivares that the generalities were interspersed with highly specific recommendations, often of an extremely radical nature, as if he drew no great distinction between the general and the particular, and put them down indiscriminately on paper just as they entered his mind.

The disconcerting disorderliness of so many of Olivares's

[24] Several versions exist, with some differences between them. Marañón, *Olivares*, app. xviii, reproduces extracts from the version printed in the eighteenth century by Valladares in his *Semanario Erudito*, xi, 162–224. I have used here the very clear copy in B.M. Eg. MS. 2053, ff. 173–218, which bears some modifications of its own, and, very unusually, a date (25 December 1624). The document will be cited as 'Great Memorandum (1624)'.

[25] f. 173.

[26] f. 206.

memoranda tends to conceal the essential logic and coherence in his assessment of the Monarchy's problems, and in his proposals for their solution. It is only when his state papers are taken together that anything like a general picture begins to be revealed. This picture is of the type that might be expected from Alamos de Barrientos's statesman-physician, who is at once concerned to diagnose the illness in the body politic and find the remedies. Spain's illness had been a serious one—*el mal ha sido grande*, as Olivares himself observed.[27] Having diagnosed it, he had various remedies to propose. But he disclaimed in advance any pretence to possess a universally applicable nostrum, to be employed irrespective of circumstances. It was almost, indeed, as if he were anticipating Melo's later criticism, when he accompanied his great plan of 1624 for the restructuring of the Spanish Monarchy with a specific warning that it was essential to avoid becoming committed to certain fixed opinions. In a matter like this, where change and instability were the order of the day, one must always be ready to change one's ground as fresh contingencies arose.[28]

How, then, did Olivares assess the character and condition of the Monarchy, with whose government he was entrusted in 1621? Inevitably he regarded Philip IV as the greatest monarch in the world, in terms of the extent and number of his many kingdoms and territories. But, with the war against the Dutch resumed at the very start of the reign, it was natural that he should see the King as surrounded by foreign rivals, jealous of his greatness. Conflict, indeed, could not be avoided, since the King was the 'principal support and defender of the Catholic religion'. For this reason he had reopened the war with the Dutch and with 'the other enemies of the Church who assist them', and it was incumbent upon the King to defend himself and attack his enemies.[29]

The foreign policy of the Spanish Crown was therefore to be guided by the dictates of religion. It would not be long, however,

[27] '*Papel del Conde Duque* . . . 4 September 1626' (see note 12), f. 115.

[28] Great Memorandum (1624), f. 214.

[29] B.M. Eg. MS. 347, ff. 56–61 (*Papel que el Conde Duque puso en manos de SM sobre* . . . *su hacienda* . . . 28 November 1621). Printed in Marañón, app. xvii.

before Olivares's enemies were accusing him of Machiavellian attempts to accommodate religion to the needs of the State—a charge which he rejected in his famous apologia, the *Nicandro*, after his fall from power. 'If the Count had indeed followed this counsel [of Machiavelli] he would have escaped involvement in wars with Swedes, Danes, and the Protestant heretics of Holland, and would have divided France. . . .'[30] It may, however, be questioned whether his practice, as distinct from his professions, did not allow of a wider degree of latitude than the purist would have been prepared to admit. An obvious test case arose in 1625, when the Council of State was faced with the question of whether Spain should assist the Huguenots of La Rochelle. On the face of it, any such proposal ran directly counter to 'conscience'. The Crown, however, attempted to invalidate this reasoning by ingeniously arguing that a diversion in support of La Rochelle would prevent a greater evil—the conversion of La Rochelle into an Atlantic outpost of the Dutch. It was unfortunate for Olivares that six out of the nine councillors were unwilling to accept the logic of this argument. Understandably, the question of help for the Huguenots was not brought again before the Council of State. But this does not quite seem to be the end of the story, for the Huguenots, it appears, were not entirely disappointed by the outcome of their approaches to the Spanish Ambassador in France.[31]

Olivares would certainly have agreed that the claims of conscience came first. But on closer inspection few proved to be as clear-cut as they appeared at first sight—just as no considerations, however apparently secular, could ever be quite dissociated from matters of religion. Even war with France could be conceived of by Olivares as a war against heretics, 'as I consider the French to be'.[32] But behind all such considerations lay a view of the world in which Castile's right to primacy was taken for granted. In a moment of extreme strain and weariness, Olivares

[30] B.M. Add. MS. 25,688, ff. 210–56, *El Nicandro*, f. 241.

[31] The La Rochelle affair is examined in Ródenas Vilar, *La Política Europea de España*, pp. 32–7.

[32] Paper of 14 June 1635, quoted by Elliott, *The Revolt*, p. 310.

casually revealed his hope that one day Castile would be 'head of the world, as it is already head of Your Majesty's Monarchy'.[33]

The commitment to greatness, however, always tended to be accompanied in Olivares's mind with a commitment to caution. In his memorandum addressed to the King in 1621 he expressed his hope that Philip (whom he was later to style 'the Great') would one day rank among the most celebrated kings in history; but he also expressed the conviction that this was not the moment for heroics. Without money, heroics were impossible, and Philip had succeeded to an empty treasury. The war with the Dutch must be fought to a victorious conclusion. But until solvency was restored, economy and reform must be the first priorities.

When he came to diagnose the conditions which made *reformación* indispensable, Olivares constantly returned to the theme that his countrymen's misfortunes sprang from their spiritual and moral deficiencies. It was the sinfulness of the people which had brought the Monarchy to its present sad pass—the worst in which it had ever found itself.[34] 'Our sins' (*nuestros pecados*) figured prominently among the phrases which Olivares liked to use. When the twenty-three famous *capítulos de reformación* were published by the Crown on 10 February 1623,[35] it was clear that the moral backslidings of the Castilians had not been overlooked. The *capítulos*—partly inspired by recommendations made by the Council of Castile in 1619[36]—represented a strange hotchpotch of proposals, in which plans for economic reform were oddly combined with measures designed to bring about a reformation of manners and morals. But the general intention behind them was clear enough. They were conceived as a programme for reform which would pave the way for the material and spiritual revival of Castile. Austerity and sobriety were to be the keynotes of this programme. The Castile of Olivares was to be a puritanical society whose inhabitants dressed soberly, communicated regularly, abstained from frivolous amusements and

[33] *Ibid.*

[34] Great Memorandum (1624), f. 175.

[35] A. González Palencia, 'La Junta de Reformación, 1618–1625', *Archivo Histórico Español* (Valladolid, 1932), v, doc. lxvi.

[36] See note 48.

from the frequenting of brothels, and devoted their lives to the public service and the common good.

To Olivares's great distress, the Castilians showed a strange reluctance to respond to his call for reformation. Over the years, he became increasingly concerned with their unrepentant waywardness. 'We Spaniards', he wrote to the young Cardinal Infante in 1632, 'are very good when we are subjected to rigorous obedience, but, when we are indulged, we are the worst people in the world.'[37] The Spain which he governed seemed to him a hopelessly undisciplined country, badly in need of the firm hand shown by the greatest of its kings—Ferdinand the Catholic. At present, nobody was punished; no proof was ever forthcoming; nobody was willing to take responsibility, and there was not a person in Spain who could resist a bribe. Discipline must be restored; and discipline required a close attention to the 'education of Spanish youth'. It was to remedy the educational deficiencies of the aristocracy that he founded the Colegio Imperial in Madrid in 1625—an abortive enterprise which signally failed in its essential purpose of instilling a sense of obedience and service into the governing class of the next generation. The continuing lack of obedience, and the dearth of true leaders, remained for Olivares the most critical weaknesses of the Monarchy, threatening it with ruin.

The great memorandum on government of 1624 constituted the most comprehensive attempt ever made by Olivares to examine, for the benefit of the King, the problems involved in the government of his difficult inheritance. In drafting this memorandum he adopted the traditional approach, which would also be followed in Richelieu's *Testament Politique*, of considering in turn each of the three orders of society. His preoccupations, also, were traditional enough—the wealth of the Church, the power of the grandees, the dangers of popular unrest. His recommendations make it clear that he believed successful government to depend on the careful preservation of a 'balance' within and between these classes. Like Philip II, Philip IV should keep the grandees at arm's length, employing *letrados* in government, and using the rest of the nobility as an additional counterweight. But it was the

[37] B.M. Add. MS. 14,007, f. 45v (27 September 1632).

people—the most dangerous of all the orders of society—who required the closest surveillance. Justice must be firmly but equitably administered; bread must be kept cheap and abundant. 'It is always advisable to pay attention to the voice of the people.'

The history of Philip IV's reign shows that, in the event, Olivares overestimated the danger of aristocratic and popular unrest in Castile, as much as he underestimated the innate resistance of the country to change. He came to power, as others have come to power, determined to make a clean break with the immediate past, and to embark on ambitious schemes, not only for administrative and fiscal reform, but also for a transformation of national attitudes. To achieve the maximum impact, he deliberately dramatized—and was to be accused of exaggerating[38] —the wretched state in which his predecessors had left the country. While this approach may, in some quarters, have raised hopes of a new dawn, it alienated those who had benefited from the careless extravagance of the Lerma régime, and aroused fear and suspicion about his future plans. By investigating the activities and the fortunes of Philip III's ministers, and by cutting down on the previously lavish distribution of grants and favours, he clearly hoped to create a climate of opinion favourable to reform. But he failed to appreciate that his actions might also have the effect of arousing a sympathy for his victims which they had never enjoyed as ministers, and of creating a misguided nostalgia for the golden age of the Duke of Lerma.

Yet on paper his policies looked convincing enough. Although they were scattered through a number of documents drafted in the early 1620s, they amounted, in effect, to a grand design covering, in natural progression, the three most critical areas of concern—the Crown's finances, the condition of Castile, and the constitutional structure and military organization of the Spanish Monarchy. All of these were, indeed, interrelated, as the *arbitristas* of Philip III's reign had repeatedly emphasized. One of them, González de Cellorigo, whose treatise of 1600 on the restoration of Spain was to be found in Olivares's library,[39] described king and kingdom

[38] *Nicandro*, f. 217.

[39] Copy of catalogue of the Conde Duque's library in the Real Academia de la Historia, Madrid, MSS. 41–5.

as *correlativos*, with the well-being of each communicating itself to the other.[40] Where Richelieu was able to think in terms of the abstract notion of the State,[41] Olivares seems to have thought in the more traditional terms of a mystical and indivisible corporate body of king and people, whose mutual interests were described by the Crown in the Castilian Cortes of 1623 as being *correlativos necesarios*.[42]

With an annual expenditure of 8 million ducats, and an annual deficit of 4 million, Olivares saw the restoration of royal solvency as the key to Spain's revival. Over and over again he returned to the need to place the royal finances on a firm foundation. But how was this to be achieved? In the first place, by economy measures—restraint in the distribution of *mercedes*, and reduction in the expenses of the royal household.[43] This was to be accompanied by a radical reform in the management of the royal finances, with the development of a national banking scheme which would end Spanish dependence on the hated foreign bankers.[44] A systematic effort was to be made to redeem the royal debts and recover alienated revenues. Finally, Castile was to be endowed with a new system of taxation, the details of which were succinctly summarized in the memorandum of 1624: new taxes were to be avoided and old ones abolished; and, if they could not be abolished, they should be reduced to a single consolidated tax, of a type which should not—unlike previous taxes—reduce Castile to ruin.[45]

These plans, like most of Olivares's plans, were not original.

[40] *Memorial de la política necesaria y útil restauración a la república de España . . .* (Valladolid, 1600), f. 28v.

[41] Etienne Thuau, *Raison d'Etat et Pensée Politique à l'Epoque de Richelieu* (Paris, 1966), p. 351. See also Dietrich Gerhard's essay on Richelieu in *The Responsibility of Power*, ed. Leonard Krieger and Fritz Stern (New York, 1968), ch. 5.

[42] *Actas de las Cortes de Castilla*, xxxviii, 129.

[43] B.M. Eg. MS. 338, ff. 136–51 (*Resumen que hizo el Rey . . . del estado de su monarquía, 1627*), f. 139v.

[44] For details, see Domínguez Ortiz, *Política y Hacienda*, part 1, c. 2, and Earl J. Hamilton, 'Spanish Banking Schemes before 1700', *The Journal of Political Economy*, lvii (1949), 134–56.

[45] Great Memorandum (1624), f. 206v.

They had been repeatedly discussed by the *arbitristas*, and had been proposed in the Cortes of Castile. But they now obtained the endorsement of royal and ministerial approval. In the Cortes of 1623, Olivares, as *procurador* for Madrid, warmly supported a proposal for the replacement of two of the most obnoxious taxes, the *millones* and the *alcabala*, by a sliding-scale flour tax. Here, at last, was the chance for reform. 'Each of us', he urged his fellow *procuradores*, 'can equal the greatest among the Greeks and Romans, who in war and peace saved and restored their republics.'[46] But the Cortes remained unconvinced. Innumerable difficulties were discovered; and a last despairing attempt in 1631 to abolish the *millones* ended in disaster when Vizcaya revolted against the salt tax which was introduced as its replacement.[47]

It was Olivares's intention that fiscal reform should go hand in hand with vigorous measures to revive the flagging Castilian economy. Greater productivity, an increase in trade, would swell the royal revenues by increasing national wealth. Here again it was the *arbitristas* who inspired his reforms. Indeed, it was one of the ironies of the Olivares régime that a government which so resolutely turned its back on the immediate past should in fact have been so deeply indebted to it. For the age of Olivares had in some respects already begun before Olivares himself came to power. During the last years of Philip III, the pressures for reform had become so strong that the Duke of Lerma had been driven, during his last months in power, to call for a report from the Council of Castile on the country's ills, and to establish a special Junta into which Olivares would breathe new life—the significantly styled *Junta de Reformación.* The Council of Castile's *consulta* of 1 February 1619 was at once a résumé of some of the *arbitristas*'s most cogent recommendations, and a blueprint for Olivares's own programme of reform. Governmental economies; fiscal reform; the encouragement of industry and agriculture; an insistence on the necessity of securing greater financial help from the other kingdoms of the Monarchy—all these measures, which were to be so enthusiastically adopted by Olivares, had already

[46] *Actas de las Cortes*, xxxix, 353–64, for Olivares's speech.

[47] Domínguez Ortiz, *Política y Hacienda*, p. 235.

been put forward as official policy by the councillors of Philip III.[48]

The deep concern of the Council of Castile and the *arbitristas* with the problem of depopulation was reflected in Olivares's own state papers, and in his decision in 1625 to create a special *Junta de Población*—one of the many Juntas he was to establish in an effort to by-pass the cumbersome machinery of the councils, and to introduce new men and new ideas into the upper echelons of government. While this Junta was designed to foster immigration and the colonization of deserted land, its terms of reference included the general encouragement of industry, trade and agriculture.[49] Behind this and other schemes for governmental intervention in the economic life of the peninsula there lay a philosophy of action inspired by an awareness, not only of Castile's innate economic weakness, but also of its backwardness relative to other parts of Europe. Olivares, like his contemporaries elsewhere, was deeply impressed by the economic successes of the Dutch; and it was with the Dutch model in mind that he set out to modernize Castile's economy and its economic attitudes.

The obstacles to change, as Olivares himself was quick to appreciate, were to be found at least as much in mental attitudes as in technical and physical difficulties. These attitudes were epitomized in the Castilian obsession with *limpieza*—purity of blood—and in the general contempt for trade and manual labour. On both these subjects Olivares was outspoken. Commenting on the question of *limpieza* in his memorandum of 1624, he expressed his astonishment and horror that, while God forgave all sins, Castilians should continue to condemn them, even to the seventh generation.[50] A year later he castigated the *limpieza* statutes as 'unjust' and 'wicked', and as 'contrary to divine law, natural law, and the law of nations. . . . In no other country in

[48] González Palencia, *Junta de Reformación*, doc. IV. The *consulta* appears to have been drafted by Diego de Corral, who also served in the Olivares administration (see L. de Corral, *Don Diego de Corral y Arellano, y los Corrales de Valladolid* (Madrid, 1905), p. 40).

[49] J. Carrera Pujal, *Historia de la Economía Española* (Barcelona, 1943), i, 522–6.

[50] f. 195v.

the world do such statutes exist.'[51] No doubt his attitude was influenced by his concern for what he called, in his memorandum of 1624, 'the public good and the whole matter of state'. He and his Jesuit adviser on economic affairs, Hernando de Salazar, were anxious to ensure that the irrelevant question of ancestry should not interfere with business activity in Castile; and from 1627, when they succeeded in associating with the royal finances a consortium of Portuguese business-men,[52] they won their point, although at the cost of a mounting campaign of vituperation against Olivares for his alleged pro-Jewish tendencies.[53] But, over and above any question of economic advantage, Olivares seems to have been moved in the *limpieza* question by genuine compassion—perhaps because he spoke not only *for* the unclean, but *with* them. Jewish blood ran in his veins, too, for his grandmother was the daughter of Lope Conchillos, secretary to Ferdinand the Catholic and Charles V, and an Aragonese *converso*.[54]

If Castilians were to forget their terrible and economically damaging obsession with purity of blood, it was no less important that they should change their disparaging views about the status of trade. The memorandum of 1624 made much of the importance of seafaring experience and mercantile activities. A supreme effort must be made to 'turn Spaniards into merchants'.[55] This was to be achieved by the creation of companies and consulates, on the model of the Dutch. The first of these, the *Almirantazgo de los Países Septentrionales*, for trade with northern Europe, was founded at Seville in October 1624.[56] Like Richelieu, whose attempts to

[51] A(rchivo) G(eneral de) S(imancas) Estado, Inglaterra, legajo 2849 (Consejo de Estado, 1 November 1625).

[52] For these Portuguese bankers (some of whom were of Jewish origin) see Domínguez Ortiz, *Política y Hacienda*, part 2, c. 3.

[53] J. Caro Baroja, *La Sociedad Criptojudía en la Corte de Felipe IV* (Madrid, 1963), p. 53.

[54] For the origins of Lope Conchillos, see J. Caro Baroja, *Los Judíos en la España Moderna y Contemporanea* (Madrid, 1962), iv, 16. Marañón, who traced a 'bureaucratic' strain in Olivares from his descent from Lope Conchillos (*Olivares*, pp. 10–12), was apparently unaware of the Jewish strain.

[55] ff. 207 and 217.

[56] A. Domínguez Ortiz, 'El Almirantazgo de los Países Septentrionales y la política económica de Felipe IV', *Hispania*, vii (1947), 272–90.

organize trading companies began in the following year,[57] he saw the trading company as the ideal agency for promoting trade and naval power. But his companies, like Richelieu's, ran into trouble from the start for they were hampered by lack of capital and lack of genuine interest, as also by the common prejudice directed against trade.[58] Neither royal decree nor royal example could change habits overnight.

The explicit challenge to established patterns of behaviour, inherent in Olivares's schemes for the economic restoration of Castile, was repeated in the most ambitious of all his plans—his grand design of 1624 for the constitutional reorganization of the Spanish Monarchy.[59] If Philip IV could succeed in bringing his various kingdoms and territories together into a single constitutional unit, he would be master of 'the greatest united empire the world has ever seen'.[60] Olivares's suggested methods for the imposition of unity and uniformity—intermarriage, a more equitable distribution of offices, and the 'Castilianization' of law—suggest here, as elsewhere in his writings, the inspiration of Alamos de Barrientos, whose *Arte de Gobernar* of 1598 made comparable proposals.[61]

While the economic weakness of Castile and the demands of imperial defence made closer co-operation between the various kingdoms a matter of urgency, Olivares was prepared to accept that real unity could not be achieved in a day. 'The force of custom [*la fuerza de la costumbre*] is so great in matters of government', he wrote, 'as often to impede and impair the best and most appropriate measures.'[62] Union was inevitably a long-term project; and, as such, Olivares consistently returned to it throughout his political career. There was, he was still insisting in 1640, no 'rule of state' so necessary or so useful as that which advocated the 'mixing' of subjects by means of marriages and by appointments

[57] A. D. Lublinskaya, *French Absolutism: the Crucial Phase* (Cambridge, 1968), p. 283.

[58] B.M. Eg. MS. 339, f. 426, *Consulta*, 1 June 1630.

[59] For the details and origins of this design, see Elliott, *The Revolt*, ch. vii.

[60] Great Memorandum (1624), f. 213.

[61] Ed. J. M. Guardia, *L'Art de Gouverner* (Paris, 1867).

[62] Great Memorandum (1624), f. 213v.

to posts in the government and in the royal household.[63] But 'rules of state' counted for little against the intransigence of Castilians who clung to their monopoly of office, just as they counted for little against the intransigence of Aragonese or Catalans who feared for the loss of their privileges. Olivares's project for military co-operation among the provinces, the Union of Arms[64]—another product of those intellectually fertile years, the early 1620s—would also founder, like his proposals for constitutional union, on the rock which has wrecked so many reforms, *la fuerza de la costumbre.*

The disasters which would overtake Olivares's programme for reform still seemed far away, however, when he presented the King, in July 1625, with a list of his achievements, together with a formal request for permission to retire.[65] Such requests to be released from the cares of office punctuated Olivares's career, only to draw forth fulsome expressions of royal appreciation for his services and an insistent demand that he should remain at his post. On this occasion, the balance-sheet presented by the Count Duke looked sufficiently impressive to justify an expression of the highest royal confidence in the minister. Since 1621, Olivares claimed, Spain's naval and military strength had been notably increased; and this had been managed, in spite of the King's unhappy financial inheritance, without resort to new taxes. The Monarchy had won great victories against its enemies; internal reforms—the founding of trading companies, inland navigation, and repopulation schemes—were being actively promoted by specially created Juntas; and the King himself, at the age of twenty, was personally handling forty-four out of every fifty *consultas.*

All this was encouraging, but Olivares admitted that there remained one great danger: the disorder of the *vellón* currency, which he feared would be 'the absolute ruin of these kingdoms'. Already in his memorandum of 1624 he had expressed his concern about *vellón*,[66] and the great Castilian monetary crisis of

[63] A.G.S. Estado, Nápoles, legajo 3263, f. 100 (*Consulta*, 30 August 1640).

[64] Elliott, *The Revolt*, pp. 204ff.

[65] B.M. Eg. MS. 2053, ff. 239–49v.

[66] f. 207.

1626–8 seemed to justify these fears. It is not, in fact, clear how far the inflation of these years is to be ascribed to chaotic monetary conditions, and how far to harvest failure and dearth.[67] Olivares himself attributed the high prices to 'the abundance of money'[68] and urged, as against the Council of Castile,[69] that stabilization of the coinage must precede any attempt to fix prices. But he was to be disappointed in his hopes of saving the situation 'without taking the knife in the hand'. Attempts to fix prices and wages by decree, and to 'consume' the *vellón* coinage by means of a specially created new banking company, both proved abortive, and on 7 August 1628 the tale of *vellón* was reduced by 50 per cent, without compensation for the holders.[70]

The financial measures adopted by the Crown in 1627 and 1628 mark an important turning-point in Olivares's political career. In January 1627 the Crown, faced with increasingly high rates of interest on its loans, had adopted drastic measures against its bankers by suspending its payments to them and by introducing as potential rivals a Portuguese consortium. In August 1628 its drastic deflationary decree had brought further relief to the Crown's finances by sharply reducing the premium on silver in terms of *vellón*. Between them, these two measures, however harsh in their consequences for private individuals, brought a substantial alleviation of the crippling fiscal burden inherited from the reign of Philip III. At this moment, for perhaps the first and only time in his career, Olivares, as a reforming minister, was presented with a real opportunity to make a new start.[71] The plans for reform were all prepared—financial reform, modernization of the Castilian economy, and structural reorganization of

[67] See F. Ugorri Casado, 'Ideas Sobre el Gobierno Económico de España en el Siglo XVII', *Revista de la Biblioteca, Archivo y Museo* (Ayuntamiento de Madrid), xix (1950), 123–230.

[68] B.M. Eg. MS. 2053, ff. 254–6v. (*Papel del Conde Duque sobre el medio de remediar los daños presentes sin llegar a tomar el cuchillo en la mano*).

[69] Domínguez Ortiz, *Política y Hacienda*, p. 38.

[70] Earl J. Hamilton, *American Treasure and the Price Revolution in Spain* (Cambridge, Mass., 1934), p. 83.

[71] Domínguez Ortiz, *Política y Hacienda*, pp. 38–9, also sees this as the critical point in Philip IV's reign.

the Monarchy. In retrospect, everything would seem to indicate that this was the moment for a decisive change of course.

It is, however, open to doubt whether Olivares himself either saw, or could be expected to see, that this was an unusually favourable conjuncture for launching out on his programme of reform. Here, as so often, domestic considerations were blurred by the claims of foreign policy. For a minister who was heir not only to the reforming traditions of the *arbitristas*, but also to the imperial traditions of Castile, opportunity beckoned at this moment more in Italy than Spain. The death of the Duke of Mantua, without succession, on 26 December 1627, seemed to offer the Spaniards a unique chance to consolidate their hold over northern Italy.[72] The Duke himself chose to leave his possessions to the French Duke of Nevers. But Gonzalo Fernández de Córdoba, the Governor of Milan, had already moved on his own initiative to partition Montferrat between Spain and Savoy.

At the beginning of 1628, therefore, Olivares was faced with the question of whether he was to accept a French succession in Mantua, with all the political and strategic implications which might ensue from this, or endorse the Governor's action and provide him with sufficient reinforcements to make sure of the fortress of Casale. His resolution of the problem, as argued in a paper of 12 January 1628, offers an extraordinary insight into his handling of one of the most critical issues which faced him in his whole ministerial career.[73] He accepted that the Duke of Nevers was the legal successor to the deceased Duke, and therefore enjoyed the strongest claim. On the other hand, the King of Spain had been publicly affronted and humiliated by Nevers's action in marrying his son to the late Duke's niece without first seeking the approval of Philip IV. It was also an undoubted fact that the peace of Italy could best be preserved if Spain enjoyed possession of Montferrat. Did Spain, then, have a case for resorting to arms?

There were, he argued, four considerations which should

[72] Fernández Alvarez, *Don Gonzalo Fernández de Córdoba*, p. 24.

[73] B.M. Eg. MS. 2053, ff. 232–8v. (*Copia del voto del Conde Duque sobre el casamiento del de Retel . . .*). This paper was apparently unknown to Fernández Alvarez.

govern the actions of princes in their mutual relations—a just cause; a just occasion; clear advantage; and adequate resources to fulfil their designs (the last two being insufficient to justify recourse to war). If these general considerations were applied to the Italian situation, it was clear that the King did not possess sufficient justice on his side to allow a formal break with Nevers; nor did he possess the means to fight a war in Italy which might last for two years. There was, on the other hand, an obvious *advantage* to be gained from adding Montferrat to Milan, and there certainly existed a *just occasion* to 'mortify' Nevers, so that he should learn to 'respect, esteem and venerate the royal dignity of Your Majesty'. It also had to be borne in mind that the Governor of Milan had already committed himself, although without instructions to do so, and that this made it less difficult to break off relations than it would otherwise have been. But the King simply did not have the resources for a long Italian war, and the Count Duke therefore proposed (as on so many occasions) what he called a 'middle way', which would at once maintain Spain's reputation, open the door to a settlement, and 'not close it to any advantages which might accrue'.

It was only to be expected that Olivares, having used the traditional scholastic arguments in examining the case for war, should have recommended that the whole issue be brought before a special Junta of theologians and jurists. He also recommended general approval for the Governor's action, coupled with a mild rebuke for his precipitation. The King, he should be told, was anxious only for a general agreement which satisfied all parties; but in the meantime he should on no account abandon any territory he had captured. 'In conclusion, I should say that nothing is more important to Your Majesty than Montferrat, except acting with justification; that to mortify the Duke of Nevers is extremely justified; and that if, as a result of this mortification, Nevers should wish to reach a settlement, with some exchange of territory, it would be both just and saintly to agree.'

It was in this way that Olivares walked sideways into war in Italy—a war which lasted for three years, and which made such demands on Spanish resources as to preclude radical reform at home. Looking back on the Mantuan War towards the end of his career, Olivares attempted to disclaim responsibility,[74] but the deviousness of his methods cannot conceal his complicity in a military action from which he anticipated great rewards. His technique was one which became second nature to him: to adopt an ostensibly middle course of action, which might, with a little luck, yield all the advantages to be expected of decisive action, while leaving him with a variety of escape-routes which would not have remained open if he had pushed the matter to extremes. On this occasion, he clearly hoped and expected that the Governor of Milan would carry off a brilliant *coup* by occupying Montferrat while policy discussions were still continuing in Madrid. Admittedly, there was a risk, but it must have seemed in January 1628 that the risk was well worth running. Spanish arms had achieved some remarkable successes in the preceding years; Richelieu's energies were absorbed in the struggle with La Rochelle; and a unique occasion had presented itself to win for Spain an impregnable position in northern Italy. To accept humiliation at the hands of Nevers, and let slip the opportunity created by Córdoba's secret agreement with Savoy, would have been a source of lasting reproach to himself and the Spanish Crown. Considerations of prestige, and the calculation of probable advantage, urged him to embark on a gamble which stood a very reasonable chance of success.

As with so many of Olivares's gambles, however, nothing worked out quite as he had planned it. He had banked on a rapid campaign by Córdoba, culminating in the triumphant capture of Casale. But he had underestimated Córdoba's difficulties, and overestimated his powers of decision and command. As a result, Spain found itself engaged in that prolonged Italian war for which Olivares had always said that it lacked the resources. It was this prolongation of the war, rather than the actual course of the military operations, which proved to be the real misfortune of the Mantuan enterprise. Richelieu was given the time both to deal with La Rochelle and to intervene in Italy. French intervention inevitably imposed new financial and military demands on Castile, and forced the further postponement of domestic reforms. Moreover, the deterioration in the Emperor's position in Germany

[74] See Elliott, *The Revolt*, p. 518.

during the intervening period meant that the peace settlement of 1631 was considerably more unfavourable to Spain than was warranted by the balance of military power in Italy itself.

By 1631, therefore, some of the possibilities which had offered themselves in 1627 had irrevocably vanished. During these years Olivares had watched with growing anguish the terrible succession of events as they seemed one after another to be slipping from his control. The economic and financial situation in Castile was deteriorating sharply in the late 1620s, and he considered for a moment the possibility of relieving the strain by making peace with the Dutch.[75] But there was no easy way of escape from the war with the Dutch, just as there was to be no easy way of escape from open war with France, once the two Monarchies had come into conflict over the affair of the Mantuan Succession. From the early 1630s, Olivares, like Richelieu, reluctantly recognized that war between France and Spain was only a matter of time. When it came in 1635, the great reform programme was no further advanced than it had been ten years earlier, and Castile had been given no respite or relief.

'The essence of war', wrote Olivares in a paper for the King which appears to date from 1637, 'can be reduced to four points—men, money, order and obedience. The cause of war is the sin of all of us; and the most natural and harmful consequence of war is confusion, disorder, and diversity of opinion.'[76] He was to spend his remaining years in office labouring to find the men and money with which to support Spain's allies, defend her territory, and launch new campaigns against the enemy. It had become an annual practice with him to draft a memorandum for the King on the military dispositions for the coming year—the number of troops likely to be available for the various theatres of war, the revenues that were to be expected, the orders that must be given.[77]

[75] Ródenas Vilar, *La Política Europea*, p. 181.

[76] B.M. Add. MS. 25,689, ff. 210–41 (*Consulta del Conde Duque a SM, 1632 poco más o menos*—but internal evidence suggests 1637). Another copy of this document, hitherto apparently unknown, is to be found in Madrid in the Real Academia de la Historia, MS. 11–219, ff. 54–76.

[77] E.g. A.G.S. Estado, legajo 2658 (13 January 1636) and legajo 2661 (1639).

Before everything else he was now a minister for war and commander-in-chief, whose every action was directed to the supreme military effort that was needed to bring victory and peace.

In times of war different methods were required of a minister from those he would use in peacetime: 'anyone who attempts to navigate in a storm as he navigates in good weather will soon lose his ship'.[78] Olivares, however, was reluctant to accept the inevitable implication of his own argument: that cherished and long-delayed projects of reform must yield precedence to fiscal and military demands. Faced, like Richelieu, with the apparent incompatibility of war and reform, he refused to believe that they could not be successfully combined. 'The principal source of our troubles', he advised the King, 'lies in people saying: "This is not the moment; wait for peace to come." '[79] So far, he argued, from war ruling out all question of reform, it made it all the more essential. Success in war was dependent on reform at home, and the fact that reforms were actually being attempted would help to maintain morale in the difficult days ahead.

What, then, could and must be done? For a moment, as he outlined yet again his great schemes for reformation, it seemed as if he had temporarily reverted to the hopeful dawn of the early 1620s. Public sins must be castigated and the educational system overhauled. But a note of bitterness had now crept into the long list of proposed measures for reform. There were too many abuses in Castile, all crying out for remedy. Too many convents attracted too many inmates with no true vocation. Too many vagabonds roamed the country—they should be set to work in the manufacturing industries, as they were in Holland. There were too many ruined gentry, and too few men of experience left, with qualities of leadership.

The liturgy of woes was made all the more poignant by Olivare's frequent comparisons between Spanish and foreign conditions. The survival of internal customs barriers in Spain was intolerable. If trade were only 'managed as it ought to be, we should see in the midst of our misfortunes as much felicity as we

[78] B.M. Add. MS. 25,689, ff. 210v–11.

[79] f. 216v.

see now in Holland, or as was once to be seen in Venice'. Why had nothing been done about the repopulation of Castile, in spite of the recommendations of the Junta? If 200 immigrant families had been settled each year since the time of its report, the problem might almost have been solved. Why, too, had nothing been done to improve internal navigation, when this had been pronounced feasible by Flemish engineers who had examined the question at the beginning of the reign? 'I am certain that no foreign visitor to Spain can fail to blame us roundly for our barbarism, when he sees us having to supply all the cities of Castile by pack-animal—and rightly so, when all Europe is most profitably experimenting with inland navigation.' Why, too, had nothing been done to liquidate the Crown's debts, or to reform the system of tax-collection, which was more fraudulent in Castile than anywhere else in Europe? 'It is possible, Sir, that seven millions in every ten are being pocketed, and the poor are paying for everything, while the rest pay nothing. . . .'

This paper of 1637—wide-ranging, ill-organized, suffused with urgency and despair—is effectively the last great testament of Olivares as a reforming minister. Henceforth he was engulfed beneath the day-to-day problems of war and finance. But periodically he emerged to produce general reports on the state of the war and the lengthening list of reverses, while all the time he poured out his hopes and fears in a stream of letters to his friends, his generals, and the Cardinal Infante. He wanted to know everything, do everything, take command of everything. He would closely follow the plans of campaign from his study, poring over the maps with which he had surrounded himself, and drawing liberally on the large store of geographical information which he had assiduously accumulated over the course of the years.[80] The war had come to dominate his life. But once the first hopes of quick victory had been shattered, he fought his war with few illusions. 'Our position is very low,' he wrote to the Cardinal Infante on 28 October 1637, 'and it is very necessary to do something by way of retaliation. The really essential thing is to achieve

[80] Juan Antonio de Vera y Figueroa, Conde de La Roca, *Fragmentos Históricos de la Vida de D. Gaspar de Guzmán* (Valladares, *Semanario Erudito*, ii, Madrid, 1787), 266–7.

a success against the Dutch. As far as we and the French are concerned, it is unlikely that either of us will be left with any of the other's territory. This at least is the general rule, though things might turn out differently.'[81]

For all the protracted point, counterpoint of negotiations with Richelieu,[82] peace, like reform, continued to elude him. In the circumstances there was no choice but to pursue the quest for men and money with all the formidable energy which remained at his command. In so far as this meant a further exploitation of the shrinking resources of Castile, it was bound to involve the further postponement of plans for reform. Paradoxically, however, the very necessities which compelled Olivares to abandon his plans for the reordering of Castile simultaneously compelled him to press ahead with his plans for the reordering of the Spanish Monarchy. The creation of a unified Monarchy, each part of which bore its fair share of the burden of defence, acquired supreme priority as the sole means of alleviating the miseries of Castile. At this critical moment, help from Catalonia and Portugal became an indispensable necessity. In 1640, by choosing to revolt rather than concur in Olivares's grand design, the Catalans and the Portuguese proved the accuracy of his diagnosis that the fundamental weakness of the Monarchy lay in lack of unity. The Monarchy's constitutional structure had proved too fragile to withstand the pressures of war once Castile was no longer in a position to bear its burdens single-handed.

The disasters of 1640, and the subsequent collapse of Spanish power in Europe, helped to confirm the verdict already being formulated by contemporaries on the statecraft of Olivares. They thought they detected in him a fatal obstinacy—a stubborn adherence to general principles which bore little relation to practical possibilities. 'In matters of state,' wrote Sir Arthur Hopton from Madrid in 1638, 'he tieth himself so obstinately to certain grounds he hath laid as he will hazard all rather than leave them.'[83] For Melo, Olivares's besetting weakness was essentially the same—instead of being pragmatic, he preferred to follow

[81] B.M. Add. MS. 14,007, f. 87.

[82] See A. Leman, *Richelieu et Olivarès*.

[83] Quoted Elliott, *The Revolt*, p. 197.

Tacitus.[84] It was easy to overlook the inconvenient fact that he was not alone in this. 'Le cardinal de Richelieu lisait et pratiquait fort Tacite', wrote Guy Patin.[85] Tacitus, after all, had his uses for the seventeenth-century statesman walking the narrow line that divided religion from expediency.

If the Count Duke did indeed tie himself 'obstinately to certain grounds he hath laid', this may well have been less because of an obsession with maxims of state than because of practical necessity. The determination to reform the life of Castile and reorganize the structure of the Monarchy remained central to his purpose; and both of these policies were dictated by the financial and military necessities of the 1620s and 1630s. No doubt he attempted too much. War and reform did indeed prove to be incompatible, as Richelieu also found. He lacked, too, the administrative machinery to implement his plans. The new Juntas proved to be the old councils, writ small; and the men appointed to them lacked the stature to perform the heroic tasks with which they were entrusted. Perhaps Olivares expected too much. Perhaps Spain really did lack 'leaders', as he had persistently complained. Or perhaps there was room for only one 'leader' in the Spain of Olivares.

Were there, then, flaws in the man which played their part in determining the unhappy outcome of events? It is possible that he was not adequately served because he did not know how to be adequately served. It is possible, too, that he lacked the capacity to transform his theoretical conceptions into tactical approaches. On three of the major issues of his political career—Mantua, Catalonia and Portugal—he displayed a tendency to bridge the gap between an idea and its execution by an act of faith. On each occasion, with just a touch of good fortune, success lay within his grasp. But on each occasion Fortune failed him, and he had nothing in reserve. Gonzalo de Córdoba waited too long before starting on campaign; the Castilian soldiers who were billeted in Catalonia over-reacted; the Portuguese nobility, for the first time in memory, failed to prove compliant. Time and again the glit-

[84] Above, note 19.

[85] Quoted Thuau, *Raison d'Etat*, p. 44.

tering prize somehow slipped from his grasp, and the diamonds of success were turned into the ashes of disaster.

Yet it is likely enough that no one else could have done any better, though it is questionable whether anyone else would have failed quite so spectacularly. There were moments in his career when the Count Duke could reasonably have complained that the stars in their courses were against him—although this itself he would have ascribed to his own sins and to those of his countrymen. Misfortunes were sent by God both to punish sin and try the faith of men, as Olivares observed when the silver fleet was reported lost in 1632. Nothing, he told the Council of State, appeared to turn out well. This persuaded him that God might want us to place more trust in His providence and omnipotence than in human ways and means. He therefore feared for the good success of any measures which might be proposed.[86] In the long run, no device, however ingenious, no maxim of state, however well-founded, could hope to prevail against the will of God. But the ways of God were inscrutable, and the prime concern of the statesman, as of every man, lay with the state of his soul. For ultimately 'solo salvarse importa'[87]—salvation is all that counts.

[86] A.G.S. Estado, legajo 2651. *Consulta*, 19 March 1632.

[87] B.M. Eg. MS. 2053, f. 34v. Letter to the Prince of Carpiñano, 20 October 1628.

Six

Time, History and Eschatology in the Thought of Thomas Hobbes

by

J. G. A. Pocock

The change from the medieval interpretative gloss *on* a passage of Scripture to the new grammatical analysis *of* the passage brought forth an entirely new question in theology. The rhetorical commentaries of the earlier period, generally concerned with delineating the intention of a phrase and never questioning any matter of textual integrity, gave way to the *disquisitiones philologicae* in which all instances of textual corruption were investigated, and the whole emphasis placed upon exact rendition. The older query, so to speak, of 'What does God mean here?' became the far more arresting question, 'What has God said here?' Allegory, mystic paraphrase, tropology and the whole formal literature of interpretation were uncompromisingly attacked as doctrinal irrelevancies by syntax and lexicography. Grammar, not speculation, became the greatest heresy of the Christian world, and unhappily no fires could be kindled to consume the *rudimenta linguae* of Hebrew and Greek.

George Newton Conklin, *Biblical Criticism and Heresy in Milton* (New York: King's Crown Press, Columbia University, 1949), pp. 1–2

The assertion that Hobbes's political philosophy is 'unhistorical', though often made and in some senses correct, is neither economical nor elegant. There are simply too many ways in which a man's thought can be said to be 'historical', and too many ways of negating each one of these statements, for the epithet alone to have any very obvious meaning. Hobbes, as is generally known, declared that you could not ground a philosophy of politics on the study of human experience as recorded in history because, as he put it, 'experience concludeth nothing universally'.[1] But this did not prevent his being interested in history; the thought even of his later years can be observed keeping pace with some of the sharpest and most advanced historical perception of his time.[2] On matters of English tenurial and Parliamentary history, he profited by his friendship with Selden[3] and went beyond that great but elusive scholar in some respects. Again, his famous characterization of the papacy as 'the ghost of the deceased Roman Empire, sitting crowned upon the grave thereof',[4] like his interpretation of the Cluniac campaign for clerical celibacy,[5] could

[1] Hobbes, *Elements of Law*, I, iv, 10 (ed. Tonnies, London, 1969, p. 16).

[2] Pocock, *The Ancient Constitution and the Feudal Law* (Cambridge University Press, 1957, and New York: W. W. Norton, 1967), ch. vii.

[3] Selden's *Titles of Honour* (1614 and 1631) is almost the only contemporary work mentioned with respect in *Leviathan* (i, 10; Oakeshott edition, Oxford: Basil Blackwell, p. 62).

[4] *Leviathan*, iv, 47 (Oakeshott, p. 457).

[5] In *Behemoth*; Hobbes argues that this was designed to separate the kingly

only have come from a vivid and freely ranging historical imagination. The epithet 'unhistorical', then, is not immediately justified and needs clarification; and this has been sensibly and acceptably provided by, for instance, M. M. Goldsmith.[6] But it should be observed that what has happened illustrates the lack of economy arising from historians' use of the rhetoric of common speech. An appropriate-seeming term occurs to someone and is used; it wins enough acceptance to become part of the conventional wisdom. But in conventional use it is discovered to bear too many possible meanings to be uniformly applicable to the evidence, and the community of historians is saddled with the necessity of discovering the sense or senses in which it can be used so as to mean something.[7] Professor Goldsmith has shown that there are indeed ways in which Hobbes's thinking may accurately be termed 'unhistorical', but the very success with which he does so inevitably if unintentionally carries the implication that he has vindicated the original adoption of the term and its use by his predecessors; and the way in which it has come into use remains uneconomical and has involved an excessive deployment of what Hobbes himself memorably termed 'insignificant speech'.[8]

Historians are condemned to this sort of thing, and it is not intended to suggest that they have any alternative to using common speech first and refining it afterwards.[9] But specialized techniques may be developed as means of cutting corners in this process and rendering it more economical, and it is part of the

[6] M. M. Goldsmith, *Hobbes's Science of Politics* (New York: Columbia University Press, 1966), pp. 232–42, 251–2.

[7] The language used here is intended to give some indication of my debt to Thomas S. Kuhn's *The Structure of Scientific Revolutions*.

[8] 'I say not this as disproving the use of universities; but because I am to speak hereafter of their office in a commonwealth, I must let you see, on all occasions by the way, what things would be amended in them; amongst which the frequency of insignificant speech is one.' *Leviathan*, i, 1 (Oakeshott, p. 8). See also i, 8 (Oakeshott, pp. 51–2).

[9] On this see J. H. Hexter, *Reappraisals in History* (London, 1961), and my review article in *History and Theory*, iii, 1 (1963).

office from the priesthood (*English Works*, vi, pp. 180–1). The interpretation may not be correct; what matters is the quality of the thought that produced it.

intention of this essay[10] to assert that one technique exists which may be applied to the question whether or not a man's thought is 'historical'. Instead of applying an epithet and then debating its use until some precise meaning for it is discovered, it should be possible to institute a critical enquiry aimed at discovering what, if any, elements that may be termed 'historical' a man's thought contained. There is, of course, one obvious difficulty in the way of such a proceeding. It may seem necessary to establish in advance canons of what constitutes 'historical' thinking, and this can all too easily lead to the sort of academic high-jump contest beloved of Hegelian and Crocean scholars, in which the bar of true historicity is raised again and again until only the fortunate candidate succeeds in leaping it. But we are not obliged to engage in such sterile olympiads. It can be shown that the language even of prehistoricist social and political thinkers carries a constant tissue of statements, explicit and implicit, about the time-structures in which society and the political order were thought of as existing, and that these consisted mainly of statements about the occurrence, recurrence and continuity of the modes of human action and cognition held to constitute social and political behaviour, as well as the divine actions and utterances which in monotheist contexts were indispensable to its understanding. Time so conceived differed from the time of the physicist or the metaphysician in being filled with—indeed, composed of—a rich texture of the acts, words and thoughts of personal and social beings; and in stating the continuities, recurrences and occurrences of which it consisted theorists frequently encountered problems which compelled them to recast their thoughts in terms of process, change and discontinuity.[11]

10 An earlier version was read to the Midwest Conference on British Studies at the University of Kansas on 26 October 1968, and at a University of Wales colloquium at Gregynog Hall on 14 March 1969. M. M. Goldsmith, Steven Schwarzschild, Quentin Skinner and William M. Lamont have helped me by criticism at various stages in its preparation; and I owe a special debt to discussion and correspondence with Patricia Springborg during the preparation of her unpublished master's thesis (Patricia M. McIntyre, 'Authority, Ecclesiastical and Civil, in Hobbes's *Leviathan*', University of Canterbury Library).

11 For two attempts to state the theory of this kind of time-awareness, see 'The

At this stage in the analysis, it becomes in principle possible to show how specific thinkers and traditions of thought have encountered problems of this kind, how they have dealt with them and what further problems have arisen in consequence of their responses; and in doing so, modes of thought may be met with which approximate to what we mean when we use such terms as 'historical'. At the cost of some looseness, we may employ such terms in exploring these intellectual developments, and to do so has the great advantage of being positive instead of evaluatory. Instead of trying to determine whether a man's thought was or was not 'historical' according to some preconceived criterion, we can trace the ways in which—rather than the extent to which—his thought had become involved in questions and answers of the kind to which such a term may possibly be illuminatingly applied; and we can concern ourselves with the substance rather than the epithet, with what his thought was rather than with what it may not have been.

The problem, then, becomes that of discerning the languages, explicit or implicit, concerning time of which Hobbes made use, what he did with them and in what ways he turned them to his characteristic purposes. There were a number of modes in which it was possible for men of his day to conceptualize society's existence in time and time itself as the dimension of social existence,[12] and of two of these at least Hobbes made significant use. It must be remembered, not only that these modes of conceptualization seem remote and primitive to minds of the twentieth century, but that they imposed cramping limitations against which minds of the seventeenth can be seen struggling, often in vain. It was, that is to say, difficult for the contemporary intellect to conceive of the sequence of events and problems in time except in

[12] I have tried to particularize them more fully in 'The Onely Politician: Machiavelli, Harrington and Felix Raab', *Historical Studies: Australia and New Zealand*, xii 46, (1966).

Origins of Study of the Past: a Comparative Approach', *Comparative Studies in Society and History*, iv, 2 (1962), and 'Time, Institutions and Action; an essay on traditions and their understanding', in Preston King and B. C. Parekh (eds.), *Politics and Experience: Essays Presented to Michael Oakeshott* (Cambridge University Press, 1968).

terms which suggested that these were accidental and irrational, that few and limited means existed whereby the human mind could understand and control them and that the means of maintaining a political system as a structure of intelligent behaviour existing in time, foreseeing its emergencies and maintaining its own stability, were correspondingly limited and the prospects of success small. One entire rhetoric, of Greco-Roman and Florentine origin—that of fortune and innovation, cycle and equilibrium—was available for the dual purpose of stressing the instability of politics in time and suggesting means by which recurrent disorder might after all be controlled; but Hobbes made little or no use of it. Instead, his thought stresses in the first place—in order to reject or minimize later—that very ancient doctrine of man's ability to understand and control the accidents of time, which was based on the concept of experience. The human mind, it was held, dealt with secular happenings by recollecting one's previous encounters, and those of other men, with phenomena resembling them and by trading on the assumption that likes recurred in like circumstances, so that responses appropriate on former occasions would prove appropriate on what appeared to be occasions of recurrence. Only further experience could test this presumption, and of that experience, even if the test were passed, only the memory would remain, so that the whole procedure would have to be gone through again on the next encounter with a similar phenomenon;[13] but a sufficiently lengthy accumulation of similar experiences would equip us with a tradition of usage looking back to its own antiquity—the doctrine of custom evolved by English common lawyers is the classic instance of this—while the individual, operating on his own experience and that which he shared with other men, might at least develop in the present the quality called 'prudence', which was in the individual and his moment what custom was in institutionalized antiquity.

[13] A classical statement of this position was coined in reply to Hobbes's *Dialogue of the Common Laws*, by Sir Matthew Hale. See Holdsworth, *History of English Law*, vol. V (London and Boston, 1924), pp. 499–513; and Pocock, *The Ancient Constitution and the Feudal Law*, *loc. cit.*, and 'Burke and the Ancient Constitution: a problem in the history of ideas', *The Historical Journal*, iii (1960).

It was of this Hobbes declared 'experience concludeth nothing universally'. He was not being particularly striking or original when he used those words; his philosophical radicalism lay in his ideas about how memory did operate to point to universal conclusions. It was a commonplace that since experience and use were based on nothing but presumption, they could never provide rational demonstration that the consequences they predicted would follow, or explanation of why they did so; and to all but the most drastic innovators, the demonstrable and the universal were interchangeable terms. But it is worth studying attentively the language in which Hobbes points out the limitations of experience and prudence, both because it indicates clearly how far secular political understanding was seen as the understanding of events in time and because it demonstrates how closely Hobbes's own views on this matter were still tied to the medieval trinity of reason, experience and faith:

> But this is certain: by how much one man has more experience of things past than another, by so much also he is more prudent and his expectations the seldomer fail him. The present only has a being in nature; things past have a being in the memory only; but things to come have no being at all, the future being but a fiction of the mind, applying the sequels of actions past to the actions that are present, which with most certainty is done by him that has most experience, but not with certainty enough. And though it be called prudence when the event answereth our expectation, yet in its own nature it is but presumption. For the foresight of things to come, which is called providence, belongs only to him by whose will they are to come. From him only, and supernaturally, proceeds prophecy. The best prophet naturally is the best guesser, and the best guesser he that is most versed and studied in the matters he guesses at, for he hath most signs to guess by. . . .
>
> As prudence is a presumption of the future, contracted from the experience of time past, so there is a presumption of things past, taken from other things, not future but past also. For he that hath seen by what courses and degrees a

> flourishing state hath first come into civil war and then to ruin, upon the sight of the ruins of any other state will guess the like war and the like courses have been there also. But this conjecture hath the same uncertainty almost with the conjecture of the future, both being grounded only upon experience.[14]

Particular events, Hobbes is saying, take place in time and we have only sense and memory to tell us of their occurrence. If we attempt to think diachronically, to reason from occurrence at one point in time to occurrence at another, we shall be compelled to rely on the presumption that one event will be attended with circumstances like those attending another which resembles it. This presumption can only be tested by experience, and we can draw no general conclusions from it. Therefore the most we can do, so long as we continue to think in this manner, is to accumulate more remembered data and more cases in which the event has confirmed the presumption. In this way the individual acquires prudence and—Hobbes could have added—society builds up traditions and customs; but the process is a quantitative and actuarial one, in which the probabilities of successful prediction grow ever greater while never attaining certainty. Certainty of prediction, or prophecy, or providence—the terms are used interchangeably—belongs only to God, because he is not an observer of events, but the author of them.

It is the time-bound nature of human intelligence which renders it incapable of predicting occurrences and events with any certainty. 'Signs of prudence are all uncertain, because to observe by experience, and remember all circumstances that may alter the success, is impossible.'[15] We inhabit a flux in which there is more going on than can be observed at one moment, and too much change to permit of our recollections remaining valid for long; it is an indication that Hobbes took a relatively stable, customary society for granted that he dealt with this problem in terms of the limitations of experience, where Machiavelli had seen it in terms

[14] *Leviathan*, i, 3 (Oakeshott, p. 16). In extended quotations, I have sometimes modified Hobbes's punctuation in ways that seem to me to make the sequence of ideas plainer to a modern eye.

[15] *Ibid.*, i, 5 (Oakeshott, p. 30).

of the difficulty of innovation in a world controlled by chance.[16] But we can escape from the flux, and enter a world of scientific certainties, if we abandon our insistence on thinking diachronically and, instead of seeking to argue from moment to moment, occurrence to recurrence, reason from premise to consequence. This will liberate us from Plato's cave, from the world of phenomenal time:

> No discourse whatsoever can end in absolute knowledge of fact, past or to come. For as for the knowledge of fact, it is originally sense and ever after memory. And for the knowledge of consequence, which I have said before is called science,[17] it is not absolute but conditional. No man can know by discourse that this or that is, has been or will be, which is to know absolutely; but only that if this be, that is; if this has been, that has been; if this shall be, that shall be; which is to know conditionally, and that not the consequence of one thing to another, but of one name of a thing to another name of the same thing.[18]

Hobbes does not even mention the possibility of knowing that if this is, that shall be; so determined is he to separate the world of logical from that of temporal consequence, the world of rationally perceived necessary consequence from the world of facts observed by sense and memory as they occur in time. Knowledge of the former world he terms 'science' or 'philosophy', knowledge of the latter 'history'.[19] From this point in the analysis we are constructing, he may be seen going on to show how knowledge of premise and consequence brings knowledge of cause and effect, knowledge of the universe of consequences, knowledge of the universe of motions. Through extension of this kind of knowledge, we discover the laws of nature that bind our consciences; we discover the necessity for a representative sovereign and are led to perform

[16] See in particular chs. ii, vi and xxiv–xxv of *The Prince*.

[17] *Leviathan*, i, 5 (Oakeshott, pp. 29–30).

[18] *Ibid.*, i, 7 (Oakeshott, p. 40).

[19] *Ibid.*, i, 9 (Oakeshott, p. 53). Professor Oakeshott, arguing that a distinction between science and philosophy is emergent in Hobbes's thought, agrees (Introduction, p. xxi) that he uses the terms synonymously.

the acts which set him up; we conclude that God exists and is all-powerful, and that the normative laws which our reason discovers must be also his commands. This complex process of making discoveries and acting upon them takes place in time—there is no action or motion in Hobbes's world which does not—but has no history; it is synchronic, observable as taking place at any and every moment, and does not necessitate that any civil society, or mankind at large, possess a past, present or future in which the stages of its development may be observed. Hobbes has followed the pattern, very common in the history of Western philosophy, of removing from the domain of political time into that of political space,[20] a removal usually carried out for precisely the reason which he gives: the sequence of events in time cannot be known with certainty sufficient to be termed 'philosophical'. Only by abandoning diachronic for philosophical thinking can we understand scientifically how political authority must come into being, or erect a system of authority on a foundation of rational certainty.

We have now uncovered and clarified a sense in which it can very properly be said that Hobbes's political philosophy is unhistorical. He distinguished between philosophy and history as two modes of knowledge and ascribed scientific or rational demonstrability only to the former. But we must be careful not to suppose we have proved too much, or to fall into this error by using the words 'philosophy' and 'history' loosely and anachronistically. Since Hobbes uses 'philosophy' as the name of one of two modes of knowledge, it clearly does not follow that phenomena which are known historically do not exist or have no relevance to politics. A more subtle error would be to suppose that 'history', which Hobbes uses to denote the world of phenomena sensed and remembered as occurring in time, denotes each and every way in which human existence in time is known or important. It may seem natural to suppose that the temporal sequential phenomena which become apparent to our perceptions embrace the totality of human history, though a philosopher of history

[20] The very valuable terminology is that of Sheldon S. Wolin, *Politics and Vision* (New York and London, 1961), *passim*. See also John W. Gunnell, *Political Philosophy and Time* (Wesleyan University Press, 1968).

would probably find this supposition naïve; but even the debate which we might hold with him would not save us from the anachronism of supposing that what Hobbes meant by 'history' embraced every way in which the seventeenth-century intellect saw human existence as carried on in time and marked by its stages. All that we have considered so far consists of Hobbes's responses to the assertion that man's temporal existence was known to him through experience; yet it is quite certain that contemporary thought saw man as having another history, known in another way. The anachronism of refusing to recognize this accounts for the extraordinary neglect and inattention paid to Hobbes's text by the whole tradition of modern scholarship.

Leviathan consists of four books, with an introduction and a conclusion. Books I and II contain the doctrine to which attention has already been given, and the rest of Hobbes's political philosophy, properly so called; and the interest of philosophers and historians of philosophy has quite rightly been focused upon them. But at midpoint in the whole work, at the end of Book II and the outset of Book III, Hobbes embarks on a new course. He states quite plainly[21] that human existence, knowledge, morality and politics must be thought of as going on in two distinct but simultaneous contexts: the one of nature, known to us through our philosophic reasoning on the consequences of our affirmations, the other of divine activity, known to us through prophecy, the revealed and transmitted words of God.

> . . . there may be attributed to God a twofold kingdom, *natural* and *prophetic*: natural, wherein he governeth as many of mankind as acknowledge his providence, by the natural dictates of right reason; and prophetic, wherein having chosen out one particular nation, the Jews, for his subjects, he governed them, and none but them, not only by natural reason, but by positive laws, which he gave them by the mouths of his holy prophets.[22]

[21] *Leviathan*, ii, 31 (Oakeshott, pp. 232–4) and iii, 32 (Oakeshott, pp. 242–3).

[22] *Ibid.*, ii, 31 (Oakeshott, pp. 233–4). The formal link is that men must hear God commanding them directly before they can in the full sense be obliged to obey him. This kind of obligation is not universal, but peculiar to the chosen or elect.

The change in mid-sentence from present to past tense indicates the major and significant alteration that has begun to occur. The Christian God operates in time, and our knowledge of prophecy is our knowledge of the time-frame and scheme of events within which he does so. There are two ways in which this comes to be the case: first, God performs acts, including acts of revelation to prophets, at various points in time; second, the words by which we have knowledge of his acts are revealed to prophets at specific moments in time, and are subsequently transmitted through tracts of time by the authority, religious or civil, on which the prophets and their words are taken to be authentically God's. Actions and words, both divine and human, prophetic and civil, join to constitute a time-scheme which is not only that within which Christian thought is inescapably conducted, but is actually that of which the Christian has knowledge. Our knowledge of God is knowledge of his acts, gained through his words, both of which are performed in time and schematize it. Hobbes therefore affirms the existence of a sacred history, which does not appear in the scheme of philosophical and historical knowledge set out in Book I, Chapter 9, but which does constitute virtually the whole of the subject-matter of Books III and IV. In these books Hobbes sets forth his perceptions of the Christian religion, or as he significantly calls it 'the prophetic kingdom of God', as a system of belief in past acts and utterances of the deity, and of expectation of future acts which those utterances foretell. Following the orthodox scheme, in short, his exposition of the Christian faith concluded with an eschatology; following certain less orthodox schemes, it is very nearly reducible to one.

The two books in which Hobbes expounds Christian faith and its sacred history are almost exactly equal in length to Books I and II;[23] yet the attitude of far too many scholars towards them has traditionally been,[24] first, that they aren't really there, second,

[23] In the first edition of *Leviathan*, the Introduction plus bks. i and ii total 193 pages, bks. iii and iv minus the Review and Conclusion 192. I am indebted to Professor Goldsmith for pointing this out.

[24] Exceptions to this all too general rule may be found in the writings of A. E. Taylor (Keith C. Brown, ed., *Hobbes Studies*, Harvard University

that Hobbes didn't really mean them. For this obviously unsatisfactory state of affairs various reasons can be suggested. In the first place, the history of thought has been too much left in the hands of philosophers, historians of philosophy and scholars who have assumed that the history of thought can be subsumed under the history of successive philosophic systems. Since Hobbes was a major philosopher, and Books III and IV of *Leviathan* are manifestly not philosophy, it has seemed simplest to leave them out; and on grounds like these scholars feel justified in producing students' editions of *Leviathan* from which Books III and IV, and of *De Cive* from which Chapters XVI and XVII, are simply omitted. In the second place, for historical reasons inclusive of that just given, scholarship has suffered until recently from a fixed unwillingness to give the Hebrew and eschatological elements in seventeenth-century thought the enormous significance which they possessed for contemporaries. In the third place, Hobbes's readers since his own lifetime have found reason to doubt if he was a man of deep personal piety and even to affirm that he was an atheist; and even the recent revival of interest in the possible role of God in his thought[25] has focused upon the theory of natural law, which forms part of his philosophy, and not upon his doctrines of prophecy and eschatology, which do not.[26] It has thus come to be a near-orthodoxy that he did not believe what he

[25] See Brown, *op. cit., passim*; Howard Warrender, *The Political Philosophy of Hobbes: His Theory of Obligation* (Oxford, 1957), F. C. Hood, *The Divine Politics of Thomas Hobbes* (Oxford, 1964) and Quentin Skinner, 'Hobbes's *Leviathan*', *The Historical Journal*, vii (1964), pp. 321–33. Some of these writings—notably Hood's—make a serious attempt to show that the thought of bks. iii and iv is implicit in i and ii, but do not focus on the analysis of prophetic content.

[26] Prophecy cannot, of course, be the object of philosophical knowledge as Hobbes understands the latter; nor does he include sacred history in his classification of the modes of that branch of knowledge (i, 9), presumably because it is not an object of sense-knowledge. His theory of knowledge determines the status of our belief in prophecy, but cannot determine the content of what we believe.

Press, 1965, pp. 35, 50, 54n.), Willis B. Glover (Brown, *op. cit.*, pp. 141–68), Oakeshott (Introduction, pp. xliv–l, lxi–lxiv) and Goldsmith (*op. cit.*, pp. 217–27, and 'A Case of Identity' in King and Parekh, eds., *op. cit.*).

wrote in the unread half of *Leviathan*, and that consequently these books have no meaning, though the fallacy should be evident of affirming that the sincerity of a man's belief in what he says suffices to determine the content of what he says or its impact upon others. Although esoteric reasons have been suggested why Hobbes should have written what he did not believe,[27] the difficulty remains of imagining why a notoriously arrogant thinker, vehement in his dislike of 'insignificant speech', should have written and afterwards defended sixteen chapters of what he held to be nonsense, and exposed them to the scrutiny of a public which did not consider this kind of thing nonsense at all. The only recourse open to the historian is to examine, not Hobbes's sincerity of conviction, but the effects which his words seem designed to produce, reconstructing the meanings which their contents would appear to have borne, first, in the thought-patterns characteristic of the time, secondly, in the thought-patterns characteristic of their author. If the effect or the intention of Books III and IV was to reduce the Christian revelation to insignificance, this will be discovered not by making prior assumptions about Hobbes's beliefs when he wrote them, but by paying attention to what he actually wrote. And, further, if we are to conclude that he esoterically intimated that Christian eschatology was nonsense, we must begin by ascertaining the ways in which it was conventionally held to make sense.

Prophecy and eschatology—to which Hobbes in effect reduces the whole body of revealed religion—were not merely a system of dogmas for believers, but a highly important component of the conceptual equipment possessed by Christian Europe. They constituted an intellectual scheme of a distinctive kind, known by an intellectual faculty unlike any we have so far considered. The greater part of their content consisted of acts which God was said to have performed in the past, or which it had been promised that he would perform in the future; and each statement of which prophecy consisted had itself been uttered by God or his prophets

[27] The classic instance is that of Leo Strauss (Brown, *op. cit.*, p. 27, n. 43). It is odd that Strauss seems to speak of the view that Hobbes meant what he said as constituting a 'prevalent practice'; belief in his theistic sincerity has surely been a minority opinion.

at a distinctive moment in time. In two ways, therefore, prophecy constituted a sacred history, and if 'prophecy' and 'revelation' were taken as interchangeable terms, it must follow that knowledge of the Christian revelation was in a sense historical knowledge. But the question must arise of how the events of this history were to be known. It would be common ground to Hobbes and a scholastic thinker that they were not accessible to reason, since they were not consequences to be inferred or deduced from a premise, and that they were equally inaccessible to experience, since their content (as distinct from their verbal utterance) did not belong to the realm of phenomena which the individual sensed and remembered for himself. They were statements, made on specific occasions and transmitted through subsequent time, which we accepted either as true or as authoritative—it was on this point that the schools divided—by means of a faculty of the mind known as faith. Faith was distinct from either reason or experience, and this must be why sacred history, to which so large a part of *Leviathan* is devoted, does not figure in the scheme of knowledge set out in Chapter IX and divided into modes of philosophy and modes of history. Experience and prudence, forms of thought appropriate to the study of natural and civil history, have no part to play in the study of revealed history.

Books III and IV, then, form in a sense Hobbes's contribution to the study of faith, both as a system of revealed truth and as a faculty of the mind. But at a much earlier point in *Leviathan*, immediately after drawing his distinction between experiential knowledge of facts and logical knowledge of the consequences of verbal affirmations, he had turned his attention to the question of what faith was; and it will aid our study of his eschatology if we keep in mind what he there said:

> When a man's discourse beginneth not at definitions, it beginneth either at some other contemplation of his own, and then it is still called opinion; or it beginneth at some saying of another, of whose ability to know the truth and of whose honesty in not deceiving he doubteth not; and then the discourse is not so much concerning the thing as

the person, and the resolution is called BELIEF and FAITH: *faith* in the man, *belief* both *of* the man and *of* the truth of what he says. So that in belief are two opinions, one of the saying of the man, the other of his virtue. . . . But we are to observe that this phrase, *I believe in* [and its Greek and Latin equivalents] are never used but in the writings of divines. Instead of them in other writings are put, *I believe him* [etc.] . . . [and] this singularity of the ecclesiastic use of the word hath raised many disputes about the right object of the Christian faith.

But by *believing in*, as it is in the creed, is meant not trust in the person, but confession and acknowledgement of the doctrine. For not only Christians, but all manner of men do so believe in God as to hold all for truth they hear him say, whether they understand it or not; which is all the faith and trust can possibly be had in any person whatsoever; but they do not all believe the doctrine of the creed.

From whence we may infer that when we believe any saying, whatsoever it be, to be true from arguments taken not from the thing itself or from the principles of natural reason, but from the authority and good opinion we have of him that hath said it, then is the speaker or person we believe in or trust in, and whose word we take, the object of our faith; and the honour done in believing is done to him only. And consequently, when we believe that the Scriptures are the word of God, having no immediate revelation from God himself, our belief, faith and trust is in the church, whose word we take and acquiesce therein. And they that believe that which a prophet relates unto them in the name of God, take the word of the prophet, do honour to him and in him trust and believe touching the truth of what he relateth, whether he be a true or a false prophet. And so it is also with all other history. . . . If Livy say the Gods made once a cow speak and we believe it not, we distrust not God therein, but Livy. So that it is evident that whatsoever we believe, upon no other reason than what is drawn from authority of men only and

> their writings, whether they be sent from God or not, is faith in men only.[28]

The last conclusion that we should draw from this passage is that Hobbes is declaring God to be non-existent or irrelevant. If we can only believe that God spoke on the authority of men who speak to us subsequently, we believe that he spoke once we accept their authority, and in so believing we invest him as well as them with the authority that comes with speaking. What Hobbes is doing is historizing faith in a new way, one of the highest relevance to politics. Faith is reposed in a system of statements and in the authors who transmit them through time, and whether we stress the statement or the author as the object of our faith, a large part of the content of the statements made and transmitted by every author, saving God himself, consists of statements about previous authors. Since once we accept that an author spoke, whether directly or on the authority of another, we invest that speaker with an authority of divine origin, it follows that the whole body of our faith is reducible to the construction of a system of authors and of authority, existing through time and resting on the statements they transmit, our opinion of the authority they have as transmitters, and the authority of the previous speakers, back to God himself, whom we accept as authors in the act of accepting any one of them. This system of authority constituted by faith differs from the system of authority constituted in the erection of the civil sovereign in that historicity is of its essence; it rests upon the transmission of words through time, words which constantly reiterate statements about previous utterances of the same words; and the individual believer becomes involved in this history as he validates and perpetuates it through faith.

There exist then in *Leviathan* two structures of authority, one as a-historical as the other is historical, and they will come into direct and potentially competitive coexistence once the commonwealth constituted in Books I and II becomes 'a Christian Commonwealth'—words which, including the article, form the title of Book III. The civil sovereign is set up by the a-historical

[28] *Leviathan*, i, 7 (Oakeshott, pp. 41–2).

processes of civil philosophy and natural reason, which among other things declare that God exists and commands obedience to the laws of nature which the sovereign also enjoins. He now finds himself faced by a new system of authority, resting upon what are accepted to be utterances of the same God, made in a past and concerning a future, but in no way deducible by the reason which set him up and validates his authority. The sovereign, and the student of civil government, must pay urgent attention to the content as well as the transmission—which, again, forms a large part of the content—of the body of revelation on which rests the structure of religious authority; the inhabitants of the a-historical world of reason must enter the historical world of faith. Since faith is reposed in the content of revelation as well as in its authors and transmitters, and since on the other hand the content of the statement transmitted affects in many ways the sort of authority possessed by those involved in its transmission, the whole content of revealed religion is potentially of concern to the civil magistrate. We shall see that this is particularly true of revelation's eschatological component.

The one thing which scholars do generally know concerning Hobbes's doctrine of prophecy is that God does not speak to us direct but mediately, through the utterances of men—the prophets and Christ in his human nature—to whom or in whom he reveals himself; and that whether God has indeed spoken direct to any man is a thing past any man's capacity to determine,[29] so that the belief we repose and publicly own in the prophets is grounded either on our opinion—which is never our knowledge—of their authenticity, or on the command of the civil sovereign once he is constituted and requires us in the name of civil peace to accept this man as prophet or this doctrine as the word of God.[30] And on the supposition, which there is no need to contest

[29] *Ibid.*, i, 7 (Oakeshott, p. 42); i, 12 (Oakeshott, pp. 77–80); i, 14 (Oakeshott, p. 90); ii, 26 (Oakeshott, pp. 186–8); iii, 32 (Oakeshott, pp. 243–6); iii, 34 (Oakeshott, pp. 254–5); iii, 36 (Oakeshott, pp. 277–85); iii, 37 (Oakeshott, pp. 286–91); Review and Conclusion (Oakeshott, p. 465).

[30] *Ibid.*, ii, 26 (Oakeshott, p. 188); iii, 32 (Oakeshott, p. 246); iii, 34 (Oakeshott, pp. 254–5); iii, 38 (Oakeshott, pp. 290–1); iii, 42 (generally, but in particular Oakeshott, pp. 327–30 and 340–1). Since some

here, that Hobbes did not show that anything except the needs of civil peace bound the will of the sovereign in decreeing matters of this sort, it is usual to drop the subject, leaving it to be inferred that the revealed prophetic word means nothing but what the sovereign ordains that it shall mean, and that the domain of prophecy has been successfully reabsorbed by that of nature, by the unhistoric rationality of the civil order and its sovereign.

But that is not how Hobbes proceeds, and if it is what he really meant then he meant something other than what he said. The history of God's prophetic word, and the future prophesied by that word, constitute the sacred history of mankind, and if Hobbes had meant that sacred history had no meaning of itself and that the sovereign might rewrite it to suit the permanent or passing needs of society, he would hardly have written chapter after chapter of exegesis with the proclaimed intention of arriving at the truth about it. Yet this is what he did, and having once acknowledged the existence of prophecy he could hardly have done less or more. The magistrate may be the supreme and unchallenged interpreter of God's word, but that is not at all the same as being its author—either in the sense of being God himself or of being one of those acknowledged as uttering that word at God's direct or even mediated command. The authority by which the sovereign interprets the prophetic word is clearly distinct from the authority by which the word is uttered; and since the word, its content, its transmission and its authors constitute a history, the secular ruler finds himself inhabiting a history which he did not make—it does not owe its being to the natural reason which produced him—and which indeed looks forward to a time when his authority will be exercised by the risen Christ. The word and the history it connotes are given him, and his authority as inter-

Jewish and all Christian kings have ruled in times when direct prophetic inspiration was in suspension or at an end, their opportunities for sitting in judgment upon true prophets have been limited. The interesting case, with which Hobbes does not deal, is that of Elisha, who conveyed the Lord's command to Jehu, authorizing him to overthrow King Joram and take his throne (in 2 Kings ix). Jehu must have exercised his own judgment as to the authenticity of this revelation by one who was already an accredited prophet.

preter begins only from acceptance of it as *datum*. Hobbes therefore, as a private man, a subject and (so he tells us) a Christian, inhabiting the same history, finds it desirable to pursue an accurate interpretation of the same data, and does not wait in mindless quiet for the sovereign to interpret it to him.

The prophetic word of God constitutes the past, present and future of mankind. At moments in the past, God spoke to prophets, who relayed his word to his peculiar people—the Jews first and the Christian elect later; it was his word commanding them, and their acceptance of him and his prophets as uttering it, which constituted the peculiar kingdom of God over them, and a peculiar kingdom thus differs in kind from a natural civil kingdom. After the deaths of the various prophets, there were—as there still are—periods of time in which the people continued to accept their word as God's and to remember them as having received and given it.[31] Sacred time, thus far, consists of moments of divine revelation and continua of human transmission. But a prophet is both a *prolocutor* who speaks in God's name—all revelation is prophecy in the sense that it is mediated through such men—and a *predictor* who foretells what is to come.[32] Some part of the content of prophecy is prediction in that it foretells a future, composed of divine actions, including the action of foretelling it, in which we believe and which we expect. The present, consequently, is a time of remembering past prophecies and expecting the future which they foretell.

But all these subdivisions of sacred history, including the future, are also subdivisions of the history of political authority. In the synchronic, a-historical world of natural civil authority, there is movement from a phase in which we know by reason what are the laws of nature and that they are also the commands of God, but are obliged by this knowledge only in conscience and *in foro interno*,[33] to a phase in which our wills and actions are lawfully obliged because there is now one Leviathan whom we have constituted with power to command us. But in the diachronic

[31] *Ibid.*, i, 7 (Oakeshott, p. 40); i, 12 (Oakeshott, p. 78); iii, 36 (Oakeshott, pp. 282–5); iii, 40 (Oakeshott, p. 312).

[32] *Ibid.*, iii, 36 (Oakeshott, pp. 275–6).

[33] *Ibid.*, i, 15 (Oakeshott, p. 103).

world inhabited by God's peculiar people, this purely natural movement does not take place, because God is active from the time of Abraham,[34] commanding men directly, not only through reason and experience, but through his word which is spoken by the prophets. Political authority is present from certain moments and it has a history—including a recorded commencement—because the prophetic word has a past, present and future and entails different modes of authority at different times.

For two reasons, the authority which God exercises over his peculiar people is a civil or political authority in the full sense of the term: first, because God is literally present and commanding the people through positive laws, peculiar to themselves, issued through his prophets; second, because the people have covenanted, at Sinai and on other occasions,[35] to obey him through his prophets, acknowledged as uttering his laws. The term 'covenant' is used here in a variant of the full Hobbesian sense. In the natural world the covenant sets up Leviathan, the mortal god, a man or men bearing the person of all other men composing the community. In the prophetic world the people covenanted with Moses to speak with God for them, and so obliged themselves to accept as God's word all that Moses told them for such.[36] Does this mean that Moses as representative sovereign constituted Israel a people in a manner no different from that of other Leviathans? Not if we accept, as there is no sign that Hobbes did not, that God spoke to Moses, for then Moses was in the prophetic world and not simply in the natural. We cannot know that God spoke to him; the authority on which we accept this must be largely his own; the faith by which we acknowledge it must be largely faith in Moses; but once we accept it Moses becomes the

[34] *Ibid.*, ii, 26 (Oakeshott, pp. 187–8); iii, 35 (Oakeshott, pp. 266–7); iii, 40 (Oakeshott, pp. 307–8). The covenant with Abraham is relatively little emphasized as compared with that with Moses.

[35] A renewal of the covenant took place under Esdras, at the return from the Captivity, but did not constitute a new civil sovereignty. *Leviathan*, iii, 40 (Oakeshott, p. 315) and iii, 42 (Oakeshott, p. 342).

[36] *Ibid.*, ii, 20 (Oakeshott, p. 134); ii, 26 (Oakeshott, p. 188); iii, 35 (Oakeshott, pp. 267–78, 270); iii, 40 (Oakeshott, pp. 308–11); iii, 42 (Oakeshott, pp. 340–1).

lieutenant of God in a way in which the civil sovereign can never be, since in the natural world God rules through reason and not through positive and peculiar command.

God exercised direct political authority—that is to say, he was king—over Israel from the time of Moses to that of Samuel. He ruled, it is true, through lieutenants of two kinds: a constituted succession of priest-kings in the line of the heirs of Aaron, and—given the people's frowardness and constant demands for signs of his will—an extraordinary and occasional succession of judges and other prophets, recognized by a far from infallible popular opinion as speaking with his voice.[37] But with the death of Eli the line of the ruling high priests ended, and the misdeeds of the children of Samuel caused the people to lose faith in the prophetic succession in a way that proved irrevocable.[38] Samuel—who was soon to pronounce the old law at an end[39]—presided over that most controversial moment in pre-Exilic history as seen through seventeenth-century Christian eyes, the election of Saul to be king in the manner of the Gentiles. Innumerable were the emphases which could be selected in interpreting this event, and Hobbes's treatment can be seen as it were suspended between two of them: emphasis that it constituted a 'rejection' and 'deposition' of God from his direct kingship over Israel, and insistence that this nevertheless occurred with his permission and consent, so that the authority of the kings was not merely natural, but had his express and positive sanction.[40] But if we compare the works on politics

[37] *Ibid.*, iii, 40 (Oakeshott, pp. 311–12).

[38] *Ibid.*, i, 12 (Oakeshott, pp. 78–9); iii, 35 (Oakeshott, p. 268); iii, 39 (Oakeshott, p. 314).

[39] *De Cive* (*English Works*, ii, p 245). Hobbes gives St Jerome as authority for this.

[40] *Elements of Law* (Cambridge University Press, 1928), pt. i, ch. 7, sec. 5, pp. 127–8: no distinction drawn between high-priests and kings. *De Cive*, xvi (*English Works*, ii, p. 245): 'the kingdom of God by way of priesthood (God consenting to the request of the Israelites) was ended'; 'new priesthood and new sovereignty . . . founded in the very concession of the people'. *Leviathan*, i, 12 (Oakeshott, p. 79): 'faith also failed; insomuch as they deposed their God from reigning over them'. ii, 20 (Oakeshott p. 134): 'when the people heard what power their king was to have, yet they consented thereto, and say thus . . . *we will be as all other nations*. . . . Here

which Hobbes is known to have composed before the outbreak of the Civil War—the *Elements of Law*, written in 1640, and *De Cive*, published in 1642—with the language published in

---

is confirmed the right that sovereigns have. . . . ' ii, 29 (Oakeshott, p. 213—passage deals with 'the infirmities of a commonwealth'): 'And as false doctrine, so oftentimes the example of different government in a neighbouring nation disposeth men to alteration. . . . So the people of the Jews were stirred up to reject God, and to call upon the prophet Samuel for a king after the manner of the nations.' iii, 35 (Oakeshott, pp. 268–9): 'after the Israelites had rejected God, the prophets did foretell his restitution; as . . . I will reign over you, and make you to stand to that covenant which you made with me by Moses, and brake in your rebellion against me in the days of Samuel and in your election of another king . . . it were superfluous to say in our prayer, *Thy kingdom come*, unless it be meant of the restoration of that kingdom of God by Christ, which by revolt of the Israelites had been interrupted in the election of Saul'. iii, 38 (Oakeshott, p. 294): 'they rebelled'. iii, 40 (Oakeshott, pp. 313–14): 'cast off by the people, with the consent of God himself. . . . And yet God consented to it. . . . Having therefore rejected God, in whose right the priests governed, there was no authority left to the priests, but such as the king was pleased to allow them; which was more or less, according as the kings were good or evil. . . . [p. 314] And afterwards, when they demanded a king after the manner of the nations, yet it was not with a design to depart from the worship of God their king . . . they would have a king to judge them in civil actions, but not that they would allow their king to change the religion which they thought was recommended to them by Moses. So that they always kept in store a pretext, either of justice or religion, to discharge themselves of their obedience, whensoever they had hope to prevail' [!]. There follows on p. 315 a confused account of the dealings of the later kings with the prophets after Samuel; Elijah and Elisha are not mentioned. iii, 41 (Oakeshott, pp. 318–19): Christ to restore the kingdom 'cut off by rebellion', but only to proclaim its future coming; Pilate accepts his claim to be king of the Jews as not contrary to the laws of Caesar. iii, 42 (Oakeshott, p. 376): 'Before the people of Israel had, by the commandment of God to Samuel, set over themselves a king, after the manner of other nations, the high-priest had the civil government, and none but he could make or depose an inferior priest. But that power was afterwards in the king. . . . Kings therefore may in like manner ordain and deprive bishops, as they shall think fit for the well-governing of their subjects.' It would on the whole appear that a kingdom of men legitimized by nature exists only in an interlude of sin and rebellion against God. The king reigns in God's absence, but that absence is caused by the king's election.

Leviathan in 1651, we shall notice an important difference of emphasis and an extension of the argument into new fields of relevance.[41] The stress in *Leviathan* falls very heavily indeed, in ways not paralleled in the earlier works, upon the idea that the supreme purpose of Christ's mission is to restore the literal and political kingdom of God upon earth that existed from Moses to Samuel; that, since the Jews have rejected Christ's invitation to re-enter this kingdom, it is now to be exercised over a new peculiar people, the Christian elect; and that through the death, ascension and promised return of Christ, the second kingdom of God is to begin only at his return and at the resurrection of the saints, which is to end this world and inaugurate a new one. Where in the first kingdom God reigned in his representatives Moses and the prophets, he will reign in the second kingdom in the person of Christ risen in his human nature and his human body; and the identity of Christ's kingship with that of Moses is insisted on so strongly that it impels Hobbes to one of the only two occasions in *Leviathan* on which he resorts to the typological mode of argument, in which Christ and his precursors are presented as reiterating and perfecting a common figurative pattern.[42] If the sole purpose of Christ's mission is to restore the immediate civil rule of God over his peculiar people which ended with the election of Saul, it might almost seem as if that event constituted a second fall of man, something which the whole process of redemption exists to undo. Hobbes does not go to these lengths, since he wishes to maintain the legitimacy of Davidic kingship over the peculiar people; though in common with the general trend of Christian interpre-

[41] Chs. xvi and xvii of *De Cive* should be carefully compared with bk. iii of *Leviathan*, and the relation between the two texts considered. If we conclude that Hobbes's interest in eschatology sharply increased between 1642 and 1651, this must have occurred during his residence at Paris, in a *milieu* not usually considered eschatologically-minded.

[42] *Leviathan*, iii, 41 (Oakeshott, pp. 316–17): the sacrificed goat and the scapegoat both 'types' of Christ; pp. 320–21: the 'similitude with Moses'—twelve elders and twelve apostles; seventy elders and seventy disciples; circumcision and baptism; the washing of lepers a 'type' of baptism. 'Seeing therefore the authority of Moses was but subordinate, and he but a lieutenant of God, it followeth that Christ, whose authority as man was to be like that of Moses, was no more but subordinate to the authority of his Father.'

tation of later Jewish history, he does not attempt to assign post-Exilic forms of political power a distinctive role in the history of prophetic authority, and the emphasis falls by default on the utterances of the Exilic prophets in foretelling Jesus as the Messiah.[43] But the fact remains that his history of prophetic authority has been projected into an eschatological future. His politics have taken on a messianic dimension, just as the messianism they entail is almost brutally political.

As Hobbes's thought enters the domain of eschatology, it begins to make use of apocalyptic: both that part of the content of acknowledged revelation which had to do with the acts of God promised for a future, and the doctrines and speculations, for historical reasons largely heterodox or heretical, which had been built up around it. He insists unremittingly on the literal and physical nature of Christ's return, the literal, physical and political character of his kingdom after the resurrection of the saints. It is to be exercised on earth,[44] and indeed from Jerusalem,[45] since 'salvation is of the Jews (*ex Judaeis*, that is, begins at the Jews)'; the speculation is of the same order as that which represented the conversion of the Jews as a necessary preliminary to a millennial *regnum Christi.* Formally, Hobbes is not a millennialist, or at least a pre-millennialist, since his kingdom of Christ follows and does not precede the end of this world;[46] but as the allusion to Jerusalem shows, his 'world to come' so closely replicates this world that the distinction tends to disappear. On an earth indistinguishable from this one, Christ in his risen human body is to reign for ever over the elect in theirs, and 'for ever' has no other meaning than that time as we know it in this life is

[43] *De Cive* (*English Works*, ii, p. 248) and *Leviathan*, iii, 40 (Oakeshott, p. 315) make the point that post-Exilic history is too confused to be of authority. iii, 36 (Oakeshott, p. 280): 'after the people of the Jews had rejected God, that he should no longer reign over them, those kings which submitted themselves to God's government were also his chief prophets', in the *prolocutor* sense presumably. iii, 42 (Oakeshott, pp. 341–2): the problem of when the Exilic prophecies became canonical.

[44] *Leviathan*, iii, 38 (Oakeshott, pp. 292–6).

[45] *Ibid.* (Oakeshott, pp. 301–3). On p. 294 it seems that the conversion of the Jews must precede the second kingdom.

[46] *Ibid.*, p. 303; also p. 295.

prolonged *ad infinitum*.[47] The risen saints will neither beget nor die; since Hobbes refuses to accept eternal torment, or any evil greater than personal death, he has the damned resurrected to face the certainty of a second and eternal death, not to be suffered before they have begotten children in the state of damnation, who will continue to all eternity the generations of men doomed to perish utterly without help from the God who visibly and humanly reigns over them.[48] Since Hobbes could as well have extinguished the damned without allowing them to breed, his theory of damnation is gratuitous; and since he knew more clearly than most men that damnation consists in the deprivation of hope, it appears more than usually abominable. Its importance, however, is that it underlines both the material and the temporal nature of his hereafter. Salvation and damnation both happen in the world of matter and of time. As Hobbes denies that eternity is a *nunc-stans* or 'eternal now', and will permit it only to be an infinite prolongation of the time we know,[49] so his 'heaven' is located in no spiritual and (until we ask where God is now) hardly any spatial realm, but essentially in time—in the infinite future of the material world.[50] It is this which links his hereafter to the millennium of the Protestant sects; Gerrard Winstanley had already shown that Christ's resurrection could be described exclusively in terms of a transformation of this world's conditions. Again, Hobbes's determination to acknowledge no processes outside the world of matter, space and time led him to follow many radical sectarians and much contemporary higher criticism[51] in propounding the doctrine of mortalism, according to which the soul could have no

[47] *Ibid.*, iv, 44 (Oakeshott, pp. 411–12): the damned to be renewed 'as long as the kind of man by propagation shall endure, which is eternally'. *Answer to Bishop Bramhall* (*English Works*, iv, p. 299): '*God's mercy endureth for ever*, and surely God endureth as long as his mercy; consequently there is duration in God, and consequently endless succession of time.'

[48] *Leviathan*, iii, 38 (Oakeshott, pp. 296–300); iv, 44 (Oakeshott, pp. 410–12).

[49] *Ibid.*, iv, 46 (Oakeshott, p. 443). *Of Liberty and Necessity* (*English Works*, iv, p. 271). *Answer to Bishop Bramhall* (*English Works*, iv, pp. 298–300).

[50] *Leviathan*, iii, 38 (Oakeshott, pp. 294–5).

[51] G. H. Williams, *The Radical Reformation* (London, 1962), *passim*. George Newton Conklin, *Biblical Criticism and Heresy in Milton* (New York: King's Crown Press, Columbia University, 1949). Nathaniel H.

existence apart from the body, but must perish with it at death and enjoy immortality only with it on resurrection.[52] This too was an apocalyptic heresy: immortality did not consist in the soul's existence outside time, but was a gift to be received by the elect in an infinite future. Clearly, what is going on is a conjunction of some kind between Hobbes's philosophical materialism and the apocalyptic and millennialist speculation reaching a high-water mark in England about the time that *Leviathan* was published, a conjunction occurring at the point where salvation could be presented as a temporal, a historical and even a millennial process; and we have to understand this conjunction if we are to understand Hobbes's political eschatology.

Among the radical sects—one has only to mention *Man's Mortalitie*, usually ascribed to the Leveller Richard Overton[53]—such a heresy as mortalism could go hand-in-hand with chiliasm and enthusiasm; the paradox of the doctrine is that it could flourish among mystics whose belief in the primacy of the spirit was so absolute that they saw spirit as immanent in matter to the point where it could by no means be separated from it. Man's spirit was his body and his body his spirit; the resurrection of the one was the resurrection of the other, and it was blasphemy to try to separate the two. Along these lines it was perfectly possible for a devout and even mystical Christian to be a systematic materialist. A hundred years after Hobbes, Joseph Priestley was to combine materialism with millennialism,[54] and in his own day one has but to think of Gerrard Winstanley to be reminded of a cluster of

[52] *Leviathan*, iii, 38 (Oakeshott, p. 292); iv, 44 (Oakeshott, pp. 407–12).

[53] John Canne's edition, giving the author as 'R.O.', was dated from Amsterdam in 1649. See W. Haller, *Liberty and Reformation in the Puritan Revolution* (New York, 1955), pp. 175–8; and for doubts about the authorship, Henry, *loc. cit.*, n. 51, above.

[54] See, as introductory to an extensive literature, 'Institutes of Natural and Revealed Religion' and 'Disquisitions Relating to Matter and Spirit', in *Theological and Miscellaneous Works of Joseph Priestley*, ed. J. T. Rutt (London, 1825), ii and iii. For the relations of science and millennialism in the eighteenth century, see Ernest Tuveson, *Millennium and Utopia* (Berkeley and Los Angeles, 1949).

Henry, 'Milton and Hobbes: Mortalism and the Intermediate State', *Studies in Philology*, xlviii (1951), pp. 234–50.

sects subscribing to varieties of materialist pantheism. Hobbes does not share the outlook of these men; it can quite conclusively be shown that his thought does not rest on belief in the primacy of the spirit, but on denial of this belief, but he has to be understood as living in the same world and belonging to the same context in intellectual history. We do not profit by treating him in isolation or by treating him in the light of ideas about materialism and atheism which belong properly to the nineteenth century.

Christianity is a prophetic religion, which cannot wholly escape from depicting the salvation of men as an event taking place in the future; and its insistence on the resurrection of the body imparts a bias towards depicting this event as taking place in the material and even social environment of human life, and therefore in the future of that environment. But these tendencies have always been combated, for reasons which are of vast importance to political thought because they have affected the views men hold of the nature and authority of the Church. St Augustine, and Catholic tradition after him, discouraged thought focused on the idea of a future collective redemption of mankind in time or at its end, and stressed that we were not told much of these things and that what we did know was better interpreted as figurative of the individual soul's redemption and ascent to God. The effect was to divert attention from the diachronic to the synchronic presentation of God's relation to men; instead of human salvation being brought about by a succession of acts performed by the eternal upon the world in time, it appeared rather in terms of the passage of numbers of souls through time to eternity—a passage performed through the actions of pure grace upon the individual's spirit, which however were usually thought of as institutionalized in the sacramental and other channels provided by the organizational Church, exercising in the world of time an authority derived from the eternal. The medieval Church thus rested largely upon the minimization of the eschatological perspective and the diversion of attention from the historical to the institutional; its philosophy correspondingly dealt in terms of the intelligibility of timeless universals in which part of God's reality was accessible to human reason.

As a tactical consequence of this, late-medieval heresy and both the magisterial and the radical Reformations, all bent on undermining the foundations of the institutional Church, commonly adopted arguments which pressed Christian thought back towards the eschatological perspective and its apocalyptic and millenarian forms. (That Calvin himself is an exception is a momentous fact in the history of English Puritanism.) If salvation came through grace, not reason, or through faith, not works, the Christian community might appear not a body of pilgrims ascending the Church's institutional ladder through time into eternity, but a body of faithful situated in time, reading God's word given in the past, commemorating Christ's Passion suffered in the past, and reposing faith in a promise which was very largely an undertaking that he would return in the future. Salvation came through this expectation and not through Christ's real presence in the immediate now of the sacramental union; but it followed both that salvation could only come about in time and that Christ himself was seen as operating diachronically. He had come in the past and would return in the future; and salvation itself might be seen as a historical process. Joachim of Calabria, or perhaps rather the Spiritual Franciscans who had adapted his teachings,[55] had depicted the three persons of the Trinity as operating through successive ages to make history a process of the reunion of man with God. In this and other ways, it happened that every statement to the effect that salvation was to be expected in time became a blow struck at the sacerdotal enemy. Eschatology, prophecy and even millennialism became weapons in the armoury of Protestantism, whether the Protestant community was seen as a secular nation organized under its prince or as a gathered congregation separated from his obedience; and modern scholars have remarked[56] that several sixteenth-century princes took a deep—and, remotely and vaguely, Joachite—interest in the idea that the authority of the Holy Spirit differed somehow from that of the Vicar of Christ. Certainly, a secular prince who had encouraged his subjects to believe that the Kingdom of God or the Age of the Spirit was at hand might live to regret it; such an expectation,

[55] Gordon Leff, *Late Medieval Heresy* (2 vols., Manchester, 1967), vol. I, pp. 68–83.

[56] Frances A. Yates, 'Queen Elizabeth as Astraea', *Journal of the Warburg and Courtauld Institute*, X (1947), pp. 27–82, esp. 78–9.

especially when couched in millennial terms, might inconveniently underline the transitoriness of his authority, and his divines might make haste to preach that the Son of Man came as a thief in the night and none knew the hour of his coming. But it was the temporal (and so the transitory) nature of his authority which had led him to encourage such ideas in the first place. Prophecy and eschatology formed a device for drawing the process of salvation more fully within the world of time, and so subjecting its outward organization to temporal authority; history (and especially sacred history) was the instrument of the secular power. The adjectives 'secular' and 'temporal' themselves indicate the primacy of time, and even the apocalyptic of Patmos or Calabria was to a surprising degree a means to secularization.

We are now in a better position to see what Hobbes was about when he made use of the rhetoric of eschatology and apocalyptic. He does not employ the language of Patmos—there are only five references to the Book of Revelation in *Leviathan* and three to the Book of Daniel, none of them very important[57]—but he is engaging in traditional anti-Papal strategy when he reduces the Christian religion to a system of prophecy. All that has happened is that God has pronounced, through the mouths of prophets, certain words in time; the occasions of these pronouncements, together with other happenings to which they refer, constitute a series of divine acts in past time; we believe that these acts were performed by believing the authors and the words which they have relayed to us; these words include foretellings and promises of a resurrection and a world to come; by believing these among other words, we ensure to ourselves a reward which will be only then, in that future. All is *logos*, and *logos* is a system of communications through time. Since salvation and even eternity are entirely temporal, there can be no Church in the sense of a spiritual institution communicating between time and an eternal now; and Hobbes denies not only purgatory, to do which was orthodox Protestantism, but the separate existence of the soul between the death and resurrection of the body, to do which was less orthodox though intellectually somewhat fashionable, in order to deny that there is a process of salvation occurring outside historical and

[57] Oakeshott, pp. 275, 278, 293, 297 (2), Revelation, 263, 299, 365, Daniel.

political time, over which the Church exercises a separate authority that must be obeyed in the here and now.

Neither the use of apocalyptic in *Leviathan*, nor its mortalism and materialist literalism, suffice to place Hobbes outside the mainstream of Protestant thinking. Protestantism was the religion of the word, and the word not only consisted in large measure of a system of prophecies concerning future time, but in its character as a series of utterances required men to think in terms of a time-scheme which it was necessary to express in an eschatological language.[58] But Hobbes's thought is anti-sectarian as well as anti-Papal, and it is here that his role in the Protestant tradition becomes visibly enigmatic. He set himself to counter the sin of Korah, Dathan and Abiram, who had rebelled against Moses on the ground that 'all the congregation are holy, every one of them'.[59] If Protestantism was the religion of the word, it was also the religion that exalted the primacy of faith, and the story need not be rehearsed here of how in Puritan thinking the life of faith had become a realm of direct spiritual experience, in which the individual might, and regularly sought to, feel himself the subject of direct action by the will and redemptive mercy of God; or how the word became the vehicle of the spirit, and the spirit—moving rather in the individual than in the congregation or the Church—the means of interpreting the word. By 1651, when *Leviathan* appeared, every possible challenge implicit in this development was being publicly articulated and the collision between private inspiration and the authority of the civil magistrate had become a staple of political debate. The far greater attention paid to apocalyptic in *Leviathan* than in *De Cive* may perhaps be a consequence of this. Puritan millennialism was essentially spiritualist: a Joachite Third Age, a Fifth Monarchist thousand-year reign of Christ and his saints were, however literally intended, modes of envisaging a day in which all the elect should be immediately and permanently possessed by the Holy Spirit. But the paradox was that this primacy of the spirit operated against the tendency

[58] For the classical modern study of this, see W. Haller, *Foxe's Book of Martyrs and the Elect Nation* (London, 1963). Michael Fixler, *Milton and the Kingdoms of God* (London, 1964), should also be consulted.

[59] *Leviathan*, iii, 40 (Oakeshott, p. 310).

of apocalyptic to draw salvation back into time and tended rather to restore the eternal now of an earlier Christian tradition. It placed the individual saint where the Church had once been, in an immediate relation to the eternal, and gave him authority originating outside time for his actions within it. There is a relationship between Hobbes's insistence that covenants must be kept[60] and the debates at Putney as to whether men might find authority in their spiritual experience for regarding engagements as superseded;[61] and William Prynne's discovery that Quakers were Franciscans in disguise is only a somewhat idiosyncratic expression of a widespread Erastian realization that the struggle against sectaries was a second front of the war against papists.[62]

Hobbes, then, set out to destroy 'enthusiasm',[63] which he considered a form of madness,[64] the sin of Korah, Dathan and Abiram, a doctrine that must place the authority of prophetic utterance at the disposal of any man who might claim it on grounds that could not be evaluated by his fellows. In attacking Bishop Butler's 'very horrid thing' he stood at the outset of a century and a half's Anglican orthodoxy, but the manner of his attack does much to explain why that orthodoxy devoted much of its energy to attacking him. He denies the reality of 'enthusiasm' or 'inspiration'—defined as the infusion of God's spirit into that of a man—by ruthlessly denying both the reality of 'spirit' in the ordinarily accepted sense of the term and the possibility of the individual's directly experiencing God except on the rarest of historic occasions. This denial was conducted by means, and we may be temp-

[60] *Ibid.*, i, 15 (Oakeshott, pp. 93–4).

[61] A. S. P. Woodhouse, *Puritanism and Liberty* (London, 1948), pp. 9–13, 25–36, 45–52, 86–95.

[62] William M. Lamont, *Marginal Prynne* (London, 1963), explains the curious but contemporary relation between apocalyptic and Erastianism in Prynne's thinking. See also his *Godly Rule: Politics and Religion, 1603–60* (London, 1969).

[63] The word is used in *Leviathan*, i, 8 (Oakeshott, p. 49) and iii, 33 (Oakeshott, p. 246). The terms 'inspiration' and 'infusion' are, however, far more common: i, 3 (Oakeshott, p. 13); i, 8 (Oakeshott, pp. 47–50); iii, 32 (Oakeshott, p. 244); iii, 34 (Oakeshott, pp. 259, 264–5); iii, 36 (Oakeshott, pp. 280–2); iv, 45 (Oakeshott, p. 429); iv, 46 (Oakeshott, p. 445).

[64] *Ibid.*, i, 8 (Oakeshott, pp. 47–50).

ted to explain it as the consequence, of Hobbes's philosophical materialism. In a universe consisting of matter and motion 'spirit' may be the name of an extremely subtle corporeal substance, or a metaphor helping to express the state of a man's thoughts and feelings, notably—but conventionally—on such occasions as he has heard God's word directly or indirectly;[65] there can be no justification for using it as a nonsense-word to express the ubiquity of a non-substance. Nor can we intelligibly use it to describe any medium of communication between God and man. When God communicates with men he does not enter their bodies himself—the only man in whom 'the Godhead dwelt bodily' was Jesus[66]—or blow an extremely subtle wind into their nostrils;[67] nor, certainly, does he communicate with them through a shared non-substantial being. He speaks to them either mediately, through words, which are systems of motions transmitted through space and time to the senses—in a phrase of St Paul's which Hobbes quotes, 'faith comes by hearing'[68]—or by supernatural revelations, of which we do not know very much, but may ask whether they are made by affecting the senses of men or, as in the case of Moses, by means altogether beyond our understanding. The men who receive these revelations—of which there have been none since the deaths of the first apostles—cannot communicate to other men the experiences by which they receive them, and it is only by opinion, faith and public authority—all of which involve the transmission of words—that others believe they were made. It is to such verbal, material, social and historical processes that a man who claims a direct 'spiritual' revelation must appeal if he wishes others to accept his claim; he cannot invoke the word 'spirit' in order to give himself authority and would do better to avoid its use altogether.

The argument has implications far beyond what can be discussed by elucidating the workings of a system of philosophical materialism. If God cannot be known to us through the operation

[65] *Ibid.*, iii, 34 (Oakeshott, pp. 255–60).

[66] *Ibid.*, iii, 36 (Oakeshott, p. 280); iv, 45 (Oakeshott, p. 429).

[67] *Ibid.*, iii, 34 (Oakeshott, p. 264). When Christ breathed on his disciples, this was a sign (p. 429).

[68] *Ibid.*, iii, 29 (Oakeshott, p. 212); iii, 43 (Oakeshott, p. 387).

of his spirit upon ours, he can be known to us, and can work upon us, only through his words, and knowledge of these words is historical knowledge; they were given to us in past time, and both their content and the faith we repose in them have been transmitted through complex social processes taking place in time and involving awareness of their earlier stages. It can be said, furthermore, that the God of revelation and faith acts upon men only through history and is present to them only in history. The God of nature and reason is known to all men through processes which involve no history; but if there have been no revelations and no miracles since the lifetimes of the Christians who knew Jesus as a man,[69] then the God who acts positively to rule and redeem his peculiar people is not immediately present to us now. We have nothing of him except his word, and these prophetic and revealed utterances were given in past time and are acting upon us only through the modes of their transmission through subsequent time. Hobbes's God—of whom Bramhall asserted, and Hobbes did not deny, that he existed wholly in time[70]—begins to resemble the *deus absconditus* of modern radical theologians and, as has been the case with some of them, his operations are entirely eschatological. He was in direct relationship with us only when he spoke to us directly; that relationship will be restored only when he speaks to us directly again, which will be—the elect know through their faith in his given word—in his second kingdom which is to come.

Hobbes's nominalism, as well as his materialism, is at work here. By nominalism may be understood—if only for elucidation of the present context—a philosophy which asserts that our knowledge is of words, denoting things that are not to be understood in themselves, so that words are at once all-important to knowledge and imperfect in the knowledge they supply. Hobbes added, of course, that philosophy was a knowledge of the relation

69 *Ibid.*, iii, 37, contains Hobbes's doctrine concerning miracles, which are extraordinary works of God designed to procure credit to an extraordinary minister speaking directly from him. Cf. *Leviathan*, iii, 32 (Oakeshott, p. 246), marginal note: 'Miracles ceasing, prophets cease, and the Scripture supplies their place.'

70 Bramhall, *Works*, iv (Oxford, 1844), pp. 523–4; Hobbes, *English Works*, iv (n. 49, above).

between ideas, arrived at by reflection on the content of words and logically certain in itself; but his system of prophecy is not a mere extension of his system of philosophy, and can be discussed without committing us to deciding how far the latter is consistent with the nominalist language which he undeniably uses. Now, a consequence of nominalism in this sense is that God is not to be known through understanding of his nature, but rather as will or power and through the revelations or prophecies—themselves words—which he wills to make known to us; and a further consequence is that these words may not be fully intelligible, and that what matters is rather the faith by which we acknowledge them to be God's words than the reason by which we apprehend their meaning.

Hobbes's God is one of whom we can know by reason only that he must exist and must be all-powerful. His nature is incomprehensible, and anything we may say about it is no more than language designed to honour his power.[71] When therefore such a God speaks to us, what is required is that we believe and acknowledge the words to be his rather than that our understanding be enriched by their contents; they can communicate to us, and their function is to communicate, primarily a reminder of his power and an injunction to obey him; and Hobbes indicates that nearly all religious and prophetic teaching is reducible to this form, including the injunction to obey and expect the kingdom of God that was and shall be over his peculiar elect. Faith in God's word is little more than acknowledgment of his power; the Ten Commandments,[72] the Old and New Testaments[73] convey little more than reminders and injunctions of that power; and, conversely, it is by the faith we repose in his word that his civil power over us, the subjection of our wills to his, is constituted. His civil and prophetic kingdom rests on a voluntary submission by the elect; we may refuse him that kingdom, or reject him after acceptance as the Jews did, by refusing or withdrawing the measure of faith necessary to constitute it. His word to the elect, given on peculiar occasions, is that his power is; the elect

[71] *Ibid.*, ii, 31, *passim*; iii, 34 (Oakeshott, p. 257).

[72] *Ibid.*, iii, 42 (Oakeshott, pp. 339–40); iv, 45 (Oakeshott, p. 424).

[73] *Ibid.*, iii, 33 (Oakeshott, p. 253).

constitute his civil kingdom by believing that he spoke this word on peculiar occasions, through the mouths of peculiar men, and addressed it peculiarly to them. Such a civil kingdom was, from Moses to Samuel, but it ceased to be; Christ, in whom we repose faith as God himself, promised the elect a restoration of that kingdom, but since it visibly does not exist at present, our faith in Christ must be our acceptance that he was God in person, restoring God's kingdom by uttering his word, but that he spoke the word and restored the kingdom in a future tense, by promising that he would come and rule again. Our relation to God is one of civil obedience. God is not here now in such a way that he can be so obeyed, but we ensure ourselves a place in his future obedience by believing that Christ was sent to promise that his kingdom would come again. God's word is invariably command, and our faith in it invariably acknowledgment of a kingdom; but at present we are acknowledging and constituting a future kingdom by believing the author of words uttered in a future tense. By believing that God, who has the power to rule, will come and rule again, we ensure ourselves a place in his kingdom. The whole structure of faith and salvation has been reduced to a system of statements in and about time. This is the inner meaning of Hobbes's premise that the one article of faith necessary to salvation is 'Jesus is the Christ'.[74]

This radical temporalization of salvation is the consequence of the sharpness of the distinctions Hobbes draws between the traditional trinity of experience, reason and faith; for this alone is sufficient to indicate that statements concerning God's relation to his peculiar people, since they cannot be universals, must be made not a-historically, but at particular times; and if faith is defined both as that by which statements of this order are accepted, and as that by which salvation is effected, then salvation becomes a matter of acceptance of a historical scheme. The content of the statements is of significance mainly as providing the scheme with a future, expectation of which becomes the principal means of salvation; but we are to be saved less because we have faith that God will save us than because we acknowledge—and thus actualize—his power to do so. In Hobbes's theology, God's

[74] *Ibid.*, iii, 43 (Oakeshott, pp. 388–93).

power is known to us far more certainly than his mercy or goodness, and we do not so much receive his grace as help to reconstitute his civil kingdom. This is not merely to temporalize Christian salvation, but to politicize it. Faith in and knowledge of God are mere acknowledgments of power; but that power is committed by words it has used, and we are committed by our faith that those words were spoken, to a scheme of its action in time.

The tactical thrust of Hobbes's argument is now clear. It is directed against new presbyter as well as old priest, and against new saint as well as old scholastic—against anyone, that is, who may claim that the process of salvation authorizes his civil actions or power in the present. The tactic of combining apocalyptic with mortalism served, as it always had, to destroy the claim that the Church possessed the keys to an individual's salvation at the hour of his death; he could be saved or damned only by an action which God was to take in the future, and the Church was merely a community of faithful expectant of that future act. Hobbes furthermore directed his radical nominalism against the claim of the schoolmen that there existed a structure of essences through which the character of the eternal might be apprehended by men in time and its actions upon time rendered accessible to reason; we shall see that he regarded the erection of this philosophy as the chief event in the history of the false church or 'kingdom of darkness'. But he also turned his nominalism against the saints with a systematic demolition of the claims of the spirit, as opposed to the temporal word, to act as the vehicle of salvation in time. The Joachite Spirituals had in their day sought to historize salvation by declaring that the Age of the Son was being superseded by the Age of the Spirit, in which God would be manifest in all men—a belief not unknown among Hobbes's contemporaries,[75] and, despite its revolutionary possibilities, capable of vesting the hierarchies of human society with sacerdotal authority. There is one point at which Hobbes's doctrine seems to echo Joachism: he suggests that God's Trinity may be known from his having been personated on earth three times—by Moses and the prophets as the Father, by Jesus as the Son, by the apostles and

[75] Gerrard Winstanley, James Nayler.

their successors as the Spirit.[76] But not only does his drastic handling of the term 'spirit' render it more than usually difficult for him to give a satisfactory account of the Third Person of the Trinity;[77] the apostolic mission is little more than to represent the Son in his absence, or rather—since we should avoid using the word 'represent' in its properly Hobbesian sense—to transmit through time the word that the Son came, redeemed us[78] and promised to return. The Christian present—the time now elapsing between the apostles and the general resurrection—is less a Kingdom of the Spirit than an era in which God is known to his peculiar people through the Word.

It follows that the apostles and their successors are not strictly prophets in either sense of the term. From Moses to Samuel there were, intermittently but frequently, prophets in the sense of *prolocutores*—men to whom God spoke and who relayed his words to the people, and through whom as well as the high priests God exercised his civil kingdom. The prophets of the Exile were *predictores*, men who exercised no civil authority, but were inspired (a metaphor, of course) to foretell the birth of Christ, by whom the kingdom would be restored. When Christ came, he did not restore the kingdom in this world but left words constituting his promise to do so in a future world; and once these words had been spoken by God himself in human form, there was no need for special revelations to other men which could merely repeat their substance. The apostles themselves, as men who had walked with God, would seem to have possessed extraordinary powers, but these were not transmissible;[79] and God ceased to perform miracles as signs of the authenticity of his word. Now that he had spoken words concerning his return, faith became a simple matter of accepting those words as spoken by him, and

[76] *Leviathan*, i, 16 (Oakeshott, p. 107); iii, 33 (Oakeshott, p. 253); iii, 41 (Oakeshott, p. 322); iii, 42 (Oakeshott, pp. 323–4). Bramhall, *Works*, iv, pp. 526–7; Hobbes, *English Works*, iv, pp. 306, 310–12, 315–17.

[77] E.g. *Leviathan*, iii, 34 (Oakeshott, p. 265).

[78] For Hobbes's account of the redemption see *Leviathan*, iii, 41 (Oakeshott, pp. 316–17). Christ's three functions, those of a redeemer, a pastor and a ruler, are to be exercised sequentially in time.

[79] *Ibid.*, iii, 42 (Oakeshott, p. 351).

this was not to be done on the authority of other men's having received a special commission to speak for him. The age of prophets ended with that of miracles. The word was no longer spoken through chosen men; it had been spoken once and for all —since its content was essentially a promise concerning a future time—and faith was now to be reposed in it as spoken, recorded and transmitted. The business of the faithful was to expect the return (and very little more). They expected that Christ would return through believing that he had said he would, and the church was that organization through which they transmitted his words, and belief in them, to one another. Faith came by hearing.

But Christ, unlike Moses, had left no Tables of the Law, civilly promulgated to the people on a public occasion; since his kingdom was not of this world, i.e. was not then or now, but to come, he could not have done so. Hobbes emphasized, what the scholarship of his age could see well enough, that the New Testament was the result of a process, through which its various books had been written, assembled and recognized as canonical, taking place over time.[80] This brought us back to the problem, with which he had dealt early in *Leviathan*, of the mechanisms of belief and faith. It was not possible altogether to separate belief in the thing spoken from belief in the person speaking—the God of Jews and Christians was therefore especially *logos*, a God who had spoken[81]—and in the world of human continuity this raised the question of the human transmitter of words formerly spoken. Hobbes's famous remark that the cause of all religious change was 'unpleasing priests'[82] was not merely a secularist's joke; he meant that loss of faith necessarily involved loss of credence in persons authorized to transmit belief-systems through social time. But this sort of credence, he had emphasized, meant our continued good opinion of the transmitters; the line of the ruling high priests had ended with the sons of Eli, that of the ruling prophets with the sons of Samuel, precisely because this opinion had been forfeited.

[80] *Ibid.*, iii, 33 (Oakeshott, pp. 252–3); iii, 42 (Oakeshott, pp. 338–9, 342, 345).

[81] For Christ as the word made flesh see *Leviathan*, iii, 36 (Oakeshott, pp. 274–5).

[82] *Ibid.*, i, 12 (Oakeshott, p. 80).

It might seem, then, that faith, necessarily a historical and a social phenomenon, rested on no other foundation than the faithful's continued good opinion of the authorized speakers and transmitters of the word; and if the Christian communities had continued as voluntary congregations of believers, this would in fact have been the case. But a great historical transformation had prevented it. Instead, it had happened, either accidentally or providentially (but Hobbes does not state how), that entire civil societies had become Christian and that civil sovereigns had been converted to Christian belief, and this had brought the entire process of the transmission and determination of faith into the domain of public acts performed by civil authority as constituting public corporations. The task of deciding what words were to be believed, what writings regarded as canonical and what authors and doctors considered authentic and authoritative, now ceased to be performed by unincorporated opinion and fell instead to the civil sovereign; faith itself, always a decision,[83] became a public act, only to be performed by one whose authority rested on neither opinion nor faith.

The sovereign's authority comes into being through the processes of natural civil reason, at least to the extent that reason makes us aware that natural laws exist, have to be obeyed and can be obeyed only in certain conditions, though Hobbes may never have made it plain how men became capable of the acts of fiction and personation by means of which the sovereign was created. At all events, he was not set up by, nor did his authority rest on, either opinion or faith, and we have already seen that there is no chapter of history which we need understand in order to understand this process. If we now ask by what kinds of intelligence the sovereign exercises his functions, that is, of course, a separate question from asking what authorizes him to perform them, and tends to divert our attention from the truth that his *raison d'être* is less to exert intelligence than to perform acts of will; but evidence can no doubt be found to indicate that Hobbes saw the sovereign's intelligence as consisting in civil philosophy rather than civil

[83] *Ibid.*, i, 7 (Oakeshott, p. 40): 'so the last opinion in search of the truth of past and future is called the JUDGMENT, or *resolute* and *final sentence* of him that *discourseth*'.

experience.[84] When we learn therefore that the sovereign, who owes his existence neither to faith nor to history, acquires an unlimited right to take the decisions of which faith consists, in the history which faith constitutes and acknowledges, it is tempting to conclude—something was said of this earlier—that the ahistorical has somehow annexed and annulled the historical, and that the sovereign's decisions in matters of faith and observance will be taken with an eye to the needs of civil society and none to the imperatives of Christian belief. But this does not seem to be correct. Reason and nature command—reason indeed tells us that God commands—that we will the existence of civil society and will to give up to the sovereign our power of privately determining our social or public actions; and when the decisions of faith become public actions of public concern, reason commands that they be taken by the sovereign, since to do otherwise would be to erect other authorities, other than civil in their origins, but now capable of challenging him on his own grounds, which the nature of civil society commands must not be done. But it does not follow that the sovereign's decisions in matters of faith will be determined solely by considerations of the well-being of society. The situation which we are studying has arisen because civil societies and their sovereigns have become involved in the historical world of faith. Since they are so involved they have brought with them the considerations and the forms of intelligence which dictate their own self-perpetuation; but all that has happened is that the mechanisms of faith, the decisions to accept certain words as spoken by God and certain men as authoritatively transmitting them, have left the sphere of opinion and entered that of public obligation. The objects on which the mind is focused in belief—the words and acts said to be those of God, the writings and teachings of men—have not altered and cannot be the objects of rational knowledge. Hobbes may perhaps be shown to have cared too little about the possibility that the sovereign would take his decisions in the field of faith for reasons of civil prudence, but he cannot be shown to have substituted either prudence or philosophy for belief. The distinctions he had formally drawn between these three modes of knowledge remained as sharp as ever.

[84] This has been the usual interpretation of his *Dialogue of the Common Laws.*

We can now see that Hobbes's religious heterodoxy[85] is of a fideist-sceptical kind, very characteristic of its age, but not to be confused with the deist rationalism of the next century. He found himself faced by scholastics who invested both God and reality with timeless attributes or essences which could be rationally known, and by saints and enthusiasts who affirmed the existence of a world of spirit, operating within time, but giving the time-dwelling individual opportunity of direct contact with the eternal. Both positions seemed to him philosophically absurd because they intruded unreal entities upon the understanding, and politically dangerous because they intruded unreal forms of authority upon the government. In reply he asserted a radically nominalist theology, entailing a God of whom nothing could be known except his existence and his infinite power, and rehearsed the great rhythms of the Way of Negation[86] in order to dismiss the God of Greek and scholastic philosophy in favour of a purely Hebrew I AM. It may be that such a God, however much we may stress his simplicity and eternity, is condemned to exist within time, since if we can know nothing of his attributes we can apprehend him solely through his acts; when Bramhall reaffirmed the scholastic doctrine of the *nunc-stans* or eternal now, Hobbes replied that he could attach no meaning whatever to this concept. But in addition there was available, and was just then at the peak of its importance in English thought, an alternative rhetoric of God, in which affirmations concerning him were made not as philosophical attributions, but as historical statements, and he was shown not as exerting a timeless intelligibility, but as affirming his relation to a peculiar people, who could be located only in history, with the result that his acts concerning them must be located there too. Hobbes embraced the concept of the Judeo-Christian elect with the effect of confining the known and positive God within history and still more drastically separating the spheres of reason and faith; a consequence was that when the 'mortal god' of political science entered the domain of faith and history, the power he exercised did not amount to a power to change or annul it.

[85] Glover (in Brown, *Hobbes Studies*, n. 24, above) has argued the case for a good deal of orthodoxy in his thought as well.

[86] *Leviathan*, ii, 31 (Oakeshott, pp. 237–8).

If a God of history could be effectively employed in answer to the God of the schoolmen, he had become a paradigm for the saints and enthusiasts, who employed revelation and apocalypse as means of asserting their immediate spiritual links with him. Hobbes employed both materialist and nominalist weapons to destroy the concept of spirit altogether and leave our contact with God confined to knowledge of his words, and the content of those words virtually confined to acts and affirmations of his power. Experience of God was conceivable only in the past and the future, the two times of the existence of his civil kingdom. To orthodox Christians this seemed, understandably and perhaps rightly, incompatible both with Christian faith as they had received it and with the existence of God as they considered they believed in him. But we cannot conclude that it was Hobbes's intention to affirm God's non-existence. He was simply denying that faith could affirm the existence of any but a God of history, and the more he repeated that denial the more he affirmed that God's reality; he was left with the irreducible concept of a God whose being was power, who was believed to have exerted power in the past and to have promised that he would return to exert power in the future, and with a conceptual system that included belief and historical authorities and from which he made no attempt to eliminate them. Having used apocalyptic against the scholastics, he could not eliminate it by further secularization; for if apocalyptic is a device for drawing God back into time, and if secularization is defined as the affirmation of the supremacy of time, then we need more than secularization to destroy apocalyptic. We need the replacement of belief by something else. Hobbes made no attempt to effect such a substitution. He treated belief with epistemological and brutal literalness, but the result was to leave intact the structure of historical authority towards which belief was directed. That structure included a future and an eschatology, and so Hobbes remained—inescapably but with no sign of a will to escape on his part—the author of two prophetic books.

The scheme of God's words and acts in time constitutes sacred history, but the stages by which the word and belief in it have been transmitted through time constitute what may be termed Christian history. This is a history of social communications and social structures, and the sensitivity to the variety of verbal and linguistic communication, characteristic both of late-Renaissance scholarship and of Hobbes's philosophy, makes him sharply aware of it. The history of belief includes both the processes by which the books of Scripture were written, disseminated, authorized and made canonical, and the processes by which Christian communities became coterminous with civil societies and the mechanisms of belief coterminous with the mechanisms of public law. There is another branch of history to which Hobbes's discoursing of religion commits him, and this is a history of error and perversion. He adopted what was long to remain the standard Protestant position that the greater part of the history of the Church consisted of Papal usurpation and its accompanying superstitions. Any polemicist who desires to reject as illegitimate the greater part of an existing and traditional order faces two simultaneous necessities, one for a necessarily somewhat anti-historical account of how things ought to be, the other for a necessarily non-normative account of how they came to be as they deplorably are; and this should warn us against being naïvely surprised when we find historical and unhistorical thinking together in such a man's works.[87] To Hobbes the Papal Church, and in no small measure the Anglican and Presbyterian Churches, all of which seemed to claim a civil authority apart from that of the civil sovereign, were prime examples of that which ought not to be but nevertheless was; and he set himself to explain the divagations from the norm which alone could account for their existence. As regards the Papal Church, there was available a well-established means of doing so. The apocalyptic history prevalent in most Protestant countries, and developed in England chiefly by John Foxe, confidently explained the rise and predicted the downfall of Roman authority by attributing it to the operations of Antichrist, a malign spiritual being operating through time and involved in the eschatology of the Book of Revelation and the subsequent commentaries thereon. This mode of explanation involved intensive reliance on allegory, typology, numerology and the rest of the apparatus of prophetic interpretation. Hobbes had no liking for

[87] I have tried to state this in greater theoretical completeness in the essay in *Politics and Experience* referred to in n. 11, above.

such intellectual pursuits; he preferred to take his metaphors singly; and, what was of far greater significance, he had carried his antipathy to talk of 'spirit' and 'spirits' to the point of denying the Devil and all his angels.[88] Apocalyptic for him was a verbal, not a spiritual mystery: not a matter of unveiling the esoteric history of the universe, but one of discovering what God had said he would do. It could therefore contain no account of what might have been done contrary to God's revealed will for mankind; and Hobbes's account of 'the kingdom of darkness', the matter of the fourth book of *Leviathan*, rests formally on his express denial that the Pope is to be in any sense identified with Antichrist. This being is indeed mentioned in Scripture, but as one who shall come claiming falsely to be the returning Christ; and however many and various the false claims of the Pope, he has never asserted anything like that.[89] Exegesis is used to destroy mystical interpretation, and the illegitimate authority of Rome is reduced at one blow from the status of spiritual iniquity to that of intellectual error and deception. But the causes of error can be discovered where the mysteries of iniquity cannot, and the way is now open for Hobbes to study the Papal usurpation as a historical phenomenon. It is plain, however, that the explanations he provides originate in the need to provide substitutes for the mystical interpretations of traditional Protestant apocalyptic. The elaborate witticisms in which the Papacy is presented as a 'kingdom of fairies'[90]—of unreal essences and authorities—do no more than erect substitutes for the rhetoric in which it appeared the kingdom of Satan and Antichrist, the Beast and the Whore; and the description of the Church as the 'ghost' of the Empire, 'sitting crowned upon the grave thereof', is both a superb historical image and a piece of secularized apocalyptic—the new Babylon arisen in place of the old and sitting upon seven hills.

[88] *Leviathan*, i, 8 (Oakeshott, pp. 50–1); iii, 34 (Oakeshott, p. 263); iii, 38 (Oakeshott, pp. 298–9); iv, 44 (Oakeshott, p. 397); iv, 45 (Oakeshott, pp. 421–2).

[89] *Ibid.*, iii, 42 (Oakeshott, pp. 364–5). Hobbes's point helps to explain the savagery of the punishments inflicted on James Nayler, who did apparently claim to be Christ.

[90] *Ibid.*, iv, 47 (Oakeshott, pp. 457–8).

The history of error, which in Hobbes takes the place of Protestant apocalyptic history, records the temporary triumph[91] of priestcraft and Gentilism. The former rests on the false assertion that the Church, in some presently constituted form, is or represents the kingdom of God spoken in the Scriptures; on this are based the claims of presbyters, bishops, and above all the Pope, to exercise authority *jure divino* or *Dei gratia*—that is, to derive it from God without the intervention of the civil sovereign. While Hobbes consistently regards Papalism as the paradigmatic and most dangerous instance of this claim, and spends more time refuting it than any other,[92] he includes in his condemnation Laudian bishops,[93] Geneva presbyters[94] and, though only by implication, self-appointed prophets and visible saints; and out of all these he builds up a history of spiritual usurpation that cannot have been read with any pleasure by the dispossessed bishops of the Interregnum. First presbyters, then bishops and finally the Bishop of Rome asserted in the first Christian centuries claims to exercise authority direct from God; and in recent English history these 'knots' upon Christian 'liberty'[95] have been untied in the reverse order to that in which they were tied up—the Papal power having been destroyed by Queen Elizabeth, that of the bishops who still claimed authority *jure divino* by the presbyterians, and lastly that of the presbyterians by an agency Hobbes does not identify:

> . . . and so we are reduced to the independency of the primitive Christians, to follow Paul, or Cephas, or

[91] *Ibid.*, iv, 46 (Oakeshott, p. 435): 'old empty bottles of Gentilism, which the doctors of the Roman Church, either by negligence or ambition, have filled up again with the new wine of Christianity, that will not fail in time to break them'.

[92] There is no Protestant counterpart to the two long refutations of Bellarmine: *Leviathan*, iii, 42 (Oakeshott, pp. 361–83); iv, 44 (Oakeshott, pp. 405–18).

[93] The references are not specific, but are to bishops claiming *jure divino* authority. E.g. *Leviathan*, iii, 42 (Oakeshott, p. 357). Hobbes's thinking here may be compared with that of Prynne; Lamont, *op. cit.*

[94] See the critique of Beza in *Leviathan*, iv, 44 (Oakeshott, pp. 406–7).

[95] Hobbes is speaking of 'Christian liberty' in the severely orthodox Protestant sense.

> Apollos, every man as he liketh best; which, if it be without contention, and without measuring the doctrine of Christ by our affection to the person of his minister (the fault which the apostle reprehended in the Corinthians), is perhaps the best . . . there ought to be no power over the consciences of men but of the Word itself, working faith in every one, not always according to the purpose of them that plant and water, but of God himself that giveth the increase.[96]

Hobbes at this moment would have been content—as one suspects the majority of Englishmen would in 1651—with a system of independent congregations under civil rule, no less than with bishops who claimed only a *jure humano* authority, and there is a relationship between this ecclesiological position and the heightening of interest in apocalyptic observable in *Leviathan*. He would not feel that this progressive undoing of the chains of spiritual usurpation presaged the imminent return of Christ, because he did not hold that even faith enabled one to predict one event from another; prophecy enjoined us to expect, but did not empower us to presage. But he had written at length about apocalyptic because this was a necessary means of destroying the spiritual usurpations that England seemed to be overcoming at the end of the Civil Wars; and he was now in a position to argue that the fallacy of spiritual jurisdiction rested on a confusion of the timeless with time. He could not accuse the ecclesiastics (even the saints) of contending that Christ in his kingdom had come again; the Papacy was not Antichrist; but he could accuse them of confounding, in his terms, the 'kingdom of grace' with the 'kingdom of glory',[97] of supposing that because a kingdom was promised for the future they could exercise in the present an authority which could only exist when the kingdom was restored. To make such a claim was to contend that the kingdom existed outside time and that they were its lieutenants within time—to repeat in another form the error of the *nunc-stans*. There was a considerable affinity

[96] *Leviathan*, iv, 47 (Oakeshott, pp. 455–6).

[97] *Ibid.*, iii, 35 (Oakeshott, p. 270); iii, 42 (Oakeshott, p. 329); iv, 44 (Oakeshott, p. 399); iv, 47 (Oakeshott, p. 451).

between this and the error of believing in the doctrine of separated essences, which provides the second theme of the history of the Kingdom of Darkness.

This theme is the history of the importation into the revelation of the true God of the errors of the 'Gentiles'—a term to all intents and purposes interchangeable with 'Greeks and Romans'.[98] The Gentiles, being ignorant of the physical processes of vision, took things which they imagined they saw for gods and disembodied spirits;[99] and later, being equally ignorant of the mental processes of the formation of ideas, took the words which they coined in excessive profusion for the names of real entities.[100] In this way was built up the kingdom of darkness, an empire of 'insignificant speech' in which men were ruled by imaginary entities, bodiless and independent of space and time, manipulated by ecclesiastics to provide themselves with spiritual authority: a kingdom of spirits, then, maintained by superstition and scholasticism; a kingdom of ghosts which can only be compared to the kingdom of fairies supposed by folk-imagination to exist as an invisible double of our world, coterminous with it. All this is the result of the importation of Greek thought and mental habit into the revelation made by God to the Jews and Christians. Hobbes's hatred of the contemporary universities is very largely a hatred of the Greek heritage which he saw them as carrying on, and which he saw as the foundation of the ecclesiastical conspiracy against civil authority and society.

Set in a different context, of course, this feature of Hobbes's thought appears as the 'new philosophy' in revolt against the old, a Galilean and Cartesian rejection of Aristotelianism. But in the context in which it occurs, it depicts Hellenic superstition in opposition to, and as encroaching upon, the prophetic religion of Moses and Christ. One would like to know more about Hobbes's ideas of the historic relation between false philosophy, prophecy and true philosophy. Did the fact that God had revealed himself to the Jews and first Christians as acting and speaking words in

98 See the account of 'Gentile' religion in *Leviathan*, i, 12 (Oakeshott, pp. 73–6).

99 *Ibid.*, i, 12 (Oakeshott, p. 71); iv, 45 (Oakeshott, pp. 418–19).

100 *Ibid.*, iv, 46 (Oakeshott, pp. 435–7).

time help save them from conceiving the erroneous belief in separated essences, which was only communicated to them by 'contagion' from the Hellenized Jews of the Diaspora, the Hellenic and Hellenistic converts of the post-Pauline era?[101] Or was the true revelation helpless to resist false philosophy until the true philosophy had been independently arrived at? Hobbes's need to construct a historical dimension to his thought does not carry him to the construction of answers to these questions. It is plain, however, that he most rigorously separated the Hellenic from the Hebraic components of his cultural tradition and went further than any major philosopher since Augustine in rejecting the former and relying upon the latter. In this he must be most sharply separated from the English and French political deists of the next century, the lineage of Toland and Voltaire—classicists to a man, who sought to reduce the God of prophecy to a theorem in philosophy and, as Hobbes would certainly have predicted, put forward predominantly republican theories of politics in so doing. Hobbes was not of the opinion that Christianity was 'reasonable' or 'not mysterious', though he defined 'mystery' with a razor as sharp as Ockham's and a good deal more recklessly wielded. The Christian mystery to him was the belief that God had spoken in history and had said that he would return in time. The God of prophecy and history was the only God of whom Hobbes would speak; the God of faith was the only God compatible with his political system.

[101] *Ibid.* (Oakeshott, pp. 419–20, 423, 430–5).

Seven

On the Historical Singularity of the Scientific Revolution of the Seventeenth Century

by

A. Rupert Hall

Since that revolution overturned the authority in science not only of the Middle Ages but of the ancient world—since it ended not only in the eclipse of scholastic philosophy but in the destruction of Aristotelian physics—it outshines everything since the rise of Christianity and reduces the Renaissance and Reformation to the rank of mere episodes, mere internal displacements within the system of medieval Christendom.

Herbert Butterfield, *The Origins of Modern Science, 1300–1800* (London, 1949), p. viii

Even before the seventeenth century ended it was becoming customary to contrast the slow progress of scientific knowledge after its inception among the Ancients, with the profound and swiftly-succeeding achievements of the Moderns since the 'revival of learning'. No reader of William Wotton's *Reflections upon Ancient and Modern Learning* (1694) could doubt where the superiority lay, despite Wotton's tactful insistence that the fabric of knowledge created by the Moderns was itself a noble 'Monument to the Memory of *Archimedes* and *Diophantus*, of *Hippocrates* and *Aristotle*, of *Herophilus* and *Galen*, by building upon their Discovery's and Improving of their Inventions'.[1] The French Academy was no less on the side of modernity than the Royal Society; in Fontenelle's words, 'les Sciences ne font que de naître, soit parce que chez les Anciens elles ne pouvoient être encore qu'assez imparfaites, soit parce que nous en avons presque entierement perdu les traces pendant les longues ténèbres de la Barbarie, soit parce qu'on ne s'est mis sur les bonnes voies que depuis environ un siècle'.[2] Thus early, too, Fontenelle and Wotton expressed the fear that the seventeenth-century age of giants must draw to a close, especially as satire and ridicule have made science their butt. In fact, of course, neither Temple's

[1] William Wotton, *Reflections upon Ancient and Modern Learning* (3rd ed., London, 1705), p. 394. See in general R. F. Jones, *Ancients and Moderns* (St Louis, 1936).

[2] B. le B. de Fontenelle, *Histoire du Renouvellement de l'Académie Royale des Sciences . . . Et les Eloges historiques* (Amsterdam, 1709), pp. 22–3.

learning nor Swift's irony weakened the eighteenth-century's complacent confidence in its learning and science, as in its art and taste; but there was no second Newton, and so there is a certain nostalgia about the sentence with which Montucla opens the second volume of his *Histoire des Mathématiques* (1758): 'Parmi les siècles qui ont successivement contribué à l'avancement des Sciences celui qui vient de s'écouler doit sans doute tenir jusqu' ici le premier rang, & cet avantage ne lui sera probablement ravi par aucun de ceux qui le suivront.'

The scientific revolution that was already passing into history had itself by no means lacked historical consciousness. While indebtedness to scholastic subtlety was scarcely ever avowed by its leaders—one finds no trace of medieval debates about the possible motion of the earth in Copernicus and no explicit allusions to medieval kinematics in Galileo—inspiration rather than authoritative precedent was drawn from the Greeks. Not to insist upon Copernicus's open statement of the Pythagoreans' precedence (so well known that he was not infrequently stated even by his best supporters to have 'revived' their hypothesis), or Galileo's frequent invocations of Archimedes, or Harvey's Aristotelianism, there was a still more striking recognition of the *prisci theologi* by Newton and his followers. In the words of J. T. Desaguliers, 'The System of the Universe, as taught by Pythagoras, Philolaus, and others of the Ancients, is the same, which was since reviv'd by Copernicus, allow'd by all the unprejudic'd of the Moderns, and at last demonstrated by Sir Isaac Newton.'[3] No one in the seventeenth century could feel quite certain that science was treading wholly new paths, rather than retreading an old course. Yet, on the other hand, though the notion of a past Golden Age must entail a subsequent decline, there was an uneasy admission that so far as techniques were concerned, the barbaric Middle Ages had seen the appearance of the ocean-going sailing-ship and its magnetic compass, of the windmill, of gunpowder, of paper and printing.

[3] J. T. Desaguliers, *The Newtonian System of the World the Best Model of Government: An Allegorical Poem* [written on the accession of George II] (Westminster, 1728), p. 2n. See in general J. E. McGuire and P. M. Rattansi, 'Newton and the "Pipes of Pan"', *Notes and Records of the Royal Society*, xxi (1966), 108–43.

If, as Bacon held, there was a relation between scientific originality and technical ingenuity, the theory of barbarism must look a bit thin.[4]

These complexities, however, were hardly important enough to modify the conventional historical judgment that natural science had been virtually re-created by the seventeenth century. When William Whewell came to compose his *History of the Inductive Sciences*, though he could write (of Leonardo da Vinci) that 'both the heliocentric doctrine and [the] truths of mechanics were fermenting in the minds of intelligent men, and gradually assuming clearness and strength, some time before they were publicly asserted', he had no doubt of a 'mental declension' produced by an obscurantist religion causing 'the almost complete blank which the history of physical science offers, from the decline of the Roman Empire, for a thousand years'. Only in the seventeenth century arrived 'the grand completion of the history of the most ancient and prosperous province of human knowledge'.[5] One might have supposed that, a little later in the nineteenth century, the final collapse of the fluid theory of heat (following on the previous downfall of the phlogiston concept) would have suggested the notion that even modern science was not necessarily infallible, especially as the great Newton's speculations about the nature of light were now known to have been mistaken. However, positivist preconceptions ensured the prevalence of the alternative historical explanation that these false theories were really mere aberrations, speculative deviations from the true inductive line of progress, a view borne out by the stability of the empirical and mathematical parts of Newton's optics.[6] Indeed, it was feasible to see the relatively late ascendancy of inductive methods and

[4] For the inventions see Stradanus, *Nova reperta* (*c.* 1590). 'Modern' is obviously always a conveniently elastic term. On the Chinese contribution see Isaac Vossius, *Variarum observationum liber* (London, 1685).

[5] William Whewell, *History of the Inductive Sciences* (London and Cambridge, 1837), ii, 123; i, 355; ii, 127.

[6] Actually such a positivist 'defence' of Newton was but half-successful, since Newton had failed both experimentally and mathematically to cope with those difficult phenomena of light with which the wave theory succeeded; but then these phenomena were only incidental to a treatment of light that was adequate in the seventeenth-century context, though not in the nineteenth.

positive knowledge in such sciences as chemistry, heat or geology as produced by the strong forces of conservatism, in turn delaying the full 'modernization' of these branches of science.

It was not until the late nineteenth or indeed the twentieth century that the inconsistencies latent in the orthodox historiography were properly explored, and the great body of neglected evidence submitted to honest examination. The causes of this fresh interest were varied. The powerful historicism of the late nineteenth century must be reckoned among them, as well as an anxiety (created by the specialization and expansion of science itself) to prove that the study of Nature was indeed a culture. Marcellin Berthelot, Raffaello Caverni, Emil Wohlwill and Pierre Duhem in the physical sciences, Karl Sudhoff and others in medicine, followed by Sarton, Singer, Thorndike and many more went back to the medieval sources, both Arabic and Latin.[7] The earlier concentration was on alchemy, medicine, and mechanics; medieval astronomy and optics came in for attention rather later.[8] From the early work, in which the most important historiographical influence was that of Duhem, three chief conclusions emerged: (1) the discussions of scientific questions in the Middle Ages were not wholly or even largely trivial or obtuse; (2) certain features or statements of 'classical' science had been anticipated in the Middle Ages; (3) there was a discernible continuity of thought extending from medieval philosophy and science into the beginnings of the scientific revolution itself.

Obviously, irrespective of the accuracy or otherwise of each of these conclusions, the first and second are more readily capable of historical verification than the last. Half a century's further effort, in which medieval texts have been elaborately surveyed, edited, and translated, has put them beyond reasonable doubt. The

[7] Chiefly, at first, those available in print. Exploration of manuscript archives had hardly begun before 1914; some medievalists (like Duhem and Sarton) relied wholly on books in print. In this respect the historians of Greek science, especially those of the German school such as Heiberg, were still far ahead, technically, of their medievalist colleagues.

[8] Even in 1906 the treatment of medieval astronomy in J. L. E. Dreyer's *History of Planetary Theories from Thales to Kepler* was inadequate; the 'Arabians' came off best.

virtually axiomatic belief of almost three centuries after Francis Bacon that medieval philosophy was meaningless verbiage is no longer held; we now know that medieval men were exacting, even adventurous, in their attempts to confirm and apply their intellectual inheritance. We know too that, in a few respects, through their critical appraisal and attention to phenomena, they formulated propositions whose real significance was understood much later. But whether or not such historical re-evaluations of medieval science also entail the replacement of the scientific revolution by a gradual process of change is another question. It is possibly not altogether a historical question. For, apart from interpretation of the historical evidence in this particular case, there seems to be good reason to believe that the rejection of conceptions long firmly held, justified by reason and even sanctified by religion, and their replacement by antithetic ones, must normally be a sudden and even violent process. Where the inertial mass is large, and the applied force becomes great, change can only occur through a crisis.

Pierre Duhem, however, threw his influence wholly in favour of gradualism—or, rather, of the overthrow of Aristotelianism by the philosophers of the thirteenth century: 'c'est alors', he wrote, 'que l'on déclare possibles, en dépit du Philosophe [Aristotle] et de son Commentateur [Simplicius] le mouvement de la Terre, la pluralité des Mondes, le vide, la grandeur infinie'.[9] From that point the triumph of the seventeenth century had slowly matured. 'Non plus que la Nature, la Science ne fait point de saut brusque.'[10] In his earlier work, convincing himself that Leonardo da Vinci was the sole vehicle by which the innovations of the fourteenth century had been transmitted to the sixteenth,[11] Duhem imagined that after nominalist philosophy had become outworn and exhausted in Paris and Oxford, it drew in the universities of Bologna and Padua fresh strength from the reviving knowledge of Greek geometry. Thus, 'Léonard de Vinci résume et condense, pour ainsi dire, en sa personne, tout le conflit

[9] Pierre Duhem, *Etudes sur Léonard de Vinci: Ceux qu'il a lus et ceux qui l'ont lu* (Paris, 1909), ii, *Avant-propos.*

[10] *Ibid.* (Paris, 1906), i, 156. This was possibly an unfortunate remark.

[11] See, for example, *ibid.* (Paris, 1906), i, 123.

intellectuel par lequel la Renaissance Italienne va devenir l'heritière de la Scholastique Parisienne.'[12] Later, in studying kinematics, he was impressed by the Aristotelian reaction and 'superstitious archaism' of the Renaissance, delaying the fruition of medieval mechanics to the time of Galileo. But to see the beginnings of modern mechanics with Galileo and his contemporaries as a genuine creation was, Duhem argued, an historical error; there was no swift triumph of modern science over medieval error; one sees rather the victory of the science born in Paris in the fourteenth century over the doctrines of Aristotle and Averroës honoured by the Italian Renaissance.[13]

Subsequent criticism has modified the status of the fourteenth-century nominalists from that of 'creators' of modern science to that of 'precursors'.[14] While it is difficult to express this idea with

[12] *Ibid.* (Paris, 1909), ii, *Avant-propos.*

[13] Just as Duhem's views of the Italian Renaissance altered, so did his conception of the medieval crisis. In the last volume of these *Etudes* he wrote: 'Si l'on voulait, par une ligne précise, séparer le règne de la Science antique du règne de la Science moderne, il la faudrait tracer, croyons-nous, à l'instant où Jean Buridan a concu cette théorie [that God imparted an initial *impetus* giving the Universe eternal motion], à l'instant où l'on a cessé de regarder les astres comme mus par des êtres divins, où l'on a admis que les mouvements célèstes et les mouvements sublunaires dépendaient d'une même Mécanique', *ibid.* (Paris, 1913), iii, vi, ix.

[14] See Marshall Clagett, *The Science of Mechanics in the Middle Ages* (Madison-London, 1959). Apart from Professor Clagett and his associates, the main scholar in this field is Dr Anneliese Maier, who was the first to challenge, on the basis of extensive reading in the manuscripts, the exaggerated claims of Duhem. His contemporary, Paul Tannery, though well apprised of the researches of Wohlwill and Duhem, continued to regard modern science as the product of an intellectual transformation; his notes for a course of lectures on the history of science in the first half of the seventeenth century run: 'Lutte definitive contre l'enseignement scholastique—introduction d'une nouvelle conception rationelle et générale de la nature—Triomphe de la physique corpusculaire' (*Memoires Scientifiques* (Paris, 1930), x, 7). See also his papers on 'Descartes physicien' (1896) and 'Galilée et les principes de la dynamique' (1901) (*ibid.* (Paris, 1926), vi, 305–19, 387–413). I cannot find that Tannery wrote of a 'scientific revolution'. Erik Nordenskiöld (*c.* 1920) referred to the 'complete revolution of the aims and methods of natural science . . . carried out by Galileo' (*The History of Biology*, tr. L. B. Eyre, 1928 (New

precision, most historians of science nowadays would agree that 'modern science was not suddenly born with Galileo, but rather emerged about that time after a long period of incubation', or with Herbert Butterfield that the scientific revolution reached 'back in an unmistakably continuous line to a period much earlier' than the Renaissance, without denying that a real intellectual revolution took place.[15] No one now supposes that, in mechanics, the medieval concepts of inertia and acceleration were identical with those formulated in the seventeenth century, or that the world-view of Oresme was identical with that of Newton; rather, the recent view maintains that there were varying degrees of analogy between the two. Consequently, no historian would now argue that seventeenth-century science was a mere reformulation of that of the fourteenth. For example, it is now recognized that many of the more adventurous notions of the high Middle Ages were never advanced as true, or even credible. No one before Copernicus believed that in physical and theological reality the earth moves. As Dr Edward Grant has pointed out, Copernicus's acceptance of this motion as a reality was a result of 'his conception of the function and role of an hypothesis', which itself entailed so great an epistemological revolution that it marks Copernicus's 'drastic departure from the scholastic tradition almost as much as his new cosmological system'.[16] Like E. A. Burtt (1925), like Herbert Butterfield (1949), and indeed like many other historians, Dr

[15] Stillman Drake, 'Mathematics, Astronomy and Physics in the Work of Galileo', in Charles S. Singleton (ed.), *Art, Science and History in the Renaissance* (Baltimore, 1968), p. 305; H. Butterfield, *The Origins of Modern Science, 1300–1800* (London, 1949), p. viii.

[16] Edward Grant, 'Late Medieval Thought, Copernicus, and the Scientific Revolution', *Journal of the History of Ideas*, xxiii (1962), 197.

York, 1946), p. 91). Abraham Wolf echoed Kant in giving the title 'The Copernican Revolution' to one of his chapters (1935). At about the same time R. G. Collingwood declared that it was Galileo who brought the modern science of Nature to maturity, and added: 'this new physical science was recognized on all hands as a genuine and secure possession of the human intellect, perhaps the greatest and most secure advance made by human knowledge since the Greeks invented mathematics' (*The Idea of Nature* (Oxford, 1945), 1961 ed., pp. 103, 112). Koyré began to speak of the 'scientific revolution' in the late 1930s.

Grant emphasizes the importance of the scientific revolution, not as the sum of particular scientific propositions, but as a total modification of what Collingwood called the 'idea of nature'—that is, an *a priori* redefinition of the objects of philosophical and scientific inquiry.

In 1953 the scholastic contribution towards the scientific revolution was stated afresh by Dr A. C. Crombie in an important book which emphasized the medieval approximation towards experimental method, exemplified rather by optics than mechanics. *Robert Grosseteste and the Origins of Experimental Science* asserted the case for gradualism against the traditional concept of the scientific revolution in strong terms, in that it seemed to be maintaining (in parallel to Duhem) the *identity* of medieval empiricism with that of the seventeenth century, and the *identity* of medieval optical theory at its height with that of Descartes. Dr Crombie seemed almost prepared to claim, with Duhem, that the seventeenth century had only to pick up where the fourteenth century had left off. In his subsequent writings, however, Crombie's views appear in a softer form; while marshalling in a telling way the evidence for gradualism (in 1969 hardly longer in dispute), and claiming what is no more than just, that medieval science was neither trivial nor without succession, Crombie has made it clear that, nevertheless, the scientific revolution did occur as the climax to a more tentative process of change and development.[17]

The historiography of *Robert Grosseteste and the Origins of Experimental Science* did not pass without criticism, on the one hand from those who have doubted whether the medieval contributions to optics discussed by Crombie were as advanced, or as influential, as the author supposed; and by those who hold (contrary, of course, to what one might call the old English tradition) that experimenting did not provide the sole, or perhaps even the major, entrance to the new world of science.[18] Probably

[17] See his contributions to Marshall Clagett (ed.), *Critical Problems in the History of Science* (Madison, 1959), pp. 70–2, 79–101; and in K. F. Drew and F. S. Lear (eds.), *Perspectives in Medieval History* (Chicago, 1963), pp. 35–57.

[18] See Carl B. Boyer, *The Rainbow: from Myth to Mathematics* (New York and

there can hardly be more question of Descartes's 'copying' from Theodoric of Freiberg than of Galileo's 'copying' from Nicole Oresme. It is more important that during the last twenty years historians of science and technology have demonstrated, beyond dispute, that in the later Middle Ages rich and fertile capacities for innovation were at work. This was no period of sterile abstraction. On the contrary, it was a time of acquisition, transmission, assimilation and experiment. Whatever is to be said of the period between the fifth century and the twelfth—in which the historian of science at any rate can as yet claim no major accomplishment[19] —when taking a general view over several centuries from the twelfth onwards it is difficult not to perceive amid all vicissitudes a continuing extension of civilization and intellect. In this historical process the maturity of scholasticism appears as a plateau, the scientific revolution as another sharp, upwards slope.

If medieval studies have, in the end, left the concept of the unique scientific revolution in the seventeenth century relatively unscathed, though rendering its occurrence less abrupt, another kind of historiography would destroy its historical character by assimilating it into a succession of such events. Whereas all participants in the older argument agreed (roughly) that there was something called 'modern science' that came into existence, either swiftly or gradually, over a definable stretch of time, in basic outline the new interpretation sees nothing but periods of relative quiescence within which ideas on any topic remain constant, separated by shorter intervals of rapid transition from one 'paradigm' to another. The argument requires the following moves to be made: firstly, the series of historical events embraced under the term 'scientific revolution' are fragmented into the Vesalian revolution, the Copernican revolution, the Harveian revolution, the Galilean revolution, and so on, as a series of discrete episodes;

[19] That technology underwent vital improvements in these early centuries as well as later is argued by Lynn White, Jnr, in *Medieval Technology and Social Change* (Oxford, 1962).

London, 1959), and Alexandre Koyré, 'Les Origines de la Science Moderne', *Diogene*, 16 (Paris, 1956), reprinted in *Etudes d'Histoire et de la Pensée Scientifique* (Paris, 1966), pp. 48–72.

secondly, it is to be recognized that 'revolutions' (of sometimes greater effect) have occurred in the eighteenth century and later, linked with the names of Lavoisier, Young-Fresnel, Darwin, Joule-Clausius, Faraday-Maxwell, Einstein, Planck, and so forth. Finally, it is argued that science is not concerned with a search for reality, but rather (to use a convenient phrase) with 'probable stories'; the scientist at any period of history (including the present, of course) cannot say whether or not any particular proposition corresponds to the real structure of the Universe, but can only explain why this proposition seems more credible than others and how it is consonant with all or most of the relevant data. As the reasons for finding any particular proposition acceptable vary, and the data change, so do scientific propositions.[20]

These revisions of the conventional historiography of science are salutary in several respects. They remind us that chemistry, geology, the biological sciences, did not assume a 'classical' form in the seventeenth century, as mechanics did; and that 'classical' mechanics was itself but an episode in the history of science. They draw attention, too, to the Whiggism of a historical narrative directed solely to tracing the lines along which the 'classical' forms of the sciences were evolved. If these 'classical' forms are no more than intermediates between Greek science and recent science (as represented by relativistic cosmology, quantum mechanics and molecular biology) then the scientific revolution can hardly be described as bringing in modern science.[21]

Nevertheless, the scientific revolution seems to remain as an historical reality. It refuses to dissolve into fragments, nor is modern science (1500–1900) so episodic as the analysis suggests. In the Renaissance period particularly there was an unbroken and inter-

[20] This paragraph attempts to epitomize, so far as I understand them, the views of Thomas S. Kuhn (*The Structure of Scientific Revolutions*, Chicago, 1962, and other writings), and other recent exponents of relativist history; see Gerd Buchdahl, 'A Revolution in Historiography of Science', *History of Science*, iv (1965), 55–69. Professor Kuhn's historiography is also noteworthy for its reintroduction of the idea of cyclic patterns in the historical process.

[21] In other words, the scientific revolution was *not* a once-for-all positive event in history; science (according to this view) has changed no less in the twentieth century than in the seventeenth.

locking series of new discoveries combined with changes in ideas, and it is quite arbitrary to resolve this into chapters concerned with discrete problems. The Copernican issue was still unsettled—indeed, the conservative view was still ascendant—when it was modified by the new physical interpretations of the Universe put forward by Tycho Brahe and Galileo, and given a fresh twist by Kepler; it was still unsettled when Galileo and Descartes (in their several ways) set this cosmological debate in a mechanical context. That early seventeenth-century interest in the science of mechanics was integrally related to the problems of the earth's movement or rest is obvious, Galileo's *Dialogue on the Two Chief Systems of the World* (1632) being the *locus classicus.* It would be trivial to point out how all this meshed with the development of pure mathematics, of optics and scientific instruments, and of experimental physics to become negatively an attack on the whole of scholastic philosophy, and positively a universal front of investigation into Nature. Newton (mathematician, experimental physicist, theoretician) did not inherit two or three half-solved problems from his predecessors, but an evolving physical science that was in a state of flux at every point. Again, the scientific revolution was united by deeper and by now well-known intellectual characteristics that appear as common elements in many individuals and varied researches. Apart from a virtually ubiquitous contempt for argument about terms and mere book-learning that led many men to emphasize the empirical foundations of knowledge;[22] apart from the frequent distinction drawn between primary and secondary qualities and, still more, the prevalence of the 'mechanical philosophy'; and apart from the fundamental conception that Nature is 'everywhere uniform and consonant to

[22] Henry Oldenburg, as Secretary to the Royal Society, in explaining its purposes, adopted an almost constant formula of this kind; see, for an early example, his letter to Hevelius of 18 February 1662/3 (A. Rupert Hall and Marie Boas Hall, *The Correspondence of Henry Oldenburg* (Madison, Milwaukee and London, 1966), ii, 25–8). The antischolastic empiricism of such apologists as Joseph Glanvill is well known. Huygens believed that the compilation of an experimental history of Nature 'à peu près suivant le dessein de Verulamius' should be the chief business of the Académie Royale des Sciences (Joseph Bertrand, *L'Académie des Sciences et les Académiciens de 1666 à 1793* (Paris, 1869), p. 9).

herself' (a conception that in itself destroyed the basis of Aristotelian science)—on all of which generalities physicists and biologists agreed—there was the mathematical analysis of phenomena which, in the opinion of Alexandre Koyré, constituted the core of the scientific revolution.

In 1939, in the first of his *Etudes Galiléenes*, Koyré made clear his commitment to the notion of a 'révolution scientifique du dix-septième siècle, profonde transformation intellectuelle dont la physique moderne, ou plus exactement classique, fut à la fois l'expression et le fruit', describing it as possibly the most important mutation in human thought since the Greek invention of the Cosmos. It was no matter of overthrowing insufficient or false theories [in discrete episodes], but of transforming 'les cadres de l'intelligence elle-même' in the replacement of one intellectual attitude, plausible enough, by another of far less plausible appearance. In particular, the scientific revolution involved a 'géométrisation de l'espace', a substitution for Aristotle's and Ptolemy's concrete cosmos of the abstract space of Euclid.[23] Over the years Koyré widened and intensified his conception that the crucial difference between the Greco-medieval and the classical concepts of physics was the latter's mathematicism. Galileo, he argued, was a Platonist, Kepler a Pythagorean, Descartes both a Platonist and a Pythagorean. Hence he insisted again and again that the changes that had brought classical science into being were neither socio-economic nor technological, nor concerned with the methodology of science (empirical or otherwise), but solely changes in the way the human mind reflected upon its natural environment.[24] He embraced the title of idealist with enthusiasm:

> Je crois, en effet (et si c'est là de *l'idéalisme*, je suis prêt à porter l'opprobre d'être un *idéaliste*) . . . que la science, celle de notre époque, comme celle des Grecs, est essentiellement *theoria*, recherche de la vérité, et que de ce fait elle a, et a

[23] Alexandre Koyré, *Etudes Galileennes* (*Actualités scientifiques et industrielles*, no. 852, Paris, 1939), i, 6–9; new issue (Paris, 1966), pp. 12–15.

[24] See the essay noted above, Note 18, and another on 'Galilée et la Revolution Scientifique' (in the same volume, pp. 176–92). Also in A. C. Crombie (ed.), *Scientific Change* (London: Heinemann, 1963), pp. 847–57.

> toujours eu une vie propre, une histoire immanente, et que c'est seulement en fonction de ses propres problèmes, de sa propre histoire qu'elle peut être comprise par ses historiens.[25]

And no student of Koyré's work can doubt that he regarded mathematical thinking as the supreme form of scientific thought.

Such an expression of the totality of intellectual change during the late Renaissance (which I find extremely convincing) compels an historian to see the scientific revolution as a great historical drama, which has its subplots and convolutions as all grand dramas do, one that works slowly towards the climax of accomplishment in the mid- to late seventeenth century. Yet to insist excessively on the role of mathematics (in the later stages of the scientific revolution particularly) may be to court the objection that the drama was partial; for if it concerned only the mathematical sciences, it could hardly have dominated the intellectual life of the age. But even the most idealist historian of science, it seems to me, need not so restrict a claim for the transcendent role of the scientific revolution, particularly in its later stages. The biological sciences were indeed transformed, though in them empiricism took the place of mathematics.[26] There is no contradiction here, for it is obvious that significant observation and experimentation are neither random, nor mechanical, nor undirected by ideas. On the contrary, it is certain that the mathematization of astronomy and optics could not have proceeded without observation and experiment, while in some aspects of physical science ideas of structure, organization and arrangement were more significant than ideas of number.[27] There was as it were a methodological spectrum in the scientific revolution, relating rather to height of achievement than to profundity of conceptual change, from the combination of weak empiricism with much

[25] Alexandre Koyré, *Etudes d'Histoire et de la Pensée Scientifique* (Paris, 1966), p. 360; the English version in *Scientific Change*, p. 856, is less emphatic.

[26] The late C. E. Raven strongly emphasized this point of view in his writings (e.g. *John Ray*, Cambridge, 1950) and took it to excess in his Gifford Lectures, *Natural Religion and Christian Theology* (Cambridge, 1953).

[27] See Cyril S. Smith and John G. Burke, *Atoms, Blacksmiths and Crystals* (Los Angeles, 1967).

mathematicism, to that of strong empiricism with little mathematics. In general, the importance of empiricism increased throughout the seventeenth century.

That there was a transformation of ideas concerning living things is borne out by the introduction of the concepts of biological mechanism and 'chemical physiology', by the abandonment of the Aristotelian theory of sexual reproduction and of spontaneous generation, by the rise of comparative anatomy, by the taking of the first steps towards a rational palaeontology and organized taxonomy, and by the results of the application of the microscope to histology (both plant and animal) as well as the parallel discovery of microscopic organisms. It is true that the grand organizing principles of modern biology, like those of modern chemistry, appeared only later. But this (only relative) insuccess is less important than the occurrence among some (not all) of the biologists, chemists and physiologists of attitudes to their work which were identical with those of their colleagues in physics. Moreover, some men (Kepler, Descartes, Charleton, Digby, Boyle, Hooke, Borelli, for example) were markedly active on both sides of the topical division; others (Willughby, Mariotte, Newton) slightly so.[28] The scientific societies, with the exception of the Accademia del Cimento, clearly behaved as though there was an active front of advance in the mainly descriptive parts of science just as in the mathematical, and saw no difference of principle between them. Men of accomplishment in biology (Perrault, Malpighi, Ray, Swammerdam, Steno, Lower, Leeuwenhoek, Tyson) were almost disproportionately praised for their industry in research, no less than for their ingenuity in interpretation. Evidently if any elements in the scientific revolution related to methodology, epistemology or metaphysics these elements affected attitudes to organic as well as inorganic nature, even though descriptive science inevitably emphasized empiricism rather than mathematicism.[29] The study of living things was,

[28] See (for one recent illustration of this argument) A. C. Crombie, 'The Mechanistic Hypothesis and the Scientific Study of Vision', in S. Bradbury and G. L'E. Turner (eds.), *Historical Aspects of Microscopy* (Cambridge, 1967).

[29] There are exceptions—for example, early notions about crystal structure.

however, very far from being wholly descriptive. Hence (as it seems to me) the attempt to reduce the historical significance of the scientific revolution by attaching to it a restrictive mathematical character would fail, on the evidence both that its universality was taken for granted by those who participated in it, and that changes in scientific thinking of a wholly non-mathematical type were analogous to those in the mathematical sciences.

In fact, of course, the analogy was deliberately pursued not only by the mechanistic physiologists (Descartes, Borelli, Croone, Willis, Sylvius) and by the iatromechanists, but by those in the eighteenth century who investigated electricity, chemistry, and the nature of heat. Whatever the originality of these investigations both experimentally and conceptually, to regard them as independent of the seventeenth-century scientific revolution or even of a parallel nature (as though Hales, Daniel Bernoulli, Black, Franklin, Haller or Lavoisier found their starting-point in out-of-date scholasticism) would be manifestly unhistorical. These men were all Boylists, Cartesians, Newtonians;[30] like Newton, they saw farther by standing on the shoulders of giants. It was, after all, from the physical scientists that chemists like Lavoisier had learned the model of science that they strove to emulate, the 'rigorous law' from which, he says, 'I have never deviated, of forming no conclusions which are not fully warranted by experiment, and of never supplying the absence of facts . . .'.[31] And a recent writer generalizes farther in declaring that 'if we are to gain a true appreciation of the ideas that increasingly underlay chemical theory as the eighteenth century progressed, it is to Newtonianism we must look'.[32] Priestley in his *History of Electricity* makes the

[30] This is particularly well brought out by I. Bernard Cohen in *Franklin and Newton* (Philadelphia, 1956) and by Amram Vartanian, *Diderot and Descartes* (Princeton, 1953).

[31] A. L. de Lavoisier, *Elements of Chemistry*, tr. R. Kerr (Edinburgh, 1790), pp. xix–xx. Lavoisier emphasizes his positive philosophy by elaborate quotations from Condorcet. My point here is not that Lavoisier was (in his own eyes) a positivist, but that his 'paradigm' was a positivist version of seventeenth-century physics.

[32] Arnold Thackray, 'Quantified Chemistry—the Newtonian Dream', in D. S. L. Cardwell (ed.), *John Dalton and the Progress of Science* (Manchester, 1968), p. 92.

point that though the enormous advances in that science since Newton's day would have astounded that great man, the seventeenth century's relative stagnation (after Gilbert) so far as electricity was concerned is to be attributed to its, and Newton's, preoccupation with other topics.[33] About the year 1800 few people doubted that all the physical sciences would follow much the same course as mechanics, optics and pneumatics at an earlier stage—an expectation borne out by the recently revealed analogies, as it then seemed, between the laws of electricity and magnetism and those of gravity.

It is perhaps less easy to show that the nineteenth-century 'revolution in biology' was in a similar way imitative of earlier achievement in different types of investigation, but continuity at least can be established. Not only did Buffon, in calculating the likely age of the earth, employ Newton's law of cooling and Stephen Hales extend seventeenth-century experimental pneumatics to the physiology of plants and animals, but there is evidently an unbroken (if not always distinguished) tradition stretching through the eighteenth century in microscopy, in the theory of animal heat, in research into reproduction. It is not belittling the originality of Darwin, Schleiden or Claude Bernard to recognize that all branches of biological knowledge were utterly different in 1800 from what they had been in 1500 (and I think one might add, in an obvious if indefinite sense, more 'scientific'); if this had not been so, the great nineteenth-century steps could hardly have been taken.

For what it is worth, the continuity and integrity of science are far more readily demonstrable in the years 1700–1850 (roughly) than in the period 1250–1550. Let it not be denied that a new age of scientific thought began about a century ago, with the almost simultaneous publication of Darwin's *Origin*, Clerk Maxwell's electromagnetic theory of light, and Mendel's studies of inheritance, with which the valency theory in chemistry, Bunsen and Kirchoff's work on spectroscopy, and the Maxwell-Boltzmann distribution-law were also closely contemporary. If it

[33] Joseph Priestley, *The History and Present State of Electricity*, 3rd ed. (London, 1785), i, xv, 32.

had ever really been the case that the Universe could seem rather simple and the tasks before science easily delimitable, this now rapidly ceased to be so. The historians of the scientific revolution cannot claim more for it than that it established 'classical' science, and to regard this as *the* type or essence of all science would clearly be an error. But that recent science has descended from 'classical' science is clear, and that is enough.

The question now remains: if the scientific revolution directed (or redirected) intellectual energy towards the comprehension of reality, was this—to put it crudely—an aberration that the recent philosophy of scientists has reversed? To take the last part of this question first, it seems to me that for a historian (at any rate) to be easily persuaded that recent science has not been concerned with realities, but only with figments, 'probable stories', or, as the Greeks said, 'saving the appearances' might be perilous. Taking for granted all the well-known limitations on the certainty of knowledge, the difference is that between the investigator who believes that there is a reality towards which scientific propositions may successively approximate, and one who regards these propositions as intellectual constructs and reality as for ever unknowable—indeed, the discussion of its nature as meaningless. Perhaps there can be no final knowledge of matter or energy as ultimate realities. For Newton and his successors knowledge of matter passed into knowledge of God, since the Universe existed under divine law and would one day be reshaped into the Heavenly City. In recent physics, banishing for ever such realities of the last century as atoms and the aether, the ultimate realities appear to be mathematical expressions about which the purest of mathematicians are themselves somewhat unhappy. Very few scientists or philosophers have chosen to deify matter, to make it final and eternal. But to refuse to do that is not to deny that ordinary exploration of the Universe is, at other levels, devoted to the pursuit of reality, and that its results are taken to be (with all the restrictions hinted at above) true and not merely conventional; the major atomic particles, the molecular structure of materials, including the living cell, the evolutionary modification of organisms by natural selection and the nuclear processes governing the life of a star—these do not seem to be regarded by those who study them (or by the world at large) as less true than any contingent proposition whatsoever.

It is generally agreed that in this respect the scientific revolution made a profound and widespread change. Ancient mathematical science, particularly, 'saved appearances', and to Aristotelians reality could not be apprehended through mathematics. Upon these ideas the Middle Ages grafted the notion that in the highest sense only revealed truth is real, and is sufficient for man. Rational enquiry could be too easily defrauded by the frailty of the human mind. What was true to sense and reason might well be supernaturally false. On theological grounds alone, Nicole Oresme in the late fourteenth century rejected the hypothesis of the earth's mobility that he found most rational.[34] After William of Ockham had categorized the idea of 'double truth' still further into the belief that statements in science are mere hypotheses or at best statements of what might be without assertion of what is,[35] nominalist physics became an exercise in 'logic accompanied by explicit disavowals that the results or assumptions had application to physical reality'.[36] In other words, philosophy was an intellectual game, only theology being concerned with truth.

Copernicus, unlike Oresme, believed in the physical reality of the earth's motions; this truth could not be demonstrated, but reason spoke for it; to believe the opposite was to credit an intellectual abomination, and this truth alone made God's cosmos simple and knowable. Like Einstein, Copernicus believed that God does not play at dice in Nature, or, as Galileo put it, God does not deceive His creation. Thus it was that in shifting the basis of reality from revelation to physical plausibility (in the words of Dr Edward Grant) Copernicus 'first mapped the new path and inspired the Scientific Revolution by bequeathing to it his own ardent desire for knowledge of physical realities'. And he remarks in a footnote that 'the significance of the quest for physical

[34] See A. Rupert Hall, *The Scientific Revolution, 1500–1800* (London, 2nd ed., 1962), pp. 56–9.

[35] See Ernest A. Moody, *The Logic of William of Ockham* (New York, 1935), p. 232.

[36] Edward Grant, 'Late Medieval Thought, Copernicus and the Scientific Revolution', in *Journal of the History of Ideas*, xxiii (1962), 207.

reality cannot be overestimated as a turning-point in the history of science'.[37] To agree with this view does not commit one to positivism—indeed, quite the opposite—since it was shared by such a devoted idealist as Koyré, for whom science as the *itinerarium mentis in veritatem* was certainly a quest for reality, and for whom the 'ontologie mathématique inspirée de Platon' was linked with the modern science of Galileo and Descartes as that which tended towards a 'connaissance réelle, bien que naturellement partielle et provisoire, du monde réel . . .'.[38] Indeed, the whole point of the distinction between mathematics and mathematical physics from Archimedes through Galileo to Newton—the whole structure of whose *Mathematical Principles of Natural Philosophy* was based on this distinction—is that physics is concerned with reality, so far as men may ascertain it.[39]

Where did this concern for reality originate? It was opposed to nominalism, it was not prompted by humanism, and it could not have been produced by the renewed classicism of the Renaissance. What other strands in contemporary thought were bridled neither by theology nor by Aristotle? What other strands believed—to fanaticism and absurdity—in the reality of its own truths? Are they to be found, perhaps, in the Hermetic and Neoplatonic traditions, which by this time had become one? Not to mention the obvious appearance of Hermeticism in the writings of some of the more mysterious, even 'uncanonical', figures of the scientific revolution (Paracelsus, Dee, Porta, Fludd), there are good grounds for discerning it in such unimpeachable heroes as Copernicus, Bruno, Francis Bacon, Kepler and Newton.[40] Of course, no one would wish to transfer all the honour of innovation once accorded Oresme to Pico della Mirandola, or that accorded Leonardo da Vinci to Marsilio Ficino. The Hermeticists were

[37] *Ibid.*, p. 220. I have drawn much from this article in these paragraphs.

[38] See in the volume mentioned above (Note 25), pp. 71, 360–1.

[39] It may be doubted whether Archimedes was really concerned with this distinction, but it is certainly significant that the seventeenth century thought that he was.

[40] But it is nevertheless absurd to qualify Newton as an alchemist and a *magus*! See the article by McGuire and Rattansi cited in Note 3, above, and Paolo Rossi, *Francis Bacon* (London, 1968; first published, 1957).

not modern scientists; arithmetology is not mathematical physics. The maximum claim is that the 'Renaissance *magus* . . . exemplifies that changed attitude of man to the cosmos which was the necessary preliminary to the rise of science'.[41] The direct and postive contribution of the Renaissance *magus* to modern science was virtually zero (the development of empiricism may show an exception), and in the person of Robert Fludd he was opposed by science in the person of Kepler and Mersenne. His contribution was roundabout, indirect, and obscure. 'Paracelsus', as Walter Pagel writes, 'though not "scientific" himself, produced scientific results from a non-scientific world of motives and thoughts. In this lies the perennial interest of his work to the historian.'[42] The same might be said of others whose positive contribution was even less than that of Paracelsus. The point here is not so much whether Hermeticism was wrong and irrational (which it was), nor whether it was a lineal precursor of modern science (which it was not), but rather that it furnished an alternative *and real* conception of Nature. It was a conception promising man limitless knowledge and power within the cosmos, one which unified the cosmos that Aristotle had divided, and one that conduced both to enquiry into the properties of things and to mathematicism. Yet at the same time it countered both the naïve empiricism and the sterile rationalism of scholastic philosophy. Perhaps one might say crudely that Hermeticism was the 'bad side' of early modern science, yielding in the seventeenth century the worst aspects of alchemy, astrology and witchcraft, but if so it may well be that this 'bad side' was indispensable to the emergence of the good, exerting a constant catalytic or fermentative action.

What seems certain is the multifarious, perhaps in some respects inconsistent, nature of the various factors ultimately resulting in the scientific revolution. It was not simply a succession of circumstances in which traditional beliefs were first questioned

[41] Frances Yates, 'The Hermetic Tradition in Renaissance Science', in *Art, Science and History in the Renaissance*, ed. Charles S. Singleton (Baltimore, 1968), p. 255; for a full study see the same author's *Giordano Bruno and the Hermetic Tradition* (London, 1964).

[42] Walter Pagel, *Paracelsus: an Introduction to Philosophical Medicine in the Era of the Renaissance* (Basel and New York, 1958), p. 347.

and then, overwhelmed by the evidence against them, rejected. Nor was it the consequence of a unique movement, such as nominalist physics or late-medieval empiricism. Not even the invocation of Platonic mathematicism will of itself explain all its manifestations—and the ascendancy of Platonism has still to be accounted for. Clearly the historian must be eclectic in his choice of causal factors: to all those mentioned so far he must add the known sterility of scholasticism, humanism and the classical revival, and Hermeticism. (And some would add the reflection of late-medieval technological progress.) As the scientific revolution came to full accomplishment in the time of Newton and Malpighi, it was the synthesis, or rather the resultant, of a whole corpus of new thoughts of those who in their day had dissented from orthodoxy—not by any means only scientific thoughts either. And it is this fact that, it seems to me, best reveals the historical singularity of the scientific revolution. Its profundity and its universality make it unique. The nineteenth-century revolution within science has transformed subsequent thinking; but the scientific revolution of the seventeenth century was itself the consequence of far-reaching and diverse changes in the texture of thought, not only in science itself, but more important outside science in the strict sense.

Eight

History and Reform in the Middle of the Eighteenth Century[1]

by

Franco Venturi[2]

[1] For a bibliography on this problem see the three volumes of *Illuministi Italiani* (Milan-Naples, 1958–65), which deal with the reformers of the various regions of Italy. See also my book, *Settecento Riformatore. Da Muratori a Beccaria* (Turin, 1969). My aim in this essay has been to reconsider and discuss one of the principal themes of these works, while referring the reader back to them for specific points of detail.

[2] Translated by Paul Ginsborg, Research Fellow of Queens' College, Cambridge.

In the activities of the Italian enlightened reformers of the eighteenth century history and reform, the study of the past and the desire to modify the present, often intertwined. Their influence upon each other, and the interaction between the two, contributed in no small way to the formation of the particular intellectual climate of the time. The connection between history and reform originated in the seminal works of men like Muratori, Maffei and Giannone. Its impetus was derived from the real difficulty of achieving concrete reforms in a land which was so fragmented and subdivided, which was the inheritor of so many traditions and memories, and which contained so extraordinary a variety of forms of government, ranging from the Papacy to the republics, from the duchies to the kingdoms. Italy in the eighteenth century was a museum—a museum which, while it enchanted travellers from abroad, left the men of the Enlightenment stupefied and indignant, and naturally inspired them all to make continual comparisons between past and present. Thus the eighteenth century in Italy was not only the age of enlightenment and the era of meticulous and deep-rooted enquiry into the geography of Italy, the forms of its society, and the economy of the country. It was also the epoch in which enlightened thinkers were often historians, and, less often, historians were men of the Enlightenment. To take just two examples: the last work of Pietro Verri, the foremost of the Lombard reformers, was a large-scale history of Milan. Carlantonio Pilati, the writer from Trento whose principal work, *Di una Riforma d'Italia*, provided both the slogan and the symbol for the second part of the eighteenth century, was also the author of a large history of the German Empire.

A comparison with the contemporary situation in other European countries is not without interest. It would be difficult for us to imagine Jean-Jacques Rousseau writing a voluminous history of Geneva, or Denis Diderot compiling a history of Paris, or even Turgot publishing a history of the German Empire (though he was one of the very few men of the French Enlightenment capable of reading German). The contrast between French *encyclopédisme* and Italian *illuminismo* is brought out very clearly by this paradoxical comparison. However, even in France, we must never forget that one of the strongest roots for the development of ideas in the eighteenth century lay in the great dispute between Dubos and Boulainvilliers over the monarchy, the nobility and the Third Estate. Montesquieu was also a great historian. Amongst the writers of the second half of the century, Condillac and his brother Mably—stimulated, it is true, by practical demands that came from Parma—were the pioneers of Enlightenment writing on political and social history. The debate on the past became more intense as the Revolution approached. In France, before and after the wonderful decade which saw the publication of the *Encyclopaedia*, past and present met, not only on an ideological and political plane, but also on that of historical understanding.

Germany shared with Italy a greater number of elements in common. The variety of political régimes, the weight of tradition, the multiplicity and difficulty of the problems of both history and reform formed obvious links between the two countries. Professor Herbert Butterfield has given us the key to the understanding of the complexities of the German situation. The school of Göttingen saw the political and historical strains of eighteenth-century German writing meet and fuse. To take only one example, Schlötzer, one of the country's most distinguished and active political writers, was also one of its most important scholars in the field of Russian history.

In England, Hume's literary output, with his *Essays* and his *History of England*, was equally divided between history and reform. Gibbon was both a great enlightened thinker and a great historian. In the Scotland of Ferguson, Robertson, Millar and Gilles the writing of history and the desire for reform went hand in hand, and thus created one of the most alive cultural centres of the eighteenth century. Such a European survey as this could be continued, from the Spain of Jovellanos to the Russia of Ščerbatov. But the general panoramas thus disclosed are too vast for it to be possible for us to hope to include in them the Italian experience. Here it will suffice to consider eighteenth-century Europe (the historiography of which has not yet been explored as much as it deserves) as a mere backdrop, and to content ourselves with concentrating at closer quarters on what happened in Italy during the decisive decades from the age of Muratori, Maffei and Giannone to that of Verri and Pilati.

Muratori intended both to reform the literature, science, morality and very *animus* of the literary world, and at the same time to introduce into the writing of history new and more critical methods and criteria.[3] The two facets of his activity, the writer and the historian, fused almost naturally together. The greatest period of his activity, from youth to middle age, saw the publication of *Della Perfetta Poesia Italiana*, the *Riflessioni sopra il Buon Gusto* and the *Rerum Italicarum Scriptores*. He was on the threshold of old age before he began to confront, with ever-increasing urgency, the problem of how to transform, not only persons, but things, not only minds, but social, judicial, political and economic structures. It was the Italian political situation between 1730 and 1748 which stirred him to action. Ravaged by the wars of the Polish and Austrian Succession, afflicted by a deep economic depression, Italy was further weakened by dynastic events which culminated in the passing away of the Medici and Farnese, and the creation of a new sovereign in southern Italy. Muratori reacted to this crisis of desperation and weakness with the *Antiquitates* (1738), the *Annali d'Italia* (1744–9), *Dei Difetti della Giurisprudenza* (1742) and *Della Pubblica Felicità* (1749). The *Antiquitates* are an extraordinary collection of studies on the economic and

[3] Sergio Bertelli, *Erudizione e Storia in Lodovico Antonio Muratori* (Naples, Istituto Italiano per Gli Studi Storici, 1960), and Lodovico Antonio Muratori, *Opere*, ed. Giorgio Falco and Fiorenzo Forti (Milan-Naples, 1964). Both these works contain full biographical details on Muratori.

social history of the medieval epoch. In the *Annali*, as Luigi Salvatorelli has rightly noted, Muratori's enlightened thinking is more in evidence than in any other of his works. He is here to be seen in the course of dissociating himself from the powerful and the fortunate in order to side with those who are forced to toil and struggle. *Dei Difetti della Giurisprudenza* is both a prudent and a moderate work, but it is also clear and precise in its sharp detachment from any illusion on the absolute value of law. The same clarity is to be found when Muratori deals with the possibility that the law should become the instrument for analysis and action in human society; and when he combines an acid critique of the Italian legal mentality with his desire to rediscover the reality under the words of the law. *Della Pubblica Felicità* is a sketch for the new age which was dawning with the end of the War of the Austrian Succession. It is an attempt to provide, for the new generation of the second half of the century, aims and methods for achieving a different and better solution to the problems of education and economics, of administration and social life.

The way which led from the *Antiquitates* to the *Pubblica Felicità* was anything but easy or straightforward. Even for a man as open-minded as Muratori it was no simple matter to pass from the writing of history to the advocacy of reform. He was sufficiently sincere and intelligent to understand and proclaim that the instruments which served to enquire into the past were not always suited for the modification of the present. The man who knew so much about the economic and social history of medieval Italy felt himself frequently disarmed when faced with the problems of his own age. He reacted by getting hold of the most modern books he could find, by availing himself of the help of acquaintances and specialists, and by researching into the new science of political economy, which in Italy as well as elsewhere was making such great advances at this time. To Carlantonio Broggia, the greatest Italian economist of the 1740s, he owed the acquaintance of Melon, and thus of the controversies the latter had aroused in France. As the *Encyclopaedia* of Diderot was soon to demonstrate, the growth of political economy was intimately linked with new techniques, with the prevailing passion for machines, and with the new study of rural economics. Muratori, up to the time he died, continued to read pamphlets, and to search through dictionaries which would allow him to take proper account of the new era of science which was dawning in the middle of the century. His experiences as a historian, as the discoverer of an Italian history so clearly distinct from the Roman world, so clearly autonomous in its slow and painstaking medieval foundations, offered him an extraordinarily sound starting-point. The last part of the *Annali* deals with contemporary events, with the revolt ot Genoa of 1746, and with the peace which was finally concluded at Aix-la-Chapelle. In it Muratori demonstrated how useful, even indispensable, the study of past history could be when it came to confronting the contemporary world. In his old age he saw the last upsurge on Italian soil of the medieval city disputes, the last struggles between Guelph and Ghibelline, the sunset of the age of the *signorie*, of the Renaissance and the Counter-Reformation. His experience as an historian of medieval Italy helped him to write the history of these contemporary events with detachment and insight. Simultaneously he was looking towards the future and preparing himself and others for the new tasks which the disastrous inheritance of the past had imposed upon the nascent Italian enlightened reformers. For the latter the importance of Muratori was immense. Twenty years later the Physiocrats were to be astonished at the relevance and vitality of his writings. In Germany his works were to be translated for many years to come. The generation of Italians who followed him seemed to divide up the spoils he had left. They retraced and developed his programme of reform, carried on his historical researches, but seldom combined the two. It was not an easy task, as has been understood by the heirs of the great eclectics, by generations dominated, for example, by a Goethe or a Croce. Those who followed Muratori often lacked his sense of balance and ended up by dividing the inheritance, by splitting up the cultural estate they had been bequeathed; each one appropriated a particular area of activity. In the eighteenth century Beccaria took over judicial reform, Verri and Pilati the desire to reform society. Antonio Genovesi revived, more than anyone else, Muratori's *encyclopédisme*, and engrained it deeply into the thought of the Neapolitan school. But history was not forgotten. Long after he was dead, Muratori forced these writers, and many of their contemporaries, into studying the medieval past and the 1,000 years from 500 to 1500.

Scipione Maffei, if perhaps he lacked Muratori's wide-ranging intellect, is, in many ways, a similar case.[4] As Arnaldo Momigliano has explained, Maffei found during the 1730s a meeting-point between his desire for political reform and his passion for history and antiquity. He declared that what needed re-evaluation was the life of the provinces, both in the Venice of his own day and the Roman Empire of the past. These territories, which at first had been colonized, had in time tended to establish their own importance and dignity in the face of the dominant city. Maffei insisted that, both in the past and the present, a rich and unexplored provincial life could and should be contrasted with the life of the capital cities. His *Consiglio Politico* (1737) was enriched by his experience in various parts of Europe, and by the history of the Roman provinces which it contained. It constituted the most lucid programme to be written in the eighteenth century of a movement for reform which accompanied the Republic of St Mark in the last period of its existence. On a historical plane the same purpose was fulfilled with his *Verona Illustrata.* In 1745 he intervened in a dispute over the old problem of usury. His work *Dell'Impiego del Danaro* was important precisely because it gave an historian's viewpoint on a theological dispute. Maffei's sense of chronological distinctions and social differences served him well here. How was he to admit that, irrespective of the era of history, the same law should determine loans, rents and interest rates? Maffei had an acute grasp of reality which enabled him to combat established judicial and theological assumptions. Calling upon history for his evidence, he demanded that the modern world should not be crushed under the weight of the ancient and medieval past. His book aroused controversy in every corner

[4] On Scipione Maffei (1675–1755), the great archaeologist, historian and writer from Verona, see Arnaldo Momigliano, 'Gli Studi Classici di Scipione Maffei', *Giornale Storico della Letteratura Italiana*, cxxxiii (1956), fasc. 403, 363ff.; and *idem*, *Secondo Contributo alla Storia degli Studi Classici* (Rome, Edizioni di Storia e Letteratura (1960), pp. 255ff. For his political ideas, see the edition of his *Consiglio Politico alla Repubblica Veneta*, ed. by Luigi Messedaglia (Verona, 'Vita Veronese', 1955).

of Italy. Nothing revealed more clearly the difficulties that were then accumulating, even during the reign of the tolerant Pope Benedict XIV, for writers like Maffei. To fuse history and reform was no easy task in Italy in the middle of the eighteenth century.

On Pietro Giannone, the one other thinker of the first half of the eighteenth century who continued to dominate the post-1750 intellectual world, much has recently been written in Italy.[5] Did the centre of Giannone's political inspiration lie in his desire to defend the State from interference by the Roman *Curia*? Or was he rather more concerned to extend historical knowledge of the fortunes of the Mezzogiorno during the millennium which preceded the eighteenth century? Was he the apologist of the *paglietti*, the Neapolitan lawyers, the *noblesse de robe* of southern Italy, or was he rather an isolated thinker grappling with the problems which were common in the 'crisis of the European consciousness', to use the expression of Paul Hazard? Recent studies, carried out primarily by Marini, Bertelli and Ricuperati, have enabled us to study more closely Giannone's ideas and life. What emerges is the lasting value of Giannone's thought, in spite of the juridical straitjacket in which, at the start of his career, he enclosed himself. What becomes clear is the breadth of his cultural experience, formed over the years by his Viennese exile, by his contact with the German scholars, with the English deists,

[5] On the extraordinary life of this jurist and philosopher (having been exiled from Naples for his *Istoria Civile*, he became a refugee in the Vienna of Charles IV. At the time of the War of the Polish Succession he was a fugitive again in northern Italy, and escaped to Geneva. He was arrested by the agents of Charles Emmanuel III of Savoy, and spent the rest of his life in Piedmontese prisons, dying in Turin in 1748), see among more recent works: Pietro Giannone, *Vita Scritta da Lui Medesimo*, ed. Sergio Bertelli (Milan, 1960); Giuseppe Ricuperati, *Le Carte Torinesi di Pietro Giannone* (Turin, Accademia delle Scienze, 1962); *idem*, 'Libertinismo e Deismo a Vienna: Spinoza, Toland, e il "Triregno"', *Rivista Storica Italiana*, lxxix (1967), fasc. iii, 628ff.; *idem.*, 'La Prima Formazione di Pietro Giannone. L'Accademia Medina-Coeli e Domenico Aulisio', *Studi sul Settecento italiano* (Naples, Istituto Italiano per gli Studi Storici, 1968), pp. 94ff.; Lino Marini, 'Documenti dell'Opposizione Curiale a Pietro Giannone (1723–1735)', *Rivista Storica Italiana*, lxxix (1967), fasc. iii, 696ff.; Sergio Bertelli, *Giannoniana. Autografi, Manoscritti e Documenti della Fortuna di Pietro Giannone* (Milan-Naples, 1968).

and the inheritors of the cosmopolitan tradition of the first decades of the century. His development from the *Istoria Civile del Regno di Napoli* to the *Triregno*, and to the works he continued to write while in prison in Turin, reveals a truly remarkable richness of subject-matter and tenacity of purpose. Giannone came to devote more and more time to one central element in his work. He tried to understand the contrast and the contact between the religious and the political history of past ages, pagan as well as Jewish and Christian. He attempted to establish a general viewpoint, from which to explain the facts as well as the myths, the actions as well as the fantasies of mankind. Obviously this attempt already contained many of the elements of the subsequent age of the Enlightenment.

When now, after two centuries, we read the *Triregno* and Giannone's posthumous works, we cannot avoid thinking that Giannone could have been the real master of the Italian Enlightenment. His claims appear stronger than those of Muratori or Maffei, both unable to escape from the world of Catholicism, or those of Vico, whose work was too original and individual to be understood by the generation which grew up after 1750. But Giannone's development was tragically stunted by the Roman Church, the Inquisition, the political narrow-mindedness of Charles Emmanuel III, the weakness of Charles of Bourbon and the cowardice of the Republic of Venice. It would be easy to continue this list of obstacles, too many to be purely fortuitous. Giannone was the major victim of the crises which racked Italy in the 1730s. When Italy's fortunes began to revive it was too late, for he had already died in a Turin prison. His historical ideas filtered through, albeit slowly, to the rest of Europe, and his opinions came to be known through English, French and German translations of his work. In Italy, for a long time, his fame rested on his juridical works, and on the polemical battle he had waged with the Roman *Curia*. The *Triregno* remained in almost complete obscurity, both in Italy and beyond the Alps. His philosophy of history aroused little interest in an epoch already dominated by Voltaire and Hume. Giannone, instead of being the first thinker of the Italian Enlightenment, remained the last of the intellectuals of the period of crisis in Italian history between the sixteenth and the eighteenth centuries. His ideas had often to make a round tour of Europe before becoming known south of the Alps. Practical obstacles had prevented him from developing along the lines he had chosen, from defining more clearly the relationship between religion and history.

Giannone died in 1748, Muratori in 1750, Maffei in 1754. Vico's life had ended in 1744. A generation passed away, and the division between the first and second half of the century is clear. The great isolated intellectuals left the stage, and the movement of the enlightened reformers took their place. Their first task was to continue to reject the historical superstitions which humanism and the more recent study of antiquity had started to overcome, and to carry on the work of revising lay and ecclesiastical traditions. In this they followed the path which Muratori, Maffei and Giannone had already opened. In Tuscany the *etruscheria* began to slow down, and became fused little by little in a more general vision of a pre-Roman Italian civilization, common to all the centres of the peninsula. The movement for the study of primitive Italy, which put the Samnites and the Pelagians alongside the Etruscans, gathered in momentum, and ran parallel with the political and religious polemical battle against Ancient and Papal Rome.

It was, however, in a less distant past that the men of the Enlightenment, at Florence, Venice and Milan, sought out with ever-greater insistence the origins of their own existence. They came increasingly to devote their attention to the more fruitful and realistic study of the recent Italian past. Thus the rediscovery of humanism, of the cultural and economic life of the great mercantile centres of the Renaissance, and even of the activities of the Protestant reformers in sixteenth-century Italy, accompanied the movement for enlightened reform. After Tuscany had fallen under imperial influence, the heritage of the Medicis was collected together at Florence by men like Lami, Mehus and Bandini.[6] At Venice Marco Foscarini, instead of writing the history of contemporary and military affairs, which the Republic had officially

[6] Mario Rosa, 'Per la Storia dell' Erudizione Toscana del '700: Profilo di Lorenzo Mehus', in *Annali della Scuola Speciale per Archivisti e Bibliotecari dell'Università di Roma*, anno ii (1962), n. 2, 41ff.

requested of him, dedicated himself to a great history of Venetian culture, science and laws. On its publication Italy was presented, perhaps for the first time, with the spectacle of a government accepting a history of ideas as a satisfactory expression of the historian's craft.[7] At Venice again it was Cardinal Querini and Gianrinaldo Carli who paved the way for a reconsideration of the heresies and heterodox religious movements of sixteenth-century Italy. Paolo Sarpi returned to the limelight, and became the most significant symbol of the ideological continuity of the Republic of St Mark.[8] At Milan, Pietro Verri created the bases for a new insight into Lombardy's past. He transferred his attention from the era of decadence under the Spanish, and concentrated instead, with great lucidity, on the fourteenth and fifteenth centuries, the age of the patricians and merchants, the epoch of prosperity and economic and political strength.[9]

The example of Pietro Verri is indicative of how new historical concepts could lead to the discovery of new fields of investigation, enquiry and research. Through the work above all of Carli and Argelati, both inspired by Muratori, numismatic scholarship was transformed on to the new plane of monetary history.[10] Argelati's essays *De Monetis Italiae*, and more especially Carli's history of the Italian Mints, attempted, in the field of economic history, what Muratori had achieved in his *Rerum Italicarum Scriptores* and his *Antiquitates*. Pagnini's history of tithes, published in Florence between 1765 and 1766, was the first example of maturity in this new type of historical writing.[11]

[7] *Della Letteratura Veneziana* (Venice, 1752), and the *Decreto dal Consiglio dei Dieci a Marco Foscarini* included in the republication of this work (Venice, 1854), p. 7.

[8] Cf. the profile of Gianrinaldo Carli (by F. Venturi) in *Illuministi Italiani*, iii, *cit.*, 419ff., and of Francesco Griselini (by Gianfranco Torcellan), *ibid.*, vii, 91ff.

[9] Pietro Verri, *Considerazioni sul Commercio dello Stato di Milano*, ed. C. A. Vianello (Milan, 1939).

[10] Gianrinaldo Carli, *Dell'Origine e del Commercio della Moneta e dell'Istituzione delle Zecche d'Italia sino al Secolo Decimo Settimo* (Venice, 1751), and Filippo Argelati, *De Monetis Italiae. Variorum Illustrium Virorum Dissertationes* (Milan, 1750).

[11] Gianfrancesco Pagnini, *Della Decima e di Varie Altre Gravezze Imposte dal Comune di Firenze. Della Moneta e della Mercatura de' Fiorentini* (Lucca, 1765–6).

At Rome the situation was different. There was no shortage of attempts to escape from the intellectual climate of the Counter-Reformation. Technical and philological activity, in fact, found particularly significant expression in the Palace of the Corsini, at Trastevere, with Bottari and Foggini. But these were Tuscans living in Rome, and their gaze was directed more towards Florence than to Rome's ecclesiastical past. Rather than concentrating on Muratori's 1,000 years, they preferred instead, as did the whole of the Roman intellectual world during the age of Benedict XIV, to rededicate themselves to the ancient world. In this way they anticipated and then accompanied Winckelmann's neo-classicism. Even in the enlightened and rational works of Piranesi and Milizia it was not medieval or more recent history, but ancient and primitive Rome which took pride of place. Rome was overcome by the fascination of the classical world.[12]

In Naples at the same time men began searching their past for an *ubi consistam*, a historical period to be restudied and to serve as a departure point for the work of reform. This was to remain a characteristic of southern historical thinking far beyond the eighteenth century. The long period of Spanish domination, in which Giannone had attempted to see something of positive value, came to appear increasingly as an age of decadence, misery and disintegration.[13] Paolo Mattia Doria had already claimed this at the beginning of the century, and the contemporaries of Tanucci and Genovesi became increasingly convinced of it. Indeed, they added new elements to Doria's general condemnation. They noted the disproportionate size of Naples and the parasitical character of its economy, a situation tragically aggravated by the concessions granted by the Spanish viceroys to the *lazzaroni* during and after Masaniello's revolt. These facts rendered increasingly difficult the

[12] E. Dammig, *Il Movimento Giansenista a Roma nella Seconda Metà del Secolo XVIII* (Vatican City, 1945); F. Venturi, 'Elementi e Tentativi di riforme nello Stato pontificio del Settecento', *Rivista Storica Italiana*, lxxv, (1963), fasc. iv, 778ff.; Francis Haskell, *Patrons and Painters. A Study in the Relations between Italian Art and Society in the Age of the Baroque* (London, 1963); *Illuministi Italiani*, vii, *cit.*, 527ff. (for Francesco Milizia).

[13] Giuseppe Galasso, *Dal Comune Medievale all'Unità. Linee di Storia Meridionale* (Bari, 1939).

task of rationalization and equalization which the absolute monarchs were at this time engaged upon elsewhere in Italy. Nor could these Neapolitan thinkers, involved as they were in a polemical battle against baronial rights and aristocratic predominance, invoke the fourteenth and fifteenth centuries as an age of glory. For in Naples these centuries had been the time of Angevin and Aragonese supremacy, and equally of aristocratic domination. Did this leave then only the Emperor Frederick II? Was he the one example of political rationality that a southern Italian could find in his own past? Giuseppe Galanti and some of his contemporaries were of this opinion. But the rule of Frederick II was obviously insufficient by itself to serve as a precedent for reform. Frederick was far too isolated and controversial a ruler to be anything more than the one light figure in a dark landscape of failed attempts, frustrated good intentions, and useless and injurious revolts. Likewise, the Longobards could not serve in southern Italy as the nucleus for a view of Italian history that elsewhere had been defended by Machiavelli, and later readopted and developed by Muratori. Similarly, it was natural that Roman history could not have the same significance at Naples that it had at Rome. Giuseppe Galanti sought refuge in the study of the Samnites, the one example, in his view, of a truly virtuous people, the southern embodiment of an ideal that elsewhere found its expression amongst the Etruscans and the Pelagians. But we are here on the fringes between history and mythology, and the direct influence of Rousseau can be discerned in Galanti's study.[14] It was exactly, however, in this zone between mythology and the eighteenth-century historian's view of the past, that there developed at Naples, with Mario Pagano and Gaetano Filangieri, a new philosophy of history, having its origins in the philosophy of Vico, and directly influenced by Nicolas-Antoine Boulanger and Adam Ferguson.[15]

[14] Giuseppe Galanti, *Saggio Sopra l'Antica Storia de' Primi Abitatori dell'Italia* (Naples, 1783).

[15] *Illuministi Italiani*, v, *cit.*, 601ff. (for Gaetano Filangieri, the well-known author of the *Scienza della Legislazione*), and pp. 783ff. (for Mario Pagano, the genial author of the *Saggi Politici*, who was executed in 1799 during the repression of the Neapolitan Republic).

The works of Muratori and Giannone were not of great import for this flight into the far-distant past and into mythology. Instead they were to make their presence felt in Naples when there arose the more humble and pragmatic historical desire to retrace the origins and roots of the laws, the political order and the economic realities of the country. A complete study of southern Italian historiography in the eighteenth century has yet to be written. One thing is certain, however: the southern Italian historians were particularly responsive to everything important that was being said or written in Europe at the time. This responsiveness was a general characteristic of Italy in the eighteenth century, but what was happening in Scotland and France seemed to hold for the south special interest and significance. A sufficient example of this is the collection made by Giuseppe Galanti of works written on the origins and nature of feudalism: the authors ranged from Robertson and Hume to Voltaire and Condillac.[16]

The new German methodology took far longer to reach Italy. While Italian translators and publishers were soon found for the general histories of Millot and George Sale, contacts with the developments in Germany in general, and Göttingen in particular, were less rapidly established.

A study on Johann-Friedrich Le Bret is in the course of being written by a young scholar, Maria Luisa Pesante. Le Bret was, without doubt, the scholar who served as one of the fundamental links between the German and Italian historical worlds. To study his life and works is to get to know, at close quarters, a series of connections and reciprocal influences in which we find the same juridical, religious and technical preoccupations which came to the fore in every part of Italy in the middle of the eighteenth century.

Of particular importance alongside the figure of the German historian Le Bret is that of the Italian Carlantonio Pilati.[17] He

[16] The collection of writings on feudalism was published by him in 1782 as one of the *Supplementi* to his version of the *Eléments d'Histoire Générale Ancienne et Moderne* of Abbot Claude-François Millot. Cf. *Illuministi Italiani*, v, *cit.*, 957ff.

[17] Born 1733 at Tassullo, a small town in the Trentino, died in 1802. Cf. *Illuministi Italiani*, v, *cit.*, 561ff.

too, from the time he was a young man, had much admired Muratori, and had begun his intellectual life under his influence. Born in the Trentino, educated at Salzburg, Pilati had had the good fortune to make the acquaintance of the famous scholar from Modena. This was in 1749, during his first journey through Italy, when Pilati was only sixteen and Muratori was in the last year of his life. Afterwards, during his adventurous formative years, Pilati seems to have travelled rapidly along the road which the thinkers of the first half of the century had already followed. He moved from the law to political philosophy and to the theory of natural law; from enlightened Christianity (which Muratori had called 'regulated devotion'), and from juridical polemical battles with the Roman *Curia* to a new conception of relations between Church and State, and to a true and deep-rooted religious reformism.

Although this aspect of his life has not yet been sufficiently studied, Pilati's sojourn at the universities of Leipzig and Göttingen was of great importance to him. In spite of the many criticisms he levelled at German academic life, there is no doubt that he learnt a great deal from it. For a time he was a professor at Leipzig; he gave lectures in German on the art of criticism and the Ancient Law, and in Italian on the history of the Empire. The great tradition of Mosheim was still very much alive at Göttingen, and Pilati came into personal contact with Michaelis, 'qui était profondement savant', as Pilati himself was to write in his *Voyages en Différens Pays de l'Europe*. In this work he also mentioned Heyne, Semler, Spalding, Jerusalem, Ernesti and Büsching. Pilati's conclusions were clear: in Germany the cultural tradition of the Protestants was distinctly superior to that of the Catholics: 'Les Allemands protestans sont infiniment plus éclairés que les catholiques.' Their education was better and was founded on 'sciences solides'. The Catholics, on the other hand, taught 'les enfants des idées qui leur gâtent le goût et la raison: on accable leur esprit de choses qui mènent a l'erreur, a la futilité, à la sottise'. The results were clearly evident. In the field of jurisprudence Thomasius, who Pilati with good reason called 'un génie', reigned supreme. In geography Büsching had written books which put to shame 'tous les livres géographiques du monde', and, similarly, protestant scholarship predominated over all the vast range of historical disciplines. The impressions and ideas that Pilati had received while in Germany continued to live with him when he returned to Trento and began, in 1758, to teach law. Soon afterwards he began again to devote himself, either in Venice or at his home in Trento, to continuous research and ceaseless intellectual enquiry.

This period in his life was to last ten years, and was to culminate with the publication at Coire, in the Grisons, of his profession of faith. It was called *Di una Riforma d'Italia, ossia dei Mezzi di Riformare i più Cattivi Costumi e le Più Perniciose Leggi d'Italia.* Voltaire was to write of it, a year after its publication, 'il n'y a guère d'ouvrage plus fort et plus hardi'. Certainly no Italian writer for a long time had appeared to expose, with such passion and forcefulness, the horrific side of the morality of the Counter-Reformation. Pilati laid bare the absurdity of a life in which superstition and the formal structure of religion seemed to have undermined the most fundamental moral values. He wrote, for example, 'we tremble to think that we may have consumed butter and milk on a day of fasting; but we have no hesitation in recounting with delight how many women we have just seduced or how many of our fellow citizens we have killed'. In the face of such attitudes, only radical reform would suffice. Every legal dispute was abandoned, as was all hope of an internal reform of the clergy. What was needed instead was the transformation of the structure of society, and the mutation of generally held beliefs. Pilati was the one Italian writer of the 1760s to propose a real and total separation of Church and State, the one writer who wished to deprive the Church of all political power, and to make it equal to any other free and spontaneous association. As far as political problems were concerned, he was close to the thinking of men like Verri, Beccaria and Genovesi when he described his ideal society as one in which men were active, useful and independent. But Pilati laid more emphasis than did anyone elese on the protestant ethic in this 'new society'. The examples of 'trouble-making England' (as the *Curia* would have it) and the German protestant countries were always before his eyes. However, in order to raise Italy anew to the level of these countries, it was not necessary, according to him, to retrace the steps of Luther and Calvin. Pilati looked rather to the Enlightenment as the force capable of giving to Italy what Protestantism had brought to England and Germany. He was decidedly an optimist, for he put his faith in the princes, and believed that, even amongst the lower classes, changes could be instituted through schools imbued with the new ideas. Every forecast that Pilati made was inspired by very real moral passion. It already seemed to him that he was about to witness the epoch in which 'all Italy shall imperceptibly change both its customs and its ways'. He believed whole-heartedly in the imminence of what, in one place, he called 'a most profound revolution' in man's thinking and the material world.

For Pilati the first consequence of what he had written was exile. His book was certainly not one that could be published in Italy. He found in the Grisons a cultural centre that was as hospitable as it was active and flourishing. It was there that he published the first and second parts of his *Riforma d'Italia.* He took up again and enlarged his concept of religious and ecclesiastical organization in his *Riflessioni d'un Italiano sopra la Chiesa* (1768). In this work the ideas of Sarpi, Giannone and Muratori fused with those of Mosheim and François Richer to create an increased insistence on the radical separation of Church and State. In the same year Pilati began the publication of a *Giornale letterario*, which must take its place alongside the *Caffé* of Verri and Beccaria as one of the most lively periodicals of eighteenth-century Italy. In it Pilati continued his struggle against 'my adversaries, those pathetic pedants, fatuous poets, infamous orators, bestial jurists and theologians inspired by the devil and their own insolence'.

It was in this periodical that Pilati gave vent most clearly to the historical problems which had constantly preoccupied him during the years he had devoted to reforming polemic. As well as reviewing books on law, letters and politics in the journal, Pilati commented on a large number of historical works. Some were German, like those of F. E. Boysen, T. Grebner, T. J. Winckelmann; others were French, like those of Mehegan, or English, like William Smith's history of New York. Previously he had not had time to concentrate on the problems of historical writing which had been posed to him by his contact with Muratori and his experience in the German universities. Now he turned his attention to them, and in 1769, again at Coire, the first volume of *La Istoria dell'Impero Germanico e dell'Italia dal Tempo dei Carolingi fino alla Pace di Vestfalia* was published. Was this a new version of the lectures he had given ten years earlier at Leipzig? It seems probable, given the discursive style of a great part of this first volume, and indeed of the second, which came out in 1772. But what concerns us most is the Preface with which he opened the work, and which was as much his historical manifesto as *Di una Riforma d'Italia* was his political and religious profession of faith.

Pilati had come to the parting of the ways between an annalist's approach and a history which was not strictly chronological, but rather followed the logic of events and problems. He had hesitated, unable to abandon traditional approaches and yet aware of the need for a new historical method. 'An Italian who writes in the vernacular and who intends to give his readers a truly vivid picture of the events he is recounting is forced, in spite of himself, to adopt the methods and order of the annalists.' What was necessary before anything else, in order to establish with confidence a new methodology, was an immense preparatory work, which would be critical of the sources and assured of the evidence. How did Pilati envisage the mixture of this indispensable work of revision and polemic with a simple narration of the events?

> Our nation is still the recipient of so many prejudices and so much false history . . . the historian who wishes to demonstrate to his readers how mistaken they are is forced to stop at every moment. He has no option but to interrupt the course of his history in order to reveal the lies and fables put forward by writers who are either cunning or stupid, in order to destroy mischievous but seemingly correct evidence, in order to show by means of tangible and verifiable arguments the truth of his own narrative, and in order to fight a continuous battle against perfidy, obstinacy, and stupidity.

Until the way was completely cleared, Pilati stressed the need to resign oneself 'to making of one's own narrative a mixture of history and annals'.

The same moral passion, the same attention to the world of truth is revealed in these words as in those which Pilati wrote, a little earlier, on Italian customs and life. Just as he had earlier demonstrated his faith in the power of the enlightened thinkers, so here he showed himself convinced of the efficacy of the critical approach which was being employed by his contemporaries. It was certainly true that an infinite number of documents 'lay hidden' in the archives 'of princes, of cities, of famous persons', and that from these papers it would be possible 'to find extraordinary illumination'. Similarly,

> a great mass of moneys, seals and other antiques which could throw the greatest possible light on our history are still buried in chancelleries and little or no use is made of them for understanding the past. Moreover, the chronology and geography of the Middle Ages, on which the course of history depends to the highest degree, are both still full of errors, confusions and uncertainties.

In spite of the work of the followers of Mabillon and of the school of St Maur and their disciples, an immense amount of research remained to be done. 'In the collections of the works of the historians of the Middle Ages made by the most famous *letterati* and historians of the present and the last century, there cannot be discerned, to put it frankly, any order, wisdom of choice, judgement or criticism.'

Pilati thus parted company with his teacher, Muratori, and the division between the first and second half of the century is reflected even in this. A more exacting critical sense was employed by Pilati in his search for a more authentic history. The struggle against falsification, against traditional lies of every sort, tended to make him both more impassioned and more efficient. Pilati had seen the 'erudite and able Signor Semler' at work in this stubborn and unyielding battle. He quoted from the latter's work entitled *Versuch den Gebrauch der Quellen in der Staats- und Kirchengeschichte der mitleren Zeiten zu Erlichtern*, published at Halle in 1761. Pilati explained to his Italian readers the criteria that Semler had devised to prepare a critical edition of the sources. Semler's method certainly seemed to him 'to be the most opportune of those it is possible to imagine', and consisted, to put it briefly, in

> making a collection of all the historians of the Middle Ages in such a way that each writer is accurately distinguished by that piece of history in which he is original and not merely a copyist. Then that all the errors committed through imprudence by a historian or his copyists should be diligently and critically indicated, and that all those writers who have written on the same subject should be wisely compared and collated.

This was an enormous task, which could only be carried out, as Pilati well understood, by a properly organized group of scholars. 'Therefore it is a great fortune for posterity that such a task has been undertaken by the most learned members of the Royal Institute for Historical Studies at Göttingen, whose work, when it is published, will kindle in the fires of medieval history the clearest of flames, and reflect immortal fame upon the scholars concerned.'

But Pilati knew that it was a difficult and very long task, and we must not be surprised that his history turned out to be more traditional than he had hoped or desired. His narrative, which went as far as the end of the thirteenth century, was more often in reality inspired by Muratori, Voltaire and Mehegan than by the nascent school of history at Göttingen. There is no doubting the vigour of his polemic when, for example, he inveighed against the function traditionally attributed to the Church in the Middle Ages. His interpretation of the beginning of the Crusades, with which these two volumes of his finished, is never less than original. But in these pages the convergence between reforming and critical zeal remains substantially no more than a programme, a hope for the future.

Pilati was yet convinced of the necessity of his attempt. It is true that his history remains that of an annalist, and far from balanced or definitive, but, when compared with the history of 'the most scholarly and most honest Muratori', the difference between the two is striking, 'and this difference is what excuses our boldness'. Pilati always tried not to compromise, not to follow a middle course, just as he did not shrink from 'dazzling the eyes of the reader' with the truth. For the times in which he was writing, in an age which, as he said, lived in expectation of 'a most profound revolution', 'prudence' was 'stupidity' and 'that middle way with which they hope to save everything is the way in which one first deceives the public and then oneself'. The truth had no more 'to travel masked through the world, so that it can be recognized only by a few, while its enemy openly and arrogantly displays itself to all, and claims to ride tyrannically over the thoughts and actions of mankind'. In spite of all the technical obstacles which he himself clearly recognized and singled out, Pilati displayed, better than any other writer of these years, the mind of the enlightened historian, and the wish to combine the desire for reform with the necessity for historical understanding.

Nine

The Duke of Newcastle and the Origins of the Diplomatic Revolution

by

the late D. B. Horn

Few eighteenth-century historians have given much thought to the foreign policy of the Duke of Newcastle, in spite of the fact that he held the key office of Secretary of State from 1724 to 1754 and continued for another two years as Prime Minister to play a major role both in the formulation and execution of British foreign policy. As long as Walpole dominated a Cabinet composed more and more clearly of second-rate politicians, most of them in the House of Lords, Newcastle's responsibility for policy was not much greater than that of Holdernesse during Newcastle's Premiership or of Carmarthen under the younger Pitt. It is true that towards the end of the Walpole era Newcastle showed signs of independence and, if we accept the testimony of the younger Horace Walpole, betrayed his master and was partly responsible for Walpole's fall from power. It was this conviction that originally inspired Horace Walpole's malicious characterization of Newcastle as vain, foolish and indeed ridiculous. Even Newcastle's few admirers had to admit that outwardly Newcastle behaved in very odd ways. Cradock wrote that it was unaccountable 'that so much as he [Newcastle] had been ridiculed by Foote on the stage . . . he could not restrain himself, even in the street, from seizing your head and holding it between his hands, whilst perhaps he would ask the most unmeaning and trifling questions'.[1]

So far as the content of Newcastle's foreign policy is concerned, he had served his apprenticeship in the 1720s under Townshend,

[1] Joseph Cradock, *Literary and Miscellaneous Memoirs*, iv (London, 1828), 119.

the arch-enemy of Austria, and therefore a firm supporter of alliance with France. After Walpole had taken over control of British foreign policy from Townshend and nominally restored the former alliance with Austria by the second Treaty of Vienna in 1731, Newcastle showed no particular enthusiasm for the restored alliance, but, like the Walpole brothers, continued to rely on the pacific professions of Cardinal Fleury. Even after he emerged from Walpole's tutelage, he had 'the strongest prepossession that the house of Austria is not worth supporting'.[2] He must therefore not be placed amongst the British politicians who were lifelong adherents of the Austrian alliance and saw in the problems which faced Maria Theresa on her accession a welcome chance to restore 'the old system'. This is sufficient to distinguish him from Carteret and to justify the Pelhams in bringing Carteret down in November 1744. Yet the Pelham brothers were more impressed by the risk that Carteret's extravagance and flamboyance would destroy the confidence of the country gentlemen in the joint Administration than hostile to his basic line of policy on the Continent. They prayed to be delivered from a warlike genius and an enterprising Minister, whose policies, if successful, would have undermined the position of the Pelhams with the King and, if unsuccessful, would have destroyed the confidence of the House of Commons in the joint Ministry. After getting rid of Carteret, Newcastle gradually took over the main lines of his foreign policy.

Admittedly this at first was partly because the forceful impulse given by Carteret to British foreign policy was so agreeable to the King that it could not be immediately reversed. The most the Pelhams could hope to do if they were to retain the support of a distrustful and suspicious monarch was gently to apply the brakes. The Pelhams concluded at Warsaw in January 1745 the negotiation which Carteret, before his fall, had begun for a joint Austro-Saxon attempt, financed by the Maritime Powers, to defeat Prussia, break off the alliance of France and Prussia, which was the main barrier to Austrian hegemony in Germany, and perhaps even to deprive Frederick of most of his gains in the First Silesian War. They were also prepared to increase the subsidies payable to

[2] *New Cambridge Modern History*, vii (Cambridge, 1957), 440.

Austria and to underwrite most of the obligations Carteret had undertaken towards Sardinia in the hope of bolstering up Austria's position in Italy. Partly no doubt to curry favour with George II, but also from a genuine conviction that Hanover was the loser by the personal union with England, the Pelhams made a generous contribution to the cost of keeping the Hanoverian army on a war footing.

Even at the outset of the Pelham Ministry it was clear that Newcastle found the mantle of Carteret much more congenial than Pelham ever did. But Pelham was so lacking in interest as well as in knowledge of the problems of foreign policy that he never ceased to depend on his brother's long experience and superior knowledge. This was indeed the basic weakness of Pelham foreign policy in the decade between the fall of Carteret and the death of Henry Pelham. Pelham, while deferring to his brother's superior lights, distrusted his judgment and frequently interfered to thwart his brother's plans. Newcastle on his side was inclined to resent the Premier's calm assumption that he was entitled to the last word upon foreign as on domestic policy, particularly when this policy threw unwelcome burdens upon the Exchequer. This built-in conflict was less serious than it might have been, owing to the position occupied in the Cabinet by Lord Chancellor Hardwicke, which enabled him to mediate between the two brothers and even sometimes to act with the consent of both as arbiter between them. Hardwicke shared Pelham's basic 'little Englander' approach to foreign policy, but had a better grasp of Continental politics and therefore a sounder appreciation of what Newcastle was trying to do. More than once his influence over Pelham ended a deadlock between the Pelham brothers and enabled Newcastle to take an important step towards the attainment of his aims on the Continent.

The fundamental divergence between Premier and Foreign Minister made particularly important the choice of the other Secretary of State. This office after the dismissal of Harrington, who had affronted the King, was held in turn by Chesterfield and Bedford. Each soon fell foul of Newcastle, who finally succeeded in securing a docile tool, Holdernesse, as Bedford's successor in 1751. At the same time he deliberately brought Carteret into the

Ministry as President of the Council, in the belief, which proved to be well founded, that the former rival of the Pelhams was no longer a danger to the Ministry, while his views on foreign policy accorded well with Newcastle's. Thus for the last three years of the Pelham Ministry, Newcastle could usually count upon the support of Hardwicke and Carteret while his colleague as Secretary of State, Holdernesse, made no attempt to follow a line of his own in foreign policy.

As long as the Austrian Succession War continued Newcastle had merely been the leader of a group in the Government pledged to continue the war. His brother-secretaries, Chesterfield and Bedford in succession, advocated the conclusion of peace at almost any price as a lesser evil than the continuation of a bloody and expensive Continental war in which our allies were more and more clearly determined to throw the principal if not the whole burden on the British Government. The collapse of the Jacobite Rebellion and the restoration of the Stadholderate in the United Provinces encouraged Newcastle to persist in this policy and even for a few months to hope for victories in the Netherlands comparable to those of Marlborough in the Spanish Succession War. Speedily undeceived by the chief advisers of the new Stadholder, who told him bluntly that they could not pay their share of the expense of carrying on the war, Newcastle hurriedly switched roles. He ceased to represent himself as the Atlas who had carried on the war almost single-handed against the opposition, overt and concealed, of his colleagues. He now saw himself as the shrewd and experienced diplomatist whose skill in negotiation could alone extricate his country from a dangerous and critical situation.

In the opinion of Sir Richard Lodge, Newcastle's conduct in the closing years of the Austrian Succession War ought to have shattered his political reputation for ever. This was certainly the opinion of the Parliamentary Opposition at the time, who enquired in a series of motions what advantages Newcastle had gained at the Peace of Aix-la-Chapelle which the Government could not have secured five years earlier by Carteret's Hanau negotiation. The longer the war lasted the clearer it became to everybody concerned that Britain could not face France 'without the active aid of the two traditional allies [Austria and the United Provinces], and he [Newcastle] had lost them both'.[3]

After the conclusion of peace on what were surprisingly good terms for his country, Newcastle, attributing his failure in the war to lack of adequate support from the United Provinces and Austria, set himself not only to restore the 'old system', but to strengthen it by a series of treaties of subsidy with states which, unlike Austria and the United Provinces, could not be expected to join the old system without pecuniary inducements. Newcastle in a very private letter to Hardwicke expounded the main lines of his foreign policy after the Peace of Aix-la-Chapelle:[4]

> France has now wisely found out that a little money well applied in peace may save millions in war and, what is the worst of all for us, enable her to continue the peace or begin a new war with almost a certainty of success whenever her interest or her ambition shall incline her to it. [France may thus reduce Britain to a state of dependency or even by another Jacobite rising overturn the constitution.] . . . I am sensible in opposition to this reasoning it will be said this may be all true and therefore we should not provoke France to exert the power she certainly has. To that I answer that if she certainly has the power she will have the inclination and . . . they would imperceptibly reduce us to a state of dependency upon them. . . . If therefore these imminent dangers are not to be avoided by any complacency on our part towards France what other means are there of doing it? I do not pretend there are any certain ones but some very probable ones [subsidy treaties] which therefore I think ought to be tried and which I am sensible if not tried sooner or later the nation will cry out for and greatly blame those who have not attempted it. . . . France at present is for peace and will not easily be drove from it and therefore this is the time to form such an alliance and party in Europe as shall enable you to make some stand, or what I would principally propose discourage France from

[3] R. Lodge, *Studies in Eighteenth Century Diplomacy* (London, 1930), p. 410.

[4] 25 August O.S. 1749, in B.M. Add. MSS. 35410, f. 126.

> beginning a new war. . . . If they go on in buying up all the powers upon the Continent when they have bought those which are to be sold they will get the others from fear, and therefore France will reasonably then conclude that they may impose what conditions they please upon us without our daring to dispute them and therefore in reality run no risk of engaging themselves in a new war; whereas if we had a tolerable system and force upon the Continent, though by no means equal to France and Prussia, the experience of the last war shows us France would not wantonly in the present circumstances engage in a new war, the event of which might be doubtful. . . .

Hardwicke's uncompromisingly negative reply[5] produced a second plea from Newcastle in which he argued: 'France will outdo us at sea when they have nothing to fear by land. . . . I have always maintained that our marine should protect our alliances upon the Continent; and they, by diverting the expense of France, enable us to maintain our superiority at sea.'[6] Even this argument seems to have left both Hardwicke and Pelham unimpressed. What in the end made it possible for Newcastle to convert his reluctant colleagues to his objective of securing a new Grand Alliance against France, buttressed by subsidies to the princes of Germany, was the twist given to the purposes of the subsidy treaties by the rising diplomatic star, Sir Charles Hanbury Williams.

While British Minister at Dresden during the war, Hanbury Williams had heard talk about securing the election of the eldest son of Maria Theresa and the Emperor Francis I as King of the Romans. This would give the Archduke Joseph the right to succeed his father as Emperor without any need for further election which France or Prussia could exploit, as they had done in 1740–1, to bring about a general war in Europe. As Hanbury Williams put it:[7]

[5] P. C. Yorke, *The Life and Correspondence of Philip Yorke, Earl of Hardwicke*, ii (Cambridge, 1913), 16–22.

[6] 2 September O.S. 1749, in B.M. Add. MSS. 35410, f. 140.

[7] P.R.O., undated memorandum, endorsed October 1749, in S.P. 88.71.

> I must own that I think the election of the King of the Romans so material a thing that I don't see how any reasonable project can be framed for the future security of the liberties of Europe without making that election one of the principal objects. I think the sum requisite is trifling in comparison with the desired end and I think the election of a King of the Romans would be a satisfactory answer to anything that could be said in Parliament against those subsidys . . . the whole would be done under His Majesty's auspices and by his own hands. He will have the glory of it and Europe the benefit.
>
> But I cannot help thinking that if something of this kind is not soon undertaken it will shortly be out of our power to do it and we may in time be obliged to spend millions in order to stop an evil which now some few thousands would prevent.

Newcastle eagerly adopted as the main point in his Continental programme the idea of securing the Archduke's election as King of the Romans, and during the next few years tried to carry it out.[8] Peace was already a British interest: country gentlemen proved willing to provide many thousands a year for the princes of Germany. What chiefly convinced them was the argument that if Britain had a firm system on the Continent, France would not dare to break the peace. Even £100,000 a year in subsidies for a few years was a cheap insurance policy against a war which would cost millions for each campaign.

English experts on foreign policy believed that the best chance of creating a real and lasting counterpoise to the Bourbon courts lay in checking and if possible reversing the separatist tendencies which had made Germany an easy prey to France for more than a century. Germany was clearly superior to France in population, natural resources and perhaps even in commercial and industrial development. All that was required was the co-ordination and direction of these resources by a dominant political authority—and in the eighteenth century this could only mean the Emperor. To

[8] Reed Browning, 'The Duke of Newcastle and the Imperial Election Plan 1749–54', in *Journal of British Studies*, vii, no. 1 (November 1967), 28–47.

secure the imperial crown for the Habsburgs for two lives might well be the first step towards the reappearance of Germany as a great power in the European balance.

British hopes were reinforced by fears. Austria was no longer the power she had been in the seventeenth century and had at least appeared to be in the early eighteenth century. The brilliant promise of the Archduke Charles's early years had ended in something not far from disaster. It is true that Maria Theresa had saved the bulk of her father's territories, but only at the cost of surrendering valuable provinces. She was now engaged on far-reaching schemes of internal reorganization, intended to transform Austria from a medieval agglomeration of territories into a modern state. In the meantime it was clear that Austria, unaided, could no longer resist France with any hope of success. France already had a strong party in Germany; if Britain did not belatedly follow the example of France and try to organize her supporters within the Empire, France might well secure complete control of the resources of Germany, with disastrous results to the balance of power and the Protestant cause in Europe.

Unfortunately, the method chosen by Newcastle to give effect to this quite rational policy was not well-adapted for the purpose. The very arguments which led Newcastle to adopt the King of the Romans scheme made certain that it would be bitterly opposed in Germany. Almost the only point on which the German princes agreed was that the present state of affairs in the Empire suited them admirably: the last thing they wanted was a real revival of the imperial authority, as was shown a generation later, when Frederick II was able to organize the *Fürstenbund* against Joseph II's ambitious schemes. Those who were not already committed to France, of course, welcomed British intervention, since they could reasonably hope to obtain subsidies from a new source. Some of them even thought they could draw subsidies simultaneously from both powers: at the worst, they could put themselves up to auction and accept the best bid available at the moment.

Even now Newcastle's difficulties were formidable, as he himself explained to a prominent Dutch politician, Charles Bentinck. After referring to 'those who are willing to triumph over me here for being as they say the *only one* who is wild enough to think at present of supporting the antient system', he continued:[9]

> You don't at all know how our affairs stand here: all the love of peace, detestation of war, etc., which you saw when you was last in England is now turned to the necessity of economy: the impossibility of giving any subsidy in time of peace: the little advantage of paying German princes who will leave you tomorrow for a better bargain with France: the weakness of the republic of Holland: the impossibility of having any assistance from thence or even of making any system or stand against France and therefore nothing was to be done but to keep quiet, pay our debts, and not *engage*. This language though very general is and ever shall be constantly opposed by *me*; and if our allies would be reasonable, take their proper share in expence: and nothing be asked but what carries certain advantage with it, with labour, pains, perseverance, and being reasonable as to the sum and pretty certain as to the effect, I may perhaps (tho' I can't answer for it) be able to do something, but in any other shape I dare not attempt it.

Newcastle's adoption of the election project, deliberately intended to bring Austria and Britain together again and make amends to Maria Theresa for Britain's desertion of Austria at the end of the war, contributed to their alienation and the break-up of the old system of alliances which it was Newcastle's intention to confirm and consolidate. It is indeed the best example of Newcastle's worst weakness as a Foreign Minister—his inability to place himself in the shoes of the statesmen with whom he was negotiating. Neither Maria Theresa nor Kaunitz was much impressed by the rather shop-soiled idea that Hanbury Williams had persuaded Newcastle to adopt. They were much better informed about the legal, constitutional and political difficulties which stood in the way of its accomplishment. They knew that it could only be secured by bribing an eminent majority of the Electoral College. They saw it as another example of British meddling in Germany

[9] Newcastle to C. Bentinck, 29 December O.S. 1749, in B.M. Add. MSS. 32819, f. 301.

and attempting to dictate policy to the Habsburgs. Newcastle made it plain that he thought he was conferring a favour on Austria by taking up the election project: Maria Theresa, on the contrary, resented the ill-advised and presumptuous attempt of the youngest of the electors to take over Habsburg leadership in the Empire. Even worse, to adopt Newcastle's plan was to expose herself to blackmail by the German princes whose votes would be required to secure the election. Worse still, Kaunitz, who already saw Austria's hope of salvation as dependent on the conclusion of an alliance with France, foresaw that Newcastle's project would result in a futile subsidy competition between Britain and France which would set Germany in uproar and make more difficult the attainment of his basic aim—the reconciliation of Austria and France and the support of France for an Austro-Russian war against Prussia.

Newcastle seems never to have had even an inkling of the causes which were responsible for the reserved attitude of Austria to his great scheme. 'The conduct of the Austrian ministers is astonishing', he wrote. 'We wish to be well with them. We show it by desiring to do their business; and rather than owe any obligation to us they will obstruct their own business and do *that* of their greatest enemies, France and Prussia. . . . This is a real truth.'[10]

Apart from the election question, the most serious cause of Austro-British friction between the wars was undoubtedly the divergence of views on the Austrian Netherlands. Two main questions were at issue here: (1) the re-establishment of the barrier against France and (2) the making of a new treaty of commerce which would reduce, if not eliminate, the privileges enjoyed by subjects of the Maritime Powers under the treaties to which Austria owed her possessions in the Netherlands. Here too Austria was much less conservative than her Dutch and British allies. She recognized that the course of the Austrian Succession

[10] Newcastle to Williams (private), 20 February 1753 in B.M. Add. MSS. 32843, f. 28. Professor Reed Browning kindly allowed me to see in typescript a chapter from his forthcoming book on Newcastle in which is discussed on the basis of papers in the Haus-Hof- und Staatsarchiv at Vienna the attitude of Maria Theresa and Kaunitz to the election project.

War had proved the futility of the attempt to contain France by an expensive system of barrier fortresses, and would no longer make a substantial contribution to their upkeep, still less to their re-establishment after the devastation wrought by Marshal Saxe in the later campaigns of the Austrian Succession War. Newcastle, on the other hand, partly influenced by the Dutch, insisted that Maria Theresa was not the independent sovereign of the Austrian Netherlands, but merely a trustee for the Maritime Powers. 'The Low Countries', he wrote, were 'a kind of common country in which we, the Dutch, and the Empress-Queen are all interested.' Austria must accept, along with the restrictions and burdens imposed upon her by the Barrier Treaty, the major responsibility for restoring and maintaining the Barrier out of the revenues she derived from the Netherlands, and she must continue to honour the commercial privileges granted by the original Barrier Treaty to British and Dutch traders there.

It was on these issues that Hanbury Williams, sent by Newcastle to Vienna in 1753 to try to restore to the Anglo-Austrian alliance the spirit of confidence and cordiality which had been lacking since the Treaty of Aix-la-Chapelle, found himself openly and dramatically at variance with the Empress-Queen. His own report of his conversations with Maria Theresa,[11] though no doubt heightened to impress his royal master,[12] may be accepted as substantially accurate:

> Her jealousy of being governed broke out very often and particularly in the whole story of the Maritime Powers having signed the preliminaries at Aix without her. . . . I also told her Imperial Majesty . . . that the King desired no superiority, but that he insisted upon equality and reciprocity; and that I was sorry to tell her Imperial Majesty that all unprejudiced persons were convinced that it was owing to some jealousy of this sort, and the want of a due confidence in the best and most powerful friend of the House

[11] Printed almost in full in W. Coxe, *Memoirs of the Administration of the Rt. Hon. Henry Pelham*, ii (London, 1829), 469–82, from P.R.O. S.P. 88.75.

[12] Joseph Yorke to Hardwicke, 7 August 1753, in B.M. Add. MSS. 35356, f. 171; Hardwicke's reply, *ibid.*, f. 175.

of Austria, that the great affair of the election of a King of the Romans had not been long ago completed, and that it was a melancholy consideration for those who were sincerely attached to the House of Austria to reflect that while the King was taking indefatigable pains and expending great sums for attaining one of the greatest benefits that could accrue to her Imperial family and to the peace of Europe, the court of Vienna had rather hindered than forwarded that great work. The Empress-Queen was warmed by what I said, and seemed to take it very ill; but I could not depart from what I was convinced was true. Your Grace had ordered me to talk with freedom and I did so.

Our conversation was still more animated upon the affair of the barrier. . . . As I am convinced that till that point is settled the connection between the House of Austria and the Maritime Powers is but precarious I was resolved to do my utmost to persuade her Imperial Majesty . . . of the injustice with which [the Maritime Powers] had been treated. This I did with a decent freedom. But I am sorry to say that I found her Imperial Majesty so prejudiced in this affair that reason had very little share in all she said. The notion of being the independent sovereign of the Low Countries is so fixed in her that it will be difficult to eradicate it. I took the liberty to tell her Majesty in so many words that she was far from being the independent sovereign of the Low Countries, that she was limited by her treaties with the Maritime Powers, which I hoped for the future at least would be no more violated. This her Imperial Majesty seemed also to take very ill; and insisted loudly, so loudly that the people in the next room heard her, that she was the sovereign of the Low Countries, and that it was her duty to protect her subjects, who had been too long oppressed by the barrier treaty and deprived of the natural privileges which all other nations enjoy. To this I replied that the treaty of the barrier was still in force, though it had certainly been violated by her Imperial Majesty. . . . I wish I could tell

> your Grace that anything I said upon this subject had made the least impression upon the Empress-Queen. . . .

Hanbury Williams's exchanges with Maria Theresa's new Chancellor, Kaunitz, were much less heated, but Kaunitz was merely paying lip-homage to Austria's old love until he could establish himself successfully in the affections of the new. By accepting the counterfeit for genuine coin, Hanbury Williams helped to prolong Newcastle's residence in a fool's paradise from which he was rudely thrust in the summer of 1755, when Austria demanded impossible terms for assisting Britain to defend Hanover and the Netherlands against France. Keith, the resident British Minister at Vienna, shared Hanbury Williams's responsibility, and to a higher degree.

In fact, Kaunitz's abandonment of hostility to France, whether he succeeded in detaching France from Prussia or not, converted Austria's alliance with Britain from the essential foundation of Austrian foreign policy into a dangerous burden, since at any moment Franco-British hostility might involve Austria in war with France. The alliance had virtually lost its *raison d'être*, and there was naturally no disposition on the Austrian side to make sacrifices for the 'common cause', since in Kaunitz's eyes that cause no longer existed. The only method of restoring to the British alliance the value it had lost would have been for Britain to commit herself to Austro-Russian antagonism to Prussia, and in particular to accede to the fourth secret article of the Treaty of 1746.[13]

Austrian demands on Britain were as unrealistic as Newcastle's expectations from Austria. Probably the most fundamental cause of the final breach between Britain and Austria was the firm British refusal to accept Kaunitz's plans for the liquidation of Prussia. All British politicians were agreed that British involvement in Continental politics and above all in expensive Continental wars were evils, justified only if they clearly served the manifest interests of Britain by reducing French power in Europe and distracting French attention from British interests

[13] D. B. Horn, *Sir Charles Hanbury Williams and European Diplomacy, 1747–1758* (London, 1930), pp. 150–1.

beyond Europe. During the last years of the Austrian Succession War it had been the policy of Newcastle himself to help Austria against France, but not against Prussia. He wanted Austria, not Prussia, as an ally, but had no intention of being drawn into war with Prussia merely to serve the interests of Austria and Russia. After peace had been made at Aix, he was ready to accede to the main treaty of the two Empresses, but refused to have anything to do with its secret clauses which would have bound Britain to join in a crusade against Prussia. It was partly as an alternative to such a dangerous and unpopular commitment that the ill-starred subsidy negotiations began between Britain and Russia. Here again, as in his dealings with Austria, Newcastle never understood the advantages which Russia hoped to attain by the conclusion of the treaty. To him, as to his lieutenant, Holdernesse, a subsidy treaty with Russia was essentially the same as a subsidy treaty with Hesse or Brunswick: it gave Britain the right to make use of a certain number of foreign troops when British interests required it. But to Russia the attraction of a subsidy treaty with Britain was that it would provide an ostensible reason for placing a body of Russian troops within easy reach of East Prussia and thus hamper Frederick the Great's freedom of political manœuvre and paralyse his military initiative, while at the same time the British subsidy would help to defray the financial costs of the operation. It was for these reasons rather than with any hope of British participation in a Russo-Austrian war against Prussia that Kaunitz made the conclusion of the treaty a prerequisite for Austrian participation in the defence of the Austrian Netherlands against France.

When in the spring of 1755 Newcastle, prompted by Kaunitz, had taken up again the negotiation for a Russian subsidy treaty, his intention had been to conciliate Austria, secure her participation in the defence of the Low Countries against France, and provide for the defence of Hanover by the implied threat that Prussian action against George II's electorate would be promptly countered by a Russian invasion of East Prussia and Brandenburg. Before the treaty had been concluded, British ideas of the use to be made of it had radically changed. Newcastle, in the course of his correspondence with Münchhausen in July 1755, claimed to have been the only begetter of the new ideas, and expounded them at considerable length and with more than his usual clarity. His basic aim as he explained it was to conclude the Russian treaty without bringing about a breach with Prussia.[14] He told the Hanoverian Ministers that their plans to organize a grand coalition for the defence of Hanover, while good in themselves, were not feasible in view of the attitude of Britain's allies and of the heavy expenses to which the British Government was already committed. Purely defensive measures, he advised them, would forestall the charge of having begun a war upon the Continent and dragged into it princes whom the British Government was not in a position to support effectively.[15] Exactly a week later he offered Münchhausen an alternative plan:[16]

> Comme j'écris à vôtre excellence dans la dernière confiance, je veux bien vous hazarder une pensée, qui me vient en tête, et que je n'ai jamais confié à personne ni ici ni dehors.
>
> Vous avez, à ce que j'espère, vû mes lettres à My Lord Holdernesse; et vous aurez compris l'impossibilité où nous sommes d'entrer dans un plan général pour la guerre sur le Continent. Ces obstacles s'augmentent journellement jusqu'au point qu'il se trouve ici quelque mécontentements même sur la convention dernièrement conclue avec le landgrave de Hesse, la plus grande Partie chez nous malheureusement regardant, à cette heure, tout traité subsidiare plutôt comme une demarche qui pouvoit entrainer et provoquer la guerre sur le Continent que comme une mesure sage, d'en prévenir les suites.
>
> Non obstant, il faut aller en avant avec nôtre traité Russien, et, si nous y réussissons (comme il y a quelque apparence, depuis l'arrivée de Monsieur le Chevalier Williams) je soumets aux lumières superieurs de Votre

14 Newcastle to Hardwicke, 26 July 1755, in B.M. Add. MSS. 32857, f. 384b. Cf. Add. MSS. 35415, f. 17.

15 Newcastle to Münchhausen and Steinberg, 18 July 1755, Niedersächsisches Staatsarchiv, Hanover, Hanover 91v. Münchhausen, i, 22.

16 Newcastle to Münchhausen, 25 July 1755, Niedersächsisches Staatsarchiv, Hanover, Hanover 91v. Münchhausen, i, 22, and B.M. Add. MSS. 32857, f. 348.

> Excellence si l'on ne pouvoit pas en faire l'usage suivant. Le Roi de Prusse craint, par dessus toutes choses, la Russie et l'accomplissement de nôtre traité avec elle. Ce traité une fois faite, ne peut on pas faire sentir au Roi de Prusse qu'en cas que Sa Majesté Prussienne ne prenne pas aucune part dans la guerre entre l'Autriche et la France et qu'elle ne permet pas que les états allemands du Roi fussent attaqués en conséquence de ces brouilleries, les trouppes que Sa Majesté est en droit de démander en vertue de son traité avec la Russie, ne seront point requises, mais tout restera, à cet égard, sur le pied, où il est à present? On épargnera par là la dépense immense des troupes Russiennes si elles étoient à notre solde et on procureroit (à ce qû'il me semble) une seureté la plus solide et la plus réelle pour les états allemandes du Roi. . . . On auroit grand raison ici de se louer de la sage mesure du traité avec la Russie si, moyennant un subside annuel pour quatre ans qui ne montera pas au delà de cent à cent trente mille livres sterling par an, on auroit pû obtenir une neutralité de la part du Roi de Prusse pendant la guerre, et une seureté entière pour les états allemandes de Sa Majesté.

While welcoming Newcastle's initiative, Münchhausen appreciated much more clearly than the proposer of the scheme the danger that its adoption might finally and fatally alienate Austria. The alternative, he pointed out to Newcastle, if pursued with care, was not incompatible with a reconciliation with Austria. Both lines of policy should be pursued concurrently until it became clearer which would best enable them to face up to France and yet preserve the peace of the Continent.[17]

Hardwicke shared Münchhausen's reservations. He wrote:

> I am anxious about that [the Russian] treaty in our present circumstances. I do not see how we can do without it or with it. When it is finished it will be made the foundation of further schemes on the Continent of which the whole expense will be thrown upon England. How this can be

[17] Münchhausen to Newcastle, 2 August 1755, Niedersächsisches Staatsarchiv, Hanover, Hanover 91v. Münchhausen, i, 22.

> accepted I know not and yet, if it should become necessary to make the requisition, it will be thought a prodigious burden for the defence of Hanover merely. I therefore extremely wish that some such scheme could take place as your grace has hinted to Münchhausen and yet I fear for the practicability [of it]. The King of Prussia may lie by and yet France may send such a force that way as may strike so much terror that the King may insist on the requisition being made. On the other hand, may not the Czarina be revolted or disgusted when she hears such a private bargain is struck up with the King of Prussia, for she certainly flatters herself with the expectation that the great subsidy of £500,000 *per annum* will come into her coffers.[18]

Other colleagues in the Cabinet were much more favourably impressed by Newcastle's scheme. Granville remarked that 'if we could keep the King of Prussia quiet for one year only it would be worth everything to us'.[19] Holdernesse, still in attendance on George II at Hanover, was not enthusiastic, but concurred reluctantly with his colleagues 'that no better use could be made of the *Russian treaty* in the *present circumstances*, I say in the present circumstances, because, if there had been any possibility of engaging England in *great* and *wise* schemes for the Continent, I could not have approved this step, but the moment *we* cannot make up our matters with *Vienna* the only thing left is to keep terms with *Prussia*'.[20] By this time Newcastle was convinced that if the Russian treaty was signed, as it probably would be, before Newcastle had explained to Frederick the Great the real intentions of the British Government in concluding it, the King of Prussia 'would fly out at once'.[21]

Once again Newcastle had jumped out of the frying-pan into the fire. To recover and strengthen the Austrian alliance after

[18] Hardwicke to Newcastle, 28 July 1755, in B.M. Add. MSS. 32857, f. 396.

[19] Newcastle to Holdernesse, *entre nous*, 1 August 1755, in B.M. Add. MSS. 32857, f. 506.

[20] Holdernesse to Newcastle, 2nd *entre nous*, 3 August 1755, in B.M. Add. MSS. 32857, f. 555.

[21] Newcastle to Hardwicke, 12 August 1755, in B.M. Add. MSS. 35415, f. 38.

Aix-la-Chapelle, he had had to adopt a plan of subsidy treaties for which there was no precedent in time of peace. He had then taken up the election project and set the Empire in uproar. To protect his German clients, he had then been driven to take up again the Russian treaty of subsidy which he had refused to negotiate earlier. By changing in July 1755 the use intended to be made of this treaty he finally convinced both Austria and Russia that a British alliance against Prussia was an impracticable dream. The more Newcastle wriggled the more he convinced both Austria and Russia that they must have the active support of France if their plans were ever to be realized.

It is unnecessary to trace here the complicated negotiation between Britain and Prussia which led to the signature of the Convention of Westminster on 16 January 1756. Neither signatory intended to make any change in the political system of Europe. Both regarded it as a temporary *ad hoc* agreement, in no way inconsistent with their long-standing treaties of alliance respectively with Austria and with France. Newcastle believed that by a diplomatic *coup* he had resolved the difficulties over Austrian participation in the defence of British interests on the Continent, which had threatened a few months earlier the total overthrow of the Austro-British alliance. Newcastle hoped Austria would receive with enthusiasm the news of his convention with Prussia.[22] Even after these hopes had been belied by the outbreak of war in the summer of 1756 between Austria and Prussia, Holdernesse explained with evident sincerity that the clauses of the Convention of Westminster

> were not meant to be, nor would they in their consequence have been detrimental to the Court of Vienna. They were intended to diminish the number of the enemies of the House of Austria; to prevent an unjust attack, on the part of France, on His Majesty's German dominions, . . . and to put the House of Austria, if necessary, in a condition to have withstood any attempts that might have been made against them in consequence of their Alliance with the

[22] That he had his doubts is evident from Holdernesse's despatch to Keith, 23 March 1756, in P.R.O. S.P. 80.197.

> King; and Time might have brought about the happiest event for the welfare of Europe, I mean a good understanding between the Courts of Vienna and Berlin.[23]

The British Government, so far from seeking to establish a new system in Europe, was still intent on remedying what Hardwicke at the end of the Austrian Succession War had described as the 'lameness' of the old system without Prussian support. Newcastle was all the more hurt when Maria Theresa told Keith that so far from providing adequately for the defence of her interests in the Netherlands, the Westminster Convention was calculated to encourage France to attack them.

Just as Britain argued that her object in signing the Convention of Westminster was to save Austria from herself, so Frederick the Great contended that he had done France good service by concluding the Convention. Since France's best hope of winning the colonial war was to avoid involvement in a simultaneous Continental war, the preservation of peace in Germany, the main aim of his agreement with Britain, was in the best interests of France; but Frederick's special pleading annoyed Louis XV and contributed to the French decision to remove Prussia from the roll of France's allies.

By August 1755 Kaunitz had reopened under more favourable auspices his negotiation with France. Some progress had been made before the signature of the Convention of Westminster, but a fundamental divergence of aim still separated France and Austria. France was pacific, and certainly anxious not to wage war on the Continent while she was engaged with Britain on the seas and in the colonies. Kaunitz, on the other hand, required the French alliance chiefly to enable Austria to wage a Continental war against Prussia with less cost to herself and a greater prospect of success. But for French indignation over the Convention of Westminster, which seemed to France yet another betrayal of her interests by Prussia, this gulf would never have been bridged. If Spain, as seemed to be the case under Ferdinand VI, had been detached from France and Prussia had betrayed her, France had no strong ally upon which she could count against Britain.

[23] Holdernesse to Stormont, 10 September 1756, in P.R.O. S.P. 88.79.

Isolation was dangerous. She was already negotiating with Russia to end the estrangement between them and undermine British influence at St Petersburg. An understanding with Austria would be helpful here as well as invaluable for its own sake. The first Treaty of Versailles was therefore signed and the Diplomatic Revolution was effected.

Contemporaries and later historians have undoubtedly exaggerated the novelty and suddenness of the alliance between Austria and France.[24] It had been proposed and seriously considered, sometimes by one party to the agreement of 1756, sometimes by the other, for many years before it actually occurred. Probably the knowledge that such attempts had been repeatedly made and had uniformly failed contributed to the general astonishment with which the first Treaty of Versailles was received in Europe.

Voltaire insisted that the Diplomatic Revolution was a natural development: 'When the English were for bearing rule, this alliance was perfectly natural, and not in the least contradictory to the Treaty of Westphalia.'[25] There was indeed on the Continent in the first half of the eighteenth century a general feeling that Britain was an aggressive power with a penchant for intervening in questions which did not concern her, usually with the intention of setting the Empire in disorder and keeping the Continental powers disunited and jealous of each other. While professing to secure the balance of power, she was really seeking to arrogate to herself a pre-eminence over all the other powers and to establish herself as the effective arbiter of Europe.[26] A common resentment against Britain certainly contributed powerfully to the reconciliation between the two leading powers of the Continent, Austria and France. Looking at the Revolution too much from the standpoint of Kaunitz, later historians have emphasized the anti-Prussian element and have unduly neglected the equally or even more important anti-British aspect.

[24] Max Braubach, *Versailles und Wien von Ludwig XIV bis Kaunitz* (Bonn, 1952), *passim*.

[25] *Supplement to the Essay on General History*, ii (London, 1764), 174.

[26] Even Prince Eugène of Savoy, who on the whole favoured the British alliance, expressed these views (Max Braubach, *Prinz Eugen von Savoyen*, iv (Munich, 1965), 335–9).

In my view, therefore, the Duke of Newcastle has an equal claim to Kaunitz for consideration as the man who really brought about the Revolution. In the previous decade he was the effective director of British foreign policy, and the line he pursued so annoyed France and Austria that they decided at last to sink their long-standing differences. He refused to help Austria against Prussia, her nearest and, as Kaunitz and Maria Theresa thought, most dangerous enemy. He refused—until too late—to buy the active assistance of Russia, which was fundamental to Kaunitz's plans. By his election schemes he set the Empire in uproar without taking any effective steps to undermine French influence. His persistent refusal to admit that Austria was sovereign in the Netherlands and his partiality for Sardinia in the politics of the Mediterranean provided Austria with additional grievances. And when Keith, the British Diplomatic Agent at Vienna, tried to explain to Newcastle the natural Austrian reaction to British policy, Newcastle declaimed about the ingratitude and impertinence of the Court of Vienna and denounced Keith as an Austrian parasite.

At the same time Newcastle was taking steps which would inevitably bring about war with France. Whatever may be said about the activities of French colonial governors and agents, the French Court was genuinely desirous of avoiding war with Britain. Contemporaries contrasted its passive, not to say supine, attitude with the violent reaction which Newcastle's acts would have met from Louis XIV. Probably the weakness of the French reaction contributed to war because it encouraged Newcastle to go further than he otherwise would have done until he had gone too far to draw back. As Pitt said in one of his philippics: 'We had provoked before we could defend, and neglected after provocation; . . . we were left inferior to France in every quarter. . . . He prayed to God that his Majesty might not have Minorca, like Calais, written on his heart.'[27] If Pitt's analysis is correct, Newcastle had surely done more than anyone else to bring Austria and France together.

When Newcastle realized that he was well on the way to war with France and that Austria would not lift a finger to help him,

[27] Horace Walpole, *Memoirs of George II* (ed. 1847), ii, 194.

he rushed headlong into the treaty of subsidy with Russia, which he had hitherto refused to conclude, in spite of repeated Austrian solicitations. It was this treaty which acted as a percussion cap and set off the train of events leading to the first Treaty of Versailles. As its negotiators intended, the Convention of St Petersburg alarmed Frederick the Great. Newcastle then exploited Prussian fears to conclude the Convention of Westminster, apparently with the idea that it could become the basis of an Austro-Russian-Prussian coalition to fight Britain's battles on the Continent. As his fellow-secretary, Holdernesse, remarked, 'As we pay the piper it is not unreasonable for us to have the tune we like.' When Keith, on orders from Newcastle, tried to explain Newcastle's latest scheme to the Court of Vienna, he was politely shown the door. Kaunitz deliberately used Newcastle's actions, not only to overcome the party at Vienna which favoured continued co-operation with Britain, but to convince France that she had been deserted by Prussia, her last important ally on the Continent, and must choose between isolation and the conclusion of an alliance with Austria. Like other French and Austrian ministers in the preceding half-century, Kaunitz had tried to reconcile France and Austria during his mission to Versailles from 1750 to 1752. He had, on his own admission when he returned to Vienna, completely failed in his self-imposed task. If he succeeded four years later, he owed his success more to the Duke of Newcastle than to anyone else.

Ten

Cavour and the Tuscan Revolution of 1859

by

Denis Mack Smith

On 27 April 1859 a peaceful revolution in Florence expelled the Grand Duke Leopold and his son Ferdinand. Some months later Piedmont annexed Tuscany. This was a considerable achievement, all the more remarkable in that it had been opposed by both France and Austria. The revolution of April 1859 is sometimes said to have been planned and organized by Cavour;[1] but the extent of his involvement requires further study.

Before 1859 Cavour's thoughts had not often travelled beyond the Apennines. He had never been in central Italy. He had no intimate friend in Tuscany, and fewer contacts there than in most other Italian regions. His ideas about its future were changeable nor were they the result of any profound thought. When Palmerston once suggested enlarging the Grand Duke's domains, he had opposed the idea,[2] because he wanted no alternative focus for Italian patriotism; yet when Louis Napoleon later repeated the suggestion, Cavour agreed that Tuscany could be allowed to annex Umbria and the Marches.[3] In negotiations with the Emperor he bid for Venice, Modena, Parma and the Romagna

[1] R. della Torre, *La Evoluzione del Sentimento Nazionale in Toscana, dal 27 Aprile 1859 al 15 Marzo 1860* (Milan, 1915), p. 23. Sergio Camerani, 'La Toscana alla Vigilia della Rivoluzione', *Archivio Storico Italiano* (Florence, 1945–6), cii, 159, 181. E. Passerin d'Entrèves, *Il Piemonte, l'Italia Centrale e la Questione Romana nel 1859–60* (Pisa, 1960), pp. 54–5, 59.

[2] Cavour to Lamarmora, 21 January 1856, *Lettere Edite ed Inedite di Camillo Cavour,* ed. Luigi Chiala, ii (Turin, 1883), 176.

[3] Cavour to Victor Emanuel, 24 July 1858, *Il Carteggio Cavour-Nigra dal 1858 al 1861*, ed. R. Commissione (Bologna, 1926), i, 105.

as possible acquisitions for Piedmont, but did not bid for Tuscany. Leopold's dynasty evidently met no rooted objection on his part, and he once seems to have considered a marriage alliance between Lorraine and Savoy.[4] He even showed solidarity with Leopold by helping him suppress Mazzini's nationalist agitation.[5] Yet he could also consider giving Tuscany to the Bourbons of Parma so as to leave Parma available for that advancement of Piedmont which was his first political principle. As late as December 1858 he was not unfavourable to the strange notion of imposing a Hohenzollern prince on Tuscany, for it would please the Germans and bring into Italy what he called 'une race qui a encore de la force et de la vigueur'.[6] All this shows a notable disinclination towards political dogmatism or doctrinaire Italian patriotism.

Cavour knew that the *ancien régime* was at its least intolerable in Tuscany. Well-to-do Florentines, appalled by the revolution of 1848, were happy that the Grand Duke had now exiled Montanelli, Guerrazzi and the radical firebrands of Leghorn, while those moderates who, to defeat radicalism, had restored Leopold in 1849 and hence caused a six-year Austrian occupation, continued thereafter to fear political change lest the Left should manage to recover power. Among this group of moderates, Marquis Ridolfi admired Cavour and resented Austria, but for him the real enemies were Guerrazzi, Mazzini and the *italianissimi* rather than Leopold.[7] Gino Capponi contributed to the Piedmontese war loan, but still accepted Leopold's divine right to rule; so did Neri Corsini; and both these titled elder statesmen feared the Austrian counter-measures which might follow if Tuscany took Piedmont's side too openly. The other leading liberal-conservatives, Peruzzi, Salvagnoli, Giorgini, Galeotti and Cambray-Digny, qualified their belief in Italy by a panic fear that the radicals might profit from any revolution, or that Leghorn

[4] F. Martini, *Confessioni e Ricordi* (*Firenze granducale*) (Florence, 1922), i, 227.

[5] Gramont to Walewski, 26 August 1856, *Archives Ministère Affaires Etrangères, Paris* (*Corresp. Politique Sardaigne*, vol. 340).

[6] Cavour to Villamarina, 17 December 1858, *Cavour-Nigra*, i, 250.

[7] Ridolfi to Cavour, 12 May 1856, *Cosimo Ridolfi e gli Istituti del suo Tempo*, ed. L. Ridolfi (Florence, 1901), p. 373.

would rebel against Florence, as had happened in the terrible days of 1848–9.

Baron Ricasoli, almost alone among the grandees who dominated Tuscan society, had long since envisaged a unified peninsula as possible one day; but he too, despite what is sometimes said, gave more weight to the immediate need to avoid revolution, and hence was far from being opposed on principle to the House of Lorraine.[8] Ricasoli, Ridolfi and Peruzzi, together with a few politically more advanced non-aristocrats, had formed a society to publish a monthly volume with the aim of educating Tuscans in *italianità*; but this Biblioteca Civile dell'Italiano found only a very restricted audience, and in practice could produce only two books a year. Some of its associates were distantly in touch with Cavour, but they often disagreed with him just as with each other.[9]

Cavour's instructions to his diplomatic representative in Tuscany, Count Boncompagni, were that Piedmont's only aim in Tuscany was to support political reform and detach the Grand Duke from Austria.[10] Boncompagni also had orders to befriend the Tuscan liberals. In November 1858 Cavour was angry to find that these liberals were in independent touch with Louis Napoleon and had the 'absurd' notion of enlarging Tuscany; for although he himself had secretly agreed with the Emperor to enlarge Tuscany, any interference with his own plans was unwelcome. His indignation was tempered only by his contemptuous belief that 'the Etruscan race' was too timid to rival Piedmont as the driving

[8] Undated letter by Corsi, *Atti della Reale Accademia delle Scienze di Torino, Classe di Scienze Morali* (November 1929), pp. 25–6. *Le Assemblee del Risorgimento, Toscana* (Rome, 1911), iii, 604–5. For Ricasoli's unitarist faith, see Carlo Pischedda, 'Appunti Riscasoliani (1853–59)', *Rivista Storica Italiana* (Naples, 1956), lxviii, 66–8.

[9] Cannarozzi does not make out a strong case when he describes their policy from 1857 to 1859 as inspired by Cavour. Cannarozzi, P. Ciro, *La Rivoluzione Toscana e l'Azione del Comitato della Biblioteca Civile dell'Italiano* (Pistoia, 1936), p. xiii.

[10] Cavour to Boncompagni, 13 January 1857, Nicomede Bianchi, *Storia Documentata della Diplomazia Europea in Italia, dall'anno 1814 all'anno 1861* (Turin, 1872), viii, 77–80. Carlo Boncompagni, *Considerazioni sull'Italia Centrale* (Turin, 1859), pp. 36–8. Cavour's private comments are quoted in *Carteggio Cavour-Salmour*, ed. R. Commissione (Bologna, 1936), p. 149.

force in Italy. He privately informed Ricasoli that Piedmont was preparing war against Austria, but added that he did not want any revolution at Florence; and when it was suggested that an artificially contrived revolt in Tuscany might serve to spark off his war, Cavour disagreed, for it was alliance not enmity that he required from Leopold. Massa, Carrara and the Romagna—in other words, Modenese and papal territory—were where he intended to 'detonate the explosion'; these areas, unlike Tuscany, were marked down for Piedmontese annexation.[11]

The circle of the Biblioteca Civile did not, of course, know his more secret thoughts. In January 1859, however, when rumours of war became common knowledge, they sent to ask him what they could do to help, and explained that lack of information and advice was embarrassing Piedmont's friends in central Italy.[12] Cavour, too, was beginning to want something more positive, for he had undertaken to give the French a plausible pretext for hostilities by making it look like a spontaneous war of liberation, not something planned, nor a war of Piedmontese aggression. When he ordered one of his embassy staff in Florence to sound out the Grand Duke's army to test its allegiance, this had to be concealed from the liberals who valued the army's loyalty as protection against leftist disorderliness: in replying to Ricasoli's friends, Cavour merely asked that they should try to make Leopold grant a constitution, and Marquis Gualterio was sent to explain why.[13]

[11] Massari's diary for 24 November 1858, *Diario dalle Cento Voci, 1858–1860*, ed. Emilia Morelli (Rocca San Casciano, 1959), p. 71. Cavour to Nigra and to Villamarina, 25 November 1858, *Cavour-Nigra*, i, 213–14. Torre asserts that Cavour in October 1858 prepared a plan for a revolution in Tuscany, *La Evoluzione del Sentimento Nazionale*, p. 23; but in fact this plan, if indeed it was ever approved by Cavour, concerned not Tuscany, but Massa, Carrara, the Romagna and the smaller central duchies, *Epistolario di Giuseppe La Farina*, ed. Ausonio Franchi (Milan, 1869), ii, 83–5.

[12] Corsi to Castelli, 15 January 1859, *Carteggio Politico di Michelangelo Castelli*, ed. Luigi Chiala (Turin, 1890), i, 179. Ricasoli to Massari, 15 January, *Carteggi di Bettino Ricasoli*, ed. Mario Nobili and Sergio Camerani (Rome, 1954), vi, 211. Ricasoli to Torelli, *ibid.*, p. 212.

[13] Massari, *Diario*, 4 and 20 January, pp. 107, 120–1. Cavour to Boncompagni, 20 January, *Una Silloge di Lettere del Risorgimento*, ed. C. Bollea (Turin, 1919), p. 139. *Carteggi di Ricasoli* (Rome, 1955), vii, 344.

This advice was received with disapproval. It suggested that Cavour meant to leave Tuscany out of his territorial realignment of Italy, or even that he favoured the Tuscan radicals—the same extremists who, in 1848–9, had won power through a constitution. Probably Cavour's advice came in fact from no deeply laid plan. It did indicate, however, that he put no great value on consulting Tuscan opinion; hence the suspicious reaction among Florentines was that they should do nothing until Piedmont committed herself publicly and irrevocably to war. Cavour was furious when they would not take his advice about a constitution. He was not even mollified when Salvagnoli sent him the proofs of a pamphlet advocating an alliance with Piedmont against Austria. The diplomatic situation was already complicated enough without these self-important Tuscans refusing to do as he required.[14]

This minor contretemps exposed a potentially dangerous weakness in Cavour's lines of communication, for evidently his aides in Piedmont were out of touch with opinion in Florence. Detached from Turin, the Tuscan moderates were developing ideas of their own. Cavour therefore turned to La Farina's National Society, whose members were pledged to support Piedmont and who represented a younger, more activist, more middle-class group than Ricasoli's. La Farina gave Cavour to believe that his society had many disciplined supporters in Tuscany, and he now told his principal agent there, Bartolommei, to agitate with the aim of forcing Leopold into an alliance with Piedmont. Cavour insisted that failure in this task would not matter, provided agitation was obvious enough to convince Europe of widespread Italian backing for his war. To those patriots who would have preferred to dethrone the dynasty, it was explained that revolution was the aim elsewhere, but not in Tuscany; here a military alliance was preferable, for it would unite moderate and extreme patriots, together with those who wanted an independent Tuscany and even some who supported the

[14] Salvagnoli to Massari, 11 January 1859, *I Toscani del '59*, ed. Raffaele Ciampini (Rome, 1959), p. 181. Massari, *Diario*, 7 February, p. 133. Salvagnoli to Panizzi, 10 February, *Lettere ad Antonio Panizzi di Uomini Illustri e di Amici Italiani*, ed. Luigi Fagan (Florence, 1880), p. 288.

Grand Duke.[15] To La Farina's chagrin, however, no demonstrations took place in response to his urgent plea. Some historians still insist that the National Society was the agency through which Cavour directed the Tuscan revolution, but in fact its practical effectiveness was slight.[16]

Cavour knew that the Tuscan aristocrats feared he might be using other channels to promote a more revolutionary policy than he ever spoke of to them. There would have been outrage had they also known that he had no qualms about getting in touch even with Guerrazzi and Montanelli. This was Cavour's natural instinct, to play different policies independently of, or indeed against, each other. While Nigra was sent to Paris to ask how far Tuscan agitation could be allowed to go, Cavour kept up a friendly correspondence with his Ambassador, Boncompagni, and more indirect contact with the Biblioteca Civile, though still trying to conceal the extent of his relations with the National Society. Boncompagni sometimes found that other people in Florence claimed to speak for the Turin Government, which was not only undignified for him, but confusing for everyone else; and there was even a junior secretary in his own embassy who for a time, no doubt on orders from Turin, seems to have been secretly working at cross-purposes with official policy. Cavour at one point tried to find a new ambassador who possessed a 'less scrupulous political conscience';[17] but no replacement could be

[15] La Farina's letters in February, *Epistolario di La Farina*, ii, 127–8, 133. Cavour to Bartolommei, Matilde Gioli, *Il Rivolgimento Toscano e l'Azione Popolare (1847–1860): dai Ricordi Familiari del Marchese Ferdinando Bartolommei* (Florence, 1905), pp. 239–40. La Farina's secret orders of 4 March are, once again, said to have been directed at Tuscany, Cannarozzi, *La Rivoluzione Toscana*, p. 273, when in fact they were sent to Sarzana for use in Massa and Carrara.

[16] Camerani's description of the 'victory of the National Society' (*Archivo Storico Italiano*, 1945–6, pp. 148, 155) cannot be accepted after Raymond Grew's *A Sterner Plan for Italian Unity: the Italian National Society in the Risorgimento* (Princeton, 1963), pp. 96, 118, 170, 196–7. Camerani restated his conclusions, slightly modified, in 'La Società Nazionale nell'Italia Centrale', *Il Movimento Unitario nelle Regioni d'Italia, Atti Società di Storia Patria* (Bari, 1963), pp. 38–41.

[17] Massari, *Diario*, 28 January, pp. 127–8. Cavour to Boncompagni, 8 February, *Lettere Edite ed Inedite di Camillo Cavour*, ed. Chiala (Turin,

found, and so Boncompagni was recalled to Turin at the end of February for talks. With him, at their own request, came Ridolfi and two others who were connected with the Biblioteca Civile.

Ridolfi, Carega and Corsi had not met Cavour before; they now had three talks with him. Marquis Carega's account, many years later, is not entirely trustworthy; but he thought he recalled Cavour's 'exact words', that Tuscans 'should do nothing except induce the dynasty to ally with Piedmont and grant a constitution', and on this point his testimony is confirmed, not only by Ridolfi's later attempt to carry out this policy, but by a contemporary account which came from Corsi.[18] Cavour strongly opposed Ricasoli's wish to start a newspaper, strangely arguing that it would divide opinion and frustrate action. Perhaps this shows that Cavour had been nettled by Ricasoli's use of this very same argument against Turin's advocacy of a campaign for a Tuscan constitution. It also exemplified his scornful attitude to Tuscans and to their inability to act in concert. In the upshot the Tuscan delegation agreed to put out a booklet with the arguments for Tuscany allying with Piedmont, and Boncompagni also promised to be less timid about using his diplomatic immunity as a cover for conspiracy.

Ricasoli was upset by the veto on a newspaper: far from causing divisions, a newspaper would be a rallying-point for all who opposed Austria; he thought, on the contrary, that it was Cavour who was dividing liberals by imposing policy from a distance where local conditions were not understood. A newspaper

[18] Carega, Francesco, 'Dal Conte di Cavour nel Febbraio 1859', *Fanfulla della Domenica*, 31 January 1892 (anno xiv, Rome, no. 5). F. D. Guerrazzi, 'Diary', 2 May 1859, *Nuova Antologia* (June 1933, Rome), cclxxxix, 330–1. Camerani correctly shows (*Archivio Storico Italiano*, 1945–6, pp. 143–5) that both accounts must have been wrong over details where they disagree, but it would need further corroboration to conclude from this, as he does, that they must therefore both have been wrong on major points where their testimony concurs.

1884), iii, 23. Boncompagni's protest is in Bianchi, *Storia Documentata*, viii, 81. For the confusion in embassy policy, cf. the police report of 15 March in *Rassegna Storica del Risorgimento* (Rome, 1929), xvi, 469; and Boncompagni to Cavour, 28 March, *Il '59 in Toscana: Lettere e Documenti Inediti*, ed. R. Ciampini (Florence, 1959), p. 51.

would educate public opinion, at the same time as it would create a useful initiative for manufacturing a crisis at any desired moment. Ricasoli accepted Cavour's decision, but here he had new evidence of an unwillingness at Turin to be seriously interested in Tuscans. Cavour just wished them to agitate, which they did not like, so as to obtain a constitution, of which they were suspicious, and in association with unknown radical forces of whom they were deeply afraid. Cavour's mind was set on annexing Italy north of the Apennines, and he wanted Ricasoli to help him do this and no more. 'These Tuscans are unbearably doctrinaire', Cavour told Massari; if they continued with their foolish plan to start a newspaper he would wash his hands of them.[19]

By mid-March, however, Cavour needed Tuscan help more than he had anticipated, for in the papal Romagna La Farina's friends once again were failing to produce the required detonating mechanism. As it was imperative to show Louis Napoleon and Europe that Italy was in a state of complete dissolution, perhaps the evidence for seething patriotic revolt could be more easily manufactured under the tolerant régime of the Grand Duke than under the eye of Austrian soldiers in Bologna. Moreover, Cavour suddenly saw the danger that England might persuade Leopold to give up his Austrian alliance: the Piedmontese had, on French advice, told England they wanted just this; but, now that the options were narrowing, a continuance of the Austro-Tuscan alliance might turn out to be the only available pretext for war. Once again, therefore, Gualterio mysteriously reappeared in Florence and the National Society was again ordered to produce some agitation, while the *burgraves* of the Biblioteca Civile were accused of cowardice and told to choose more active leaders than Ridolfi and Ricasoli. Cavour then tried hopefully to convince Louis Napoleon that Tuscany must be in a ferment of unrest;[20] but his case was unconvincing.

A more authentic success was that the Biblioteca Civile on

[19] Massari, *Diario*, 8 March, p. 164.

[20] Cavour to Boncompagni, 13 March, 'Cavour e Boncompagni nella rivoluzione Toscana del 1859', ed. Beniamino Manzone, *Il Risorgimento Italiano, Rivista Storica* (Turin, 1909), ii, 210–11. Nigra to Cavour, 10 March, *Cavour-Nigra*, ii, 78; Cavour to Prince Napoleon, 16 March, *ibid.*,

21 March published a much-applauded manifesto of liberal, pro-Piedmontese opinion. *Toscana e Austria* stated that Tuscany should accept Cavour's lead in excluding Austria from the peninsula. Ricasoli, Ridolfi and Peruzzi publicly signed this pamphlet, but they made difficulties when Cavour also asked for a letter which he could publish as proof that the best-known names of Tuscany were behind him. They were reluctant to compromise themselves in a collective statement, partly perhaps because it might be read as political criticism of Leopold, but partly because Capponi, Corsini and Galeotti feared that the moderates were going too far. This was an unfortunate division. When time went by, with nothing which Cavour could show to the Emperor as evidence of agitation, and indeed almost no communication from Tuscany of any kind, he sharply accused the moderates of *lèse patrie.*[21]

Lack of communication went both ways. On Cavour's side it was understandable, for this was perhaps the most difficult month of his whole life; yet it had unfortunate results which showed that his type of empirical statesmanship carried some inherent defects. Boncompagni on 18 March asked how to act if Leopold fled from Florence or if popular insurrection broke out; but Cavour had no time to answer, and anyway counted on Leopold staying. The Turin Government still had established no unified chain of command, and advice continued to reach Florence in various senses through various agencies: the regular Tuscan postal service had been bribed to carry secret messages, which may explain why the Tuscan police could read Ricasoli's letters and even Boncompagni's despatches.[22] A much more

[21] Cavour to Boncompagni, 3 April, *Il Risorgimento Italiano, Rivista Storica* (1909), p. 213. Boncompagni's earlier reports of 15 and 28 March are given in *Il '59 in Toscana*, ed. Ciampini, pp. 43–4, 49. Farini to Boncompagni, early April, *Epistolario di Luigi Carlo Farini*, ed. Luigi Rava (Bologna, 1935), iv, 246.

[22] Diary of Landucci, 'La Toscana alla Vigilia del 27 Aprile 1859', ed. Giacomo Lumbroso, *Rassegna Storica del Risorgimento* (Rome, 1933), xx, 96. Report of police spy to Landucci, 20 March, Cannarozzi, *La Rivoluzione Toscana*, p. 203.

p. 99; Cavour to Nigra, 19 March, *ibid.*, p. 117. Report of 16 March, *Il Risorgimento Italiano nell'Opera, negli Scritti, nella Corrispondenza di Piero Puccioni*, ed. Mario Puccioni (Rome, 1932), p. 61.

serious difficulty was that, though Cavour repeatedly demanded incessant 'agitation', he specifically barred any *émeute.* Legal petitions were needed, but never on any account *moti in piazza*; street demonstrations would not only revive fears of another 1848, but they could easily get out of control, and above all they would antagonize Louis Napoleon, who needed to feel that Cavour was fully in charge of what was a socially conservative movement. The advice against mob demonstrations was repeated often and firmly.[23] In effect, however, much as this advice delighted the moderates, it disarmed the activists among Cavour's followers, and local elements of the National Society were now left to work with little central direction.[24] It simultaneously strengthened those anti-French radicals who had no scruples about defying Cavour and taking revolution into the streets.

Uncertainty also existed over the volunteer soldiers who were leaving in small batches to join Garibaldi and the regular army in Piedmont. Capponi, Peruzzi, Bastogi, Ricasoli, and above all Bartolommei, subscribed to help these volunteers, and the Grand-ducal Government raised no serious opposition to recruitment. Besides the motive of Italian patriotism, many conservatives no doubt had a common interest with Leopold's ministers in wanting these hotheads out of the country.[25] Cavour's view seems to have changed more than once. He needed volunteers, especially from the upper classes; he knew his shortage of troops in Piedmont, and the arrival of some central-Italian recruits would demonstrate support for his cause. But sometimes his agents preferred to discourage enlistment, because there were counter-arguments for keeping the activists at home, and because the regular Piedmontese

[23] Louis Napoleon's wishes were conveyed by Nigra from Paris on 1 March, *Cavour-Nigra*, ii, 47; Cavour's replies, later in March, *ibid.*, pp. 122, 150. For Cavour's warnings to La Farina against *moti in piazza*, see *Epistolario di La Farina*, ii, 91, 151; for his warning to Boncompagni, 20 March, *Il '59 in Toscana*, ed. Ciampini, p. 45.

[24] The National Society's committees at Leghorn and Florence were working at cross-purposes: *Rassegna Storica del Risorgimento* (1929), xvi, 455, 458; Gioli, *Il rivolgimento toscano*, p. 232.

[25] Ermolao Rubieri, *Storia intima della Toscana dal 1 Gennaio 1859 al 30 Aprile 1860* (Prato, 1861), pp. 35, 384-5.

Army was most unwelcoming to any volunteer units.[26] Early in April, however, Cavour was again worrying that the volunteers from central Italy were too few to impress the French. Such contradictions helped to create uncertainty about what was required.[27]

Confusion over the volunteers and over the permitted limits of agitation left the field open to radical elements around Ermolao Rubieri and Giuseppe Dolfi, who had fewer inhibitions than either Biblioteca Civile or National Society about disobeying orders from Turin. Dolfi, the baker and *capopopolo*, was the most widely liked and respected citizen in Florence. Rubieri, the intellectual, wanted a united nation, not just a kingdom of northern Italy, and hence aimed to supplant the dynasty. He believed that Cavour's Piedmontese preconceptions and undertakings to the French made him less than a wholly effective guide. Rubieri and his *ad hoc* 'party of action' were neither Mazzinians nor social revolutionaries. They respected Ricasoli and were friendly with Bartolommei; but they were more consistent than the latter in wanting to keep the volunteers for action at home, and they had no scruples about planning an *émeute* in alliance with Cironi and the Mazzinian republicans.[28]

Ricasoli's circle, on the other hand, was proving under the stress of events to be divided and disorganized; its members were reluctant to accept responsibility or agree about action; they were 'weak people, men of words, not deeds, who will probably end up as before by giving way to the republicans'.[29] They were good

[26] General Lamarmora's opposition was noted in Provenzali's report from Turin to Lenzoni, 30 March, *Archivio di Stato, Florence* (Sardegna, no. 60). But Boncompagni was already trying to discourage recruitment, Malenchini to Corsi, 21 March, *Pasqua di Liberazione, Raccolta di Documenti . . . sul 27 Aprile 1859*, ed. V. Soldani (Florence, 1909), p. 55.

[27] Farini to Boncompagni, *Epistolario di Farini*, iv, 247. Bardesono (Cavour's secretary) to Casarini, 3 April, E. Masi, *Fra Libri e Ricordi di Storia della Rivoluzione Italiana* (Bologna, 1887), pp. 113–14. Pepoli to Castelli, 9 April, *Carteggio di Castelli*, i, 188.

[28] D. Mack Smith, 'La Rivoluzione Fiorentina del 27 Aprile 1859', in *Inghilterra e Toscana nell'Ottocento* (Florence, 1968), pp. 80–90.

[29] Marco Tabarrini, *Diario 1859–1860*, ed. Antonio Panella (Florence, 1959), 5 April, p. 9.

patriots in their fashion, but feared that war would mean rioting and a dangerous disintegration of the Tuscan Army; it might mean an Austrian invasion, and they still had no way of telling that France would give more than diplomatic help. Nor were any of them ready to countenance the idea of Piedmontese annexation which eventually prevailed. They sometimes were deeply suspicious of each other, though most of them distrusted and feared the National Society, while they looked on Guerrazzi and Dolfi with disdain and horror.[30]

Cavour, contrary to what is sometimes asserted, was still hoping for Tuscany, and possibly even Naples, to ally with him in fighting against Austria. On 12 April he therefore decided to let Leopold into the biggest secret of all, and explained privately, perhaps injudiciously, that France had secretly promised to join him in a war to liberate Italy; also that moral support had been promised to them by Russia, Prussia and England; and hence Tuscany would be wise to join the big battalions. Leopold was unimpressed, having checked with the Russians that the story was untrue.[31] Apparently Boncompagni was not informed of this move by Cavour, but, after reminding Turin that he still had no orders what to do in an emergency, the Piedmontese Ambassador at last received what he had asked for a month earlier. When war began he should formally ask Leopold for an alliance.[32] If re-

[30] Peruzzi to Ricasoli, 17 April, *Carteggi di Ricasoli,* ed. Nobili-Camerani, vi, 265–6. Ferrière-le-Vayer from Florence to Walewski, 20 April, quoting Galeotti, *Le Relazioni Diplomatiche fra la Francia e il Granducato di Toscana,* ed. Armando Saitta, iii serie (6 January 1858 to 14 July 1860) (Rome, 1959), iii, 121.

[31] Canofari's despatch from Turin to Naples and Provenzali's of 12 April to Florence were both published by Nicomede Bianchi, 'Il Conte Camillo di Cavour: Documenti Editi e Inediti', in *Rivista Contemporanea* (Turin, April 1863), xxxiii, 29–30. The denial by Russia was reported by Boncompagni to Cavour, 24 April, Bianchi, *Storia Documentata*, viii, 87.

[32] An alliance, of course, would have excluded any chance of Piedmont annexing Tuscany. Chiala, perhaps for this reason, is sure that Cavour had no wish for an alliance, *Lettere di Cavour*, iii, p. clxvi. Camerani similarly thinks that Cavour felt safe in offering an alliance because he was quite certain that Leopold would never accept, *Archivio Storico Italiano* (1945–6), pp. 155–9; but it is hard to explain, if so, what there was to gain in allowing Boncompagni to go on trying for an alliance until the last moment,

pulsed, he should try to terrify the Grand Duke into leaving the country. Failing that, he should still not promote anything so dangerous as a revolution by the local Italian patriots, but should incite the Army to a *pronunciamento*, after which he would intervene to proclaim the dictatorship of Victor Emanuel. Cavour now realized that it might prove wrong to have taken so many volunteers from Tuscany, where they might have exerted a useful pressure at this critical stage.[33] Boncompagni, who had reported that efforts to win over the Army were proving ineffective, was now instructed to be deceitful and give the Army officers a private reassurance that there was no intention of promoting a *pronunciamento* or undermining their loyalty to Leopold.

Although Cavour had these many irons in the fire, it was not any of his friends but Dolfi and Rubieri who eventually sponsored the decisive events of 27 April. Boncompagni and the liberal aristocrats, though some of them later tried to erase the fact from public memory, fervently hoped that the dynasty of Lorraine could be saved. At one point they had agreed to hold meetings with Rubieri and even with Cironi, but only so as to discover the plans of the opposition and halt any anti-dynastic revolution. Wehn Rubieri on the 24th realized this and refused to accept their leadership, the terrible moment of anarchy seemed to have arrived, and the Biblioteca Civile simply dissolved.[34] Corsini, Ridolfi, Peruzzi, Capponi, Galeotti, Matteucci, Salvagnoli and Cambray-Digny, all made strenuous individual efforts between 24 and 27 April to win the Grand Duke to an alliance with Piedmont and so avert the popular movement which they all feared; nor is there

[33] Cavour to Boncompagni, 11 April, *Il Risorgimento Italiano, Rivista Storica* (1909), pp. 215–16. Farini to Ridolfi, 11 April, ed. Camerani, *Archivio Storico Italiano* (1945–6), p. 167. Cavour to Massimo d'Azeglio, 14 April, *Lettere di Cavour*, ed. Chiala, vi, 384.

[34] Rubieri, *Storia Intima*, pp. 50–1, 57–60.

Bianchi, *Storia Documentata*, viii, pp. 84, 90–1. Louis Napoleon certainly would have liked Leopold to join the Franco-Piedmontese side, and to secure this was ready to guarantee the Grand Duke's throne, *Cavour-Nigra*, ii, p. 172; Nerli from Paris to Lenzoni, 26 April, *Rivista Contemporanea* (April 1863, Turin), p. 29. An alliance would, equally, have been good politics for Cavour, quite apart from the fact that he was still allowing France to dictate policy.

any doubt that this pressure-group was concerted by Ricasoli and Boncompagni. Ricasoli and Salvagnoli, perhaps the two closest to Cavour of the group, were so anxious for this alliance that they would have accepted less than an open espousal by Leopold of the Piedmontese cause.[35] Even quite late on the 26th, after hostilities had begun in Lombardy, and when at Dolfi's house in Florence the time-table of the revolution was being decided, Ricasoli personally visited Leopold's ministers to make a final plea, but failed. Fearing the worst, he refused to collaborate in the Grand Duke's overthrow, but overnight left for Turin, hurriedly abandoning the revolution to take its course.[36]

Some historians still argue that, whatever may be true of the aristocratic liberals in Florence, Cavour had designed an insurrection, even down to details, and indeed that a fortnight earlier he had ordered the National Society to put a long-prepared plan into action. But Cavour did not want a real insurrection in Tuscany; he would certainly have liked to avoid the *moto in piazza* of 27 April, and his note of a fortnight earlier made this quite clear. Not only had Louis Napoleon insisted on Cavour keeping the Tuscan movement within legal and constitutional bounds, but the National Society was in any case too disorganized and probably far too small and unpractical to make a reliable instrument of revolt. If there did exist any plan, it was not carried out, and members of the society acted in ways which showed that

[35] Corsini to Guicciardini, 25 April, A. Salvestrini, *I Moderati Toscani e la Classe Dirigente Italiana (1859–1876)* (Florence, 1965), p. 15. Ferrière's reports to Walewski, *Le Relazioni Diplomatiche fra la Francia e il Granducato*, ed. Saitta, iii, 121, 128. Leopoldo Galeotti, *L'Assemblea Toscana*, 2nd ed. (Florence, 1859), p. 90. Anon. (Peruzzi), *La Toscane et ses Grands-Ducs Austrichiens* (Paris, 1859), pp. 112–13. Antonio Panella, 'Un po' più di luce su una "Storia di Quattro Ore" ', *Ad Alessandro Luzio, gli Archivi di Stato Italiani: Miscellanea di Studi Storici* (Florence, 1933), ii, 257–65.

[36] Ricasoli has sometimes been thought to have been at the head of the revolutionaries, Torre, *La Evoluzione del Sentimento Nazionale*, p. 37. But his activity can now be followed in 'Un Carteggio Inedito di Bettino Ricasoli', ed. A. Sapori, *Rivista delle Biblioteche e degli Archivi* (Florence, 1926), xxxvi, 4–6; and *Carteggi di Ricasoli*, vi, 267–71, vii, 344. Panella shows that Ricasoli altered one of the relevant documents later, *Ad Alessandro Luzio*, ii, 262.

there was still no effective central direction. Cavour was not sure until 21 April that the war would even start. Certainly he hoped that, if hostilities began, there would be sympathetic movements elsewhere in Italy; but any independent rising by the party of action was to be rigorously avoided, while his own preparations for a revolt were in practice confined to a modest operation in the Modenese districts of Massa and Carrara, adjoining the Piedmontese frontier.

On 24 April Boncompagni followed instructions and again asked Leopold for an alliance after confirming that Piedmont had no intention of violating his rights of sovereignty.[37] Meanwhile, at Turin, Mezzacapo was told to enlist any volunteers from the Papal States, and Ulloa had to hold himself ready to reorganize the Tuscan Army in the event of joint action. Cavour further informed Paris that he had sent agents to Tuscany to prepare a movement in support of the war,[38] but we know nothing that these anonymous people did, and probably his communication was just designed to help frustrate any eleventh-hour attempt by the French to stop the fighting. From La Farina, who would surely have communicated any official call to revolt, there came only the news that the National Society no longer existed.[39] Not until late on the 26th did Malenchini arrive with Cavour's go-ahead to associate with the radicals in their movement to coerce the Grand Duke; and this must have been a last-minute change of plan, for Malenchini was suddenly diverted to Florence when on his way to join Garibaldi. Cavour probably took this decision when he heard from Crespi that the party of action had the upper hand in Florence. Malenchini's orders were that Cavour urgently wanted the various parties to settle their differences and above all win over the Army; but, as can be seen from Boncompagni's conduct the next day, Malenchini must also have brought confirmation of the belief that an alliance with the Grand Duke

[37] Boncompagni to Lenzoni, 24 April, *Cronaca degli avvenimenti d'Italia nel 1859*, ed. Antonio Zobi (Florence, 1859), i, pp. 393, 395.

[38] Cavour's telegram to Prince Napoleon, 23 April, A. Comandini, *Il Principe Napoleone nel Risorgimento* (Milan, 1922), p. 118.

[39] La Farina to Ridolfi, 24 April, ed. Camerani, *Archivio Storico Italiano* (1945–6), p. 177. Masi, *Fra libri e ricordi*, p. 118.

would still be welcome if feelings at Florence would permit it.[40]

Malenchini's arrival and, perhaps even more, the news that French troops were moving into Piedmont gave authoritative support to the huge popular demonstration which Rubieri and Dolfi had arranged for 27 April; yet when the leading aristocrats were invited late on the 26th to associate their names with this demonstration, they absolutely refused, and in fact it took place in spite of them. While the mob fraternized with the soldiers, Boncompagni's role on the 27th was mainly to provide an extra-territorial residence where revolutionaries and aristocrats could meet and discuss a compromise policy.[41] Towards midday, Leopold agreed under severe pressure to accept the Italian cause and appoint a liberal government. Rubieri was for refusing this and overthrowing the dynasty; but here Boncompagni intervened in order to make quite clear first where the Army officers stood. When it was obvious that even the more liberally-minded officers supported the Grand Duke, the Piedmontese Minister encouraged Ridolfi and Peruzzi to form a government under Leopold, and certainly must have felt that such was Cavour's wish.[42]

[40] For the activity of Malenchini on the 26th, there is a tantalizing single sentence by Boncompagni, *Il Risorgimento Italiano, Rivista Storica* (1909), p. 222; another in Yorick, *Uomini e Fatti d'Italia* (Florence, 1921), p. 62; another in A. Giannelli, *Lettere di Giuseppe Mazzini ad Andrea Giannelli* (Prato, 1888), i, 103; another in *Ricordi di Michelangelo Castelli (1847–1875)*, ed. L. Chiala (Turin, 1888), p. 226. Cironi's diary suggests that Malenchini's action was chiefly addressed to introducing Victor Emanuel's name into the revolutionary proclamation, Ludmilla Assing, *Vita di Pietro Cironi* (Prato, 1865), p. 167. Rubieri mentions him only *en passant* in *Storia Intima*, pp. 66–9. The plan of revolution had already been decided, and what Malenchini brought was Cavour's permission for ex-members of the dissolved National Society to associate with it.

[41] Passerin d'Entrèves accepts that both Boncompagni and La Farina's National Society played a dominant part in the revolt as part of a master plan by Cavour to confront Louis Napoleon with a convincing example of Italian patriotism, *Il Piemonte, l'Italia Centrale e la Questione Romana nel 1859–60*, p. 55. But Cavour and La Farina had too many other things to think of, and were not closely enough in touch with events in Florence, while Boncompagni, perhaps wisely, merely tried to keep the options open until he could exert some influence as a mediator.

[42] Boncompagni to Cavour, 29 April, *Il Risorgimento Italiano, Rivista Storica*

The liberal-conservative aristocrats were fully behind this move. Anxious to retain Tuscan independence, they were determined to keep the dynasty if possible, but in any case their main fear was of 'the reds', against whom the Grand Duke was their best defence.[43] In Ricasoli's absence from Florence, Corsini therefore agreed to Leopold's request to form a ministry. This decision was then discussed at Boncompagni's house, where Rubieri and Malenchini opposed it, but they gave way when Ridolfi and the aristocratic party, supported by Boncompagni, agreed to join Corsini on the one condition that Leopold would abdicate in favour of his son. Corsini thought such a condition altogether excessive. He came round only when he saw it as the one chance of securing broad agreement and saving the dynasty. What defeated this consensus and allowed Dolfi's revolution to proceed was the unexpected decision by Leopold and Ferdinand to leave the country rather than accept abdication.

The collapse of the dynasty was greeted with joy in the crowded streets, though, despite subsequent legend, it was far from welcome to Corsini, Ridolfi, Peruzzi and those who now found themselves the leaders of free Tuscany.[44] Cavour was seldom one to be caught entirely by surprise, and quickly adapted his plans to this new situation. General Ulloa was already waiting near Genoa to come to organize the Tuscan Army, using funds

[43] Corsini to Galeotti, 27 April, 'Lettere di Neri Corsini a Leopoldo Galeotti', ed. B. Biagiarelli, *Rassegna Storica Toscana* (Florence, 1958), iv, 43.

[44] Corsini, the next day, stated publicly that 'in these brief four hours everything might have been saved, but in fact everything was lost', *Storia di Quattro Ore, Dalle 9 Antimeridiane alle 1 Pomeridiane del 27 Aprile 1859* (Florence, 1859), p. 16. Ridolfi, too, did what he could on the 27th to save the dynasty, and spoke of Leopold's withdrawal as a 'grave misfortune' for the country, *Breve Nota a Una Storia di Quattro ore Intorno ai Fatti del 27 Aprile 1859* (Florence, 1859), p. 14. Peruzzi agreed with the French Ambassador that the events of the 27th were a victory for the democrats over the Biblioteca Civile, Ferrière's reports of 30 April and 4 May, *Le Relazioni Diplomatiche*, ed. Saitta, iii, 139, 142. Rubieri noted how, at Boncompagni's house, the moderates were at first stunned by the defeat of their policy, *Storia Intima*, p. 92.

(1909), p. 223. M. Carletti, *Quattro Mesi di Storia Toscana dal 27 Aprile al 27 Agosto 1859* (Florence, 1859), p. 22.

appropriated by Cavour from the secret service account; and now, when news arrived of the Grand Duke's departure, the Cabinet in Turin suddenly decided that Ulloa should if possible assume 'une espèce de dictature militaire'.[45] The French, however, realized that it would be rash to spoil the general appearance of spontaneity by thus imposing a dictator from outside, and an urgent telegram from Paris stopped Cavour's abrupt decision to confer full powers on such an entirely incompetent man.

Meanwhile, Boncompagni, improvising on his own initiative and despite his embarrassing position as Ambassador to the Grand-ducal Court, assumed a certain degree of power to make the change-over as easy as possible. It may even be that he prevented Leopold abdicating at the last minute and saving the day for his son.[46] He also helped to form a provisional government which purposely excluded Rubieri and the party of action. Rubieri, having achieved his aim of destroying the old régime, agreed to stand down in the interests of patriotic unity.[47] Peruzzi's election as head of government was then decided inside the Piedmontese Embassy, and Rubieri secured a pseudo-legitimacy for this election by obtaining the public approval of such members of the Florentine municipal administration as could be induced to agree.[48]

[45] Cabinet minute for 27 April, Ernesto Artom, *L'Opera Politica del Senatore I. Artom nel Risorgimento Italiano* (Bologna, 1906), pt. 1, 246. Cavour's telegrams to Prince Napoleon, 27–8 April, and the latter's reply, 'L'Italie Libérée', ed. Frédéric Masson, *Revue des Deux Mondes* (Paris, 1923), xciii, 570–1. Cavour's telegram to Boncompagni, and a note about funds for Ulloa, are in *Archivio di Stato, Turin (Gabinetto Min. Interno 1848–60, cart. 29).*

[46] G. Cecconi, *Il 27 Aprile* (Florence, 1892), p. 54. Boncompagni himself says that, after securing the Army's consent, he intervened to prevent a printer publishing Leopold's final protest, *Il Risorgimento Italiano, Rivista Storica* (1909), p. 224.

[47] Rubieri, *Storia Intima*, pp. 100–2. One contemporary commentator looked back on 27 April as *la journée des dupes*, since 'opponents of the dynasty, though they won the day, did not capture power, while the *dinastici* were beaten and yet were able to take over government', ed. Renato Carmignani, 'Opinioni e Problemi in Toscana nel 1859–60', *Rassegna Storica del Risorgimento* (Rome, 1959), xlvi, 398.

[48] After some difficulty, Rubieri got the consent of a third of the Council members, *I Casi della Toscana nel 1859 e 1860, Narrati al Popolo da Una Compagnia di Toscani* (Florence, 1864), p. 84.

Cavour soon knew that Ricasoli's friends, however fearful of absorption by Piedmont, were far more afraid of the radical Left;[49] and he learnt from Ricasoli that extra troops were badly needed to prevent further popular agitation.[50] On the 28th he agreed to send these soldiers, provided that Peruzzi formally asked for French and Piedmontese protection.[51] But Boncompagni, following previous instructions, had already persuaded Peruzzi to request that Victor Emanuel would act as dictator of Tuscany: Peruzzi clearly explained that this dictatorship would be just for the duration of the war and on condition of preserving, or later restoring, local autonomy. Cavour in reply, changing his former policy in response to French wishes, would accept no more than full powers over the Army; he further agreed to appoint Boncompagni as Royal Commissioner to exercise an undefined protectorship over Tuscany, but allowing local self-government, and specifically leaving Tuscans free to decide their own future when the war was over.

Cavour later admitted that it would have been better to accept dictatorial powers, and he blamed this mistake on Paris, as he later blamed Boncompagni for not disregarding the letter of his instructions and acting as a dictator.[52] If it was a mistake, part of the explanation is that Cavour was now not only Prime Minister, but Foreign Minister, Minister of the Interior, and Minister for Army and Navy, so that he had little enough time for these unexpected developments so far away from Turin. His first principle had to be that he could not afford to antagonize Louis Napoleon, who wanted a conservative policy in Tuscany; nor would he wish to add to his other troubles a gratuitous fight

[49] Peruzzi to Minghetti, *c.* 1 May, Lilla Lipparini, *Minghetti* (Bologna, 1942), i, 299.

[50] Ricasoli had warned Turin on 18 April that Piedmontese troops might be needed in an emergency, *Carteggi di Ricasoli*, vi, 266. His notes of a meeting he had with Cavour on 28 April were published by Jarro, *Vita di Ubaldino Peruzzi* (Florence, 1891), p. 108.

[51] Cabinet minute in E. Artom, *L'Opera Politica del I. Artom*, p. 247.

[52] Farini to Boncompagni, 7 May, *Epistolario di Farini*, iv, 253. That it was a mistake was agreed by Pallavicino on 24 May, *Memorie di Giorgio Pallavicino* (Turin, 1895), iii, 520; by Cavour on 8 June, *Cavour-Nigra*, ii, 215; and by the King, *Le Relazioni Diplomatiche*, ed. Saitta, iii, 186.

with the Tuscan aristocracy, who firmly believed in local autonomy. From Peruzzi he now heard that the revolution of 27 April had been the work of dangerous radicals who were far from reconciled to Piedmontese policy; to defeat them he would need to back their opponents—in other words, the autonomists who wanted Florence a capital city with its own separate court life. Cavour can have been in little doubt, for he had few ambitions on their side of the Apennines; it was Modena, Bologna and Ancona which he was chiefly anxious to annex.[53] The usefulness to him of Tuscany was, first, for its moral support, secondly, for its Army, which was badly needed in Lombardy, and, thirdly, as a base from which General Mezzacapo could prepare a movement in the papal Romagna. It is almost certain that Cavour, had he planned to take Tuscany instead of letting policy wait on events, would have chosen more decisive men than Ulloa and Boncompagni, and would have briefed them better about Piedmontese intentions; moreover, he would hardly have waited until war was beginning before he appointed Minghetti, an outsider from central Italy, as Chief Secretary at the Turin Foreign Office; nor, if he could have foreseen these events, would he have left it till May to set up Farini in a new department dealing with 'annexed and protected' provinces. The likelihood is that the Florentine revolution was largely unexpected and hence that the events of 27 April reinforced his natural liking for an empirical policy. This would help to explain why his emergency decision to assume dictatorial powers was changed, and then changed back again.

Early in May, Boncompagni did try to obey Cavour's changed orders and recover greater authority, but he could not find a single person in Florence who combined being acceptable to Piedmont with a willingness to co-operate in what must now have seemed a threat to self-government. Capponi, Matteucci and Galeotti enlisted the French Ambassador to persuade Boncompagni to drop his plan and confirm Tuscany's right to be autonomous,[54] while Corsini and Peruzzi called on the British Ambassador with

[53] Farini to Boncompagni, 14 May, *Epistolario di Farini*, iv, 260–1.

[54] Ferrière-le-Vayer to Walewski, 10 May, *Le Relazioni Diplomatiche*, ed. Saitta, iii, 148.

a similar purpose.[55] Perhaps, if the National Society had been as important as is usually said, the Royal Commissioner might have found support from the *lafariniani*, but they had produced not a single leader of real stature, and in general were treated by the aristocracy and by Boncompagni as of little account. As for the real radicals, those who it was now agreed had done most to bring about the revolution,[56] their brief grasp of power had at all costs to be loosened, especially since their talk of a much larger Italy resembled Mazzini's doctrine of national unity. As Cavour reassured the French Minister, 'la cause de l'indépendance de l'Italie ne pourrait qu'être compromise par le concours du parti demagogique'. 'Son langage, à cet égard', reported the Minister, 'a été des plus explicites.'[57] Failing to obtain respectable local support for a non-political administration under his own control, Boncompagni on 11 May had to change direction and fall back on what Ricasoli termed 'the usual people', with an autonomous Government led by Ricasoli, Ridolfi and Salvagnoli.

Not a single one of the leading names in Tuscany yet subscribed to any policy of fusion with Piedmont. Nor, probably, did Cavour himself. He knew that he had, if possible, to avoid repeating the mistake of 1848, when so many Italian patriots had been alienated by the fear of Piedmontese ambition, nor should he antagonize too early those who wanted a federal solution for the Italian problem. The Tuscan autonomists were, as Cavour himself admitted, the most widely admired Italians in Europe. Also their roots were deep. 'Tuscany is small', wrote Galeotti, 'but it is all we have'; the common cause would merely be weakened if Piedmont were to treat this province as annexed and subordinate territory.[58]

55 Scarlett to Malmesbury, 6 and 11 May, Public Record Office F.O. 79/204.

56 Corsi to Salvagnoli, 8 May, 'remember that it was the common people who carried out the revolution, while we just watched from the window', ed. Mario Puccioni, *L'Unità d'Italia nel Pensiero e nell'Azione del Barone Bettino Ricasoli* (Florence, 1932), p. 31. Ferrière reported that the *parti unitaire* was very weak in Florence, and that the real supporters of Piedmont were, paradoxically, the old republicans, 18 May, *Le relazioni diplomatiche*, ed. Saitta, iii, 153–4.

57 La Tour d'Auvergne from Turin to Walewski, 5 May, *Archives Ministère Affaires Etrangères* (Sardaigne, vol. 346).

58 Galeotti to Massimo d'Azeglio, 19 May, *Carteggio Politico tra Massimo*

So Ricasoli's Government received Cavour's renewed promise that Tuscan autonomy would be respected. Moreover, two official representatives from Florence, Marquis Corsini and Count Cambray-Digny, were individually reassured on this head by Minghetti, Farini, and also by Louis Napoleon himself. The bait was even held out that an independent Tuscany, possibly under a relative of Victor Emanuel, might be expanded after the war to include Modena, Umbria and the Marches.[59]

At first Cavour must have thought this a minor matter. A much more serious problem was to hasten the arrival of Tuscan soldiers to help in the war. These soldiers were urgently needed, and the delay in sending them was more his own fault than he would acknowledge, for he deliberately kept full powers over the Tuscan Army; General Ulloa, the military commander, was Cavour's personal choice and had been imposed on Tuscany without consultation; General Mezzacapo was also appointed by Turin to a separate military command in Florence, so incidentally causing much confusion, and another Piedmontese officer became Military Governor of the strategically vital port-town of Leghorn. Peruzzi and Ricasoli repeatedly and urgently begged Cavour to send yet another experienced Piedmontese soldier to act as Minister of War in Florence, but there was a month's unaccountable delay before this man arrived, and in the meantime no one

[59] Corsini from Turin to Galeotti, 14 May, *Rassegna Storica Toscana*, 1958, p. 44. Corsini to Ridolfi, 17 May, Poggi, *Memorie Storiche*, iii, 14. Cambray-Digny to Ridolfi, 25 May, *Carteggio politico di L. G. de Cambray-Digny (Aprile-Novembre 1859)*, ed. G. Baccini (Milan, 1913), p. 34. The idea of an enlarged Tuscany was quite widespread: Cavour had toyed with it favourably at Plombières; so had Salvagnoli (Bianchi, *Storia Documentata*, viii, pp. 15–16), Corsi (*Nuova Antologia*, June 1933, p. 330), and Guerrazzi (Agostino Savelli, *Leonardo Romanelli e la Toscana del suo tempo*, Florence, 1941, p. 409). So at various times did Ridolfi and Peruzzi.

---

d'Azeglio e Leopoldo Galeotti dal 1849 al 1860, ed. Marcus de Rubris (Turin, 1928), p. 136. Cavour to Victor Emanuel, 18 May, *Cavour-Nigra*, ii, 197. *Lettere di Gino Capponi e di Altri a Lui*, ed. Alessandro Carraresi (Florence, 1899), iii, 239. Poggi, a ministerial colleague of Ricasoli's, recalls a 'tacit agreement between the various parties that Tuscany would not be joined to Piedmont', Enrico Poggi, *Memorie Storiche del governo della Toscana nel 1859–60* (Pisa, 1867), i, 67.

in the Tuscan Government understood enough about military matters to give orders which made much sense.

It is equally true, however, that Ricasoli delayed the despatch of troops by putting preservation of domestic order above fighting against Austria. He feared to introduce mass conscription or increase recruitment above the normal 2,000 a year, since Army service was highly unpopular even for this war of national liberation, and there was a fear that the Grand Duke's supporters would stage a counter-revolution if the war went badly.[60] Ricasoli therefore thought it unwise to arm the peasants, and he had to recognize that middle- and upper-class citizens regarded it as their traditional right to buy themselves out of military service. Even a civic guard would be too dangerous to permit, because it would give too much power to ordinary townsmen. On the other hand, he not only insisted on appointing many more policemen than had been required by the 'oppressive' Government of Leopold, but he thought it prudent to raise police pay above that of comparable rank in the Army. It was also ordered that punishments for offences against property had to be especially severe and publicly administered.[61] Not until 25 May did Ricasoli decide to declare war on Austria—the declaration contained an unfortunate reference to Cavour having 'initiated hostilities', which caused some embarrassment in Turin, where the accepted story was one of Austrian aggressiveness against peace-loving Piedmont.

Ricasoli's unwillingness to recruit enough Tuscans was aggravated in Piedmontese eyes by his reiterated demand for 2,000 troops from Turin to help him keep order. Cavour, though at first he agreed to send this force, had to back down as soon as serious fighting began and he discovered what modern war meant in practice. But without troops, warned Galeotti and Lambruschini, the reds and blacks would create havoc. 'Cavour understands nothing of the situation', complained an indignant

[60] Ferdinando Martini, *Confessioni e Ricordi 1859–1892* (Milan, 1929), ii, 6–8. Peruzzi to Minghetti, May, Lipparini, *Minghetti*, i, 299.

[61] Edicts of 18–20 May, *Atti e Documenti Editi e Inediti del Governo della Toscana dal 27 Aprile in Poi* (Florence, 1860), i, 123, 129, 133. When a militia was finally set up after the war was over, all those in receipt of daily wages were excluded, 23 July, *ibid.*, p. 361.

Ricasoli. The Countess Cambray-Digny, with unconscious irony, even urged her husband in Turin to enforce upon Cavour that the Piedmontese had a duty to save the liberal aristocrats who had carried out the Florentine revolution, and a duty to put down their enemies: by their enemies were meant Dolfi and Rubieri, who in fact had forced an extremely reluctant aristocracy into accepting a revolution that the moderates had not wanted. The 'reds', the 'Jacobins', the *parti demagogique*, these were the real enemy against which Piedmontese troops were expected to leave the battlefields of Lombardy.[62]

As well as Cavour's unwillingness to send troops, it was resented at Florence that he declined to receive an official Tuscan embassy. Cavour had not in fact fully appreciated that, by refusing Tuscany's offer of dictatorship, he had permitted or even encouraged the setting up of a largely independent administration with its own Foreign Office and diplomatic representatives. When told by Boncompagni that Salvagnoli was coming to Turin as an official representative, he now refused in blunt terms to accept him as such.[63] So Salvagnoli decided to stop instead at Alessandria, an intermediate railway station on the way to Turin, the place where Victor Emanuel and Napoleon had their headquarters. This was an unexpected misfortune for Cavour, who had told the King almost nothing about the revolution in Florence; for Victor Emanuel, who knew nothing of Cavour's policy, was ill-equipped to argue against sending French soldiers to Tuscany if Piedmont had none available. Contrary to what used to be thought, Salvagnoli in requesting French soldiers was speaking officially for Ricasoli, and probably with Boncompagni's

[62] Galeotti to Massari, 13 May, *I Toscani del '59*, ed. Ciampini, p. 92. Virginia Cambray-Digny to her husband, 22 June, *Carteggio del Conte Senatore L. G. de Cambray Digny e della Contessa Virginia, dal 16 Maggio al 13 Luglio 1859* (Florence, 1910), p. 71. Lambruschini to Ricasoli, 15 May, *Carteggi di Ricasoli*, viii, 51. Ricasoli's letters of 15 and 21 May, *ibid.*, pp. 44, 85. Salvagnoli's views against Dolfi, Rubieri and Bartolommei were noted by Cipriani, 'Alla Memoria di Napoleone Terzo Imperatore', *Il Risorgimento Italiano, Rivista Storica* (Turin, 1911), iv, 428. Salvagnoli to Ricasoli, 12 May, 'Carteggio Inedito Salvagnoli-Ricasoli', ed. Angiola Doria, *ibid.* (Turin, 1925), xviii, 658.

[63] Massari, *Diario dalle cento voci*, 11, 15 and 16 May, pp. 237, 240–1.

approval. Bringing French troops to Tuscany was no new idea, but had long since been suggested to Turin by Salvagnoli, and the possibility had been readily admitted by Cavour when Ricasoli saw him on 28 April. The Tuscans could not be expected to know that Cavour's views had changed in the interim; nor had they any reason to think that Piedmontese policy, which desperately required French troops in Lombardy, might object to them further south.[64]

On 17 May it was decided at Alessandria that Prince Napoleon would lead a French force to Tuscany, and this fact has made some people attribute to Louis Napoleon the aim of placing his cousin on the Tuscan throne. In view of later events, however, it is an unlikely story. Military considerations had already compelled the French to think of sending troops to create a diversion in Tuscany on the Austrian flank.[65] If Louis Napoleon also had a political motive, more likely it was that he guessed—from the King's inability to tell him about Cavour's policy—that Piedmont might herself have secret ambitions in central Italy.[66] French interests were against making Piedmont too large: to permit annexation of Tuscany by Cavour was no part of Louis Napoleon's plan, and indeed it would have seemed a breach of the Plombières Agreement; nor were the French eager to see revolution spreading through the Papal States. Prince Napoleon's force would be an insurance against this, at the same time as it would help to organize military provision in Tuscany and stop

[64] Ricasoli's letter of 21 May to Salvagnoli (*Carteggi di Ricasoli*, viii, 85) shows that the latter's request must have been previously concerted in Florence. The contrary view had previously been taken by Aurelio Gotti, *Vita del Barone Bettino Ricasoli* (Florence, 1894), p. 280; by D. Guccerelli and E. Sestini, *Bettino Ricasoli, i suoi Tempi, la sua Opera* (Florence, 1950), pp. 84–5, and by Torre, *La Evoluzione del Sentimento Nazionale*, p. 113.

[65] Prince Napoleon, memorandum of 25 April, Comandini, *Il Principe Napoleone nel Risorgimento*, p. 120. This was common knowledge at Florence, said Galeotti to Massari, *c.* 1 June, *I Toscani del '59*, ed. Ciampini, p. 90.

[66] Cavour's preparations for the Papal States are shown by his note of 2 May to General Mezzacapo, and Farini's of the same date, Ugo Pesci, *Il Generale Carlo Mezzacapo e il suo Tempo* (Bologna, 1908), pp. 61–3.

the kind of socialist or Mazzinian movement which was the Emperor's private nightmare.[67]

Military considerations are probably enough to explain why Louis Napoleon, after consulting the King and the Prince, decided to send not 2,000 but 10,000 troops; to deceive the Austrians, he even called it an army corps.[68] The fact that he could decide this within a few hours of Salvagnoli's arrival suggests that it was already premeditated and that Ricasoli's request for help was merely a pretext. The Emperor probably suspected that Cavour would be annoyed, for Prince Napoleon received his orders twenty-four hours before Turin was so much as informed. Cavour would not want his French ally calling the political tune in central Italy, especially as this was exactly what Mazzini had prophesied would follow from Piedmontese subservience to the Emperor. Just possibly Cavour had deliberately not co-ordinated his Tuscan policy with the French, hoping that they would be too preoccupied with the war to notice his private ambitions. More likely, however, he still had not had time to devise any policy: at all events, if a credible policy did exist he had concealed it not only from the French, but from the King and Ricasoli. Either way, however, he had allowed the initiative to be taken out of his hands.

Only late on 18 May did Salvagnoli reach Turin and inform Cavour about Prince Napoleon's expedition. Presumably he also brought the information that Louis Napoleon had spoken of a possible long-term solution which preserved an independent and

[67] Louis Napoleon to Prince Napoleon, 17 May, Comandini, *Il Principe Napoleone*, p. 126. The Prince's subsequent report on his mission was published in *La Nazione*, 19 July 1859 (Florence), p. 1. Massari already on 19 May thought that Louis Napoleon must have had antecedent plans to send troops to Tuscany, and noted the interesting point that Salvagnoli was not expecting Cavour to be annoyed, *Diario*, p. 245.

[68] It is still quite generally assumed that an army corps was sent, though in fact the greater part of the Fifth Corps remained in Lombardy. With equal implausibility, it is also still asserted, in explanation of Cavour's anger, that Salvagnoli *persuaded* the French to send such a large force; see Passerin d'Entrèves, *Il Piemonte, l'Italia Centrale . . . nel 1859–60*, p. 59; S. Camerani, 'Il Principle Napoleone e la Toscana', *Miscellanea in Onore di Roberto Cessi* (Rome, 1958), iii, 336–8.

enlarged Tuscany under a new but probably non-French dynasty.[69] Cavour's public anger over this news may well have been wholly or partly feigned, for he quickly saw some possible advantage to be gained from it.[70] The next day he hastened to Alessandria to discover the Emperor's views at first hand. He told others he was hoping to stop the expedition, but more likely he was merely determined not to let the political future of Tuscany go by default. From Alessandria he then travelled to Genoa to see Prince Napoleon, who, friendly as ever to Piedmont, had already sent to advise Cavour to use the Emperor's change of plan as a pretext for demanding outright annexation of Tuscany.[71] Returning to Alessandria, the Prime Minister was able to secure an undertaking that France had no political ambitions in central Italy. It is always assumed that he also persuaded the Emperor that only by allowing Piedmont to push her alternative claims would the rest of Europe be reconciled to the existence of French troops in Tuscany. Almost certainly, however, this clever suggestion by Prince Napoleon was accepted by the Emperor merely as a ruse to deceive the diplomats, for there is no reliable indication that he entertained the possibility of actual Piedmontese annexation.[72]

[69] Salvagnoli, from Alessandria, to Ricasoli, 17 May, *Il Risorgimento Italiano, Rivista Storica* (1925), xviii, 658. This telegram is not included with Salvagnoli's three letters of this week to Ricasoli in *Carteggi di Ricasoli*, viii, 69–70.

[70] Cavour's exchange of telegrams with Lamarmora on 18 May, indicating that there were no disadvantages and some positive advantages in this new development, is in *La Guerra del 1859: Documenti*, ed. Ufficio Storico . . . Stato Maggiore (Rome, 1910), ii, 25. According to Massari's diary, this was *after* Cavour had shown his displeasure to Salvagnoli. He had good reasons for wanting to bully Salvagnoli, and certainly would not have wanted to tell him, as he told Lamarmora, that Prince Napoleon's expedition could be welcomed as hastening plans for a revolution in the Romagna.

[71] Prince Napoleon to Cavour, 9 a.m., 19 May, *Cavour-Nigra*, ii, 200.

[72] Napoleon to Prince Napoleon, 20 May, Comandini, *Il Principe Napoleone*, p. 131. Napoleon to Prince Napoleon, 25 May, Ernest d'Hauterive, *Napoléon III et le Prince Napoléon* (Paris, 1925), pp. 171–2: this despatch was not printed by Comandini. The possibility that Cavour was in league with Prince Napoleon against the Emperor would square with the fact that Cavour told Salmour not to discuss Piedmont's Italian policy with the Emperor, but to see the Prince instead, *Carteggio Cavour-Salmour*, pp. 188–9.

Cavour seized on the fact that French troops in Tuscany would mean strong British support for Piedmont there. So he now told Boncompagni to change direction and prepare the ground secretly for 'fusion', while not showing too much regard for anyone who disagreed.[73] The French Foreign Office was privately reassured that, since there were not many 'fusionists' in Tuscany, no one could possibly assume that Piedmont meant to annex Tuscany; if facts ever appeared to suggest the contrary, that was merely a blind to allay any fears about French intentions.[74]

Nigra and Cipriani were at once sent to support Boncompagni in working for annexation, and this was almost certainly no blind; the sudden vision of new possibilities was such that, in the excitement of the moment, Cavour also sent secret orders for an uprising to begin all through Lombardy and in the Papal States.[75] Meanwhile, in Piedmont, he tried to convince Salvagnoli and Corsini that, if avoidance of anarchy and sedation of revolution was their wish, this would best be gained by surrendering Tuscan autonomy. Fear of the Left, the same fear which had

[73] Cavour to Boncompagni, 20 May, *Cavour-Nigra*, ii, 202–3.

[74] La Tour d'Auvergne, from Turin to Walewski, 20 May, *Archives Ministère Affaires Etrangères*, vol. 346. Massari, who was close to Cavour, thought that he did not intend seriously to annex Tuscany, but just to sacrifice it at a peace conference for something better, *Diario*, pp. 248–9. The French Foreign Office 'did not recognize the authority exercised by Sardinia in Tuscany', wrote Cowley from Paris to Malmesbury, quoting Walewski, *Further Correspondence Respecting the Affairs of Italy, Parliamentary Papers*, xxxii (London, 1859), p. 25. Camerani rather assumes that Cavour's campaign for annexation arose out of a mistaken but sincere fear of Prince Napoleon's ambition, and does not consider the possibility that Cavour had arranged with the Prince to use the latter's suspected ambition as a pretext for annexation by Piedmont ('L'Annessione in Toscana', p. 21 of offprint from *Atti del Convegno Tosco-Romagnolo Tenuto a Forlì e Rocca San Casciano l'11–12 Giugno 1960*). Camerani's view that Prince Napoleon had no serious ambitions in Tuscany is now broadly accepted, though not entirely by Carlo Pischedda, 'Il '59 Toscano', *Rivista Storica Italiana* (Naples, 1960), lxxii, 74.

[75] Pallavicino, *Memorie*, iii, 520. Boncompagni to Minghetti, 25 May, Lipparini, *Minghetti*, i, 149. Cipriani was hardly a good choice of agent: on 29 July he was telling Walewski that he would do anything to help France if French interests demanded the return of Leopold to Tuscany, *Archives Ministère Affaires Etrangères*, vol. 346.

made these moderates try to save the Grand Duke on 25–6 April, now pushed them closer to Piedmont; and they were still allowed to go on thinking that, after the war, Tuscany might regain her independence under a prince of Savoy, even perhaps with more territory than before.[76]

At Florence, however, the moderates saw the situation very differently when they found Nigra apparently plotting with the very 'reds' against whom they sought protection. When Nigra did not accept Ricasoli's invitation to come and explain his mysterious visit, it could only seem that this was on Cavour's orders—in other words, that the Piedmontese were using Nigra and Prince Napoleon to by-pass the *burgraves* and undermine Ricasoli's Government. When the Prince openly spoke at Leghorn in favour of Piedmontese annexation, Cavour's excuse about French ambitions could be seen as a mere cover, and suspicion of Piedmontese 'aggrandisement mania' was thereby increased, while Nigra's furtive activity antagonized 'toutes les notabilités aristocratiques, scientifiques, littéraires et politiques du pays et le sentiment général'.[77] Boncompagni quickly warned the King that Nigra's annexationist propaganda was having this unfortunate effect; Victor Emanuel thereupon informed the Emperor, who sharply told his cousin to obey orders and leave all these political questions till the war was won. The King, too, evidently without consulting Cavour, informed Florence that the annexation campaign was mistaken and must cease. Nigra beat a hasty retreat.[78]

[76] Corsini to Ridolfi, 22 and 24 May, Poggi, *Memorie Storiche*, iii, 17, 19. Ridolfi to Cambray-Digny, 28 May, *Carteggio Politico . . . Aprile-Novembre 1859*, pp. 45–6.

[77] Ferrière to Walewski, 24 May, *Le relazioni diplomatiche*, ed. Saitta, iii, 158. 'Aggrandisement mania' was Cambray-Digny's phrase to Ricasoli, 28 May, *Carteggio Politico . . . Aprile-Novembre 1859*, p. 48.

[78] Minghetti's note after a Foreign Office meeting is in 'Un'Agenda di Marco Minghetti (26 Maggio–11 Giugno 1859)', ed. U. Marcelli, *Convivium* (Turin, July 1959), xxvii, 460. Cambray-Digny's letters from his wife, 26 and 27 May, *Carteggio del Conte Senatore Guglielmo de Cambray-Digny*, pp. 31–3. Tabarrini, *Diario* for 25 May, p. 42. Boncompagni tactfully tried to retrieve the situation by telling Tuscans that the idea of annexing Tuscany to Piedmont came not from Cavour, but from Prince Napoleon, despatch to Cavour, 28 May, *Cavour-Nigra*, ii, 211.

Cavour was evidently caught unawares by this reaction; he had also quite underestimated the feelings of *toscanità* which lay behind Salvagnoli's mission and Nigra's fiasco. When he now advocated 'fusion' and 'annexation', this might please his friends at Turin, but it was poor tactics with Tuscans who resented being bossed and who (said Ridolfi's secretary) 'by tradition and language think themselves more Italian than other Italians'. *The Times*'s correspondent noted irritation at the idea of ultra-civilized Tuscany being annexed to semi-barbarian Piedmont. One mistake, said Galeotti, was that Cavour believed La Farina's self-justificatory propaganda about the strength of the National Society in Tuscany. It was the same mistake as Piedmont made in 1848, commented Ridolfi—namely, to set up gratuitous antagonism by trying to swallow Tuscany as a snake swallows a frog. Corsi agreed. So did Peruzzi, who pointed out the damage done by Piedmont going back on her pledged word to allow Tuscany to decide her own future after the war. Others, so the Prince explained, were particularly alarmed to find that the main supporters of annexation were their *bêtes noires* on the Left, 'la canaille (c'est à dire les patriotes)'; and there was even a reaction towards considering surrender to France or Leopold as a possible refuge. The only convinced 'fusionists' in Tuscany, said another observer, were Ricasoli and Bartolommei, and even they were now wavering.[79]

Ricasoli's belief in *un'Italia forte* was known in Turin; but unfortunately he was one of the people Cavour could not abide, and this may be one explanation of why these two men repeatedly seemed to be going out of their way just to thwart each other. The 'iron Baron' lacked finesse as much as he lacked subservience. He had strong views. He had presumed to disagree with Cavour over several issues in February and March; now he condemned as a 'massive error' Cavour's devious decision to campaign through Nigra for annexation, as it merely threw into disrepute what had

[79] Nocchi to Cambray-Digny, 24 May, *Carteggio Politico . . . Aprile-Novembre 1859*, pp. 27–8. Ridolfi to Cambray-Digny, 25 May, *ibid.*, pp. 36–7. Peruzzi to Minghetti, 10 June, Salvestrini, *I Moderati Toscani . . . (1859–1876)*, pp. 39–43. Vieusseux to Mayer, 26 May, Arturo Linaker, *La Vita e i Tempi di Enrico Mayer, con Documenti Inediti* (Florence, 1898), i, 270–1. Galeotti to Massari, 1 June, *I Toscani del '59*, ed. Ciampini, pp. 89–90. Prince Napoleon to Cavour, 27 May, *Cavour-Nigra*, ii, 210.

been a growing enthusiasm for the Italian cause. He concluded that Cavour would be wise to speak more of 'Italy' and less of 'Piedmont'; the demand for annexation had been 'a far worse example of municipalism than they can ever find to criticize in Tuscany', and it demonstrated Cavour's 'great lack of political sense'. Ricasoli probably intended that these wounding phrases should be seen by the King. On 27 May he put out a public statement that Tuscan policy still remained true to the original agreement with Piedmont, which postponed all political matters until the war was over.[80]

Cavour must have been annoyed to discover that the King had overruled him and taken Ricasoli's part, but at once accepted the inevitable. He confessed that the Tuscan question was unexpectedly proving the most intricate question raised by the war.[81] Worst of all was that the French had been alerted to his wish for more territorial acquisitions than had been stipulated either at Plombières or in the secret treaty of January 1859. Louis Napoleon had promised the British that it would not be a revolutionary war, yet now he found the Piedmontese encouraging revolution for purposes of aggrandizement. In central Italy they had incorporated Massa and Carrara and tried to annex the Lunigiana. In the Garfagnana they were already refusing petitions for local autonomy. The annexation of Lombardy and the rest of Modena was just about to be proclaimed, and there was clearly some idea of taking part or most of the Papal States.[82] But the French, on

[80] It was published in the *Monitore* of 28 May, and quoted by Eugenio Albéri, *La Politica Napoleonica e Quella dell Governo Toscano* (Paris, 1859), p. 8. Ricasoli to Corsini, 25 and 31 May, *Carteggi di Ricasoli*, viii, 103–4, 137–8. For his feelings against the words 'fusion' and 'annexation', *ibid.*, p. 232.

[81] Cavour to Boncompagni, end May, *Il Risorgimento Italiano, Rivista Storica* (1909), p. 226.

[82] Farini to Torre at Florence, 15 May, *Epistolario di Farini*, iv, 264. Walewski's notes to La Tour d'Auvergne in Turin, 26 May, 4 and 8 June, *Archives Ministère Affaires Etrangères*, vol. 346. Ferrière's reports from Florence to Walewski, *Le Relazioni Diplomatiche*, ed. Saitta, iii, 163–4, 173. Minghetti's notes for 26 May, 6, 7 and 10 June, *Convivium* (1959), pp. 461, 465, 467: Minghetti, who was Secretary-General of the Turin Foreign Office, still insisted that Piedmont did not want to annex Tuscany, only the Romagna.

whom the main burden of the war had fallen, cannot have been pleased to find Cavour secretly playing at revolutionary politics instead of giving them more help; certainly this fact was not unimportant in preparing their decision to back out of the war and leave him isolated.[83]

The Piedmontese meanwhile had the sorrow of realizing that their brief annexation campaign had probably been unnecessary as well as inopportune, for Tuscany 'lacked the elements needed for a separate existence', and the pro-autonomy *burgraves* were obviously a small minority. Much more urgent than these untimely schemes of political union was immediate Tuscan help against Austria; and such help was still gravely defective. Ulloa's volunteer division was looked upon suspiciously by some people in Tuscany as a potential political danger, and Ricasoli would not even recall reservists for fear of provoking opposition: these were two reasons why the Grand Duke's army (which had been about 13,000) could not be substantially enlarged. Cavour asked for 15,000 effectives, but Ulloa said he could possibly produce 12,000; and Boncompagni, supporting Ulloa, agreed that no more could be found without larger-scale conscription, which would mean using force and so prejudicing the fortunes of the revolution. Prince Napoleon, who technically held the post of supreme military commander in Florence, thought on the other hand that 35,000 men should and could have been quickly sent to the front: he told Cavour that Tuscany was making no serious preparations at all for the war, but was simply relying on France and Piedmont doing all that was needed.[84]

Cavour reacted scathingly. If Tuscany could have sent even 15,000 men, the moral effect would have been so great that he was still ready to divert 3,000 Piedmontese troops to keep order at Florence. But if the Tuscans rejected annexation and sent no help,

[83] Louis Napoleon's statement about this to Pepoli is in *Lettere di Cavour*, ed. Chiala, iii, p. ccxxxviii; and, in another version, by Massari, *Diario*, p. 301.

[84] Jérome Ulloa, *Observations sur l'Ouvrage 'Campagne de l'Empereur Napoléon III en Italie'* (Paris, 1865), pp. 11–16. Prince Napoleon to Cavour, 27 May, *Cavour-Nigra*, ii, 209–10. Boncompagni to Prince Napoleon, 11 June, *La Guerra del 1859, Documenti*, ed. Stato maggiore, ii, 43. General Niccolò Giorgetti, *Le Armi Toscane e le Occupazioni Straniere in Toscana (1537–1860)* (Città di Castello, 1916), iii, 582–91.

he would not provide a single policeman. Since they had preferred to invite French soldiers, let them ask France. He was sarcastic over their lack of military ardour. He spoke harshly of Ulloa, and not too well of Prince Napoleon. Even more he blamed Boncompagni, who had first favoured annexation against Cavour's wishes, then opposed it when Cavour was favourable, and was now about to change his mind once more just when Cavour was again changing his. Boncompagni ought to have disregarded formal orders and set up a *de facto* dictatorship.

Ricasoli and his colleagues, on the contrary, were full of pride over their achievement. They were delighted when Cavour gave up his campaign for annexation, for this would attract Tuscany to much more confident support of the Italian cause. They now realized, moreover, that active support was urgent, for the French victory of Magenta on 4 June and the capture of Milan warned them that they might arrive too late to claim any credit. The Emperor's proclamation from Milan on 8 June was addressed to 'Italians' (whereas Victor Emanuel's on 9 June made the mistake of being just to 'Lombards'), and this was inaccurately interpreted to mean a significant change in French policy. As Austrian rule in central Italy crumbled, allowing Parma and Modena to be liberated, there was mounting enthusiasm at Florence; and enthusiasm apart, if any Italian nation was really going to be made, even if reaching no further south than Ancona, *Toscanina* would have to join it or else be left impotent against revolution or reaction.

Among those Tuscans who responded readily to this message were Dolfi and the democrats who had long since learnt from Mazzini to believe in a united Italy. After Peruzzi on 27 April had refused to share office with Rubieri, these radicals had remained politically in the background; now some people thought their mood more dangerous than in April as they saw the moderates behave so feebly. As the French Minister in Florence put it, Dolfi, 'le président de la société de secours mutuels des boulangers', was now the Ciceruacchio of Florence and in a position to terrify the moderates by threatening 'la vengeance des clubs';[85] and Ricasoli well knew the danger of letting these Jacobins keep a monopoly of the unitarist faith. As the French

[85] Ferrière to Walewski, 14 June, *Le Relazioni Diplomatiche*, ed. Saitta, iii, 178.

troops were moving to Lombardy, this left Florence unarmed; there was a sudden fear of social unrest, of patriotic demonstrations by the mob, a fear of the *rossi*, who had already defeated the *onesti* on that memorable 27 April and might do so again.[86] The middle-aged men in power were also afraid of being displaced by a younger, more radical generation of Italian patriots if they did not emerge from their lethargic irresolution and modify their autonomism to fit the quick march of events.[87] Parallel to this was a fear that Leghorn, Siena, Lucca and Pisa, by tradition impatient of Florentine hegemony, might get ahead of the regional capital in declaring for Italy, and indeed might see this as a way of depreciating Florence. The Leghorn municipality was in fact quick to pass a vote for Italy on 10 June by nine votes to six, whereas Florence could not be persuaded to follow suit until six weeks later.[88]

Ricasoli was a fervent unitarist after Magenta, seeing how Tuscany could help to pave the way to a new state of Italy and so avoid the indignity of Piedmontese annexation.[89] When he discovered an address of loyalty in circulation, hailing Victor Emanuel as King of Italy, he and Salvagnoli boldly signed it and on 8 June asked the other ministers to sign too. He must have known that this would meet opposition; Ridolfi and Poggi were in fact very hostile, and the French Minister, by threatening to break off relations, forced the withdrawal of the address.[90] Four days later, however, Ricasoli persuaded the Cabinet to approve

[86] Salvagnoli to Ricasoli, 20 June, *Il Risorgimento Italiano, Rivista Storica* (1925), p. 659. Corsini to Cambray-Digny, 16 June, *Carteggio Politico . . . Aprile-Novembre 1859*, p. 76. Cambray-Digny, quoted by Massari, *Diario*, 17 June, p. 273. Salvagnoli to Cavour, 16 June, Puccioni, *L'unità d'Italia nel Pensiero del Barone Ricasoli*, p. 71.

[87] This age-differential was raised by *The Times* correspondent on 30 May (issue of 6 June), when tilting against the 'arcadian doctrinaires of the Georgofili society' who monopolized government under Ricasoli.

[88] *Archivio di Note Diplomatiche, Proclami, Manifesti, Circolari . . . Referibili all'Attuale Guerra contro l'Austria* (Milan, 1859), p. 232. Bartolommei's apology for not being able to persuade Florence to act earlier is in *La Nazione* of Florence, 20 July 1859.

[89] Ricasoli to Salvagnoli, 12 June, *Carteggi di Ricasoli*, viii, 186.

[90] Ferrière's reports of 7 and 9 June, ed. Georges Bourgin, *Bolletino Senese di*

a more noncommittal appeal to Italian patriotism after warning a reluctant Ridolfi that anything less might precipitate another *moto in piazza.*

Boncompagni informed Turin by telegram of this development. He himself signed the new appeal, though he felt guilty about acting in a hurry and without instructions. As he explained to Cavour, Tuscans must not be allowed to think Piedmont indifferent to the national idea; moreover, Ricasoli's proposal was the one sure method of dishing the democrats, who were now a real danger. Unfortunately, however, Cavour had just been seeing Louis Napoleon in Milan, where he had been roundly told not to go on providing gratuitous evidence of Franco-Piedmontese intentions of aggrandizement. He therefore replied to Boncompagni that he could not accept Ricasoli's decision of 12 June. Apart from French views, there was in any case a growing feeling in Turin that Tuscany, by virtue of Boncompagni's presence as Royal Commissioner, had a dependent status and must not take such autonomous initiatives. There was resentment also at Ricasoli's back-door welcome for Mazzini's notion of a united Italy instead of 'fusion' with Piedmont; and it seemed particularly impertinent at a time when Ricasoli's Government was still begging for Piedmontese money and soldiers.

It is ironic to find former autonomists furious with Cavour for this new veto. Twice now he had refused what they had thought of as almost over-generous acts of self-sacrifice by Florence; and once he had shown his own preference for forcibly imposing annexation on them by somewhat underhand means. They could resent all this, yet they had to admit that he now held most of the cards. A new kingdom of 12 million people was suddenly taking shape, and Tuscany, if she did not join, would be left behind as another insignificant Monaco. At last the *burgraves* of Florence were able to feel the true realities of the situation, to understand what was involved in the war, how it required from them an active participation which would cost money, men, and the acceptance of discipline and sacrifice. Only the Piedmontese

---

Storia Patria (Siena, 1953), lviii, 284–7. Poggi, *Memorie Storiche del Governo della Toscana nel 1859–60*, i, 81–99.

Army could defend them against Austria in future; and financially, too, they now feared Tuscany might be unviable on her own.[91] Even Ridolfi and Capponi, who until lately had still envisaged the possibility of the war creating an enlarged Grand Duchy under Ferdinand, were changing their minds, and the presence of Ferdinand at Austrian headquarters now made him apparently impossible.[92]

One motive for this change was a growing fear that the *parti avancé*, the *unitari rossi*, might use what Ricasoli contemptuously called the *popolaccio* to organize further *émeutes* and snatch power from the moderates. Aristocratic circles may have noted with alarm that Boncompagni was trying to get in touch with Dolfi. Owing to their fear of arming the citizenry in a civic militia, no force existed to control the mob once Prince Napoleon had departed. Even Bartolommei and the relics of the National Society saw good reason to forestall Dolfi's patriotic demonstrations and avoid the appearance of yielding to popular coercion. As Tabarrini, Ricasoli's faithful follower, noted in his diary, the bulk of the non-political aristocracy at last began to fear what might happen if the Italian cause should win, and fear was a powerful incentive to action: 'cowardly as ever, they will stoop to any degradation to avert the anger of the common people'.

[91] Corsini from Milan to Capponi, 10 June, *Lettere e Documenti del Barone Bettino Ricasoli*, ed. Marco Tabarrini and Aurelio Gotti (Florence, 1888), iii (28 April–7 November 1859), 102–4. Vincenzo Ricasoli to his brother, 15 June, *Carteggi di Ricasoli*, ed. Nobili-Camerani, viii, 202. Corsini from Brescia to Galeotti, 20 June, *Rassegna Storica Toscana* (1958), pp. 47–8. Corsini to Ridolfi, 20 June, Poggi, *Memorie Storiche*, iii, 23–4. Cambray-Digny from Turin to Corsini, *Carteggio Politico . . . Aprile-Novembre 1859*, pp. 110–12.

[92] *The Times* of 18 June (p. 12) printed Scarlett's despatch from Florence of 2 June, which quoted Ridolfi's private communication about supporters of the old dynasty being in a majority at Florence. Ferrière later confirmed that Ridolfi had once spoken in the same sense to him, but by 14 June was changing, *Le Relazioni Diplomatiche*, ed. Saitta, iii, 179, 197. Ridolfi, however, made a public disclaimer of Scarlett's statement, 23 June, *Atti e Documenti . . . del Governo della Toscana*, i, 247. Scarlett on 26 June, in another private despatch, confirmed the accuracy of his original report; but he too, in his despatch of 16 June, noted that Ridolfi and Capponi were changing their views, Public Record Office, F.O. 79/205.

Pazzi, Gherardesca, Ginori, Strozzi, Franceschi, old and famous names not much in evidence hitherto, now re-emerged to associate themselves with the benefits of a revolution which they had done more to hinder than promote.[93] There was already a move by interested parties to use this brief interregnum to reduce mortgage rates, taxes and welfare payments, and to diminish the power of the clergy.[94] Now there was also a rush by these noble families to become *italianissimi* before the main political issue could be decided by popular vote of their tenants—and by 'i pizzicagnoli, i medicuzzi, i dottoruzzi di legge' that they both despised and feared.[95]

The attitude towards Piedmont, too, was a mixture of admiration, gratitude, but also real fear and resentment. Many were the complaints at Florence against what was held to be Cavour's ill-defined, changeable, and indeed dishonest and double-faced succession of policies.[96] Even now, though on 13 June Cavour ordered that Ricasoli's appeal to Italian patriotism must be suppressed, two days later he gave this order a quite different twist, hinting that a 'spontaneous' manifestation by Tuscan citizens in favour of fusion with Piedmont might still not come amiss, so long as Ricasoli and the Government had nothing to do with it and so long as it could be privately brought to the Emperor's

[93] These names had been notably absent from the *Consulta* appointed on 11 May, *Atti e Documenti*, i, 88–9; but they were among the deputies chosen on 7 August, *Le Assemblee del Risorgimento, Toscana*, iii, 657–8. Tabarrini, *Diario*, 14 August, p. 76. L. Galeotti, *L'Assemblea Toscana: Considerazioni* (Florence, 1859), p. 46.

[94] *Atti e Documenti*, i, 203–5, 282. Ginori to Ricasoli, *Carteggi di Ricasoli*, viii, 95–7.

[95] This phrase was in Corsini's letter to Capponi of 10 June, *Lettere . . . del . . . Ricasoli*, ed. Tabarrini-Gotti, iii, 103. Massari, *Diario*, 14 June, pp. 271–2, and 17 June, *ibid.*, p. 273. Cambray-Digny to his wife, 21 June, and from his wife, 24 June, *Carteggio del Conte Senatore Guglielmo di Cambray-Digny*, pp. 69, 78. Salvagnoli to Cambray-Digny, 23 June, *Carteggio Politico . . . Aprile-Novembre 1859*, p. 120.

[96] Giorgini to Cambray-Digny, 21 June, *Carteggio Politico . . . Aprile-Novembre 1859*, p. 113–14. Lambruschini to Cambray-Digny, 28 June, *ibid.*, p. 138. Peruzzi to Cambray-Digny, Salvestrini, *I Moderati Toscani . . . (1859–1876)*, p. 50.

attention.[97] More interestingly still, Cavour on 14 June seems to have tried to outbid Ricasoli in a confidential circular which spoke of his own aim to make an Italian kingdom united by race, language and geography.[98] Ricasoli was quite unaware that he might have stimulated such a remarkable development in Piedmontese policy, but refused to be entirely deterred by Cavour's veto on his own proclamation of *italianità*; on 17 June he therefore declared publicly for a strong, united Italy. In private he repeated his repudiation of such politically insulting words as 'annexation' or 'fusion'. Despite Salvagnoli's objections, he privately sought the help of Dolfi, whose influence in Florence was enormous and who had stronger views than anyone on this matter. Forcibly suppressing alternative manifestations of opinion, Ricasoli spent a week obtaining from individual municipal councils an impressive list of declarations for Italy, to support that of Leghorn.[99] Boncompagni protested, but vainly. All he could do was to summon the 'principal agitators' and beg them to cry for Victor Emanuel, not as 'King of Italy', but as 'the Italian King'—this formula would perhaps placate Turin by its disassociation from Mazzinian notions of national unity.[100]

But by this time Cavour had been forced by the French to back down once more and oppose even the spontaneous declara-

[97] Cavour to Boncompagni, 15 June, Bianchi, *Storia Documentata*, viii, 507–8. Cavour's feelings about Ricasoli are partly explained by the apparent paradox that Boncompagni could describe the strong man of Tuscany as representing at once 'il concetto più toscano', and 'la parte più fervida nelle idee Italiane'—which made him doubly suspect. Boncompagni to Cavour, 14 June, Bianchi, *op. cit.*, p. 506, and Boncompagni to Minghetti, 21 June, Salvestrini, *op. cit.*, p. 44.

[98] Zobi, *Cronaca degli Avvenimenti d'Italia nel 1859*, i, 735–6.

[99] Ricasoli's declaration, 17 June, *Atti e Documenti*, i, 228–30, and his note to the prefects, 19 June, *ibid.*, pp. 236–8. Rubieri referred to Ricasoli's meeting with Dolfi, *Storia Intima*, pp. 259–61. Corbett accused the Government of using 'unscrupulous' police measures to secure a favourable vote, despatch of 20 July, *F.O. Confidential Print* (10 September), p. 43. Tabarrini mentioned his secret refusal to obey Boncompagni, *Diario*, 18 June, p. 53. Ricasoli's own attitude is forcibly expressed in letters, 20 June–3 July, *Carteggi di Ricasoli*, viii, pp. 221, 242–3, 256, 273, 280.

[100] Boncompagni to Cavour, 16 June, *La Guerra del 1859, Documenti*, ed. Stato maggiore, ii, 114–16.

tions for Piedmont which he had wanted a few days before. The Emperor had been becoming increasingly reproachful of the Piedmontese leaders, especially for the poor military support which he was receiving. Cavour had once been misled by the National Society into thinking of 150,000 soldiers as his contribution to the allied command; La Farina even spoke of 300,000; but with some difficulty only 60,000 had been produced, in flagrant breach of the Franco-Piedmontese Treaty. Moreover, La Farina's adherents in occupied territory, interpreting orders too strictly, were still in all appearance more anxious to stop *émeutes* than to encourage popular movements against Austria. Ulloa's Tuscan Army was not ready for action; nor could rich Tuscany produce even enough money to buy munitions, because Ricasoli feared that higher taxes would lead to a counter-revolution. Far from contributing effectively to the common cause, the Tuscans were still asking for French soldiers to be left in Florence, and this made nonsense of Cavour's promise to the French about eager popular support for a war of national liberation.

Not only was Louis Napoleon bearing the brunt of hostilities, but the French Foreign Office discovered that Piedmont had again been working against France for annexation in Tuscany and the Papal States. The Catholic world was outraged, and this was a great blow to the Emperor, for the Pope had been given formal assurances against it.[101] The French were also offended by Ricasoli's talk of Italian unity.[102] Moreover, Cavour's note of 14 June, as well as hinting at a stronger Italian kingdom than France wanted to admit, also declared that the Great Powers ought not to emerge from the war with enlarged frontiers, and this could be read as intending to deny France her stipulated pound of flesh in Savoy and Nice.[103] Cavour tried to parry some of the

[101] Walewski to La Tour d'Auvergne, 18 June and 2 July, *Archives Ministère Affaires Etrangères*, vol. 346.

[102] Tabarrini, *Diario*, 22 June, pp. 55–6. Cavour to Vigliani, 27 June, *Lettere di Cavour*, ed. Chiala, iii, 97–8. Peruzzi to Cambray-Digny, Salvestrini, *I Moderati Toscani . . . (1859–1876)*, p. 52. Corsini from Milan to Galeotti, 17 July, *Lettere Politiche di Bettino Ricasoli, Ubaldino Peruzzi, Neri Corsini e Cosimo Ridolfi*, ed. A. Morpurgo and D. Zanichelli (Bologna, 1898), p. 120. *Ricordi di Castelli*, pp. 314, 318.

[103] Walewski's anger at this note, and his ominous reply that Cavour 'fait le

more obvious French criticisms by again putting the blame on Boncompagni and promising to dismiss him; in the meantime, urgent orders were sent to Florence that Ricasoli's campaign for Italian unity was intolerable and indeed that no further political decisions of any kind could be permitted.[104]

It was easy for him to blame subordinates, but what the French objected to was the policies, or rather the lack of consistent and effective policy, which they found at Turin. In the Romagna, for instance, the party of action had been told to expect Piedmontese support, though they were left in the lurch when they were brave enough to rebel. Turin continued to express disapproval of popular insurrection and of an indiscriminate increase in the volunteers, yet also was grieved at the implications of poor recruitment and humiliated when the Austrians were allowed to escape unharassed by local insurgents.[105] This seemed to show muddle on Cavour's part and an unwillingness to support France adequately. Nor were Ulloa and Mezzacapo able to bring the armies of central Italy into action even during the last stages of the war. Gualterio, Torelli, De Cavero and Cipriani were all sent to Florence by Cavour to supervise these troops; but, whatever their instructions, they also brought confusion, for there was both an absence of central planning and a distrust of local initiative. If the Tuscan Army remained disorganized, this was partly due to Cavour's order that its whole structure and regulations had to be altered before it was sent to the front. Prince Napoleon, partly because of this fact, could make no impact on the incapable Ulloa, and eventually was astonished to find that Mezzacapo had secret orders from Turin not to fit into the French plan of attack.

104 Corsini to Ricasoli, 30 June, *Carteggi di Ricasoli*, viii, 267–8. Massari, *Diario*, 6 July, p. 292.

105 Cavour in conversation to Finali, Gaspare Finali, *Memorie* (Faenza, 1955), p. 120. Cavour to Farini, 3 July, *La Liberazione del Mezziogiorno: Carteggi di Cavour* (Bologna, 1954), v, 435. For his dislike of volunteer units, *Lettere di Cavour*, ed. Chiala, iii, 80.

---

compte sans l'hôte', was reported by Antonini to the Neapolitan Government, 1 July, ed. Bianchi, *Rivista Contemporanea* (Turin, April 1863), pp. 31–2.

Mezzacapo's force had been left, perhaps on purpose, as an anomaly, with orders arriving sometimes from Boncompagni, sometimes from Prince Napoleon, La Farina or Gualterio; and at the end of May a direct command from Cavour suddenly over-ruled Boncompagni and ordered its transference to Piedmont.[106] This order was militarily questionable and administratively im-possible to execute: worse still, its motivation must have been partly anti-French, for Prince Napoleon was kept completely in the dark and allowed to go on thinking that Mezzacapo came under his immediate command. The Prince had once been Cavour's most loyal supporter, but lack of support in Tuscany now turned him into an advocate of ending the war,[107] and no doubt his views on this subject had an important impact on the Emperor. When a disorganized revolt finally broke out in the Papal States, Mezzacapo's division, whose main function had been to stand ready to help such a movement, had orders to do nothing and in fact stood idle while papal forces mounted their counter-revolution.[108]

Cavour did not excel as an administrator. He was unwilling to go far enough in delegating minor executive responsibilities; yet, as his colleagues knew, he held too many portfolios in his own hand,[109] and subordinates were sometimes abandoned to

[106] Telegrams of 26 and 29 May, *La Guerra del 1859, Documenti*, ed. Stato maggiore, ii, 96, 116–20. Minghetti's note of 30 May, *Convivium* (1959), p. 463. Boncompagni to Minghetti, 25 May, and Pepoli to Boncompagni, 22 May, Lipparini, *Minghetti*, i, 159–60.

[107] Peruzzi to Cambray-Digny, 16 June, *Carteggio Politico . . . Aprile-Novembre 1859*, p. 78. Massari, *Diario*, 14 July, p. 300. *The Times* of 4 August mentioned the effect of Prince Napoleon's melancholy tale to the Emperor about 'the want of any real sympathy on the part of the people of Central Italy in the cause for which they were alleged to be so enthusiastic'. Peruzzi reported from Paris on 26 July about the feeling there against Piedmontese 'egoism', 'ambition' and 'desire for aggrandizement', *I Toscani del '59*, ed. Ciampini, p. 17.

[108] Cavour's attitude to Mezzacapo's division is discussed by Giulio del Bono, *Cavour e Napoleone III: le Annessioni dell'Italia Centrale al Regno di Sardegna (1859–60)* (Turin, 1941), pp. 87–101; and by Umberto Marcelli, *Cavour diplomatico, dal congresso di Parigi a Villafranca* (Bologna, 1961), pp. 352–61.

[109] Dabormida to Lamarmora, 10 June, *Lettere di Cavour*, ed. Chiala, iii, 94. Minghetti to E. d'Azeglio (wrongly dated here, but perhaps *c.* 21 June),

improvise major points of policy independently of or even against each other.[110] He himself was able to keep an open mind on most issues and be ready for whatever changes that events might suggest; but a procedure which worked excellently in peacetime, when the problem could be tackled on the single level of diplomacy, worked less well when the required skills were those of wartime administration. Lack of time to think and plan was one reason for his contrariness with Ricasoli and for Tuscan policy being sometimes allowed to go by default. So far as we know, his Cabinet colleagues did not want to bring Tuscany into the new kingdom of northern Italy,[111] and probably they were not even presented with the issue as one that required decision. As for Minghetti, who was the chief executive in the Foreign Office, he had to agree that Cavour's policy towards Tuscany was more than just empirical: it was muddled and hence ineffective.[112]

What Minghetti had particularly in mind was the repeated changing of plans which resulted from an attempt to follow the whims of the French Emperor. The tremendous burden of administration left Cavour's great talent for diplomacy with no other field of action than that of Franco-Piedmontese relations. Here the first problem was how to understand Louis Napoleon, then how to defer to him without losing all political autonomy, and, thirdly, how to deceive him and still keep that deceit secret. Cavour's long-term policy in central Italy had to be kept secret because it was not identical with that of France; hence, perhaps, the continuous anxiety to modify his public short-term policy to

110 His Ambassador in England, for example, was left largely on his own. One despatch of 24 June, omitted for some reason from the official *Carteggio Cavouriano*, shows Azeglio suggesting to Palmerston that an independent state of central Italy might possibly be created to balance an enlarged Piedmont in the north, Bianchi, *Storia Documentata*, viii, 515. Palmerston, on the contrary, was already way ahead of Azeglio and looking to the union of Tuscany and the Papal Romagna with Piedmont, Azeglio to Cavour, 4 July, *ibid.*, p. 526.

111 General Fanti to Castelli, 16 October 1862, *Carteggio Politico di Castelli*, i, 452.

112 Minghetti to Farini, 30 June, Marcelli, *Cavour Diplomatico*, p. 372.

Carteggi e Documenti Diplomatici Inediti di E. d'Azeglio, ed. A. Colombo (Turin, 1920), ii, 195.

conform with Louis Napoleon's wishes; and the results of this changeableness and duplicity were an indecisiveness of action and an absence of programme. This indecisiveness he imposed on successive Tuscan governments after the revolution of 27 April, a fact which not only caused frustration and misunderstanding among Tuscan liberals, but created a vacuum of power in which it was hard for him to control events or to recapture the initiative. A pragmatic strategy based on expediency and intuition, though hitherto he had shown that it could sometimes work admirably in the hands of a single master politician, could not possibly be so effective when events became too complex for one man's mind and energy.

Cavour had to resign in July when the French, on whom he had built his war policy, concluded the Armistice of Villafranca without consulting him. The Emperor, contrary to what is usually believed, had first asked the King's advice, and Victor Emanuel accepted the armistice even when an overworked and somewhat unbalanced Cavour advised him to reject it. Louis Napoleon was thus able to revive Leopold's claim to Tuscany. The news of this setback arrived in a Florence which was already angry, divided and suspicious: the last two envoys sent to Tuscany by Cavour, Massimo d'Azeglio and La Farina, were received frostily, because there was by now a conviction that the interests of Tuscany were never much of a consideration at Turin.[113]

Ricasoli, too, had been meeting quite strong opposition from his colleagues. Peruzzi, Ridolfi, Poggi, Capponi, Giorgini, Lambruschini, Galeotti—all had doubts about what seemed his undue partiality towards Piedmont.[114] Many Tuscans, following

[113] Salvagnoli to Ricasoli, 8 July, 'Carteggio Inedito Salvagnoli-Ricasoli', *Il Risorgimento Italiano, Rivista Storica* (1925), xviii, 661. La Farina from Florence to Giusti, 26 July, *Epistolario di La Farina*, ii, 193.

[114] Tabarrini, *Diario*, 26 June, pp. 57–8. Ferrière's reports of 22 June and 6 July, *Le relazioni diplomatiche*, ed. Saitta, iii, 186, 202. As Corbett wrote some months later to Lord John Russell: 'The Tuscans are proud of their history and of their civilization, which they consider superior to that of any other part of Italy, and are not, I believe, generally disposed to see their country absorbed by a kingdom which they have only lately become accustomed to look upon as Italian, and whose inhabitants they consider as their inferiors in intelligence and intellectual culture', January 1860, Public Record Office, F.O. 79/213.

Ricasoli's lead, would now have been ready to accept what they preferred to call 'union' with Turin, not 'fusion'; but, as Cavour's chances of forming a large Italian kingdom receded, there was a revival of all the old feelings against becoming just 'an appendix of Piedmont'. Better than union perhaps would be a prince of the House of Savoy ruling an autonomous Tuscany; failing that, the Duke of Parma would do; and some of the moderates were even able to recognize Ferdinand of Lorraine as a possibility if this would win European sanction for an enlarged Grand Duchy incorporating the other central Italian states.[115]

Eight months later, Piedmontese annexation of Tuscany at last became a fact. It was then possible to see that, during the interim, Ricasoli's energy and obstinacy had kept a larger concept of Italy vigorously alive at Florence as a programme of practical politics; and Cavour himself, though his personal feelings towards Ricasoli became even more hostile, was deeply appreciative of this fact. The revolution of 27 April could then be seen to have been a decisive event in the political education of the Tuscan aristocracy.[116] Under Ricasoli's guidance they had subsequently been enabled to take and keep power as a result of Austria's defeat by France and Piedmont. Finally, in 1860, when the balance of power in Europe had changed again, and when Cavour took his next step towards merging Piedmont into a greater Italy, they overcame their former fears and accepted the political implications of a common nationality.

[115] Ridolfi to Peruzzi, 31 July, *I Toscani del '59*, ed. Ciampini, p. 32. Jarro, *Vita di Ubaldino Peruzzi*, p. 79. Binda to Walewski, 5 August, ed. S. Mastellone, 'Gli agenti Francesi in Italia e la Politica del Walewski dopo Villafranca', *Rivista Storica Italiana* (Naples, 1951), lxiii, 390–2. The return of the old dynasty met a fair amount of support even at Turin, Massari, *Diario*, 24 July, p. 311, and 11 August, p. 334. Indeed, King Victor Emanuel tried to trade this as a concession in return for Austrian surrender of Venice to Piedmont, Hudson from Turin to Lord John Russell, 1 October 1859, *Le Relazioni Diplomatiche fra la Gran Bretagna e il Regno di Sardegna* (Rome, 1962), vii, 219.

[116] 'In quel giorno si decise la scelta, per l'Italia risorta, tra federalismo e stato unitario', Luigi Salvatorelli, *Spiriti e Figure del Risorgimento* (Florence, 1961), p. 318.

Eleven

Bibliography of Sir Herbert Butterfield's Writings (to 1968)

by

R. W. K. Hinton

Short reviews and some clearly ephemeral and repetitive pieces have been excluded, but otherwise this bibliography professes to include all Professor Butterfield's published work until the date of his retirement.

For books, only the dates of first editions and revised editions are given.

1924

The Historical Novel: An Essay, Cambridge and New York.

1927

'A French Minister at Vienna 1806–7', *Cambridge Historical Journal*, 2.

1929

The Peace Tactics of Napoleon 1806–8, Cambridge; New York, 1930.

1931

The Whig Interpretation of History, London; New York, 1951.

Ed. *Select Documents of European History*, vol. III, 1715–1920, London.

1933

'History and the Marxian Method', *Scrutiny*, I (March). Repr. in *History and Human Relations*, below, 1951.

'Bolingbroke and the "Patriot King" ', *Cambridge Review*, 54 (10 March). 3 pp.

1937

'Lord North and Mr Robinson', *Cambridge Historical Journal*, 5.

1939

Napoleon, London. Revised, 1940. New York, 1956.

1940

The Statecraft of Machiavelli, London; New York, 1956.

1941

'Napoleon and Hitler', *Cambridge Review*, 62 (6 June).

1942

Review: 'Capitalism and the Rise of Protestantism', W. Temple, *Christianity and Social Order. Cambridge Review*, 63 (23 May).

1943

'The History Teacher and Over-Specialisation', *Cambridge Review*, 65 (27 November).

1944

The Englishman and His History, Cambridge.

The Study of Modern History. Inaugural lecture as Professor of Modern History in the University of Cambridge. London.

1945

'Tendencies in Historical Study in England', *Irish Historical Studies*, 4.

1946

'The Journal of Lord Acton: Rome 1857', *Cambridge Historical Journal*, 8.

'Notes on the Way: The History of Science', 'Notes on the Way: An Antidote to Dogmatic History', *Time and Tide*, 27 (5 and 12 January).

Review: D. Mathew, *Acton: The Formative Years. English Historical Review*, 61.

1947

'The Yorkshire Association and the Crisis of 1779–80', *Transactions of the Royal Historical Society*, 4th Series, 29.

'Reflections on the Predicament of Our Time', *Cambridge Journal*, 1.

'Limits of Historical Understanding', *Listener*, 37 (26 June). A broadcast talk.

'The Birkbeck Lectures on Luther, delivered by E. Gordon Rupp', *Cambridge Review*, 68 (24 May). See 1954, below.

1948

Lord Acton, Historical Association General Series, 9, London.

'The Teaching of English History', *Cambridge Journal*, 2 (October).

'The Protestant Church and the West', *Listener*, 39 (24 June). A broadcast talk. Repr. as 'The Protestant View of Church and State' in *The Western Tradition* (British Broadcasting Corporation, Vox Mundi Books), London, 1949.

'A Bridge Between the Arts and the Sciences', *Listener*, 40 (15 July). A broadcast talk.

Review: 'The "Teach Yourself History" Library', A. L. Rowse, *The Use of History*; and other works in the same series. *History*, 33.

1949

The Origins of Modern Science 1300–1800, London; New York, 1951. Revised, London, 1957. Trans., Spanish, 1958; Italian, 1962; Polish, 1963; Danish, 1964.

George III, Lord North and the People 1779–80, London.

Christianity and History, London; New York, 1950. Trans., German, 1952; Norwegian, 1952; Chinese, 1953; Swedish, 1954; French, 1955; Spanish, 1957; Finnish, 1957; Italian, 1958.

'Charles James Fox and the Whig Opposition in 1792', *Cambridge Historical Journal*, 9.

'The Christian and Academic History', 'The Christian and the Biblical Interpretation of History', 'The Christian and the Marxian Interpretation of History', 'The Christian and the Ecclesiastical Interpretation of History', *Christian Newsletter*, nos. 333, 336, 341 (16 March, 27 April, 6 July).

'Official History: Its Pitfalls and its Criteria', *Studies: An Irish Quarterly Review of Letters, Philosophy and Science*, 38. Repr. in *History and Human Relations*, below, 1951.

1950

'Europe, History of', *Chambers Encyclopaedia*, 5.

'The Historian and the History of Science', *Bulletin of the British Society for the History of Science*, 1.

'Gasquet and the Acton-Simpson Correspondence', with A. Watkin, *Cambridge Historical Journal*, 10.

'Die Gefahren der Geschichte', *Geschichte in Wissenschaft und Unterricht*, 1. Repr. as 'The Dangers of History' in *History and Human Relations*, below, 1951.

'The Tragic Element in Modern International Conflict', *Review of Politics*, 12. Repr. in *History and Human Relations*, below, 1951.

'The Christian Idea of God', *Listener*, 44 (23 November). A broadcast talk.

'Notes on the Way: The Predicament of Central Europe', 'Notes on the Way: the Predicament that leads to War', *Time and Tide*, 31 (14, 21 January).

1951

History and Human Relations, London; New York, 1952. Include revised versions of 'History and the Marxian Method' (1933), 'Official History' (1949), 'The Dangers' (1950) and 'The Tragic Element' (1950).

Christianity in European History, Riddell Memorial Lectures in the University of Durham, London, three lectures. First ed. in hard covers, London, 1952.

The Reconstruction of an Historical Episode: The History of the Enquiry into the Origins of the Seven Years War, David Murray Lecture in the University of Glasgow, Glasgow. Repr. in *Man on his Past*, below, 1955.

'Dante's View of the Universe', 'Newton and His Universe', in *The History of Science: Origins and Results of the Scientific Revolution*, London and Glencoe, Ill. A collection of broadcast talks.

'The Scientific versus the Moralistic Approach in International Affairs', *International Affairs*, 27.

'The Contribution of Christianity to our Civilization', *Methodist Recorder*, 3 May 1951.

1952

Liberty in the Modern World, Chancellor Dunning Lectures in Queen's University, Kingston, Ontario. Toronto.

1953

Christianity, Diplomacy and War, London.
'Acton and the Massacre of St Bartholomew', *Cambridge Historical Journal*, 11. Repr. in *Man on his Past*, below, 1955.
'Lord Acton', *Cambridge Journal*, 6 (May 1953).
'Prospect for Christianity', *Religion in Life* (New York), 22.
Review: G. Sarton, *A History of Science*, vol. I. *Scientific American*, 188 (February).

1954

'The Seventeenth Century', *Encyclopaedia Americana*, 24, New York.
'Renaissance Art and Modern Science', *University Review* (Dublin), 1.
Review: E. G. Rupp, *The Righteousness of God: Luther Studies*. *Cambridge Review*, 75 (13 February). And see 1947, above.

1955

Man on His Past: The Study of the History of Historical Scholarship, Wiles Trust Lectures in Queen's University, Belfast. Cambridge. Also includes reprints of 'The Reconstruction of an Historical Episode' (1951) and 'Acton and the Massacre of St Bartholomew' (1953). With a new Preface, Beacon Press, Boston, Mass., 1960.
'The Role of the Individual in History', *History*, 40.
The Historical Association 1906–1956. A pamphlet published by the Historical Association. Anonymous, but with Foreword by H. Butterfield, who was President. Reprinted 1957 with a new Foreword, together with the Jubilee Addresses delivered in January 1956, including 'History in the Twentieth Century' by H. Butterfield.
Review: A. J. P. Taylor, *Bismarck*. *Cambridge Review*, 77 (5 November).
Review: 'Holstein's Memoirs and Historical Criticism', *The*

Holstein Papers, vol. I, ed. N. Rich and M. H. Fisher. *Encounter*, no. 24 (September).

1956

History as the Emancipation from the Past. Address at the London School of Economics and Political Science, London.

'The History of the Historical Association', *History Today*, 6.

Review: J. Brooke, *The Chatham Administration 1766–8. Cambridge Review*, 78 (1 December).

1957

George III and the Historians, London. Revised, New York, 1959.

Historical Development of the Principle of Toleration in British Life Robert Waley Cohen Memorial Lecture, London.

'George III and the Namier "School"', *Encounter*, no. 43 (April).

Review: 'The Originality of the Namier "School"', J. B. Owen, *The Rise of the Pelhams. Cambridge Review*, 78 (25 May). See also a letter in the same vol., 15 June.

Letters in connection with *George III and the Historians: New Statesman*, 54 (30 November); *Times Literary Supplement*, 13 December; *Cambridge Review*, 79 (17 May 1958).

1958

Introduction to Machiavelli, *The Prince*, trans. W. K. Marriott, Everyman, London.

'George III and the Constitution', *History*, 43.

'God in History', in *Steps to Christian Understanding*, ed. R. J. W. Bevan, London.

1959

'From Revolution to Second Empire', in *A Short History of France from Early Times to 1958*, ed. J. Hampden Jackson, Cambridge.

'The Colleges and Halls of the University: Peterhouse', in *Victoria County History of Cambridgeshire and the Isle of Ely*, 3.

'The History of Science and the Study of History', *Harvard Library Bulletin*, 13.

'Macaulay as Historian', *Methodist Recorder*, 31 December.

Review: 'Professor Chabod and the Machiavelli Controversies', F. Chabod, *Machiavelli and the Renaissance. Historical Journal*, 2.

1960

International Conflict in the Twentieth Century, London, New York. Trans., Spanish, 1961.

'Historiography', in Hebrew. In *Encyclopaedia Hebraica*, 14, Jerusalem, Tel Aviv.

'The History of the Writing of History', *Rapports du XI Congrès International des Sciences Historiques*, Stockholm.

'The Scientific Revolution', *Scientific American*, 203.

Review: L. Thorndike, *A History of Magic and Experimental Science: the Seventeenth Century*. *English Historical Review*, 75.

1961

History and Man's Attitude to the Past: Their Role in the Story of Civilization. Address to the School of Oriental and African Studies, London.

'Acton: His Training, Methods and Intellectual System', in *Studies in Diplomatic History and Historiography in Honour of G. P. Gooch*, ed. A. O. Sarkissian, London.

'Sir Lewis Namier as Historian', *Listener*, 65 (18 May).

'George Peabody Gooch', *Contemporary Review*, 200 (October).

'Reflections on Religion and Modern Individualism', *Journal of the History of Ideas*, 22.

'The Springs of Discovery', *Observer*, 9 July.

Review: B. Bonsall, *Sir James Lowther and the Cumberland and Westmorland Elections, 1745–1775*. *Historical Journal*, 4.

Review: S. Watson, *The Reign of George III*. *Historical Journal*, 4.

1962

The Universities and Education Today, Lindsay Memorial Lectures at the University College of North Staffordshire, London.

Charles James Fox and Napoleon: The Peace Negotiations of 1806, Creighton Lecture in History in the University of London, London.

Review: 'The History of the East', *Historical Writing on the Peoples of Asia*, vols. 1, 2 and 3. *History*, 47.

1963

'Charlotte Brontë and Her Sisters in the Crucial Year', *Brontë Society Transactions*, 14.

Review: 'British Foreign Policy, 1762–5', *The Fourth Earl of Sandwich: Diplomatic Correspondence 1763–1765*, ed. F. Spencer. *Historical Journal*, 6.

1964

Human Nature and the Dominion of Fear, Christian C.N.D. Pamphlet no. 3.

1965

The Present State of Historical Scholarship, Inaugural Lecture as Regius Professor of Modern History. Cambridge.

Moral Judgments in History, Foundation Oration at University of London Goldsmith's College.

'Some Reflections on the Early Years of George III's Reign', *Journal of British Studies* (Trinity College, Hartford, Conn.), 4.

'England in the Eighteenth Century', in *A History of the Methodist Church in Great Britain*, ed. R. Davies and G. Rupp, vol. 1, London.

'Sir Edward Grey in July 1914', *Historical Studies*, 5 (ed. J. L. McCracken), London.

'In Memoriam Winston Churchill', *Cambridge Review*, 86 (6 February).

Review: Sir Lewis Namier and J. Brooke, *History of Parliament: The House of Commons 1754–1790*, vols. 1–3. *English Historical Review*, 80.

Review: *Historical Writing on the Peoples of Asia*, vol. 4. *History*, 50.

1966

Introduction to H. Temperley, *The Foreign Policy of Canning 1822–1837*, second ed., London.

'History as the Organisation of Man's Memory', in *Knowledge Among Men . . .*, commemorating the 200th anniversary of the birth of James Smithson. Ed. P. H. Oehser, Washington, D.C.

'The Balance of Power', and 'The New Diplomacy and Historical Diplomacy', in *Diplomatic Investigations*, ed. H. Butterfield and M. Wight, London.

Review: 'Lord Acton's Correspondence with Döllinger', *Ignaz v. Döllinger Briefwechsel mit Lord Acton*, Bd. 1, ed. V. Conzemius. *Historical Journal*, 9.

1967

'Christianity and Politics', *Orbis, a Quarterly Journal of World Affairs* (Univ. of Pennsylvania), 10.

'Thirty Years' Work in Irish History: the Eighteenth Century', *Irish Historical Studies*, 15.

'Delays and Paradoxes in the Development of Historiography', in *Studies in International History; Essays Presented to W. N. Medlicott*, ed. K. Bourne and D. C. Watt, London.

1968

'Narrative History and the Spadework Behind It', *History*, 53.

'G. P. Gooch', *Contemporary Review*, 213 (November).

Introduction to H. Temperley, *Frederic the Great and Kaiser Joseph*, second ed., London.

Index

Acton, Lord, 3–4, 4–5, 6, 14–15, 19
Adams, Henry, 5
Ailred of Rievaulx, 31
Aix-la-Chapelle, Peace of, 250–1, 259, 260
Alamos de Barrientos, 124–5, 127, 136
Alaric the Visigoth, 27
Alexander I, Tsar of Russia, 8
Almirantazgo de los Paises Septentrionales, 135
Anabaptists, attitude to church music, 54
Andreas, Willy, 82n.
Anglicans, 23
Annali d'Italia, Muratori, 227, 229
Anselm, 21
Antichrist, Protestant concept of, 193–4
Antiquitates, Muratori, 226–7, 234
Apocalyptic, Hobbes' use of, 173–6, 179–80, 186, 192–4, 196
Aquinas, Thomas, 26, 29
Arabian contribution to scientific revolution, 204 and n.
Archimedes, 219 and n.
Argelati, Filippo, 234
Aristotelianism, 202, 205–6, 218
Aristotle, 29, 206, 220; *see also* Aristotelianism
Augustinian canons, 20
Augustinism, 20; *see also* St Augustine
Austin friars, 20
Austria:
  alliance with France, 256–68
  British relations with, 247–8, 254–68
  policy towards Prussia, 259–60, 265, 267, 268
  role in Tuscan revolution of 1859, 271, 278
Austrian Succession, War of the, 249–251, 256–7
Authority, Hobbes' concept of, 164–74 and n., 182–3, 189–98
Averroës, 206
Azeglio, Massimo d', 312

Bach, J. S., 58–60, 62
Bacon, Francis, 219
Badoer, Giovanni Francesco, 93n., 94
Baïf, Jean-Antoine de, 42
Barbaro, Daniele, 109
Barford, P. T., 59n.
Bartolommei, 275, 280, 281, 294n., 304n., 306
Basil the Great, 25
Bastogi, 280
Bayreuth, Wagner Theatre, 72
Beccaria, 229, 239, 240
Bedford, Secretary of State, 249, 250
Beethoven, 62–7, 70, 73
Bekker, Paul, 66
Bellarmine, 195n.

Bembo, Zaccaria, 88–9 and n., 90, 93n., 94–5, 98–9, 104n., 113
Benedict XIV, Pope, 231, 235
Benevoli, Orazio, 56
Bernardo, Niccolò, 89n., 94
Bernary, P., 57n.
Bernoulli, Daniel, 215
Bertelli, Sergio, 231
Berthelot, Marcellin, 204
Beza, 195n.
Biblioteca Civile dell'Italiano, 273, 276, 278–9, 283, 287n.
Biological sciences, scientific revolution in, 213–17
Black, 215
Blois, Treaty of, 83
Boethius, 41
Boncompagni, Count, 273, 276–7, 279, 282–3 and n., 283–4, 285, 286–287 and n., 288–92 and n., 294–5, 298, 299, 302, 303, 305, 306, 308n., 309–10
Borelli, 214, 215
Borromeo, St Carlo, 47
Bottari, 235
Boulanger, Nicolas Antoine, 236
Bouwsma, William J., 113n., 114n.
Boyle, Robert, 214
Boysen, F. E., 240
Bragadin, Francesco, 85n.
Brahe, Tycho, 211
Brentano, Bettina, 63–5
Broggia, Carlantonio, 228
Brown, Peter, 23
Browne, Sir Thomas, 54–5
Browning, Reed, 256n.
Bruno, 219
Buchdahl, Gerd, 210n.
Buffon, 216
Bunsen, 216
Burtt, E. A., 207–8
Büsching, 238–9
Butterfield, Herbert:
  approach to historical problems, 5–8, 9–11
  concept of diplomatic history, 7–8
  concept of sin, 3–6, 29
  concept of the Renaissance, 13–14
  on Enlightenment in Germany, 226
  on origins of scientific revolution, 207–8
  political bias, 11–12, 15
  Yorkshire patriotism, 5

Caffè, 240
Calvin, 20, 44–5 and n., 47, 178
Calvinists, 23, 45–6, 54, 55, 57
Cambray-Digny, 272–3, 283–4, 292
Camerani, 276n., 277n., 282n., 298n.
Cánovas del Castillo, 120 and n.
Canudo, Riccardo, 73
Capello, Paolo, 85, 89, 94, 101n., 104
Capponi, Gino, 272, 279, 280, 283–4, 290, 306 and n., 313
Carega, 277
Carli, Gianrinaldo, 234
Carpi, Alberto Pio da, 93 and n.
Carteret, 248–51
Catalonia, 145, 146
Catherine de' Medici, 6–7
Caverni, Raffaello, 204
Cavour:
  attitude to Tuscan expansion, 291–2 and n., 294
  attitude to volunteer units in Piedmont, 280–1 and n., 293–5, 302–3, 308–10 and n., 311n.
  control of Tuscan army, 289, 292–294
  involvement in Tuscan revolt, 272–8, 279–80, 284–5
  move towards annexation of Tuscany, 298–301 and n.
  policy towards Papal states, 295 and n., 301
  policy towards Tuscan demand for Piedmontese troops, 293–5, 302–303
  reaction to outbreak of Tuscan revolution, 287–91

relations with Louis Napoleon, 278–279, 280 and n., 281, 282–3n., 284, 286n., 289, 295–8 and n., 305, 308–10, 312–13
relations with Ricasoli, 300–1, 307–308 and n., 314
relations with Tuscan radicals, 275–276, 285–6
scheme for alliances against Austria, 282–3 and n., 285–6
weaknesses of policy, 211–12 and n.
Cessi, Roberto, 115n.
Charles V, 81, 83, 84 and n., 91, 97–9, 102
Charles IX, King of France, 42
Charleton, 214
Chesterfield, Secretary of State, 249, 250
Chiala, 282n.
Church music:
growth of extra-liturgical forms, 56–57, 61–2
modern revival, 75–6
Reformation attitudes to, 43–5, 47, 51–5
Roman Catholic policy towards, 46–7, 56–7, 75–6
Wagner's concept of, 69–70
Cipriani, 298 and n., 310
Cironi, 281, 283, 286n.
City of God, St Augustine, 20–1, 27–8
Clagett, Marshall, 206n.
Classicism, 221
Clement VII, Pope, 84 and n., 86–101 and n., 101–2, 111, 113
Colegio Imperial, Madrid, 130
Collegio of Venice, 87, 89, 91, 92, 96, 105–6 and n.
Collingwood, R. G., 206–7n.
Conchillos, Lope, 135 and n.
Condillac, 226
Confessions, St Augustine, 24–5, 28–32 48–9, 51
Consiglio Politico, Maffei, 230
Contarini, Alvise (Aloysii), 109–10 and n., 115n.
Contarini, Marcantonio, 93n., 94
Cooper, M., 73n.
Copernicus, 202, 207–8 and n., 211, 218–19
Córdoba, Gonzalo Fernández de, 139, 141
Corner, Giorgio, 85, 107–8, 111–12
Corral, Diego de, 134n.
Corsi, 277, 300
Corsini, Neri, 272, 279, 283–4, 287 and n., 290–1, 292, 298–9
Courville, Thibault de, 42
Coverdale, Bishop, 45
Cozzi, Gaetano, 107n., 109n., 110n., 113n., 115n.
Crew, Raymond, 276n.
Crombie, A. C., 208
Croone, 215

De Cavero, 310
De Cive, Hobbes, 162, 171–3 and n., 180
De Monetis Italiae, Argelati, 234
Dee, 219
Dei Difetti della Giurisprudenza, Muratori, 227, 228
Dell'Impiego del Danaro, Maffei, 230
Della Pubblica Felicità, Muratori, 227, 228
DeMott, B., 77n.
Dent, E. J., 61n.
Desaguliers, J. T., 202 and n.
Descartes, 6, 211, 212, 214, 215
Di Una Riforma d'Italia, Pilati, 239–40
Diderot, 226, 228
Digby, 214
Diplomatic history, 7–8
Dolfi, Giuseppe, 281, 282, 283, 284, 294n., 303, 306, 308n.
Dominican order, 20, 23
Doria, Paola Mattia, 235
Dorian Mode, 39
Dreyer, J. L. E., 204n.
Dubos, 226
Duhem, Pierre, 204 and n., 205–6 and n.

Dungannon, 15
Durr, A., 59n.

Ehses, Stephan, 84n., 86n., 91n., 97n.
Elements of Law, Hobbes, 171–3 and n.
Elizabeth, Empress of Russia, 6
Empiricism in scientific revolution, 212–17
Enchiridion, 20n.
Encyclopaedia, Diderot, 226, 228
Enlightenment in Europe, 225–7
Erasmus, 43–4, 47
Eschatology:
  Hobbes' doctrine of, 162, 163–4, 173–6 and n., 179–83
  in medieval thought, 177
  Protestant concept of, 178–9
Eugène of Savoy, Prince, 266n.
Eylau, Battle of, 8–9

Faith, Hobbes' concept of, 164–74 and n., 182–3, 185–6, 189–98
Farini, 290
Ferdinand, Archduke, 83, 93–4, 96, 100n.
Ferdinand, son of Archduke Leopold of Tuscany, 271, 287, 306
Ferguson, Adam, 227, 236
Ferrara, Duke of, 87 and n., 93 and n.
Ficino, Marsilio, 49–50, 219
Filangieri, Gaetano, 236
Florence:
  conduct of diplomacy, 86n., 103 and n., 104–5, 106
  growth of Enlightenment, 233
  see also Tuscany
Fludd, Robert, 219–20
Fluid theory of heat, 203
Foggini, 235
Fontenelle, B. le B. de, 201
Foscari, Marco, 87, 90, 93–4, 111
Foscarini, Marco, 233–4
Fox, Charles James, 13
Foxe, John, 193

France:
  alliance with Austria, 256–68
  British policy towards, 247–8, 250–5, 256–7, 259–60, 262
  Encyclopédisme, 226
  relations with Prussia, 265
  role in Tuscan revolution of 1859, 271, 274, 295, 302, 304, 308–11 and n.; *see also* Louis Napoleon
Franceschi, 307
Francis I, King of France, 81, 86, 91
Franklin, 215
Frederick the Great, 6, 11, 248–9, 260, 262, 263, 264–5, 268
Frederick II of Swabia, 236

Gabrieli, Andrea and Giovanni, 55
Galanti, Giuseppi, 236, 237
Galeotti, 272–3, 279, 283–4, 290, 300, 313
Galilei, Vincenzo, 48, 56
Galileo, 206–7 and n., 209, 211, 212, 218, 219
Gattinara, Chancellor to Charles V, 81 and n.
Geistliche Musik, 56–7
Genovesi, Antonio, 229, 235, 239
George II, King of England, 248, 249
George III, King of England, 9–13
George III and the Historians, Butterfield, 10–12
George III, Lord North and The People, Butterfield, 9–10
Germany:
  British policy towards unification, 253–4
  Enlightenment in, 226
Gherardesca, 307
Giannone, Pietro, 231–3 and n., 235, 237, 240
Gibbon, 226–7
Giberti, Matteo, 91, 96 and n., 111
Gietmann, G., 62n.
Gilbert, Felix, 86n., 103n., 105n., 115–116n.

Ginori, 307
Giorgini, 272–3, 313
Giornale letterario, Pilati, 240–1
Glanvill, Joseph, 211n.
Goethe, 63–5
González de Cellorigo, 131–2
Goldsmith, M. M., 152 and n., 153n., 161n.
Göttingen, Enlightenment in, 226, 237, 238, 243
Grace, Augustinian concept of, 22–3, 27
Grant, Edward, 207–8
Granville, 263
Grebner, T., 240
Gregorian chant, 75–6
Griffiths, Gordon, 47n.
Gritti, Andrea, Doge of Venice, 85–6, 107–9, 111
Gualterio, Marquis, 274, 278, 310
Guerrazzi, 272, 276, 282
Guicciardini, Francesco, 82, 83n., 84n., 85n., 107–9, 110, 114
Gunpowder, invention of, 202–3

Habsburgs, factor in Venetian diplomacy, 94, 95, 113
Hadrian VI, Pope, 84
Hales, Stephen, 215, 216
Haller, William, 215
Hanbury-Williams, Charles, 252–5, 257–9
Handel, 56, 62
Hanover, Newcastle's policy on defence of, 260–4
Hardwicke, Lord Chancellor, 249, 250, 252, 262–3, 265
Harmony, concepts of musical and cosmic, 39–41, 49–50, 57–8, 60
Harrington, Secretary of State, 249
Harvey, William, 202
Haydn, 62 and n.
Hazard, Paul, 231
Henry VIII, King of England, 83, 100n.
Hermeticism, 219–20
Hippo, excavations at, 23
Historical thinking, criteria for assessment of, 153–4
History, writing of:
  growth of monetary history, 234
  historiographical problems, 9–13
  introduction of ethical judgments, 2–5
  parallel with demands for reform, 225–44
Hobbes, Thomas:
  attitude to Papal authority, 193–6
  concept of covenant, 170–1 and n., 181–2
  concept of kingdom of God, 164–74 and n., 184–6, 187–8
  concept of relation between faith, history, and authority, 164–74 and n., 182–3, 189–98
  concept of relation between time and experience, 154–60
  distinction between experience, faith, and reason, 158–9, 185–6, 190
  distinction between history and philosophy, 159–60
  doctrine of eschatology, 162, 163–4, 173–6 and n., 179–83
  doctrine of miracles, 182 and n., 187
  doctrine of mortalism, 175–6, 180, 186
  doctrine of prophecy, 162 and n., 163–4, 164–74 and n., 179–81, 187–8
  doctrine of the Trinity, 186–7
  exposition of Christian faith and its history, 160–4
  historical perception, 151–2 and n.
  nominalism, 183–4, 186, 191
  philosophical materialism, 175–7 and n., 181–3
  rejection of Greek and scholastic philosophy, 191–2, 197–8
  theory of damnation, 175 and n.
  use of apocalyptic, 173–6, 179–80, 186, 192–4, 196

Holdernesse, Secretary of State, 249–50, 260, 263, 264–5, 268
Hooke, 214
Huguenots of La Rochelle, 128, 141
Humanism, humanists, 41–3 and n., 46, 49–50, 221
Hume, David, 226
Hume, Martin, 120
Hutton, J., 54n.
Huxley, Aldous, 67
Huygens, 211n.

Imitation of Christ, St Augustine, 28
Istoria Civile del Regno di Napoli, Giannone, 232
Italy:
growth of Enlightenment, 233–4
growth of interest in reform, 225–6, 227–37; *see also individual writers*
links with German historiographical traditions, 237–43
political and economic problems in eighteenth century, 227–8, 232

Jansenism, 20, 23
Jesuits, 23
Joachin of Calabria, 178, 186
Joseph, Archduke, 252–3; *see also* Romans, Kingship of

Kaunitz, 255–6, 259, 260, 265–6, 267, 268
Keith, British Minister in Vienna, 259, 267, 268
Kepler, 40–1, 211, 212, 214, 219, 220
Kingdom of God, Hobbes' concept of, 164–74 and n., 184–6, 187–8
Kirchoff, 216
Koenigsberger, Dorothy, 42n.
Koyré, Alexandre, 212–13, 219
Kretschmayr, 115n.
Kuhn, Thomas S., 210n.

La Farina, 275–6 and n., 278, 280n., 285, 286n., 300, 309, 313
La Istoria dell'Impero Germanico e dell Italia, Pilati, 241–2
La Rochelle, Huguenot movement in, 128, 141
Lamarmora, General, 281n.
Lambruschini, 293, 313
Lamont, William M., 153n.
Lannoy, Charles de, 97n.
Lavoisier, 215 and n.
Le Bret, Johann-Friedrich, 237
Leeuwenhoek, 214
Leghorn, 272–3, 292, 304, 308
Leibnitz, 40–1, 58, 68
Lenau, Nikolaus, 65
Leonardo da Vinci, 38–9, 49, 55, 203, 205–6, 219
Leopold, Grand Duke of Tuscany, 271, 278, 286–7, 288, 313
Lerma, Duke of, 131, 133
Leviathan, Thomas Hobbes, 160–7
Limpieza statutes, 134–5
Lombardy, annexation by Piedmont, 301
Lord, Robert, 9
Louis XII, King of France, 83
Louis XV, King of France, 265
Louis Napoleon, Emperor of France, 271, 273, 278–9, 280 and n., 282–3n., 284, 286n., 288, 292, 295–8 and n., 299, 303, 305, 308–10, 312–13
Lower, 214
Luther, Martin, 20, 51–2, 56
Lydian Mode, 39

Mably, 226
Machiavelli, 157–8
Maffei, Scipione, 230–1, 232, 233
Magenta, Battle of, 303
Magic and music, 49–51
Magna Carta, 11
Magnetic compass, introduction of, 202–3
Maier, Anneliese, 206n.
Malenchini, 285–6 and n., 287
Malipiero, Gasparo, 85

Malpighi, 214
Mantua, succession problems, 139–42, 146
Montucla, 202
Marañón, Dr Gregorio, 120
Maria Theresa, Empress of Austria, 6, 248, 254, 255–6, 257–9, 265
Marini, Lino, 231
Mariotte, 214
Mass in C, Beethoven, 62
Massari, 296n., 298n.
Mathematical sciences, scientific revolution in, 212–17
Matteucci, 283–4, 290
Maxwell-Boltzmann distribution law, 216
Mazzini, 272
Medici, The, 84n., 86n., 87, 104–5
Mei, Girolamo, 43, 48
Mehegan, 240, 243
Melo, Francisco Manuel de, 123–5, 127, 145–6
Melody, in musical theory of Schopenhauer, 68
Mendel, Gregor, 216
Messiah, Handel, 56
Mezzacapo, 285, 292, 310–11
Middle Ages:
  concept of reality, 218
  contribution to scientific revolution, 202, 204–9, 221
Milan:
  capture by Louis Napoleon, 303
  in foreign policy of Olivares, 139–41
  significance in Venetian diplomacy, 83, 84, 86, 88, 92, 94n., 97–8 and n., 100n., 107–8
Milan, Dukedom of, 83, 87
Milizia, 235
Millennialism, 174, 175–7 and n., 178–179, 180
Minghetti, 290, 301n., 312
Missa Solemnis, Beethoven, 62, 70
Mocenigo, Alvise, 85, 89, 93, 94, 104, 113
Mocenigo, Leonardo, 85n., 89 and n., 94, 101n.
Modes, Platonic, 39–40, 41
Modena, annexation by Piedmont, 301
Molek, F. J., 62n.
Momigliano, Arnaldo, 230
Montanelli, 272, 276
Montesquieu, 226
Montferrat, 139–41
Moro, Gabriele, 85, 100–1 and n., 104
Morone, Girolamo, 94n.
Morosini, Andrea, 109, 112–13 and n., 115 and n.
Morosini, Maria, 92, 85 and n.
Mortalism, doctrines of, 175–7, 180, 186
Mosheim, 238, 240
Motu proprio, 61n., 75–6 and n.
Mozart, 62 and n.
Muratori, 227–30, 232, 233, 234, 236, 237, 238, 240, 242, 243
Music and religion:
  attitudes of Romantic movement, 67–70
  attitudes to emotional impact, 38, 39–41, 43–58, 60–2, 66
  classical concept of, 39–41, 68–9
  conflicts over relationship of words to music, 41–51, 55, 60, 70
  effects of secularization of music, 37–38, 71–2
  Erasmus' concept of, 43–4
  extra-liturgical traditions, 56–7, 61–62, 75–6
  Ficino's concept of, 49–50
  impact of Beethoven, 62–7
  Luther's concept of, 51–2, 56
  metaphysical theories, 67–85
  puritanism in, 43–6, 54–5, 57, 60
  Renaissance humanism in, 41–3 and n., 46, 49–50
  St Augustine's concept of, 48–9, 51, 70
  significance of modern developments, 76–8
  universal link with ritual, 37–8

Namier, Lewis, 4, 9–13
Naples, 83, 91–2, 97, 98, 99, 102, 107–108, 235–7
Napoleon, 5, 7–8
Napoleon, Prince, 295–8 and n., 299 and n., 302, 303, 310–11 and n.
National Society, 275–6 and n., 278, 280 and n., 284–5, 286n., 291, 300, 306, 309
Navagero, Andrea, 109
Nayler, James, 194n.
Neoplatonism, 26, 41, 48, 57, 58
Neri, St Filippo, 56
Netherlands:
  Austrian policy in, 250, 256–9, 260
  polyphonic musical traditions, 46
Newcastle, Duke of:
  consequences of foreign policy, 266–268
  policy after Peace of Aix-la-Chapelle, 251–2, 260, 264
  policy in Austrian Succession War, 249–51, 260
  policy on subsidy treaties, 251, 252, 260–4, 267–8
  policy towards election of King of Romans, 252–3, 254–5, 256, 264
  relations with Pelham brothers, 249
Newman, Cardinal, 19, 29
Newton, Isaac, 202, 203–4 and n., 207, 211, 214–16, 217, 219 and n.
Nevers, Duke of, 139–41
Nigra, 276, 280n., 298, 299
Nominalism, contribution to scientific revolution, 205–7
  in philosophy of Hobbes, 183–4, 186, 191
Nordenskiöld, Erik, 206

Oldenburg, Henry, 211n.
Olivares:
  concept of government and monarchy, 122–7, 130–2
  concern with depopulation problems, 134, 144
  constitutional policies, 136–7, 145, 146
  contemporary evaluation of, 120–2 and n., 145–6
  fiscal and reforming policies, 129–30, 132–4, 137–9, 143, 144, 146
  foreign policies, 127–8, 139–42, 142–145
  Great Memorandum of 1624, 126, 129, 130–1, 132, 135, 136, 137
  opposition to *limpieza* statutes, 134–5
  personal difficulties, 119–20
  policy on trade, 135–6, 143–4
  pro-Jewish tendencies, 135 and n.
  relationship with Philip IV, 120 121–2, 137
Opera, influence on church music, 56, 57
Optics, science of, 203–4 and n., 208
Oratorio, 56
Oresme, Nicole, 207, 209, 218, 219
Origen, 25
Origins of Modern Science, The, Butterfield, 13–14
Overton, Richard, 176 and n.

Pagano, Mario, 236
Pagel, Walter, 220
Pagnini, Gianfrancesco, 234
Palestrina, 47–8, 76n.
Panella, Antonio, 284n.
Papacy:
  Hobbes' attitude to authority of, 193–196
  Protestant concept of, 193–4
  Venetian relationship with, 84 and n., 86–101 and n., 101–2, 111, 113
Papal States, 295 and n., 301, 309, 311
Paper, invention of, 202–3
Paracelsus, 219–20
Parma, 86–7
Paruta, Paolo, 82, 109, 110–12 and n., 114n.
Patin, Guy, 146
Pavia, 92–4, 99

Pavia, Battle of, 81
Pazzi, 307
Peace Tactics of Napoleon, The, Butterfield, 7–9
Pelagius, 22 and n., 30
Pelham brothers, 248–50, 252
Pembo, Pietro, 109
Perrault, 214
Peruzzi, 272–3, 279, 280, 283–4, 286–287 and n., 288, 289, 290–1, 300, 313
Pesante, Maria Luisa, 237
Pesaro, Girolamo da, 85n., 88, 89, 95–96, 98–9, 104, 113
Petrarch, 14, 31
Philip III, King of Spain, 131–2, 133–134
Philip IV, King of Spain, 120–3
Philosophy, relationship to theology, 25–6
Phlogiston theory of heat, 203
Piacenza, 87
Pico della Mirandola, 219
Piedmont:
  aggrandizement in central Italy, 301, 309–10
  annexation of Tuscany, 271, 298–301, 313–14
  attitude to recruitment of volunteer army units, 280–1 and n., 293–5, 302–3, 308–10 and n.
Pilati, Carlantonio, 225–6, 229, 237–244 and n.
Pio, Alberto, da Carpi, 93 and n.
Piranesi, 235
Pischedda, Carlo, 298n.
Pitt, William, 11
Pius X, Pope, 61n., 75–6
Plato, 25–6, 29, 39–40, 41, 57
Platonism, 26, 49–50, 55, 67–9, 221
Plotinus, 26, 29
Poggi, 304, 313
Politain, 14
Polyphony, 41–2, 46
Porta, 219
Portugal, 145, 146
Possidius, 30
Pregadi, in Venice, 82, 86, 87–9 and n., 92–6, 97–9, 100–1, 105–6 and n., 107, 115n.
Priestley, Joseph, 176–7, 215–16
Printing, invention of, 202–3
Priuli, Matteo, 85n.
Proclus, 26
Prophecy:
  Hobbes' doctrine of, 162 and n., 163–4, 167–74 and n., 179–81, 187–8
  Protestant concept of, 178–9
Protestantism:
  attitude to music, 43–5, 47, 51–5, 76
  contribution to Enlightenment, 238–240
Prussia:
  Newcastle's policy towards, 248–9, 260–8
  relations with France, 265
Prynne, William, 181
Psalm-singing in Calvinist worship, 45
Puritanism in music, 43–6, 54–5, 60
Pythagoras, theory of harmony, 40–1, 58

Quadrivium, in medieval education, 41
Queller, Donald E., 82n.
Querini, Cardinal, 234

Rameau, 60
Ranke, 15
Raven, C. E., 213n.
Ray, 214
Reformation, impact on church music, 43–5, 47, 51–4
Renaissance, the:
  classicism, 6, 13–14
  Hermeticism, 219–20
  impact on music, 38–47
Rerum Italicarum Scriptores, 234
Revelation, in Hobbes' doctrine of faith, 164–74 and n., 182–3

Ricasoli, Baron, 273, 276–7, 279, 280, 281–2, 283–4 and n., 291, 293–5 and n., 300–1, 303, 304–9, 313–14
Richelieu, Cardinal, 130, 132, 135–6, 141, 146
Richer, François, 240
Ricuperati, Giuseppe, 231
Ridolfi, Marquis, 272, 273, 277, 279, 283–4, 286–7 and n., 291, 304, 306 and n., 313
Robert Grosseteste and the Origins of Experimental Science, A. C. Crombie, 208
Rolland, Romain, 66
Roman Catholicism, Catholics:
  argument for separation from state in Italy, 238–40
  concept of church music, 46–7, 56–57, 62, 75–6
  influence of St Augustine, 23, 36
Romans, Kingship of, election controversy, 252–3, 254–5, 256, 264
Romantic movement, concept of music, 67–70
Rossini, 71–2
Rowley, Samuel, 54
Rubieri, Ermolao, 281, 282, 286–7 and n., 288 and n., 294n.
Russia:
  British subsidy treaty negotiations, 260–4, 267–8
  policy towards Frederick the Great, 260
Ruville, Albert von, 10–11, 12

Sacchi, Marco, 57
St Augustine:
  background and early career, 21–2
  concept of grace, 22–3, 27
  concept of music, 48–9, 51, 61n.
  concept of redemption, 177
  extent of influence, 19–21, 27, 28–31
  gifts as philosopher, 25–7
  gifts as preacher, 23–5
  political thought, 27–8
St Bartholomew, Massacre of, 6–7
St Mark's, Venice, musical traditions, 55–6
St Petersburg, Convention of, 268
St Theresa of Avila, 29, 31
Ste Thérèse of Lisieux, 29
Salazar, Hernando de, 135
Salvagnoli, 272–3, 275, 283–4, 291, 294–5 and n., 296 and n., 298–9, 304, 308
Salvatorelli, Luigi, 228
Sarpi, Paolo, 234, 240
Sarton, George, 204
Savi, in government of Venice, 88, 93, 94, 95–6, 102, 105 and n.
Schlötzer, 226
Schlözer, Tatiana, 74
Scholasticism, contribution to scientific revolution, 204–9, 221
Schopenhauer, 67–9
Schwarzschild, Steven, 153n.
Science, origins and development of modern, 13–14
Scientific revolution of the seventeenth century:
  characteristics in physical and biological sciences, 212–17
  classical contribution to, 202–3, 204n., 205–6
  concept of continuing process, 209–210 and n.
  concern with comprehension of reality, 217–21
  discoveries of Renaissance period, 210–11
  historiography of, 204–6
  historical consciousness, 201–2
  medieval origins, 204–5 and n.
  Newton's contribution, 203–4 and n.
  unique character of, 220–1
Scriabin, Alexander, 74–5
Semler, 242–3
Seven Years' War, 6
Sforza, Francesco, Duke of Milan, 83, 91, 94n., 97 and n., 108, 113n.
Shakespeare, 41n., 54

Singer, Charles, 204
Skinner, Quentin, 153n.
Smith, William, 240
Soliloquies, St Augustine, 33
Springborg, Patricia, 153n.
Steno, 214
Strauss, Leo, 163n.
Strauss, Richard, 72–3
Stravinsky, 57
Strozzi, 307
Sudhoff, Karl, 204
Swannerdam, 214
Sylvius, 215

Tacitus, 124–5, 145–6
Tannery, Paul, 206n.
Tanucci, 235
Taylor, A. E., 161n.
Ten, Council of, in Venice, 87, 89, 105
Theology, relationship to philosophy, 25–6
Thomasius, 238
Thorndike, Lynn, 204
Tilsit, Treaty of, 8–9
Time, Hobbes' concept of experience and, 154–60
Torelli, 310
Tractatus in Johannem, St Augustine, 24–25
Trent, Council of, 46–7, 56
Trevisan, Andrea, 85n., 89n., 94, 101n., 104
Trevisan, Domenico, 85, 94, 111–12, 113
Triregno, Giannone, 232
Tron, Luca, 85n., 89 and n., 94, 95, 99, 101n.
Tron, Sante, 85n.
Tuscany:
- annexation by Piedmont, 271, 298–301, 313–14
- attempts to form alliance with Piedmont, 283–4
- attempts to preserve autonomy, 290–2 and n., 294
- attitude to Garibaldi, 280–2 and n.
- declaration of war against Austria, 293
- demands for Piedmontese troops to keep order, 293–5, 302–3
- establishment of militia, 293 and n.
- events of 27 April 1859, 284–7
- growth of support for united Italy, 303–10
- policy of moderates, 272–3, 275, 281–282, 283, 287, 294, 299, 303–4, and n.
- role of aristocracy in revolution of 1859, 286–7, 306–7, 314
- support for volunteer units for Piedmont, 280–1 and n., 283, 292–4, 302–3, 308–9

Tyson, 214

Ulloa, General, 285, 287–8, 290, 292, 302, 309, 310
Union of Arms, 137

Valier, Agostino, 110n.
Vellón, currency problems, 137–8
Venice:
- alliance with Charles V, 83
- alliance with Francis I, 82–104
- conduct of diplomacy, 89 and n., 101–6
- Enlightenment in, 233–4
- historiography of, 82, 106–16
- relations with Papacy, 84 and n., 86–101 and n., 101–2
- sources for Renaissance history, 82 and n.
- terms of alliance with France, 100 and n.

Venier, Domenico, 88, 93n., 94
Venier, Marcantonio, 85
Verona Illustrata, Maffei, 230
Veronese, *Marriage of Cana*, 55
Verri, Pietro, 225, 229, 234, 239, 240
Versailles, First Treaty of, 266
Vico, 232, 233, 236

Victor Emmanuel, King of Piedmont, 294, 299, 301, 313, 314n.
Vienna, Treaty of, 1731, 248
Villafranca, Armistice of, 313
Voltaire, 239, 243, 266

Wagner, Richard, 65–6, 69–72, 77–8
Wagner Theatre, Bayreuth, 72
Walewski, 309–10n.
Walker, D. P., 42n., 48n., 49n., 50
Walpole, Horace, 7, 13, 247, 248
Walter, Johannes, 52
Warsaw argeement, 1745, 248–9
Weber, Max, 37–8, 77
Werckmeister, Andreas, 58
Westminster, Convention of, 264–5, 268
Whewell, William, 203
White, Lynn, Jnr, 209n.
Willaert, 55
William of Ockham, 218
Willis, 215
Willughby, Francis, 214
Winckelmann, J. J., 235, 240
Windmill, invention of, 202–3
Winstanley, Gerrard, 175, 176–7
Wohlwill, Emil, 204, 206n.
Wolf, Abraham, 206–7n.
Wotton, William, 201

Zarlino, choirmaster of St Mark's, Venice, 48
Zwingli, 52–4, 70
Zwinglians, 53–4, 57

Printed in Great Britain
by Amazon

36718320R00196